lonely planet

GREEK

Travel Phrasebook & Dictionary

Credits

Production Editor Sofie Andersen
Language Writer Thanasis Spilias

Thanks

Marc Backwell, Fergal Condon, Gwen Cotter, Helen Iatrou, Kellie Langdon, Saralinda Turner, Clifton Wilkinson

Published by Lonely Planet Global Limited
CRN 554153

Digital Depot, Roe Lane off Thomas Street, Dublin
D08 TCV4, Ireland (EU authorised representative)

9th Edition – Sep 2026
ISBN 978 1 80653 124 0

Cover Image Ancient Greek vase. Kamira/Shutterstock
Printed in China 10 9 8 7 6 5 4 3 2 1

Contact lonelyplanet.com/contact

Make the most of this phrasebook...

Anyone can speak another language! It's all about confidence. Don't worry if you can't remember your school language lessons or if you've never learnt a language before. Even if you learn the very basics, your travel experience will be the better for it. You have nothing to lose and everything to gain when the locals hear you making an effort.

FINDING THINGS IN THIS BOOK

For easy navigation, this book is in sections. The **Basics** chapters are the ones you'll thumb through time and again. The **Practical** section covers travel situations like catching transport and finding a bed. The **Social** section gives you conversational phrases, pick-up lines, the ability to express opinions – so you can get to know people. **Food** has a section all of its own: gourmets and vegetarians are covered and local dishes feature. **Safe Travel** equips you with health and police phrases, just in case. Remember the colours of each section and you'll find everything easily; or use the comprehensive **Index**. Otherwise, check the two-way traveller's **Dictionary** for the word you need.

BEING UNDERSTOOD

Throughout this book you'll see coloured phrases on each page. They're phonetic guides to help you pronounce the language. You don't even need to look at the language itself, but you'll get used to the way we've represented particular sounds. The pronunciation chapter in Basics will explain more, but you can feel confident that if you read the coloured phrase slowly, you'll be understood.

COMMUNICATION TIPS

Body language, ways of doing things, sense of humour – all have a role to play in every culture. 'Local talk' boxes show you common ways of saying things, or everyday language to drop into conversation. 'Listen for' boxes supply the phrases you may hear. They start with the language (so local people can point out what they want to say to you) and then lead in to the pronunciation guide and the English translation.

CONTENTS

About Greek

ΕΙΣΑΓΩΓΗ

Aristotle, Homer, Plato, Sappho, Herodotus and Alexander the Great can't all be wrong in their choice of language – if you've ever come across arcane concepts such as 'democracy', exotic disciplines like 'trigonometry' or the neurosis termed 'the Oedipus complex', then you'll have some inkling of the widespread influence of Greek language and culture. With just a little Modern Greek under your belt, you'll have a richer understanding of this language's impact on contemporary Western culture.

Greek is the official language of Greece and a co-official language of Cyprus, in addition to being spoken by emigrant communities in Turkey, Australia, Canada, Germany and the United States, and elsewhere across the globe. In total, there are over 13 million Greek speakers worldwide.

Modern Greek constitutes a separate branch of the Indo-European language family, with Ancient Greek its only (extinct) relative. The first records of written Ancient Greek were found in the fragmentary Linear B tablets, dating from the

AT A GLANCE

Language name: Greek

Name in language:
Ελληνικά e·li·ni·*ka*, *Νέα Ελληνικά* ne·a e·li·ni·*ka* (Greek, Modern Greek)

Language family:
Indo-European (Hellenic branch)

Key countries:
Greece, Cyprus

Approximate number of speakers:
13 million worldwide

Close relatives:
Ancient Greek

Donations to English:
anarchy, astronomy, cosmos, democracy, drama, logic, politics and many more

official language
For more details, see the introduction.
Adriatic Sea
Italy
Albania
North Macedonia
Macedonia
Thrace
Seres
Drama
Kavala
Komotini
Alexandroupolis
Sea of Marmara
Thracian Sea
Veria
Thessaloniki
Kozani
GREECE
Northeastern Aegean Islands
Corfu
Corfu
Ioannina
Epiros
Larisa
Thessaly
Volos
Sporades
Lesvos
Mytilini
Ionian Islands
Lefkada
Lamia
Sterea Ellada
Evia
Skyros
Aegean Sea
Ionian Sea
Halkida
Chios
İzmir
Kefallonia
Patras
Thiva (Thebes)
Athens
Piraeus
Zakynthos
Corinth
Andros
Samos
Türkiye
Peloponnese
Ikaria
MEDITERRANEAN SEA
Nafplio
Saronic Gulf Islands
Mykonos
Naxos
Kalamata
Sparta
Mirtoön Sea
Cyclades
Amorgos
Kos
Milos
Dodecanese
Rhodes
Rhodes
GREECE
Türkiye
Kythira
Santorini (Thira)
Sea of Crete
Karpathos
Hania
MEDITERRANEAN

14th to the 12th centuries BCE. By the 9th century BCE, the Greeks had adapted the Phoenician alphabet to include vowels – the first alphabet to do so – and the script in use today came to its final form some time in the 5th century BCE. The Greek script was the foundation for the Cyrillic script (used in Slavic languages) and the Latin alphabet (used in English and other European languages).

Although written Greek may have been remarkably stable over the millennia, the spoken language has evolved considerably. In the 5th century, the dialect spoken around Athens (known as 'Attic') became the dominant speech as a result of the city-state's cultural and political prestige. Attic gained even greater influence as the medium of administration for the vast empire of Alexander the Great, and remained the official language of the Eastern Roman Empire and the Orthodox Church after the demise of the Hellenistic world. Once the Ottoman Turks took Constantinople in 1453, the Attic dialect lost its official function. In the meantime, the common language – known as *Koine* (Κοινή ki·*ni*) – continued to evolve. It developed a rich history of popular songs (δημοτικά τραγούδια ţhi·mo·ti·*ka* tra·*ghu*·ţhia) and absorbed vocabulary from Turkish, Italian, Albanian and other Balkan languages.

When an independent Greece returned to the world stage in 1832, it needed to choose a national language. Purists advocated a slightly modernised version of Attic known as *Καθαρεύουσα* ka·tha·*re*·vu·sa (from the Greek word for 'clean'), which no longer resembled the spoken language. *Koine*, or *laiki* as it was also known (λαϊκή la·i·*ki* means 'popular'), had strong support as it was spoken and understood by the majority of Greeks – in the end, this was the language which gained official recognition. By the mid-20th century, *Koine/laiki* was known as 'demotic' and continued in daily use. It was banned during Greece's military dictatorship (1967-74) but then reinstated as the official language of the Hellenic Republic.

This book gives you the practical phrases you need to get by in Greek, as well as all the fun, spontaneous phrases that can lead to a better understanding of the people and their culture. Once you've got the hang of how to pronounce Greek words, the rest is just a matter of confidence. Local knowledge, new relationships and a sense of satisfaction are on the tip of your tongue. So don't just stand there, say something!

ABBREVIATIONS USED IN THIS BOOK

a	adjective	n	neuter (after Greek)
acc	accusative	n	noun (after English)
f	feminine	nom	nominative
gen	genitive	pl	plural
inf	informal	pol	polite
lit	literal	sg	singular
m	masculine	v	verb

BASICS

Pronunciation

ΠΡΟΦΟΡΑ

The pronunciation of Greek is easy to master, as most of the sounds correspond to those found in English. Use the coloured pronunciation guides to become familiar with them, and then read directly from the Greek when you feel more confident.

VOWEL SOUNDS

Greek vowels are pronounced separately even when they're written in sequence, eg ζώο *zo*·o (animal). You'll see though in the table below that some letter combinations correspond to a single sound – ουρά (queue) is pronounced u·*ra*.

When a word ending in a vowel is followed by another word that starts with the same or a similar vowel sound, one vowel is usually omitted and the two words are pronounced as if they were one – Σε ευχαριστώ se ef·kha·ris·*to* becomes Σ' ευχαριστώ sef·kha·ris·*to* (Thank you). Note that the apostrophe (') is used to show that two words have been joined together.

Symbol	English Equivalent	Greek Example	Transliteration
a	car	αλλά	a·*la*
e	bet	πλένομαι	*ple*·no·me
i	lid	πίσω, πόλη, υποφέρω, είδος, οικογένεια, υιός	*pi*·so, *po*·li, i·po·*fe*·ro, *i*·thos, i·ko·*ye*·ni·a, i·*os*
o	lot	πόνος, πίσω	*po*·nos, *pi*·so
u	put	ουρά	u·*ra*
ia	nostalgia	ζητιάνος	zi·*tia*·nos
io	ratio	πιο	pio

CONSONANT SOUNDS

Most Greek consonant sounds are also found in English – only the guttural gh and kh might need a bit of practice. Double consonants are only pronounced once – άλλος *a* · los (other).

Symbol	English Equivalent	Greek Example	Transliteration
b	bed	μπαρ	bar
d	dog	ντομάτα	do·*ma*·ta
dz	adds	τζαμί	dza·*mi*
f	fit	φως, αυτή	fos, af·*ti*
g	gap	γκαρσόν	gar·*son*
gh	guttural sound, between goat and loch	γάτα	*gha*·ta
h	heat	χέρι	*he*·ri
k	kit	καλά	ka·*la*
kh	loch (guttural sound)	χαλί	kha·*li*
l	let	λάδι	*la*·ţhi
m	mat	μαζί	ma·*zi*
n	not	ναός	na·*os*
ng	singer	ελέγχω	e·*leng*·kho
p	pin	πάνω	*pa*·no
ps	lapse	ψάρι	*psa*·ri
r	red (trilled)	ράβω	*ra*·vo
s	sad	στυλό	sti·*lo*
t	top	τι	ti
th	theatre	θέα	*the*·a
ţh	the	δεν	ţhen
ts	hats	τσέπη	*tse*·pi
v	vase	βίζα, αύριο	*vi*·za, *av*·ri·o
y	yes	γέρος	*ye*·ros
z	zoo	ζέστη	*ze*·sti

WORD STRESS

Most Greek words have only one stressed syllable, but some have two. Stress can fall on any of the last three syllables. In our pronunciation guides, the stressed syllable is always in italics, but in written Greek, the stressed syllable is always indicated by an accent over the vowel, eg καλά ka·*la*.

If a vowel is represented by two letters, it's written on the second letter, eg ζητιάνος zi·*tia*·nos (beggar). If the accent is marked on the first of these two letters, they should be read separately, like in Μάιος *ma*·i·os (May). Where two vowels occur together but are not stressed, a diaeresis (¨) is used to indicate that they should be pronounced separately, eg λαϊκός la·i·*kos* (popular). When stress falls on a capitalised vowel (like in Έχασα *e*·ha·sa (I lost)), the accent is written to the left of the letter.

INTONATION

Intonation in mainland Greece is rather flat, except in questions, when the voice is raised at the end of the sentence. Many island dialects have a more 'singing' intonation.

☑ SPELLBOUND

You may have noticed that sometimes two Greek letters in combination form one single consonant sound – the combination of the letters μ and π makes the sound b, and the combination of the letters ν and τ makes the sound d. This is particularly the case when each combination appears at the start of a word – in the middle of a word they sound more like the 'mb' in 'amber' and the 'nd' in 'indigo' respectively. In this book, we've used the same symbols regardless of the position of these letters within a word – you'll be understood just fine if you follow our pronunciation guides.

READING & WRITING

The Greek writing system was simplified in 1982, when the old stress symbols and aspiration marks (ie an accent indicating that a sound is pronounced with a puff of air before it) were abolished, although they may still be found in old books.

The Modern Greek alphabet consists of 24 letters. Their pronunciation is shown in the box below for spelling purposes, eg when you need to spell your name to book into a hotel. Many of the letters of the Greek alphabet are also used in the Roman alphabet. Some letters, however, are a little misleading – they look like English letters but are pronounced very differently. For more information, see the consonant table on p12 and the box on p34.

Greek punctuation uses the same symbols as in English, except for the question mark – this is written as a semicolon (;).

Greek Alphabet

Α α *al*·pha	Β β *vi*·ta	Γ γ *gha*·ma	Δ δ *ţhel*·ta
Ε ε *ep*·si·lon	Ζ ζ *zi*·ta	Η η *i*·ta	Θ θ *thi*·ta
Ι ι *yio*·ta	Κ κ *ka*·pa	Λ λ *lam*·ţha	Μ μ mi
Ν ν ni	Ξ ξ ksi	Ο ο o·*mi*·kron	Π π pi
Ρ ρ ro	Σ σ/ς* *sigh*·ma	Τ τ taf	Υ υ *ip*·si·lon
Φ φ fi	Χ χ hi	Ψ ψ psi	Ω ω o·*me*·gha

* The letter Σ has two forms for the lower case – σ and ς. The second one is used at the end of words.

A-Z Phrasebuilder

ΚΑΤΑΣΚΕΥΗ ΦΡΑΣΕΩΝ

CONTENTS

The index below shows the grammatical structures you can use to say what you want. Look under each function – in alphabetical order – for information on how to build your own phrases. For example, to tell the taxi driver where your hotel is, look for **giving instructions** and you'll be directed to information on **negatives**, **prepositions** and **requests**. A glossary of grammatical terms is included at the end of this chapter to help you.

Abbreviations like nom and acc in the literal translations for each example refer to the case of the noun or pronoun – this is explained in the glossary and in **case**.

ADJECTIVES & ADVERBS

Describing People/Things

Adjectives in Greek normally come before the noun, just like in English. They take different endings to agree with the noun they qualify (see **case**, p19, **gender**, p21, and **plurals**, p24) – we've given their standard forms below. Adjectives are shown in the nominative form in lists throughout this book and in the **dictionary** (p207) – these forms won't always be strictly correct within a sentence, but you'll still be understood. To find out more, see **case** (p19).

	masculine	feminine	neuter
singular	κα**λός** δρόμος ka·*los* *ţhro*·mos good road	κα**λή** τύχη ka·*li* *ti*·hi good fortune	κα**λό** ποτό ka·*lo* po·*to* good drink
plural	κα**λοί** δρόμοι ka·*li* *ţhro*·mi good roads	κα**λές** τύχες ka·*les* *ti*·hes good fortunes	κα**λά** ποτά ka·*la* po·*ta* good drinks

Adverbs normally end with the sound a (eg καλά ka · *la* 'well').

He filled in the form quickly.

Συμπλήρωσε το έντυπο γρήγορα. — si·*bli*·ro·se to e·di·po *ghri*·gho·ra
(lit: filled-in the-acc form-acc quickly)

ARTICLES

Naming People/Things

The Greek words for 'a' and 'an' change form to agree in gender and case with the noun they refer to.

		masculine		feminine		neuter	
indefinite article (a/an)	nom	ένας	e·nas	μια	m·*ia*	ένα	e·na
	acc	ένα(ν)	e·na(n)	μία	*mi*·a	ένα	e·na
	gen	ενός	e·*nos*	μίας	*mi*·as	ενός	e·*nos*

The Greek equivalents of 'the' also change form according to the noun – see also **case**, **gender** (p21) and **plurals** (p24).

			masculine		feminine		neuter	
definite article (the)	nom	sg	ο	o	η	i	το	to
		pl	οι	i	οι	i	τα	ta
	acc	sg	το(ν)	to(n)	τη(ν)	ti(n)	το	to
		pl	τους	tus	τις	tis	τα	ta
	gen	sg	του	tu	της	tis	του	tu
		pl	των	ton	των	ton	των	ton

Articles alway come before the noun:

a road	**ένας** δρόμος	e·nas *ţhro*·mos
the road	**ο** δρόμος	o *ţhro*·mos

BE

Making Statements

The verb είμαι *i*·me (be) changes depending on who or what is the subject (doer) of the sentence. These are the forms for the present and past tenses.

present			past		
I am	είμαι	*i*·me	I was	ήμουν	*i*·mun
you are sg inf	είσαι	*i*·se	you were sg inf	ήσουν	*i*·sun
you are sg pol	είστε	*i*·ste	you were sg pol	ήσαστε	*i*·sa·ste
he/she/it is	είναι	*i*·ne	he/she/it was	ήταν	*i*·tan
we are	είμαστε	*i*·ma·ste	we were	ήμαστε	*i*·ma·ste
you are pl	είστε	*i*·ste	you were pl	ήσαστε	*i*·sa·ste
they are	είναι	*i*·ne	they were	ήταν	*i*·tan

The future tense is formed by placing the word θα tha (will) in front of the present tense forms.

I'll be there tomorrow.

Θα είμαι εκεί αύριο.	tha *i*·me e·*ki* *av*·ri·o

(lit: will be there tomorrow)

CASE

Doing Things • Indicating Location • Naming People/Things • Possessing

Greek uses four different cases, usually shown by word endings, to indicate a noun's role and its relationship to other words in the sentence. Adjectives, articles, demonstratives and pronouns also change their form to agree with the noun they go with.

nominative nom – shows the subject of a sentence

The car won't start.

Το αυτοκίνητο δεν αρχίζει.	to af·to·*ki*·ni·to ţhen ar·*hi*·zi

(lit: the-nom car-nom doesn't start)

accusative acc – shows the direct object of a sentence

Please bring the menu.

Παρακαλώ φέρε το μενού.	pa·ra·ka·*lo* *fe*·re to me·*nu*

(lit: please bring the-acc menu-acc)

genitive gen – shows possession or the indirect object of a sentence

What's the address of the hotel?

Ποια είναι η διεύθυνση του ξενοδοχείου;	pia *i*·ne i ţhi·*ef*·thin·si tu kse·no·ţho·*hi*·u

(lit: which is the-nom address-nom of the-gen hotel-gen)

vocative voc – to address someone directly

Officer, I think there's been a mistake.

Κύριε, νομίζω ότι έχει γίνει κάποιο λάθος	*ki*·ri·e no·*mi*·zo *o*·ti *e*·hi *yi*·ni *ka*·pio *la*·thos

(lit: sir-voc I-think that has been some-nom mistake-nom)

BASICS A–Z PHRASEBUILDER

Greek nouns in the **dictionaries** (p207), the **menu decoder** (p175) and word lists in this book are given in the nominative case. You can use this form as a default and, although this won't always be grammatically correct within sentences, you'll still be understood.

DEMONSTRATIVES

Indicating Location • Naming People / Things • Pointing Things Out

The words for 'this' and 'that' in Greek change their endings depending on the form of the noun they determine (see **case**, p19, **gender**, and **plurals**, p24). We've only given the nominative forms here – in most cases you'll be understood just fine.

		masculine		feminine		neuter	
this	sg	αυτός	af·*tos*	αυτή	af·*ti*	αυτό	af·*to*
	pl	αυτοί	af·*ti*	αυτές	af·*tes*	αυτά	af·*ta*
that	sg	εκείνος	e·*ki*·nos	εκείνη	e·*ki*·ni	εκείνο	e·*ki*·no
	pl	εκείνοι	e·*ki*·ni	εκείνες	e·*ki*·nes	εκείνα	e·*ki*·na

Does this train go to Lamia?

Πηγαίνει αυτό το τρένο στη Λαμία; — pi·*ye*·ni af·*to* to *tre*·no sti la·*mi*·a

(lit: goes this-nom the-nom train-nom to Lamia-acc)

That bag is mine.

Εκείνη η τσάντα είναι δική μου. — e·*ki*·ni i *tsa*·da *i*·ne ţhi·*ki* mu

(lit: that-nom the-nom bag-nom is mine)

This is my bag.

Αυτή η σάκα είναι δική μου. — af·*ti* i sa·ka *i*·ne ţhi·*ki* mu

(lit: this-nom the-nom bag-nom is mine)

GENDER

Naming People / Things

Greek nouns have gender – masculine **m**, feminine **f** or neuter **n**. You need to learn the grammatical gender for each noun as you go, but you can often identify it by the noun's ending as shown in the table below. Adjectives, articles and pronouns take the same gender to agree with the noun they qualify.

common noun endings				
masculine	sg	**-ας** πατέρας pa·*te*·ras father	**-ης** ναύτης *naf*·tis sailor	**-ος** δρόμος *thro*·mos road
	pl	**-ες** πατέρες pa·*te*·res fathers	**-ες** ναύτες *naf*·tes sailors	**-οι** δρόμοι *thro*·mi roads
feminine	sg	**-α** πόρτα *por*·ta door	**-η** τύχη *ti*·hi fortune	
	pl	**-ες** πόρτες *por*·tes doors	**-ες** τύχες *ti*·hes fortunes	
neuter	sg	**-μα** όνομα *o*·no·ma name	**-ι** αγόρι a·*gho*·ri boy	**-ο** ποτό po·*to* drink
	pl	**-τα** ονόματα o·*no*·ma·ta names	**-α** αγόρια a·*gho*·ria boys	**-α** ποτά po·*ta* drinks

HAVE

Possessing

The verb έχω *e*·kho (have) only changes form according to who or what is the subject (doer) of the sentence. To form the future tense (as in the example on p22), just place the word θα tha (will) in front of the present tense forms.

present			past		
I have	έχω	e·kho	I had	είχα	*i*·kha
you have sg inf	έχεις	e·his	you had sg inf	είχες	*i*·hes
you have sg pol	έχετε	e·he·te	you had sg pol	είχατε	*i*·kha·te
he/she/it has	έχει	e·hi	he/she/it had	είχε	*i*·he
we have	έχουμε	e·khu·me	we had	είχαμε	*i*·kha·me
you have pl	έχετε	e·he·te	you had pl	είχατε	*i*·kha·te
they have	έχουν	e·khun	they had	είχαν	*i*·khan

I'll have no money by the end of my trip!

Δεν θα έχω χρήματα με το τέλος του ταξιδιού! — ţhen tha e·kho *khri*·ma·ta me to *te*·los tu tak·si·*ţhiu*

(lit: not will I-have money-acc with the-acc end-acc the-gen trip-gen)

NEGATIVES

Giving Instructions • Negating

To make a statement negative, add the word δεν ţhen (not) before the verb:

I speak Greek.

Μιλώ Ελληνικά. — mi·*lo* e·li·ni·*ka*

(lit: speak Greek)

I don't speak Greek.

Δεν μιλώ Ελληνικά. — ţhen mi·*lo* e·li·ni·*ka*

(lit: not speak Greek)

In commands, use the word μην min (not) instead:

Don't swim here.

Μην κολυμπάς εδώ. — min ko·li·*bas* e·*ţho*

(lit: not swim here)

Note that, unlike English, Greek has double negatives:

I don't want anything.
Δεν θέλω τίποτε. ţhen *the*·lo *ti*·po·te
(lit: not want nothing)

PERSONAL PRONOUNS

Doing Things • Making Statements

In Greek, there are two words for 'you' – an informal one, εσύ e·*si* (used with friends, younger people or family members), and a formal one, εσείς e·*sis* (used when addressing strangers, authority figures or older people). In this phrasebook we've used the form of 'you' (and the verb form) appropriate for each situation.

	subject nom			
I	εγώ		e·*gho*	
you sg inf	εσύ		e·*si*	
you sg pol	εσείς		e·*sis*	
he/she/it	αυτός/αυτή/αυτό		af·*tos*/af·*ti*/af·*to*	
we	εμείς		e·*mis*	
you pl	εσείς		e·*sis*	
they m/f/n	αυτοί/αυτές/αυτά		af·*ti*/af·*tes*/af·*ta*	
	direct object acc		**indirect object gen**	
me	με	me	μου	mu
you sg inf	σε	se	σου	su
you sg pol	σας	sas	σας	sas
him/her/it	τον/την/το	ton/tin/to	του/της/του	tu/tis/tu
us	μας	mas	μας	mas
you pl	σας	sas	σας	sas
them m/f/n	τους/τις/τα	tus/tis/ta	τους	tus

Greek pronouns vary according to case – the subject or doer of an action is in the nominative case while the object is in the accusative or genitive case.

Both direct and indirect object pronouns are placed before the verb. If you have both in a sentence, the indirect pronoun comes first. In commands, they come after the verb.

I gave my passport to him.

Του έδωσα το διαβατήριό μου. — tu e·ţho·sa to ţhia·va·*ti*·ri·o mu
(lit: him-gen I-gave the-acc passport-acc my)

I gave it to him.

Του το έδωσα. — tu to e·ţho·sa
(lit: him-gen it-acc I-gave)

It's not necessary to use a subject pronoun in Greek, as verb endings show who the subject is. A subject pronoun can be used for emphasis or when there's no verb in the sentence.

I go to school everyday.

Πηγαίνω στο σχολείο κάθε μέρα. — pi·*ye*·no sto skho·*li*·o *ka*·the *me*·ra
(lit: go-I to school-acc every day)

***I* did it.**

Εγώ το έκανα. — e·*gho* to e·ka·na
(lit: I-nom it-acc did)

PLURALS

Naming People/Things

Plural nouns take different endings depending on gender – see the table under **gender** (p21) for the most common ones. Adjectives, articles, demonstratives and pronouns also have plural forms to agree with the plural noun.

POSSESSIVES

Possessing

Possession can be expressed not only with the verb 'have' but with possessive pronouns and adjectives as well.

The possessive adjectives (my, your, his etc) are placed after the noun, with the definite article before the noun (see also **articles**, p17). They don't change for case, gender or number.

possessive adjectives		
my	μου	mu
your sg inf	σου	su
your sg pol	σας	sas
his/her/its	του/της/του	tu/tis/tu
our	μας	mas
your pl	σας	sas
their	τους	tus

I've lost my car keys.

Έχασα τα κλειδιά του αυτοκινήτου μου. — e·kha·sa ta kli·*ţhia* tu af·to·ki·*ni*·tu mu

(lit: lost the-acc keys-acc the-gen car-gen my)

Possessive pronouns (mine, yours etc) are formed by adding the word δικός/δική/δικό thi·*kos*/thi·*ki*/thi·*ko* m/f/n in front of the possessive adjective. This word agrees in gender and case with the noun it refers to – endings are the same as those the adjectives take (see **adjectives & adverbs**, p17). To keep things simple we've only given the nominative case in the next table.

possessive pronouns			
	masculine	feminine	neuter
mine	δικός μου ţhi·*kos* mu	δική μου ţhi·*ki* mu	δικό μου ţhi·*ko* mu
yours sg inf	δικός σου ţhi·*kos* su	δική σου ţhi·*ki* su	δικό σου ţhi·*ko* su
yours sg pol	δικός σας ţhi·*kos* sas	δική σας ţhi·*ki* sas	δικό σας ţhi·*ko* sas
his/hers/its	δικός του/της/του ţhi·*kos* tu/tis/tu	δική του/της/του ţhi·*ki* tu/tis/tu	δικό του/της/του ţhi·*ko* tu/tis/tu
ours	δικός μας ţhi·*kos* mas	δική μας ţhi·*ki* mas	δικό μας ţhi·*ko* mas
yours pl	δικός σας ţhi·*kos* sas	δική σας ţhi·*ki* sas	δικό σας ţhi·*ko* sas
theirs	δικός τους ţhi·*kos* tus	δική τους ţhi·*ki* tus	δικό τους ţhi·*ko* tus

Those bags are ours.

Εκείνες οι τσάντες είναι δικές μας. — e·*ki*·nes i *tsa*·des *i*·ne ţhi·*kes* mas

(lit: those-nom the-nom bags-nom are ours)

PREPOSITIONS

Giving Instructions • Indicating Location • Pointing Things Out

Many prepositions require the noun used after them to be in a particular case (see **case**, p21) – σε se (to/at/in), από a·*po* (from), με me (with), για yia (for), προς pros (towards), κάτω από *ka*·to a·*po* (under), πάνω σε *pa*·no se (on) are all followed by the accusative. The genitive is used after μεταξύ me·tak·*si* (between).

I'd like to book a seat to Athens.

Θα ήθελα να κρατήσω μια θέση για την Αθήνα. — tha *i*·the·la na kra·*ti*·so mia *the*·si yia tin a·*thi*·na
(lit: I-would like to book a seat-acc for the-acc Athens-acc)

What's the difference between 1st and 2nd class?

Ποια είναι η διαφορά μεταξύ πρώτης και δεύτερης θέσης; — pia *i*·ne i ţhia·fo·*ra* me·tak·*si* *pro*·tis ke *ţhef*·te·ris *the*·sis
(lit: which is the-nom difference-nom between first-gen and second-gen class-gen)

QUESTIONS

Asking Questions

To ask a yes/no question, just raise the intonation at the end of a sentence. Note that Greek uses a semicolon (;) instead of a question mark.

The bus stop is over there.

Η στάση του λεωφορείου είναι εκεί πέρα. — i *sta*·si tu le·o·fo·*ri*·u *i*·ne e·*ki* *pe*·ra
(lit: the-nom stop-nom the-gen bus-gen is there over)

Is the bus stop over there?

Η στάση του λεωφορείου είναι εκεί πέρα; — i *sta*·si tu le·o·fo·*ri*·u *i*·ne e·*ki* *pe*·ra
(lit: the-nom stop-nom the-gen bus-gen is there over)

The subject and the verb are often reversed in questions (see **word order**, p31). You can also start a question with a question word – the verb comes in the second place, just like in English. The table on the next page lists the main question words.

question words		
How?	Πώς;	pos
How many?	Πόσοι/Πόσες/Πόσα; **m/f/n pl**	*po*·si / *po*·ses / *po*·sa
How much?	Πόσος/Πόση/Πόσο; **m/f/n**	*po*·sos / *po*·si / *po*·so
What?	Τι;	ti
When?	Πότε;	*po*·te
Where?	Πού;	pu
Who?	Ποιος/Ποια/Ποιο; **m/f/n sg** Ποιοι/Ποιες/Ποια; **m/f/n pl**	pios / pia / pio pii / pies / pia
Which?	Ποιος/Ποια/Ποιο; **m/f/n sg** Ποιοι/Ποιες/Ποια; **m/f/n pl**	pios / pia / pio pii / pies / pia
Why?	Γιατί;	yi·a·*ti*

How do you pronounce this?
Πώς προφέρεις αυτό; — pos pro·*fe*·ris af·*to*
(lit: how you-pronounce this-acc)

How much is it?
Πόσο κάνει; — *po*·so *ka*·ni
(lit: how-much makes)

When's the first bus?
Πότε είναι το πρώτο λεωφορείο; — *po*·te *i*·ne to *pro*·to le·o·fo·*ri*·o
(lit: when is the-nom first-nom bus-nom)

Who is that?
Ποιος είναι εκείνος; — pios *i*·ne e·*ki*·nos
(lit: who-nom is that-nom)

Why can't I board this train?
Γιατί δεν μπορώ να ανεβώ σ'αυτό το τρένο; — yia·*ti* ţhen bo·*ro* na a·*ne*·vo saf·*to* to *tre*·no
(lit: why not can to board to-this-acc the-acc train-acc)

REQUESTS

Giving Instructions

A simple and polite way to make a request is to use the verb as found in the table on p30, in its second-person present form, followed by παρακαλώ pa · ra · ka · *lo* ('please'). Use the informal (singular) form with people you know well, and the polite (plural) form with others.

Would you please open the window?

ανοίγεις το παράθυρο, παρακαλώ; sg inf (lit: open the window please)	a·*ni*·yis to pa·*ra*·thi·ro pa·ra·ka·*lo*

Would you please open the window?

ανοίγετε το παράθυρο, παρακαλώ; pl pol (lit: open the window please)	a·*ni*·ye·te to pa·*ra*·thi·ro pa·ra·ka·*lo*

For the negative form, see **negatives** (p22).

VERBS

Doing Things

The dictionary form of all Greek verbs ends in -ω · o or -ομαι o · me, which is the present tense form of the first person singular (like in 'I eat'). The ending -ω represents 'active' verbs (which show someone actively doing something – πηγαίνω pi · *ye* · no 'go'), while -ομαι is for 'stative' verbs (which show a state or condition, and don't require movement – κάθομαι *ka* · tho · me 'sit'). These endings change according to the subject of the sentence. Sometimes changes in the verb stem (the form of the verb before the ending) occur, but if you use the endings shown on the next page, you'll be understood just fine.

Present

Active and stative verbs have different sets of endings.

	active verb eg 'write'		stative verb eg 'think'	
dictionary form	γράφω	*ghra*·fo	σκέφτομαι	*skef*·to·me
I	γράφ**ω**	*ghra*·fo	σκέφτ**ομαι**	*skef*·to·me
you sg inf	γράφ**εις**	*ghra*·fis	σκέφτ**εσαι**	*skef*·te·se
you sg pol	γράφ**ετε**	*ghra*·fe·te	σκέφτ**εστε**	*skef*·tes·te
he/she/it	γράφ**ει**	*ghra*·fi	σκέφτ**εται**	*skef*·te·te
we	γράφ**ουμε**	*ghra*·fu·me	σκεφτ**όμαστε**	skef·*to*·ma·ste
you pl	γράφ**ετε**	*ghra*·fe·te	σκέφτ**εστε**	*skef*·tes·te
they	γράφ**ουν**	*ghra*·fun	σκέφτ**ονται**	*skef*·ton·de

Past

The past tense endings for all verbs are provided below. There are some irregularities, however – as the stress in the verb moves back to the third syllable from the end, the prefix ε e· (augment) is added to the verb when there are fewer than three syllables. Also, the final letter before the ending sometimes changes.

	all verbs eg 'write'	
I	έγραψ**α**	e·ghra·psa
you sg inf	έγραψ**ες**	e·ghra·pses
you sg pol	γράψ**ατε**	*ghra*·psa·te
he/she/it	έγραψ**ε**	e·ghra·pse
we	γράψ**αμε**	*ghra*·psa·me
you pl	γράψ**ατε**	*ghra*·psa·te
they	έγραψ**αν**	e·ghra·psan

Future

The easiest way to express an action in the future is by using the present tense forms and adding the word θα tha (will) in front of them.

I'll send you a postcard every day.

Θα σου στέλνω μία κάρτα κάθε μέρα. — tha su *stel*·no *mi*a *kar*·ta *ka*·the *me*·ra

(lit: will you-gen send a-acc postcard-acc every day)

WORD ORDER

Asking Questions • Making Statements • Negating

While the sentence order of subject–verb–object is most common in Greek, all other combinations are correct too – the word order is relatively free as Greek uses case (meaning that different word endings express the role of a word in the sentence). You might notice, however, that emphasised words are usually at the beginning of the sentence (see also **negatives**, p22, and **questions**, p27).

The cashier didn't give me the correct change.

Ο ταμίας δεν μου έδωσε τα σωστά ρέστα. — o ta·*mi*·as then mu e·tho·se ta so·*sta* *re*·sta

(lit: the-nom cashier-nom not me-gen gave the-acc correct-acc change-acc)

The cashier didn't give me the correct change.

Δεν μου έδωσε τα σωστά ρέστα ο ταμίας. — then mu e·tho·se ta so·*sta* *re*·sta o ta·*mi*·as

(lit: not me-gen gave the-acc correct-acc change-acc the-nom cashier-nom)

Note that the indirect object comes before the direct object.

GLOSSARY

active verb	a verb that involves someone actively doing something – 'he **travelled** for many moons'
adjective	a word that describes something – '**ancient** hero'
adverb	a word that explains how an action was done – 'he **heroically** set out to find his father'
article	the words 'a', 'an' and 'the'
case (marking)	word ending that shows the role of the thing or person in the sentence
demonstrative	a word that means 'this' or 'that'
gender	Greek nouns can be masculine, feminine or neuter
imperative	a command – '**prove** to me that you are Odysseus'
noun	a thing, person or idea – 'an odyssey'
number	whether a word is singular or plural – 'journey' or 'journeys'
object (direct)	the thing or person that's directly affected by the action – 'Penelope offered **dinner** to her suitors'
object (indirect)	the person in the sentence that benefits from an action – 'Penelope offered **them** dinner'
personal pronoun	a word that means 'I', 'you', etc
possessive pronoun	a word that means 'mine', 'yours', etc
preposition	a word like 'for' or 'before' in English
stative verb	a verb that doesn't require movement – 'Penelope **missed** her husband very much'
subject	the thing or person that does the action – '**the suitors** took advantage of her hospitality'
tense	marking on the verb that tells you whether the action is in the present, past or future – 'travel**led**'
verb	the word that tells you what action happened – 'Odysseus **disguises** himself as a beggar'
verb stem	the part of a verb which does not change – like 'charm' in 'charmed' and 'charming'

Language difficulties

ΓΛΩΣΣΙΚΕΣ ΔΥΣΚΟΛΙΕΣ

Do you speak (English)?
Μιλάς (Αγγλικά); — mi·*las* (ang·gli·*ka*)

Does anyone speak (English)?
Μιλάει κανείς (Αγγλικά); — mi·*la*·i ka·*nis* (ang·gli·*ka*)

Do you understand?
Καταλαβαίνεις; — ka·ta·la·*ve*·nis

Yes, I understand.
Ναι, καταλαβαίνω. — ne ka·ta·la·*ve*·no

No, I don't understand.
Όχι, δεν καταλαβαίνω. — o·hi ţhen ka·ta·la·*ve*·no

I (don't) understand.
(Δεν) καταλαβαίνω. — (ţhen) ka·ta·la·*ve*·no

Pardon?
Συγνώμη; — sigh·*no*·mi

I speak (English).
Μιλάω (Αγγλικά). — mi·*la*·o (ang·gli·*ka*)

I don't speak Greek.
Δεν μιλάω Ελληνικά. — ţhen mi·*la*·o e·li·ni·*ka*

I speak a little.
Μιλάω λίγο. — mi·mi·*la*·o *li*·gho

Let's speak Greek.
Ας μιλήσουμε Ελληνικά. — as mi·*li*·su·me e·li·ni·*ka*

TONGUE-TIED

If you're after a challenge, try this tongue twister for size.

Ο παπάς ο παχύς έφαγε παχιά φακή.
Γιατί, παπά παχύ, έφαγες παχιά φακή;
o pa·*pas* o pa·*his* e·fa·ye pa·*hia* fa·*ki*
yia·*ti* pa·*pa* pa·*hi* e·fa·yes pa·*hia* fa·*ki*
(The fat priest ate thick lentil soup.
Why, fat priest, did you eat thick lentil soup?)

I would like to practise Greek.
Θα ήθελα να εξασκήσω τα Ελληνικά μου. — tha *i*·the·la na ek·sa·*ski*·so ta e·li·ni·*ka* mu

What does (*μώλος*) mean?
Τι σημαίνει (μώλος); — ti si·*me*·ni (*mo*·los)

How do you ...?	Πώς ...;	pos ...
pronounce this	προφέρεις αυτό	pro·*fe*·ris af·*to*
write 'Madhuri'	γράψεις 'Μαδουρή'	*ghrap*·sis ma·ţhu·*ri*
Could you please ...?	Θα μπορούσες παρακαλώ να ...;	tha bo·*ru*·ses pa·ra·ka·*lo* na ...
repeat that	το επαναλάβεις	to e·pa·na·*la*·vis
speak more slowly	μιλάς πιο αργά	mi·*las* pio ar·*gha*
write it down	το γράψεις	to *ghrap*·sis

☑ ALPHABET SOUP

Some Greek letters might look like English ones, but they're pronounced quite differently.

upper case	lower case	pronunciation
Β	β	v
Η	η	i
Ρ	ρ	r
Υ	υ	i
Χ	χ	h
Ν	ν	n
Ξ	ξ	ks
Σ	σ/ς	s
Ω	ω	o

See the box on p14 for the full Greek alphabet.

Numbers & Amounts

ΑΡΙΘΜΟΙ ΚΑΙ ΠΟΣΑ

CARDINAL NUMBERS

απόλυτοι αριθμοί

In Greek, some numbers (one, three, four, and numbers linked to them like 21 and 13) change according to gender – that is, they have different forms when the noun they're associated with is masculine **m**, feminine **f** or neuter **n**. When simply counting, you use the neuter form.

1	ένας/μία/ένα **m / f / n**	e·nas / *mi*·a / e·na
2	Δύο	*ţhi*·o
3	τρεις/τρία **m&f / n**	tris / *tri*·a
4	τέσσερις **m&f**	*te*·se·ris
	τέσσερα **n**	*te*·se·ra
5	πέντε	*pe*·de
6	έξι	*ek*·si
7	εφτά	ef·*ta*
8	οχτώ	okh·*to*
9	εννέα	e·*ne*·a
10	δέκα	*ţhe*·ka
11	έντεκα	e·de·ka
12	δώδεκα	*ţho*·ţhe·ka
13	δεκατρείς **m&f**	ţhe·ka·*tris*
	δεκατρία **n**	ţhe·ka·*tri*·a
14	δεκατέσσερις **m&f**	ţhe·ka·*te*·se·ris
	δεκατέσσερα **n**	ţhe·ka·*te*·se·ra
15	δεκαπέντε	ţhe·ka·*pe*·de
16	δεκαέξι	ţhe·ka·*ek*·si
17	δεκαεφτά	ţhe·ka·ef·*ta*
18	δεκαοχτώ	ţhe·ka·okh·*to*
19	δεκαεννέα	ţhe·ka·e·*ne*·a
20	είκοσι	*i*·ko·si
21	είκοσι ένας/μία **m / f**	*i*·ko·si e·nas / *mi*·a
	είκοσι ένα **n**	*i*·ko·si e·na

22	είκοσι δύο	*i*·ko·si *ţhi*·o
30	τριάντα	tri·*a*·da
40	σαράντα	sa·*ra*·da
50	πενήντα	pe·*ni*·da
60	εξήντα	ek·*si*·da
70	εβδομήντα	ev·ţho·*mi*·da
80	ογδόντα	ogh·*ţho*·da
90	ενενήντα	e·ne·*ni*·da
100	εκατό	e·ka·*to*
200	διακόσια	ţhia·*ko*·sia
1000	χίλια	*hi*·lia
1,000,000	ένα εκατομμύριο	e·na e·ka·to·*mi*·rio

ORDINAL NUMBERS

τακτικοί αριθμοί

Ordinals agree in gender with the noun they're associated with.

1st	πρώτος/πρώτη **m/f**	*pro*·tos / *pro*·ti
	πρώτο **n**	*pro*·to
2nd	δεύτερος/δεύτερη **m/f**	*ţhef*·te·ros / *ţhef*·te·ri
	δεύτερο **n**	*ţhef*·te·ro
3rd	τρίτος/τρίτη/τρίτο **m/f/n**	*tri*·tos / *tri*·ti / *tri*·to
4th	τέταρτος/τέταρτη **m/f**	*te*·tar·tos / *te*·tar·ti
	τέταρτο **n**	*te*·tar·to
5th	πέμπτος/πέμπτη **m/f**	*pemp*·tos / *pemp*·ti
	πέμπτο **n**	*pemp*·to
6th	έκτος/έκτη/έκτο **m/f/n**	*ek*·tos / *ek*·ti / *ek*·to
7th	έβδομος/έβδομη **m/f**	*ev*·ţho·mos / *ev*·ţho·mi
	έβδομο **n**	*ev*·ţho·mo
8th	όγδοος/όγδοη **m/f**	*ogh*·ţho·os / *ogh*·ţho·i
	όγδοο **n**	*ogh*·ţho·o
9th	ένατος/ένατη/ένατο **m/f/n**	*e*·na·tos / *e*·na·ti / *e*·na·to
10th	δέκατος/δέκατη **m/f**	*ţhe*·ka·tos / *ţhe*·ka·ti
	δέκατο **n**	*ţhe*·ka·to

A QUICK COUNT

Just as the ordinal numbers have gender in Greek, so too do the abbreviations for '1st', '2nd', '3rd' etc. Masculine ordinals take the abbreviation ος, feminine ordinals take η, and the neuter ones ο. For example '7th' can be written 7ος, 7η, or 7ο depending on gender.

FRACTIONS

κλάσματα

a quarter	ένα τέταρτο **n**	e·na *te*·tar·to
a third	ένα τρίτο **n**	e·na *tri*·to
a half	μισό **n**	mi·*so*
three-quarters	τρία τέταρτα **n pl**	*tri*·a *te*·tar·ta
all	όλα **n pl**	*o*·la
none	τίποτε	*ti*·po·te

USEFUL AMOUNTS

χρήσιμα ποσά

The words for 'How much?' and 'How many?' take different forms for the gender of the noun they refer to, as shown below.

How much?	Πόσος/Πόση **m/f**	*po*·sos/*po*·si
	Πόσο; **n**	*po*·so
How many?	Πόσοι/Πόσες **m/f**	*po*·si/*po*·ses
	Πόσα; **n**	*po*·sa
How much water?	Πόσο νερό; **n**	*po*·so ne·*ro*
How much sugar?	Πόση ζάχαρη; **f**	*po*·si *za*·kha·ri
How many men?	Πόσοι άντρες; **m**	*po*·si *a*·dres
How many women?	Πόσες γυναίκες; **f**	*po*·ses yi·*ne*·kes

I'd like (a) ...	Θα ήθελα ...	tha *i*·the·la ...
Please give me (a) ...	Παρακαλώ δώσε μου ...	pa·ra·ka·*lo* ţho·se mu ...
(100) grams	(εκατό) γραμμάρια	(e·ka·*to*) ghra·*ma*·ria
half a dozen	μισή ντουζίνα	mi·*si* du·*zi*·na
dozen	μια ντουζίνα	mia du·*zi*·na
half a kilo	μισό κιλό	mi·so ki·*lo*
kilo	ένα κιλό	e·na ki·*lo*
bottle	ένα μπουκάλι	e·na bu·*ka*·li
jar	ένα βάζο	e·na *va*·zo
tin	ένα κουτί	e·na ku·*ti*
packet	ένα πακέτο	e·na pa·*ke*·to
slice	μια φέτα	mia *fe*·ta
few	λίγα	*li*·gha
less	λιγότερο	li·*gho*·te·ro
(just) a little	(μόνο) λιγάκι	(*mo*·no) li·*gha*·ki
lot	πολύ	po·*li*
many	πολλά	po·*la*
more	πιο πολύ	pio po·*li*
some ...	μερικά ...	me·ri·*ka* ...

To find out how to put these amounts to use, see **self-catering**, p171.

WHAT'S IN A NAME?

Although Greeks have moved around their own country and emigrated worldwide, you can sometimes tell from their surnames where they originally come from. People whose name ends in -ακης -a · kis are from Crete, -ατος -a · tos from Cephallonia, -ιδης -i · ţhis from Macedonia, and -πουλος -pu · los from the Peloponnese.

Time & Dates

ΩΡΑ ΚΑΙ ΗΜΕΡΟΜΗΝΙΕΣ

TELLING THE TIME

λέγοντας την ώρα

Telling the time in Greek is straightforward. For 'It's ... o'clock' simply say είναι *i*·ne (lit: it-is) followed by the number, then η ώρα i *o*·ra (lit: the hour). Note that η ώρα is optional. To give times after the hour, say the number of hours, then και ke (lit: and) and the number of minutes. For times before the hour, say the number of hours, then παρά pa·*ra* (lit: minus) and the minutes. Instead of 30 or 15 minutes, say μισή mi·*si* (half) for the half hour and τέταρτο *te*·tar·to for a quarter hour.

What time is it?
Τι ώρα είναι; — ti *o*·ra *i*·ne

It's (ten) o'clock.
Είναι (δέκα) η ώρα. — *i*·ne (*th*e·ka) i *o*·ra

Five past (ten).
(Δέκα) και πέντε. — (*th*e·ka) ke *pe*·de

Quarter past (ten).
(Δέκα) και τέταρτο. — (*th*e·ka) ke *te*·tar·to

Half past (ten).
(Δέκα) και μισή. — (*th*e·ka) ke mi·*si*

Quarter to (ten).
(Δέκα) παρά τέταρτο. — (*th*e·ka) pa·*ra* *te*·tar·to

Twenty to (ten).
(Δέκα) παρά είκοσι. — (*th*e·ka) pa·*ra* *i*·ko·si

At what time ...?
Τι ώρα ...; — ti *o*·ra ...

At (ten).
Στις (δέκα). — stis (*th*e·ka)

At (7.57pm).
Στις (7.57μ.μ.). — stis (ef·*ta* ke pe·*ni*·da ef·*ta* to *vra*·di)

SHORT TIMES

The times 'am' and 'pm' are written 'π.μ.' (to a·*po*·gevma) and 'μ.μ.' (to *vra*·di), but the full names are πριν το μεσημέρι prin to me·si·*me*·ri (am) and μετά το μεσημέρι me·*ta* to me·si·*me*·ri (pm).

THE CALENDAR

το ημερολόγιο

Monday	Δευτέρα	ţhef·*te*·ra
Tuesday	Τρίτη	*tri*·ti
Wednesday	Τετάρτη	te·*tar*·ti
Thursday	Πέμπτη	*pemp*·ti
Friday	Παρασκευή	pa·ra·ske·*vi*
Saturday	Σάββατο	*sa*·va·to
Sunday	Κυριακή	ki·ria·*ki*

January	Ιανουάριος	i·a·nu·*a*·ri·os
February	Φεβρουάριος	fev·ru·*a*·ri·os
March	Μάρτιος	*mar*·ti·os
April	Απρίλιος	a·*pri*·li·os
May	Μάιος	*ma*·i·os
June	Ιούνιος	i·*u*·ni·os
July	Ιούλιος	i·*u*·li·os
August	Αύγουστος	*av*·ghu·stos
September	Σεπτέμβριος	sep·*tem*·vri·os
October	Οκτώβριος	ok·*tov*·ri·os
November	Νοέμβριος	no·*em*·vri·os
December	Δεκέμβριος	ţhe·*kem*·vri·os

What date is it today?
Τι ημερομηνία είναι σήμερα; — ti i·me·ro·mi·*ni*·a *i*·ne *si*·me·ra

It's (18 October).
Είναι (18 Οκτωβρίου). — *i*·ne (ţhe·ka·okh·*to* ok·tov·*ri*·u)

spring	άνοιξη f	a·nik·si
summer	καλοκαίρι n	ka·lo·*ke*·ri
autumn	φθινόπωρο n	fthi·*no*·po·ro
winter	χειμώνας m	hi·*mo*·nas

PRESENT

παρόν

now	τώρα	*to*·ra
today	σήμερα	*si*·me·ra
tonight	το βράδι	to *vra*·ţhi
this week	αυτή την εβδομάδα	af·*ti* tin ev·ţho·*ma*·ţha
this ...	αυτό το ...	af·*to* to ...
morning	πρωί	pro·*i*
afternoon	απόγευμα	a·*po*·yev·ma
month	μήνα	*mi*·na
year	χρόνο	*khro*·no

PAST

παρελθόν

(three days) ago	(τρεις μέρες) πριν	(tris *me*·res) prin
day before yesterday	προχτές	prokh·*tes*
since (May)	από (το Μάιο)	a·*po* (to *ma*·i·o)
yesterday ...	χτες το ...	khtes to ...
morning	πρωί	pro·*i*
afternoon	απογευμα	a·*po*·yev·ma
evening	βράδι	*vra*·ţhi
last night / week	την περασμένη νύχτα/εβδομάδα	tin pe·raz·*me*·ni *nikh*·ta / ev·ţho·*ma*·ţha
last month / year	τον περασμένο μήνα/χρόνο	ton pe·raz·*me*·no *mi*·na / *khro*·no

FUTURE

μέλλον

tomorrow ...	αύριο το ...	av·ri·o to ...
morning	πρωί	pro·*i*
afternoon	απόγευμα	a·*po*·yev·ma
evening	βράδι	*vra*·ţhi
tomorrow	αύριο	*av*·ri·o
day after tomorrow	μεθαύριο	me·*thav*·ri·o
next week	την επόμενη εβδομάδα	tin e·*po*·me·ni ev·ţho·*ma*·ţha
next month	τον επόμενο μήνα	ton e·*po*·me·no *mi*·na
next year	τον επόμενο χρόνο	ton e·*po*·me·no *khro*·no
in (six days)	σε (έξι μέρες)	se (*ek*·si *me*·res)
until (June)	μέχρι (τον Ιούνιο)	*meh*·ri (ton i·*u*·ni·o)

DURING THE DAY

κατά τη διάρκεια της ημέρας

afternoon	απόγευμα n	a·*po*·yev·ma
dawn	αυγή f	av·*yi*
day	ημέρα f	i·*me*·ra
evening	βράδι n	*vra*·ţhi
midday	μεσημέρι n	me·si·*me*·ri
midnight	μεσάνυχτα n pl	me·*sa*·nikh·ta
morning	πρωί n	pro·*i*
night	νύχτα f	*nikh*·ta
sunrise	ανατολή του ήλιου f	a·na·to·*li* tu *i*·liu
sunset	δύση του ήλιου f	*ţhi*·si tu *i*·liu

☑ BUT THE MOST IMPORTANT TIME OF THE DAY...

... is probably the μεσημεριανή ανάπαυση me·si·*me*·ria·*ni* a·*na*·paf·si (siesta). Don't miss out!

Money

ΧΡΗΜΑΤΑ

How much is it?
Πόσο κάνει; — *po*·so *ka*·ni

It's (12) euros.
Κάνει (δώδεκα) ευρώ. — *ka*·ni (*ţho*·ţhe·ka) ev·*ro*

It's free.
Είναι δωρεάν. — *i*·ne ţho·re·*an*

Can you write down the price?
Μπορείς να γράψεις την τιμή; — bo·*ris* na *ghrap*·sis tin ti·*mi*

Do you accept ...?	Δέχεσαι ...;	*ţhe*·he·se ...
credit cards	πιστωτικές κάρτες	pi·sto·ti·*kes* *kar*·tes
debit cards	χρεωστικές κάρτες	khre·os·ti·*kes* *kar*·tes

Where's a/an ...?	Πού είναι ...;	pu *i*·ne ...
automated teller machine	μια αυτόματη μηχανή ανάληψης χρημάτων	mia af·*to*·ma·ti mi·kha·*ni* a·*na*·lip·sis khri·*ma*·ton
foreign exchange office	ένα γραφείο αλλαγής χρημάτων	e·na ghra·*fi*·o a·la·*yis* khri·*ma*·ton

TALKIN' ABOUT MONEY

The official currency in Greece is the ευρώ ev · *ro* (euro), which is made up of 100 λεπτά lep · *ta* (cents). Some vendors are also happy to take foreign currencies.

What's the ...?	Πόσο είναι …;	*po*·so *i*·ne ...
charge	το κόστος	to *kos*·tos
exchange rate	η τιμή συναλλάγματος	i ti·*mi* si·na·*lagh*·ma·tos
I'd like to ...	Θα ήθελα να …	tha *i*·the·la na ...
cash a cheque	εξαργυρώσω μια επιταγή	ek·sar·yi·*ro*·so mia e·pi·ta·*yi*
change money	αλλάξω χρήματα	a·*lak*·so *khri*·ma·ta
get a cash advance	κάνω μια ανάληψη σε μετρητά	*ka*·no mia a·*na*·lip·si se me·tri·*ta*
withdraw money	αποσύρω χρήματα	a·po·*si*·ro *khri*·ma·ta
I'd like ..., please.	Θα ήθελα …, παρακαλώ.	tha *i*·the·la ... pa·ra·ka·*lo*
my change	τα ρέστα μου	ta *re*·sta mu
a refund	μια επιστροφή χρημάτων	mia e·pi·stro·*fi* khri·*ma*·ton
to return this	να επιστρέψω αυτό	na e·pi·*strep*·so af·*to*

There's a mistake in the bill.
Υπάρχει κάποιο λάθος στο λογαριασμό. — i·*par*·hi *ka*·pio *la*·thos sto lo·gha·riaz·*mo*

Do I need to pay upfront?
Χρειάζεται να πληρώσω από πριν; — khri·a·ze·te na pli·*ro*·so a·*po* prin

I don't have that much money.
Δεν έχω τόσα πολλά χρήματα. — ţhen e·kho *to*·sa po·*la* *khri*·ma·ta

PRACTICAL

Transport

ΣΥΓΚΟΙΝΩΝΙΑ

GETTING AROUND

κυκλοφορώντας

Which ... goes to (Athens)?	Ποιο ... πηγαίνει στην (Αθήνα);	pio ... pi·*ye*·ni stin (a·*thi*·na)
Is this the ... to (Athens)?	Είναι αυτό το ... για την (Αθήνα);	*i*·ne af·*to* to ... yia tin (a·*thi*·na)
boat	πλοίο	*pli*·o
bus	λεωφορείο	le·o·fo·*ri*·o
ferry	φέρυ	*fe*·ri
plane	αεροπλάνο	a·e·ro·*pla*·no
train	τρένο	*tre*·no
When's the ... (bus)?	Πότε είναι το ... (λεωφορείο);	*po*·te *i*·ne to ... (le·o·fo·*ri*·o)
first	πρώτο	*pro*·to
last	τελευταίο	te·lef·*te*·o
next	επόμενο	e·*po*·me·no

What time does it leave?
Τι ώρα φεύγει; — ti *o*·ra *fev*·yi

What time does it get to (Thessaloniki)?
Τι ώρα φτάνει στη (Θεσσαλονίκη); — ti *o*·ra *fta*·ni sti (the·sa·lo·*ni*·ki)

How long will it be delayed?
Πόση ώρα θα καθυστερήσει; — *po*·si *o*·ra tha ka·thi·ste·*ri*·si

Is this seat free?
Είναι αυτή η θέση ελεύθερη; — *i*·ne af·*ti* i *the*·si e·*lef*·the·ri

That's my seat.
Αυτή η θέση είναι δική μου. — af·*ti* i *the*·si *i*·ne ţhi·*ki* mu

Please tell me when we get to (Thessaloniki).

Παρακαλώ πέστε μου όταν φτάσουμε στη (Θεσσαλονίκη).	pa·ra·ka·*lo* *pe*·ste mu *o*·tan *fta*·su·me sti (the·sa·lo·*ni*·ki)

How long do we stop here?

Πόση ώρα θα σταματήσουμε εδώ;	*po*·si *o*·ra tha sta·ma·*ti*·su·me e·*ţho*

Are you waiting for more people?

Περιμένεις για περισσότερο κόσμο;	pe·ri·*me*·nis yia pe·ri·*so*·te·ro *koz*·mo

Can you take us around the city, please?

Μπορείς να μας πας γύρω στην πόλη, παρακαλώ;	bo·*ris* na mas pas *yi*·ro stin *po*·li pa·ra·ka·*lo*

How many people can ride on this?

Πόσοι άνθρωποι μπορούν να ανεβούν σ'αυτό;	*po*·si *an*·thro·pi bo·*run* na a·ne·*vun* saf·*to*

Can you take me as well?

Μπορείς να πάρεις και εμένα;	bo·*ris* na *pa*·ris ke e·*me*·na

TICKETS

εισιτήρια

Where do I buy a ticket?

Πού αγοράζω εισιτήριο;	pu a·gho·*ra*·zo i·si·*ti*·ri·o

Do I need to book?

Χρειάζεται να κλείσω θέση;	khri·a·ze·te na *kli*·so *the*·si

A bunch of (10) tickets, please.

Μια δέσμη από (δέκα) εισιτήρια, παρακαλώ.	mia *ţhez*·mi a·*po* (*ţhe*·ka) i·si·*ti*·ri·a pa·ra·ka·*lo*

Do you have a timetable (in English)?

Έχεις ένα πρόγραμμα (στα αγγλικά);	e·his e·na *pro*·ghra·ma (sta ang·gli·*ka*)

Can I get a tourist rail pass?

Μπορώ να έχω ένα τουριστικό πάσο για το τρένο;	bo·*ro* na e·kho e·na tu·ri·sti·*ko* *pa*·so yia to *tre*·no

A ... ticket to (Patras).	Ένα εισιτήριο ... για την (Πάτρα).	e·na i·si·*ti*·ri·o ... yia tin (*pa*·tra)
1st-class	πρώτη θέση	*pro*·ti *the*·si
2nd-class	δεύτερη θέση	*ţhef*·te·ri *the*·si
child's	παιδικό	pe·ţhi·*ko*
deck class (ferry)	κατάστρωμα	ka·*ta*·stro·ma
one-way	απλό	a·*plo*
return	με επιστροφή	me e·pi·stro·*fi*
student's	μαθητικό	ma·thi·ti·*ko*
tourist class	τουριστική θέση	tu·ri·sti·*ki* *the*·si

I'd like a/an ... seat.	Θα ήθελα μια θέση ...	tha *i*·the·la mia *the*·si ...
aisle	στο διάδρομο	sto *ţhia*·ţhro·mo
(non)smoking	στους (μη) καπνίζοντες	stus (mi) kap·*ni*·zo·des
window	στο παράθυρο	sto pa·*ra*·thi·ro

LISTEN FOR

Ακυρώστε το εισιτήριο.	a·ki·*ro*·ste to i·si·*ti*·rio	**Punch the ticket.**
ακυρώθηκε	a·ki·*ro*·thi·ke	**cancelled**
απεργία f	a·per·*yi*·a	**strike**
αυτό	af·*to*	**this one**
εκείνο	e·*ki*·no	**that one**
γεμάτο	ye·*ma*·to	**full**
καθυστέρησε	ka·thi·*ste*·ri·se	**delayed**
θυρίδα αγοράς εισιτιρίων f	thi·*ri*·ţha a·gho·*ras* i·si·ti·*ri*·on	**ticket window**
πλατφόρμα f	plat·*for*·ma	**platform**
πρόγραμμα n	*pro*·ghra·ma	**timetable**
ταξιδιωτικός πράκτορας m	tak·si·ţhio·ti·*kos* *prak*·to·ras	**travel agent**

Is there (a) ...?	Υπάρχει ...;	i·*par*·hi ...
air conditioning	έρκοντίσιον	er·kon·*di*·si·on
blanket	κουβέρτα	ku·*ver*·ta
sick bag	σακούλα εμετού	sa·*ku*·la e·me·*tu*
toilet	τουαλέτα	tu·a·*le*·ta

Can I get a sleeping berth?
Μορώ να έχω μια θέση με κρεβάτι; — bo·*ro* na e·kho mia *the*·si me kre·*va*·ti

How much is it?
Πόσο κάνει; — *po*·so *ka*·ni

How long does the trip take?
Πόσο διαρκεί το ταξίδι; — *po*·so ţhi·ar·*ki* to tak·*si*·ţhi

Is it a direct route?
Πηγαίνει κατ'ευθείαν; — pi·*ye*·ni ka·tef·*thi*·an

Can I get a stand-by ticket?
Μπορώ να μπω στον κατάλογο αναμονής για εισιτήριο; — bo·*ro* na bo ston ka·*ta*·lo·gho a·na·mo·*nis* yia i·si·*ti*·ri·o

What time should I check in?
Τι ώρα να έρθω στον έλεγχο; — ti *o*·ra na *er*·tho ston e·leng·kho

I'd like to ... my ticket, please.	Θα ήθελα να ... το εισιτήριό μου παρακαλώ.	tha *i*·the·la na ... to i·si·*ti*·ri·*o* mu pa·ra·ka·*lo*
cancel	ακυρώσω	a·ki·*ro*·so
change	αλλάξω	a·*lak*·so
punch	επικυρώσω	e·pi·ki·*ro*·so

IT'S NOT ROULETTE

If Athenian locals talk about μονά-ζυγά mo·*na*·zi·*gha* (odds-evens) and δακτύλιος ţhak·*ti*·lios (rings), they refer to traffic restrictions put in place in Athens to help minimise the notorious νέφος *ne*·fos (smog). The system is called 'odds-evens' because certain cars can enter the 'ring' (a restricted zone) on even or odd days of the month. The boundaries of the ţhak·*ti*·lios are marked with yellow hexagonal signs.

LUGGAGE

αποσκευές

Where can I find a/the ...?	Πού μπορώ να βρω ...;	pu bo·*ro* na vro ...
baggage claim	το χώρο αποσκευών	to *kho*·ro a·pos·ke·*von*
left-luggage office	φύλαξη αποσκευών	*fi*·lak·si a·pos·ke·*von*
luggage locker	τη φύλαξη αντικειμένων	ti *fi*·lak·si a·di·ki·*me*·non
trolley	ένα καροτσάκι	e·na ka·rot·*sa*·ki
My luggage has been ...	Οι αποσκευές μου έχουν ...	i a·pos·ke·*ves* mu e·khun ...
damaged	πάθει ζημιά	*pa*·thi zi·*mia*
lost	χαθεί	kha·*thi*
stolen	κλαπεί	kla·*pi*

That's (not) mine.
Αυτό (δεν) είναι δικό μου. — af·*to* (ţhen) *i*·ne ţhi·*ko* mu

Can I have some coins/tokens?
Μπορώ να έχω μερικά κέρματα/κουπόνια; — bo·*ro* na e·kho me·ri·*ka* *ker*·ma·ta/ku·*po*·nia

LISTEN FOR

αποσκευές χειρός f pl	a·pos·ke·*ves* hi·*ros*	**carry-on baggage**
διαβατήριο n	ţhi·a·va·*ti*·ri·o	**passport**
κάρτα επιβίβασης f	*kar*·ta e·pi·*vi*·va·sis	**boarding pass**
κουπόνι n	ku·*po*·ni	**token**
μεταβίβαση f	me·ta·*vi*·va·si	**transfer**
πτήση τσάρτερ f	*pti*·si *tsar*·ter	**charter flight**
τράνζιτ n	*tran*·zit	**transit**
υπέρβαρο n	i·*per*·va·ro	**excess baggage**

PLANE

αεροπλάνο

Where does flight (10) arrive / depart?
Πού προσγειώνεται/ απογειώνεται η πτήση (δέκα); — pu pros·yi·*o*·ne·te / a·po·yi·*o*·ne·te i *pti*·si (*ţhe*·ka)

Where's (the) ...?	Πού είναι ...;	pu *i*·ne ...
airport shuttle	το λεωφορείο του αεροδρομίου	to le·o·fo·*ri*·o tu a·e·ro·ţhro·*mi*·u
arrivals hall	η αίθουσα των αφίξεων	i e·thu·sa ton a·*fik*·se·on
departures hall	η αίθουσα των αναχωρήσεων	i e·thu·sa ton a·na·kho·*ri*·se·on
duty-free shops	τα αφορολόγητα	ta a·fo·ro·*lo*·yi·ta
gate (9)	η θύρα (εννέα)	i *thi*·ra (e·*ne*·a)

BUS & COACH

λεωφορεία, τρόλεϋ και πούλμαν

How often do buses come?
Κάθε πότε έρχονται τα λεωφορεία; — *ka*·the *po*·te *er*·kho·de ta le·o·fo·*ri*·a

Does it stop at (Iraklio)?
Σταματάει στο (Ηράκλειο); — sta·ma·*ta*·i sto (i·*ra*·kli·o)

What's the next stop?
Ποια είναι η επόμενη στάση; — pia *i*·ne i e·*po*·me·ni *sta*·si

I'd like to get off (at Iraklio).
Θα ήθελα να κατεβώ (στο Ηράκλειο). — tha *i*·the·la na ka·te·*vo* (sto i·*ra*·kli·o)

Where's the trolley bus stop?
Πού είναι η στάση του τρόλεϋ; — pu *i*·ne i *sta*·si tu *tro*·le·i

city a	αστικό	a·sti·*ko*
intercity a	υπεραστικό	i·pe·ra·sti·*ko*
local a	τοπικό	to·pi·*ko*

TRAIN & METRO

τρένο και μετρό

Where's the nearest metro station?
Πού είναι ο πιο κοντινός σταθμός του μετρό; — pu *i*·ne o pio ko·di·*nos* stath·*mos* tu me·*tro*

Which line goes to (the port)?
Ποια γραμμή πηγαίνει (στο λιμάνι); — pia ghra·*mi* pi·*ye*·ni (sto li·*ma*·ni)

What station is this?
Ποιος σταθμός είναι αυτός; — pios stath·*mos* *i*·ne af·*tos*

What's the next station?
Ποιος είναι ο επόμενος σταθμός; — pios *i*·ne o e·*po*·me·nos stath·*mos*

Does it stop at (Kalamata)?
Σταματάει στην (Καλαμάτα); — sta·ma·*ta*·i stin (ka·la·*ma*·ta)

Do I need to change?
Χειάζεται να αλλάξω; — khri·a·ze·te na a·*lak*·so

Is it direct/express?
Είναι κατ'ευθείαν/εξπρές; — *i*·ne ka·tef·*thi*·an/eks·*pres*

Which carriage is ...?	Ποια άμαξα είναι (για) ...;	pia a·mak·sa *i*·ne (yia) ...
1st class	πρώτη θέση	*pro*·ti *the*·si
for dining	φαγητό	fa·yi·*to*
for (Kalamata)	την (Καλαμάτα)	tin (ka·la·*ma*·ta)

NORTH & SOUTH

On Greek maps and road signs, 'N' stands for Νότια *no*·ti·a (south) and 'B' stands for βόρια *vo*·ri·a (north).

SHIP

πλοίο

Where's the port/port police?

Πού είναι το λιμάνι/ λιμεναρχείο; — pu *i*·ne to li·*ma*·ni/ li·me·nar·*hi*·o

Can I have the ferry timetable?

Μπορώ να έχω το πρόγραμμα του φέρι; — bo·*ro* na e·kho to *pro*·ghra·ma tu *fe*·ri

Where does the ship to (Chios) leave from?

Από πού φεύγει το πλοίο για τη (Χίο); — a·*po* pu *fev*·yi to *pli*·o yia ti (*hi*·o)

When is the next ship for (Naxos)?

Πότε είναι το επόμενο πλοίο για τη (Νάξο); — *po*·te *i*·ne to e·*po*·me·no *pli*·o yia ti (*nak*·so)

Does this ferry go to (Rhodes)?

Πηγαίνει αυτό το φέρι στη (Ρόδο); — pi·*ye*·ni af·*to* to *fe*·ri sti (*ro*·ţho)

How many hours is it to (Milos)?

Πόσες ώρες είναι για τη (Μήλο);
po·ses *o*·res *i*·ne yia ti (*mi*·lo)

How many stops does the ship make?

Πόσες στάσεις κάνει το πλοίο;
po·ses *sta*·sis *ka*·ni to *pli*·o

Where can I get a taxi boat?

Πού μπορώ να νοικιάσω μια βάρκα με βαρκάρη;
pu bo·*ro* na ni·*kia*·so mia *var*·ka me var·*ka*·ri

Where can we rent a boat?

Πού μπορώ να νοικιάσω μια βάρκα;
pu bo·*ro* na ni·*kia*·so mia *var*·ka

I'd like a/an ...	Θα ήθελα ...	tha *i*·the·la ...
cabin for one/two	μια καμπίνα για ένα/δύο	mia ka·*bi*·na yia *e*·na/*ţhi*·o
inside/outside cabin	μια εσωτερική/εξωτερική καμπίνα	mia e·so·te·ri·*ki*/ek·so·te·ri·*ki* ka·*bi*·na

What's the sea like today?

Πώς είναι η θάλασσα σήμερα;
pos *i*·ne i *tha*·la·sa *si*·me·ra

Are there life jackets?

Υπάρχουν σωσίβια;
i·*par*·khun so·*si*·vi·a

What island is this?

Ποιο νησί είναι αυτό;
pio ni·*si* *i*·ne af·*to*

What beach is this?

Ποια παραλία είναι αυτή;
pia pa·ra·*li*·a *i*·ne af·*ti*

I feel seasick.

Αισθάνομαι ναυτία.
co·*tha*·no·mo naf·*ti*·a

cabin	καμπίνα f	ka·*bi*·na
caïque (large fishing boat)	καΐκι n	ka·*i*·ki
captain	καπετάνιος m	ka·pe·*ta*·nios
car deck	χώρος για αυτοκίνητο στο κατάστρωμα m	*kho*·ros yia af·to·*ki*·ni·to sto ka·*ta*·stro·ma
catamaran	καταμαράν f	ka·ta·ma·*ran*
cruise	κρουαζιέρα f	kru·a·zi·e·ra
deck	κατάστρωμα n	ka·*ta*·stro·ma
excursion boat	εκδρομική βάρκα f	ek·ţhro·mi·*ki var*·ka
ferry	φέρι n	*fe*·ri
hammock	αιώρα f	e·o·ra
hydrofoil	ιπτάμενο δελφίνι n	ip·*ta*·me·no ţhel·*fi*·ni
inter-island boat	πλοίο συγκοινωνίας μεταξύ νησιών n	*pli*·o si·gi·no·*ni*·as me·tak·*si* ni·*sion*
jolly roger	βάρκα πλοίου f	*var*·ka *pli*·u
lifeboat	ναυαγοσωστική λέμβος f	na·va·gho·so·sti·*ki lem*·vos
life jacket	σωσίβιο n	so·*si*·vi·o
muster station	χώρος συγκέντρωσης m	*kho*·ros si·*ge*·dro·sis
purser's office	γραφείο λογιστή n	ghra·*fi*·o lo·yi·*sti*
sailing boat	ιστιοφόρο n	i·sti·o·*fo*·ro
small fishing boat	μικρή βάρκα για ψάρεμα f	mi·*kri var*·ka yia *psa*·re·ma
yacht	γιωτ n	yiot

TAXI

ταξί

I'd like a taxi ...	Θα ήθελα ένα ταξί ...	tha *i*·the·la e·na tak·*si* ...
at (9am)	στις (εννέα π.μ.)	stis (e·*ne*·a to pro·*i*)
now	τώρα	*to*·ra
tomorrow	αύριο	*av*·ri·o

Where's the taxi rank?
Πού είναι η στάση για ταξί; — pu *i*·ne i *sta*·si yia tak·*si*

Is this taxi available?
Είναι αυτό το ταξί ελεύθερο; — *i*·ne af·*to* to tak·*si* e·*lef*·the·ro

Please put the meter on.
Παρακαλώ βάλε το ταξίμετρο. — pa·ra·ka·*lo* *va*·le to tak·*si*·me·tro

How much is it (to Petroupoli)?
Πόσο κάνει (για Πετρούπολη); — *po*·so *ka*·ni (yia pe·*tru*·po·li)

Please take me to (this address).
Παρακαλώ πήγαινέ με σε (αυτή τη διεύθυνση). — pa·ra·ka·*lo* pi·ge·*ne* me se (af·*ti* ti ţhi·*ef*·thin·si)

How much do you charge for the luggage?
Πόσο χρεώνεις για τις αποσκευές; — *po*·so khre·*o*·nis yia tis a·pos·ke·*ves*

Please ...	Παρακλώ ...	pa·ra·ka·*lo* ...
slow down	πήγαινε πιο σιγά	*pi*·ye·ne pio si·*gha*
stop here	σταμάτα εδώ	sta·*ma*·ta e·*ţho*
wait here	περίμενε εδώ	pe·*ri*·me·ne e·*ţho*

CAR & MOTORBIKE

αυτοκίνητο και μοτοσικλέτα

I'd like to hire a/an ...	Θα ήθελα να ενοικιάσω ένα ...	tha *i*·the·la na e·ni·ki·*a*·so *e*·na ...
4WD	φορ-ουιλ ντράιβ	for·ghu·*il* *dra*·iv
automatic	αυτόματο	af·*to*·ma·to
car	αυτοκίνητο	af·to·*ki*·ni·to
manual	με ταχύτητες	me ta·*hi*·ti·tes
motorbike	μοτοσικλέτα	mo·to·si·*kle*·ta

with ...	με	me ...
air conditioning	έρκοντίσιον	er·kon·*di*·si·on
a driver	οδηγό	o·ţhi·*gho*

How much for daily/weekly hire?
Πόσο νοικάζεται την ημέρα/εβδομάδα; — *po*·so ni·*kia*·ze·te tin i·*me*·ra/ev·ţho·*ma*·ţha

Does that include insurance/mileage?
Αυτό συμπεριλαμβάνει ασφάλεια/χιλιόμετρα; — af·*to* si·be·ri·lam·*va*·ni as·*fa*·li·a/hi·*lio*·me·tra

Can I take the car on a ferry?
Μπορώ να πάρω το αυτοκίνητο στο φέρι; — bo·*ro* na *pa*·ro to af·to·*ki*·ni·to sto *fe*·ri

Do you have a guide to the road rules in English?
Έχετε οδικό κώδικα κυκλοφορίας στα Αγγλικά; — e·he·te o·ţhi·*ko* *ko*·ţhi·ka ki·klo·fo·*ri*·as sta ang·gli·*ka*

Do you have a road map?
Έχετε οδικό χάρτη; — e·he·te o·ţhi·*ko* *khar*·ti

What's the speed limit?
Ποιο είναι το όριο ταχύτητας; — pio *i*·ne to *o*·ri·o ta·*hi*·ti·tas

Is this the road to (Lamia)?
Είναι αυτός ο δρόμος για (τη Λαμία); — *i*·ne af·*tos* o *ţhro*·mos yia (ti la·*mi*·a)

Where's a petrol/gas station?
Πού είναι ένα πρατήριο βενζίνας; — *pu* *i*·ne e·na pra·*ti*·ri·o ven·*zi*·nas

Fill it up, please.
Γεμίστε το, παρακαλώ. — ye·*mis*·te to pa·ra·ka·*lo*

LOOK FOR

Απαγορεύεται η είσοδος	a·pa·gho·*re*·ve·te i *i*·so·ţhos	**No Entry**
Διόδια	ţhi·*o*·ţhi·a	**Toll**
Είσοδος	*i*·so·ţhos	**Entrance (Motorway/Freeway)**
Έξοδος Εθνικής Οδού	*ek*·so·ţhos e·th·ni·*kis* o·*ţhu*	**Exit Motorway/Freeway**
Προσοχή	pro·so·*hi*	**Drive With Care**
Μονόδρομος	mo·*no*·ţhro·mos	**One-Way**

LISTEN FOR

άδεια οδήγησης f	a·thi·a o·*thi*·yi·sis	**driver's licence**
βενζίνα f	ven·*zi*·na	**petrol/gas**
δωρεάν	tho·re·*an*	**free a**
επί τόπου ασφάλεια f	e·*pi to*·pu as·*fa*·li·a	**on-the-spot insurance**
παρκόμετρο n	par·*ko*·me·tro	**parking meter**
Πράσινη κάρτα f	*pra*·si·ni *kar*·ta	**Green Card (international third-party insurance)**
χιλιόμετρα n pl	hi·*lio*·me·tra	**kilometres**

diesel	ντίζελ n	*di*·zel
leaded	μολυβδούχος f	mo·liv·*thu*·khos
LPG	υγραέριο n	igh·ra·e·ri·o
premium unleaded	σούπερ αμόλυβδος f	*su*·per a·*mo*·liv·thos
regular	απλή f	ap·*li*
unleaded	αμόλυβδος f	a·*mo*·liv·thos

Can you check the ...?	Μπορείς να κοιτάξεις ...;	bo·*ris* na ki·*tak*·sis ...
oil	το λάδι	to *la*·thi
tyre pressure	την πίεση των τροχών	tin *pi*·e·si ton tro·*khon*
water	το νερό	to ne·*ro*

(How long) Can I park here?

(Πόση ώρα) Μπορώ να παρκάρω εδώ; — (*po*·si o·ra) bo·*ro* na par·*ka*·ro e·*tho*

Do I have to pay?

Πρέπει να πληρώσω; — *pre*·pi na pli·*ro*·so

I need a mechanic.
Χρειάζομαι μηχανικό. — khri·a·zo·me mi·kha·ni·*ko*

I've had an accident.
Είχα ένα ατύχημα. — *i*·kha *e*·na a·*ti*·hi·ma

The car / motorbike has broken down (at Corinth).
Το αυτοκίνητο/μοτοσικλέτα χάλασε (στην Κόρινθο). — to af·to·*ki*·ni·to / mo·to·si·*kle*·ta *ha*·la·se (stin *ko*·rin·tho)

The car / motorbike won't start.
Το αυτοκίνητο/μοτοσικλέτα δεν αρχίζει. — to af·to·*ki*·ni·to / mo·to·si·*kle*·ta ţhen ar·*hi*·zi

I have a flat tyre.
Μ'έπιασε λάστιχο. — *me*·pia·se *la*·sti·kho

I've lost my car keys.
Έχασα τα κλειδιά του αυτοκινήτου μου. — *e*·ha·sa ta kli·*ţhia* tu af·to·ki·*ni*·tu mu

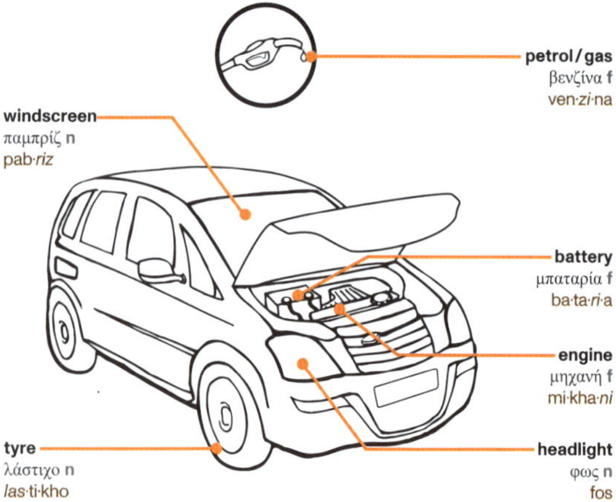

I've locked the keys inside.

Κλείδωσα τα κλειδιά μου στο αυτοκίνητο	*kli*·ţho·sa ta kli·*ţhia* mu sto af·to·*ki*·ni·to

I've run out of petrol/gas.

Μου τελείωσε η βενζίνα.	mu te·*li*·o·se i ven·*zi*·na

Can you fix it (today)?

Μπορείς να το επισκευάσεις (σήμερα);	bo·*ris* na to e·pis·ke·*va*·sis (*si*·me·ra)

How long will it take?

Πόση ώρα θα κάνει;	*po*·si *o*·ra tha *ka*·ni

BICYCLE

ποδήλατο

I'd like ...	Θα ήθελα ...	tha *i*·the·la ...
my bicycle repaired	να επισκευάσω το ποδήλατό μου	na e·pis·ke·*va*·so to po·*ţhi*·la·*to* mu
to buy a bicycle	να αγοράσω ένα ποδήλατο	na a·gho·*ra*·so e·na po·*ţhi*·la·to
to hire a bicycle	να νοικιάσω ένα ποδήλατο	na ni·*kia*·so e·na po·*ţhi*·la·to

I'd like a ... bike.	Θα ήθελα ένα ...	tha *i*·the·la e·na ...
mountain	ποδήλατο για βουνό	po·*ţhi*·la·to yia vu·*no*
racing	ποδήλατο κούρσας	po·*ţhi*·la·to *kur*·sas
second-hand	μεταχειρισμένο ποδήλατο	me·ta·hi·riz·*me*·no po·*ţhi*·la·to

How much is it per day?

Πόσο κοστίζει την ημέρα;	*po*·so ko·*sti*·zi tin i·*me*·ra

How much is it per hour?

Πόσο κοστίζει την ώρα;	*po*·so ko·*sti*·zi tin *o*·ra

Do I need a helmet?

Χρειάζομαι κράνος; — khri·a·zo·me *kra*·nos

Is there a bicycle-path map?

Υπάρχει χάρτης για δρόμο ποδηλάτου; — i·*par*·hi *khar*·tis yia *ţhro*·mo po·ţhi·*la*·tu

Is this road OK for bicycles?

Είναι αυτός ο δρόμος κατάλληλος για ποδήλατα; — *i*·ne af·*tos* o *ţhro*·mos ka·*ta*·li·los yia po·*ţhi*·la·ta

I have a puncture.

Τρύπησε η ρόδα μου. — *tri*·pi·se i *ro*·ţha mu

GUT FEELINGS

Greeks tend to get pretty physical when they talk about their emotions:

I'm not impressed.

Δεν μου γεμίζει το μάτι. — ţhen mu ye·*mi*·zi to *ma*·ti

(lit: It doesn't fill my eye.)

I can't stand him/her.

Δεν τον/την χωνεύω. — ţhen ton/tin ho·ne·*vo*

(lit: I can't digest him/her.)

I've had enough of you.

Μ'έπρηξες. — *me*·prik·ses

(lit: You've made me swollen.)

I regretted it.

Μου βγήκε από τη μύτη. — mu *vyi*·ke a·*po* ti *mi*·ti

(lit: It came out of my nose.)

He/She put me under pressure.

Μου βαλε τα δυο πόδια σ' ένα παπούτσι. — *mu*·va·le ta ţhio *po*·ţhia se·na pa·*put*·si

(lit: He/She put both my feet in one shoe.)

Border Crossing

ΠΕΡΝΩΝΤΑΣ ΤΑ ΣΥΝΟΡΑ

I'm ...	Είμαι ...	*i*·me ...
in transit	τράνζιτ	*tran*·zit
on business	για δουλειά	yia ţhu·*lia*
on holiday	σε διακοπές	se ţhia·ko·*pes*
I'm here for (three) ...	Είμαι εδώ για (τρεις) ...	*i*·me e·*ţho* yia (tris) ...
days	μέρες	*me*·res
weeks	εβδομάδες	ev·ţho·*ma*·ţhes
months	μήνες	*mi*·nes

I'm going to (Limassol).
Πηγαίνω στη (Λεμεσό). — pi·*ye*·no sti (le·me·*so*)

I'm staying at (the Xenia).
Μένω στο (Ξενία). — *me*·no sto (kse·*ni*·a)

The children are on this passport.
Τα παιδιά είναι σ'αυτό το διαβατήριο. — ta pe·*ţhia* *i*·ne saf·*to* to ţhia·va·*ti*·ri·o

LISTEN FOR

άδεια f εξαγωγής	a·ţhi·a ek·sa·gho·*yis*	**export permit**
βίζα f	*vi*·za	**visa**
διαβατήριο n	ţhia·va·*ti*·ri·o	**passport**
μόνος m	*mo*·nos	**alone**
οικογένεια f	i·ko·*ye*·ni·a	**family**
ομάδα f	o·*ma*·ţha	**group**
ταυτότητα f	taf·*to*·ti·ta	**ID card**

Can you stamp a separate paper instead of the passport?

Μπορείτε να σφραγίσετε ένα χωριστό χαρτί αντί για το διαβατήριο;	bo·*ri*·te na sfra·*yi*·se·te e·na kho·ri·*sto* khar·*ti* a·*di* yia to ţhia·va·*ti*·ri·o

Where can I get a travel permit for (Mt Athos)?

Πού μπορώ να πάρω μια άδεια ταξιδιού για (το Άγιο Όρος);	pu bo·*ro* na *pa*·ro mia *a*·ţhi·a tak·si·*ţhiu* yia (to *a*·yi·o *o*·ros)

AT CUSTOMS

στο τελωνείο

I have nothing to declare.

Δεν έχω τίποτε να δηλώσω.	ţhen e·kho *ti*·po·te na ţhi·*lo*·so

I have something to declare.

Έχω κάτι να δηλώσω.	e·kho *ka*·ti na ţhi·*lo*·so

Do I have to declare this?

Πρέπει να το δηλώσω αυτό;	*pre*·pi na to ţhi·*lo*·so af·*to*

That's (not) mine.

Αυτό (δεν) είναι δικό μου.	af·*to* (ţhen) *i*·ne ţhi·*ko* mu

I didn't know I had to declare it.

Δεν ήξερα πως έπρεπε να το δηλώσω.	ţhen *ik*·se·ra pos e·pre·pe na to ţhi·*lo*·so

I have a doctor's certificate for this medication.

Έχω πιστοποιητικό γιατρού για αυτό το φάρμακο.	e·kho pis·to·pi·i·ti·*ko* yia·*tru* yia af·*to* to *far*·ma·ko

LOOK FOR

Αφορολόγητα	a·fo·ro·*lo*·yi·ta	**Duty-Free**
Έλεγχος Διαβατηρίων	e·len·ghos ţhia·va·ti·*ri*·on	**Passport Control**
Καραντίνα	ka·ran·*di*·na	**Quarantine**
Τελωνείο	te·lo·*ni*·o	**Customs**
Μετανάστευση	me·ta·*na*·stef·si	**Immigration**

Directions

ΟΔΗΓΙΕΣ

Where's (the tourist office)?
Πού είναι (το τουριστικό γραφείο); — pu *i*·ne (to tu·ri·sti·*ko* ghra·*fi*·o)

What's the address?
Ποια είναι η διεύθυνση; — pia *i*·ne i ţhi·*ef*·thin·si

How far is it?
Πόσο μακριά είναι; — *po*·so ma·kri·*a* *i*·ne

How do I get there?
Πώς πηγαίνω εκεί; — pos pi·*ye*·no e·*ki*

What street is this?
Ποιος δρόμος είναι αυτός; — pios *ţhro*·mos *i*·ne af·*tos*

What village is this?
Ποιο χωριό είναι αυτό; — pio kho·*rio* *i*·ne af·*to*

Can you show me (on the map)?
Μπορείς να μου δείξεις (στο χάρτη); — bo·*ris* na mu *ţhik*·sis (sto *khar*·ti)

It's ...	Είναι …	*i*·ne ...
close	κοντά	ko·*da*
behind ...	πίσω …	*pi*·so ...
here	εδώ	e·*ţho*
in front of ...	μπροστά από …	bros·*ta* a·*po* ...
near ...	κοντά …	ko·*da* ...
next to ...	δίπλα από …	*ţhip*·la a·*po* ...
on the corner	στη γωνία	sti gho·*ni*·a
opposite ...	απέναντι …	a·*pe*·na·di ...
straight ahead	κατ'ευθείαν	ka·tef·*thi*·an
there	εκεί	e·*ki*

north	βόρεια	*vo*·ri·a
south	νότια	*no*·ti·a
east	ανατολικά	a·na·to·li·*ka*
west	δυτικά	ţhi·ti·*ka*

LISTEN FOR

χιλιόμετρα	hi·*lio*·me·tra	**kilometres**
λεπτά	lep·*ta*	**minutes**
μέτρα	*me*·tra	**metres**

avenue	λεωφόρος f	le·o·*fo*·ros
lane	πάροδος f	*pa*·ro·ţhos
street	οδός f	o·*ţhos*
by bus / taxi	με λεωφορείο/ταξί	me le·o·fo·*ri*·o / tak·*si*
on foot	με τα πόδια	me ta *po*·ţhia
Turn ...	Στρίψε ...	*strip*·se ...
at the corner	στη γωνία	sti gho·*ni*·a
at the traffic lights	στα φανάρια	sta fa·*na*·ria
left	αριστερά	a·ris·te·*ra*
right	δεξιά	ţhek·si·*a*

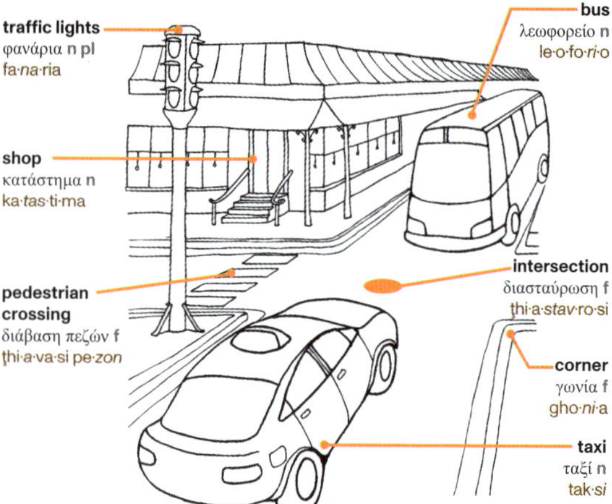

Accommodation

ΚΑΤΑΛΥΜΑ

FINDING ACCOMMODATION

βρίσκοντας κατάλυμα

Where's (a) ...?	Πού είναι ...;	pu *i*·ne ...
bed and breakfast	κατάλυμα με πρόγευμα	ka·*ta*·li·ma me *pro*·ghev·ma
camping ground	χώρος για κάμπινγκ	*kho*·ros yia *kam*·ping
guesthouse	ξενώνας	kse·*no*·nas
(3-star) hotel	ξενοδοχείο (τριών αστέρων)	kse·no·ţho·*hi*·o (tri·*on* a·*ste*·ron)
mountain refuge	ορεινό καταφύγιο	o·ri·*no* ka·ta·*fi*·yi·o
pension	πανσιόν	pan·*sion*
room for rent	δωμάτιο για νοίκιασμα	ţho·*ma*·ti·o yia *ni*·kiaz·ma
self-contained apartment	ξεχωριστό διαμέρισμα	kse·kho·ri·*sto* ţhi·a·*me*·riz·ma
some traditional accommodation	παραδοσιακό κατάλυμα	pa·ra·ţho·si·a·*ko* ka·*ta*·li·ma
youth hostel	γιουθ χόστελ	yiuth *kho*·stel

LOCAL TALK

dive	βουτιά f	vu·*tia*
rat-infested	γεμάτο ποντίκια	ye·*ma*·to po·*di*·kia
top spot	ωραιότατο σημείο n	o·re·o·ta·to si·*mi*·o

Can you recommend somewhere ...?	Μπορείτε να συστήσετε κάπου ...;	bo·*ri*·te na si·*sti*·se·te *ka*·pu ...
cheap	φτηνό	fti·*no*
good	καλό	ka·*lo*
nearby	κοντινό	ko·di·*no*
romantic	ρομαντικό	ro·ma·di·*ko*

What's the address?
Ποια είναι η διεύθυνση; — pia *i*·ne i ţhi·*ef*·thin·si

For responses, see **directions**, p63.

BOOKING AHEAD & CHECKING IN

κλείσιμο θέσης από πριν και εγκατάσταση

I'd like to book a room, please.
Θα ήθελα να κλείσω ένα δωμάτιο, παρακαλώ. — tha *i*·the·la na *kli*·so e·na ţho·*ma*·ti·o pa·ra·ka·*lo*

I have a reservation.
Έχω κάνει κάποια κράτηση. — e·kho *ka*·ni *ka*·pia *kra*·ti·si

My name's ...
Με λένε ... — me *le*·ne ...

For (three) nights / weeks.
Για (τρεις) νύχτες/ εβδομάδες. — yia (tris) *nikh*·tes / ev·ţho·*ma*·ţhes

From (2 July) to (6 July).
Από (τις δύο Ιουλίου) μέχρι (τις έξι Ιουλίου). — a·*po* (tis *ţhi*·o i·u·*li*·u) *me*·khri (tis *ek*·si i·u·*li*·u)

LISTEN FOR

Πόσες νύχτες;	*po*·ses *nikh*·tes	**How many nights?**
διαβατήριο n	ţhia·va·*ti*·ri·o	**passport**
γεμάτο	ye·*ma*·to	**full**
κλειδί n	kli·*ţhi*	**key**
ρεσεψιόν f	re·sep·*sion*	**reception**

LOOK FOR

Ελεύθερα δωμάτια	e·*lef*·the·ra ţho·*ma*·ti·a	**vacancy**
Μπάνιο	*ba*·nio	**bathroom**
Πλήρες	*pli*·res	**no vacancy**

Do you have a ... room?	Έχετε ένα ... δωμάτιο	e·he·te e·na ... ţho·*ma*·ti·o
single	μονό	mo·*no*
double	διπλό	ţhi·*plo*
twin	δίκλινο	*ţhi*·kli·no

How much is it per ...?	Πόσο είναι για κάθε ...;	*po*·so *i*·ne yia *ka*·the ...
night	νύχτα	*nikh*·ta
person	άτομο	*a*·to·mo
week	εβδομάδα	ev·ţho·*ma*·ţha

Can I see it?
Μπορώ να το δω; — bo·*ro* na to ţho

I'll take it.
Θα το πάρω. — tha to *pa*·ro

Do I need to pay upfront?
Χρειάζεται να πληρώσω από πριν; — khri·a·ze·te na pli·*ro*·so a·*po* prin

Can I pay by ...?	Μπορώ να πληρώσω με ...;	bo·*ro* na pli·*ro*·so me ...
credit card	πιστωτική κάρτα	pi·sto·ti·*ki* *kar*·ta

For other methods of payment, see **shopping**, p77.

REQUESTS & QUERIES

παρακλήσεις και ερωτήσεις

When/Where is breakfast served?
Πότε/Πού σερβίρεται το πρόγευμα; — *po*·te/pu ser·*vi*·re·te to *pro*·yev·ma

Please wake me at (seven).
Παρακαλώ ξύπνησέ με στις (εφτά). — pa·ra·ka·*lo* *ksip*·ni·se me stis (ef·*ta*)

Do you ... here?	... εδώ;	... e·*tho*
arrange tours	Κανονίζετε ξεναγήσεις	ka·no·*ni*·ze·te kse·na·*yi*·sis
change money	Αλλάζετε χρήματα	a·*la*·ze·te *khri*·ma·ta

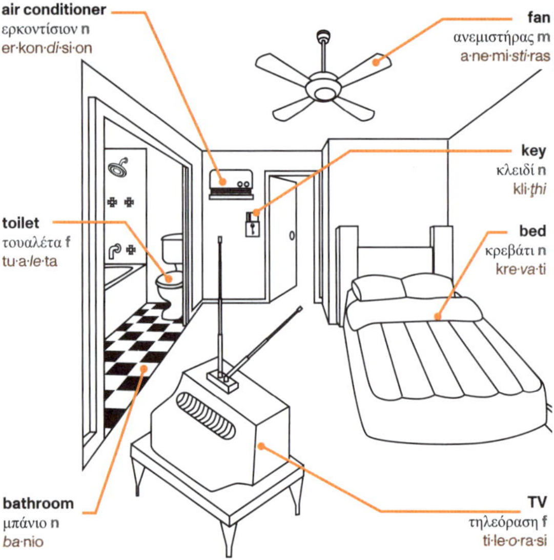

Can I use the ...?	Μπορώ να χρησιμοποιήσω ...;	bo·*ro* na khri·si·mo·pi·*i*·so ...
kitchen	την κουζίνα	tin ku·*zi*·na
laundry	το πλυντήριο	to pli·*di*·ri·o
telephone	το τηλέφωνο	to ti·*le*·fo·no
Do you have a/an ...?	Έχετε ...;	e·he·te ...
lift/elevator	ασανσέρ	a·san·*ser*
laundry service	υπηρεσία πλυντηρίου	i·pi·re·*si*·a pli·di·*ri*·u
message board	πίνακα μηνυμάτων	*pi*·na·ka mi·ni·*ma*·ton
safe	χρηματοκιβώτιο	khri·ma·to·ki·*vo*·ti·o
swimming pool	πισίνα	pi·*si*·na
Could I have (a/an) ..., please?	Μπορώ να έχω ... παρακαλώ;	bo·*ro* na e·kho ... pa·ra·ka·*lo*
extra blanket	μια κουβέρτα ακόμη	mia ku·*ver*·ta a·*ko*·mi
my key	το κλειδί μου	to kli·*ţhi* mu
mosquito net	μια κουνουπιέρα	mia ku·nu·*pie*·ra
receipt	μια απόδειξη	mia a·*po*·ţhik·si

Is there hot water all day?
Υπάρχει ζεστό νερό όλη την ημέρα; — i·*par*·hi ze·*sto* ne·*ro* o·li tin i·*me*·ra

Is there a message for me?
Υπάρχει μήνυμα για μένα; — i·*par*·hi *mi*·ni·ma yia *me*·na

Can I leave a message for someone?
Μπορώ να αφήσω ένα μήνυμα για κάποιον; — bo·*ro* na a·*fi*·so e·na *mi*·ni·ma yia *ka*·pion

I'm locked out of my room.
Κλειδώθηκα έξω από το δωμάτιό μου. — kli·*ţho*·thi·ka *ek*·so a·*po* to ţho·*ma*·ti·o mu

COMPLAINTS

παράπονα

It's too ...	Είναι πάρα πολύ ...	*i*·ne *pa*·ra po·*li* ...
bright	φωτεινό	fo·ti·*no*
cold	κρύο	*kri*·o
dark	σκοτεινό	sko·ti·*no*
expensive	ακριβό	a·kri·*vo*
noisy	θορυβώδες	tho·ri·*vo*·ţhes
small	μικρό	mi·*kro*
The ... doesn't work.	... δεν δουλεύει.	... ţhen ţhu·*le*·vi
air conditioner	Το ερκοντίσιον	to er·kon·*di*·si·on
fan	Ο ανεμιστήρας	o a·ne·mi·*sti*·ras
toilet	Η τουαλέτα	i tu·a·*le*·ta

Can I get another (blanket)?
Μπορώ να πάρω μια άλλη (κουβέρτα); — bo·*ro* na *pa*·ro mia *a*·li (ku·*ver*·ta)

This (pillow) isn't clean.
Αυτό (το μαξιλάρι) δεν είναι καθαρό. — af·*to* (to mak·si·*la*·ri) ţhen *i*·ne ka·tha·*ro*

A KNOCK AT THE DOOR...

Who is it?
Ποιος είναι; — pios *i*·ne

Just a moment.
Μια στιγμή. — mia stigh·*mi*

Come in.
Περάστε. — pe·*ra*·ste

Come back later, please.
Έλα αργότερα, παρακαλώ. — e·la ar·*gho*·te·ra pa·ra·ka·*lo*

CHECKING OUT

αναχώρηση

What time is checkout?
Τι ώρα είναι η αναχώρηση; — ti *o*·ra *i*·ne i a·na·*kho*·ri·si

Can I have a late checkout?
Μπορώ να φύγω αργά; — bo·*ro* na *fi*·gho ar·*gha*

Can you call a taxi for me (for 11 o'clock)?
Μπορείτε να καλέσετε ένα ταξί (για τις έντεκα); — bo·*ri*·te na ka·*le*·se·te e·na tak·*si* (yia tis e·de·ka)

I'm leaving now.
Φεύγω τώρα. — *fev*·gho *to*·ra

Can I leave my bags here?
Μπορώ να αφήσω τις βαλίτσες μου εδώ; — bo·*ro* na a·*fi*·so tis va·*lit*·ses mu e·*ţho*

There's a mistake in the bill.
Υπάρχει κάποιο λάθος στο λογαριασμό. — i·*par*·hi *ka*·pio *la*·thos sto lo·gha·riaz·*mo*

Could I have my ..., please?	Μπορώ να έχω ... παρακλώ;	bo·*ro* na e·kho ... pa·ra·ka·*lo*
deposit	την προκαταβολή μου	tin pro·ka·ta·vo·*li* mu
passport	το διαβατήριό μου	to ţhia·va·*ti*·rio mu
valuables	τα κοσμήματά μου	ta koz·*mi*·ma·*ta* mu

I'll be back ...	Θα επιστρέψω ...	tha e·pi·*strep*·so ...
in (three) days	σε (τρεις) μέρες	se (tris) *me*·res
on (Tuesday)	την (Τρίτη)	tin *tri*·ti

I had a great stay, thank you.
Είχα υπέροχη διαμονή, ευχαριστώ. — *i*·kha i·*pe*·ro·hi ţhi·a·mo·*ni* ef·kha·ri·*sto*

I'll recommend it to my friends.
Θα το συστήσω στους φίλους μου. — tha to si·*sti*·so stus *fi*·lus mu

CAMPING

κάμπινγκ

Do you have (a) ...?	Έχετε ...	e·he·te ...
electricity	ηλεκτρισμό	i·lek·triz·*mo*
laundry	πλυντήριο	pli·*di*·ri·o
site	χώρο	*kho*·ro
shower facilities	εγκαταστάσεις για ντουζ	e·ga·ta·*sta*·sis yia duz
tents for hire	τέντες για νοίκιασμα	*te*·des yia *ni*·kiaz·ma
How much is it per ...?	Πόσο κοστίζει για κάθε ...;	*po*·so ko·*sti*·zi yia *ka*·the ...
caravan	τροχόσπιτο	tro·*kho*·spi·to
person	άτομο	*a*·to·mo
tent	τέντα	*te*·da
vehicle	αυτοκίνητο	af·to·*ki*·ni·to

Can I camp here?
Μπορώ να κατασκηνώσω εδώ; — bo·*ro* na ka·ta·ski·*no*·so e·*ţho*

Can I park next to my tent?
Μπορώ να παρκάρω δίπλα στην τέντα μου; — bo·*ro* na par·*ka*·ro *ţhi*·pla stin *te*·da mu

Who do I ask to stay here?
Ποιον ρωτάω για να μείνω εδώ; — pion ro·*ta*·o yia na *mi*·no e·*ţho*

Could I borrow ...?
Μπορώ να δανειστώ ...; — bo·*ro* na ţha·ni·*sto* ...

Is it coin-operated?
Λειτουργεί με κέρματα; — li·tur·*yi* me *ker*·ma·ta

Is the water drinkable?
Είναι το νερό πόσιμο; — *i*·ne to ne·*ro* *po*·si·mo

A CHANCE TO BE POLITE

When you're making a request, make it sound more polite by starting your question with μήπως *mi*·pos, the equivalent of the English 'Do you, by any chance, ...?'.

Do you, by any chance, have a room with a view?

Μήπως έχετε ένα δωμάτιο με θέα;	*mi*·pos e·hete e·na ţho·*ma*·tio me *the*·a

See the **phrasebuilder** (p29) for more on requests.

RENTING

νοικιάζοντας

I'm here about the ... for rent.	Είμαι εδώ για το ... που νοικιάζεται.	*i*·me e·*ţho* yia to ... pu ni·*kia*·ze·te
Do you have a/an ... for rent?	Έχεις ένα ... για νοίκιασμα;	e·his e·na ... yia *ni*·kiaz·ma
apartment	διαμέρισμα	ţhi·a·*me*·riz·ma
house	σπίτι	*spi*·ti
room	δωμάτιο	ţho·*ma*·ti·o
I'm here about the ... for rent.	Είμαι εδώ για την ... που νοικιάζεται.	*i*·me e·*ţho* yia tin ... pu ni·*kia*·ze·te
Do you have a ... for rent?	Έχεις μια ... για νοίκιασμα;	e·his mia ... yia *ni*·kiaz·ma
cabin	καμπίνα	ka·*bi*·na
villa	έπαυλη	e·pav·li
furnished	με έπιπλα	me e·pi·pla
partly furnished	με λίγα έπιπλα	me *li*·gha e·pi·pla
unfurnished	χωρίς έπιπλα	kho *ris* e·pi·pla

STAYING WITH LOCALS

διαμονή με τους ντόπιους

Can I stay at your place?

Μπορώ να μείνω στο σπίτι σου;	bo·*ro* na *mi*·no sto *spi*·ti su

Is there anything I can do to help?

Μπορώ να κάνω κάτι για να βοηθήσω;	bo·*ro* na *ka*·no *ka*·ti yia na vo·i·*thi*·so

I have my own ...	Έχω το δικό μου ...	e·kho to ţhi·*ko* mu ...
mattress	στρώμα	*stro*·ma
sleeping bag	σλίπινγκ μπαγκ	*sli*·ping bag

Can I ...?	Μπορώ να ...;	bo·*ro* na ...
bring anything for the meal	φέρω κάτι για το φαγητό	*fe*·ro *ka*·ti yia to fa·yi·*to*
do the dishes	πλύνω τα πιάτα	*pli*·no ta *pia*·ta
set/clear the table	στρώσω/μαζέψω το τραπέζι	*stro*·so / ma·*zep*·so to tra·*pe*·zi
take out the rubbish	βγάλω έξω τα σκουπίδια	*vgha*·lo *ek*·so ta sku·*pi*·ţhia

Thanks for your hospitality.

Ευχαριστώ για τη φιλοξενία σας.	ef·kha·ri·*sto* yia ti fi·lok·se·*ni*·a sas

If you're dining with your hosts, see **eating out**, p157, for additional phrases.

☑ FOREIGN VISITORS

Punctuality for social engagements is not taken as seriously as you might be used to. An invitation for 9pm means that most people won't show up before 9.30pm. An evening coffee can sometimes extend to dinner, and not end until after midnight.

Shopping

ΨΩΝΙΑ

LOOKING FOR ...

ψάχνοντας για ...

Where's ...?	Πού είναι ...;	pu *i*·ne ...
a department store	ένα κατάστημα	e·na ka·*ta*·sti·ma
the flea market	το παζάρι	to pa·za·ri
the food market	η αγορά τροφίμων	i a·gho·*ra* tro·*fi*·mon
a kiosk	ένα περίπτερο	e·na pe·*rip*·te·ro
the street market	η λαϊκή αγορά	i la·i·*ki* a·gho·*ra*
a supermarket	ένα σούπερ-μάρκετ	e·na *su*·per *mar*·ket
a souvenir shop	ένα κατάστημα με σουβενίρ	e·na ka·*ta*·sti·ma me su·ve·*nir*

On which day is the street market held?
Ποια μέρα έχει λαϊκή; — pia *me*·ra e·hi la·i·*ki*

Where can I buy (a padlock)?
Πού μπορώ να αγοράσω (μια κλειδαριά); — pu bo·*ro* na a·gho·*ra*·so (mia kli·ţha·*ria*)

For phrases on **directions**, see p63.

LISTEN FOR

Μπορώ να σας βοηθήσω;
bo·*ro* na sas vo·i·*thi*·so — **Can I help you?**

Τίποτε άλλο;
ti·po·te *a*·lo — **Anything else?**

Όχι, δεν έχουμε.
o·hi ţhen *e*·khu·me — **No, we don't have any.**

Να το τυλίξω;
na to ti·*lik*·so — **Shall I wrap it?**

MAKING A PURCHASE

αγοράζοντας κάτι

I'm just looking.
Απλά κοιτάζω. — a·*pla* ki·*ta*·zo

I'd like to buy (an adaptor plug).
Θα ήθελα να αγοράσω (ένα μετασχηματιστή). — tha *i*·the·la na a·gho·*ra*·so (e·na me·ta·shi·ma·ti·*sti*)

Can I look at it?
Μπορώ να το κοιτάξω; — bo·*ro* na to ki·*tak*·so

Do you have any others?
Έχετε άλλα; — e·he·te *a*·la

How much is it?
Πόσο κάνει; — *po*·so *ka*·ni

Can you write down the price?
Μπορείς να γράψεις την τιμή; — bo·*ris* na *ghrap*·sis tin ti·*mi*

Does it have a guarantee?
Έχει εγγύηση; — e·hi e·*gi*·i·si

Could I have it wrapped?
Μπορείς να μου το τυλίξεις; — bo·*ris* na mu to ti·*lik*·sis

Could I have a bag/receipt, please?
Μπορώ να έχω μια τσάντα/ απόδειξη, παρακαλώ; — bo·*ro* na e·kho mia *tsa*·da/ a·*po*·ţhik·si pa·ra·ka·*lo*

Can I have it sent overseas?
Μπορείς να το στείλεις στο εξωτερικό; — bo·*ris* na to *sti*·lis sto ek·so·te·ri·*ko*

Can you order it for me?
Μπορείς να το παραγγείλεις για μένα; — bo·*ris* na to pa·ra·*gi*·lis yia *me*·na

Can I pick it up later?
Μπορώ να το πραλάβω αργότερα; — bo·*ro* na to pa·ra·*la*·vo ar·*gho*·te·ra

It's faulty.
Είναι ελαττωματικό. — *i*·ne e·la·to·ma·ti·*ko*

LOCAL TALK

bargain	ευκαιρία **f**	ef·ke·*ri*·a
rip-off	γδάρσιμο **n**	*ghţhar*·si·mo
sale	έκπτωση **f**	*ek*·pto·si
specials	προσφορές **f pl**	pros·fo·*res*

Do you accept ...?	Δέχεστε ...;	*ţhe*·he·ste ...
credit cards	πιστωτικές κάρτες	pi·sto·ti·*kes* *kar*·tes
debit cards	χρεωστικές κάρτες	khre·o·sti·*kes* *kar*·tes

I'd like ..., please.	Θα ήθελα ..., παρακαλώ.	tha *i*·the·la ... pa·ra·ka·*lo*
a refund	επιστροφή χρημάτων	e·pi·stro·*fi* khri·*ma*·ton
my change	τα ρέστα μου	ta *re*·sta mu
to return this	να επιστρέψω αυτό	na e·pi·*strep*·so af·*to*

BARGAINING

παζάρεμα

That's too expensive.
Είναι πάρα πολύ ακριβό. — *i*·ne *pa*·ra po·*li* a·kri·*vo*

I don't have that much money.
Δεν έχω τόσα πολλά χρήματα. — ţhen e·kho *to*·sa po·*la* *khri*·ma·ta

Do you have something cheaper?
Έχεις κάτι πιο φτηνό; — e·his *ka*·ti pio fti·*no*

Can you lower the price?

Μπορείς να κατεβάσεις την τιμή;	bo·*ris* na ka·te·*va*·sis tin ti·*mi*

How much for (two)?

Πόσο κάνει για (δύο);	*po*·so *ka*·ni yia (*ţhi*·o)

I'll give you (five euros).

Θα σου δώσω (πέντε ευρώ).	tha su *ţho*·so (*pe*·de ev·*ro*)

BOOKS & READING

βιβλία και διάβασμα

Is there an English-language bookshop/section?

Υπάρχει ένα βιβλιοπωλείο/ τμήμα Αγγλικής γλώσσας;	i·*par*·hi e·na viv·li·o·po·*li*·o/ *tmi*·ma ang·gli·*kis ghlo*·sas

Can you recommend a book for me?

Μπορείς να μου συστήσεις ένα βιβλίο;	bo·*ris* na mu si·*sti*·sis e·na viv·*li*·o

Do you have Lonely Planet guidebooks?

Έχετε βιβλία-οδηγούς του Λόνλι Πλάνετ;	e·he·te viv·*li*·a·o·ţhi·*ghus* tu *lon*·li *pla*·net

Do you have ...?	Έχεις ένα ...;	e·his e·na ...
a book by (Nikos Kazantzakis)	βιβλίο (του Νίκου Καζαντζάκη)	viv·*li*·o (tu *ni*·ku ka·za·*dza*·ki)
an entertainment guide	οδηγό διασκεδάσεων	o·ţhi·*gho* ţhias·ke·*ţha*·se·on

I'd like a ...	Θα ήθελα ...	tha *i*·the·la ...
dictionary	ένα λεξικό	e·na lek·si·*ko*
newspaper (in English)	μια εφημερίδα (στα Αγγλικά)	mia e·fi·me·*ri*·ţha (sta ang·gli·*ka*)
notepad	ένα μπλοκ για σημειώσεις	e·na blok yia si·mi·o·sis

CLOTHES

ρούχα

My size is ...	Το νούμερό μου είναι ...	to *nu*·me·ro mu *i*·ne ...
(40)	(σαράντα)	(sa·*ra*·da)
small	μικρό	mi·*kro*
medium	μεσαίο	me·se·o
large	μεγάλο	me·*gha*·lo

Can I try it on?
Μπορώ να το προβάρω; — bo·*ro* na to pro·*va*·ro

It doesn't fit.
Δε μου κάνει. — ţhe mu *ka*·ni

ELECTRONIC GOODS

ηλεκτρονικά είδη

Where can I buy duty-free electronic goods?
Πού μπορώ να αγοράσω αφορολόγητα ηλεκτρονικά είδη; — pu bo·*ro* na a·gho·*ra*·so a·fo·ro·*lo*·yi·ta i·lek·tro·ni·*ka* *i*·ţhi

Is this the latest model?
Είναι αυτό το τελευταίο μοντέλο; — *i*·ne af·*to* to te·lef·*te*·o mo·*de*·lo

Is this (240) volts?
Είναι αυτό (240) βολτ; — *i*·ne af·*to* (ţhia·*ko*·sia sa·*ra*·da) volt

I need an adaptor plug.
Χρειάζομαι ένα μετασχηματιστή. — khri·a·zo·me e·na me·ta·shi·ma·ti·*sti*

☑ BOY-WORDS & GIRL-WORDS

Some phrases in this book are marked with **m/f** – they refer as a rule to the speaker. Follow the **m** (masculine) form if you're a 'he' and the **f** (feminine) form if you're a 'she'.

HAIRDRESSING

κομμωτήριο

I'd like (a) ...	Θα ήθελα ένα ...	tha *i*·the·la e·na ...
blow wave	στέγνωμα με πιστολάκι	*stegh*·no·ma me pis·to·*la*·ki
colour	βάψιμο	*vap*·si·mo
haircut	κούρεμα	*ku*·re·ma
my beard trimmed	ψαλίδισμα στο μούσι μου	psa·*li*·ţhiz·ma sto *mu*·si mu
shave	ξύρισμα	*ksi*·riz·ma

Don't cut it too short.
Μην τα κόψεις πολύ κοντά. — min ta *kop*·sis po·*li* ko·*da*

Please use a new blade.
Παρακαλώ χρησιμοποίησε καινούργιο ξυράφι. — pa·ra·ka·*lo* khri·si·mo·*pi*·i·se ke·*nur*·yio ksi·*ra*·fi

Shave it all off!
Ξύρισέ τα όλα. — *ksi*·ri·se ta *o*·la

I should never have let you near me!
Δεν θα έπρεπε ποτέ να σε αφήσω κοντά μου! — ţhen tha *e*·pre·pe po·*te* na se a·*fi*·so ko·*da* mu

barber	κουρέας m	ku·*re*·as
beauty salon	ινστιτούτο αισθητικής n	in·sti·*tu*·to es·thi·ti·*kis*
for both sexes	και για τα δύο φύλα	ke yia ta *ţhi*·o *fi*·la
men's hairdresser	κομμωτής για άντρες m	ko·mo·*tis* yia *a*·dres

women's hairdresser	κομμωτής για γυναίκες m	ko·mo·*tis* yia yi·*ne*·kes

MUSIC

μουσική

I'm looking for something by (Anna Vissi).
Ψάχνω για κάτι (της Άννας Βίσση). — *psakh*·no yia *ka*·ti (tis *a*·nas *vi*·si)

What's his/her best recording?
Ποια είναι η καλύτερη ηχογράφησή του/της; — pia *i*·ne i ka·*li*·te·ri i·kho·*ghra*·fi·*si* tu/tis

PHOTOGRAPHY

φωτογραφικά

Can you ...?	Μπορείς να ...;	bo·*ris* na ...
develop digital photos	εμφανίσεις ψηφιακές φωτογραφίες	em·fa·*ni*·sis psi·fi·a·*kes* fo·to·ghra·*fi*·es
recharge the battery for my digital camera	φορτίσεις την μπαταρία για την ψηφιακή μου μηχανή	for·*ti*·sis tin ba·ta·*ri*·a yia tin psi·fi·a·*ki* mu mi·kha·*ni*

Do you have ... for this camera? Έχεις ... για αυτή τη φωτογραφική μηχανή; e·his ... yia af·*ti* ti fo·to·ghra·fi·*ki* mi·kha·*ni*

batteries μπαταρίες ba·ta·*ri*·es

memory cards κάρτες μνήμης *kar*·tes *mni*·mis

I need a cable to connect my camera to a computer.
Χρειάζομαι ένα καλώδιο για να συνδέσω τη μηχανή μου στο κομπιούτερ. khri·a·zo·me e·na ka·*lo*·ţhi·o yia na sin·*ţhe*·so ti mi·kha·*ni* mu sto kom·*piu*·ter

I need a cable to recharge this battery.
Χρειάζομαι ένα καλώδιο για να φορτίσω αυτή τη μπαταρία. khri·a·zo·me e·na ka·*lo*·ţhi·o yia na for·*ti*·so af·*ti* ti ba·ta·*ri*·a

Do you have disposable (underwater) cameras?
Έχεις (υποβρύχιες) φωτογραφικές μηχανές μιας χρήσης; e·his (i·pov·*ri*·hi·es) fo·to·ghra·fi·*kes* mi·kha·*nes* mias *khri*·sis

When will it be ready?
Πότε θα είναι έτοιμο; *po*·te tha *i*·ne e·ti·mo

How much is it?
Πόσο κάνει; *po*·so *ka*·ni

I need a passport photo taken.
Θέλω να βγάλω φωτογραφία για διαβατήριο. *the*·lo na *vga*·lo fo·to·ghra·*fi*·a yia ţhia·va·*ti*·ri·o

I'm not happy with these photos.
Δεν είμαι ικανοποιημένος/ ικανοποιημένη με αυτές τις φωτογραφίες. **m/f** ţhen *i*·me i·ka·no·pi·i·*me*·nos/ i·ka·no·pi·i·*me*·ni me af·*tes* tis fo·to·ghra·*fi*·es

I don't want to pay the full price.

Δεν θέλω να πληρώσω ολόκληρη την τιμή.	ţhen *the*·lo na pli·*ro*·so o·*lo*·kli·ri tin ti·*mi*

REPAIRS

επισκευές

Can I have my ... repaired here?	Μπορώ να επισκευάσω εδώ ...;	bo·*ro* na e·pi·ske·*va*·so e·*ţho* ...
backpack	το σάκο μου	to *sa*·ko mu
camera	τη φωτογραφική μηχανή μου	ti fo·to·ghra·fi·*ki* mi·kha·*ni* mu
shoes	τα παπούτσια μου	ta pa·*pu*·tsia mu
sunglasses	τα γιαλιά μου του ήλιου	ta yia·*lia* mu tu *i*·liu

When will my ... be ready?	Πότε θα είναι έτοιμα τα ...;	*po*·te tha *i*·ne e·ti·ma ta ...
glasses	γυαλιά μου	yia·*lia* mu
shoes	παπούτσια μου	pa·*put*·sia mu
sunglasses	γυαλιά μου του ήλιου	yia·*lia* mu tu *i*·liu

When will my camera be ready?

Πότε θα είναι έτοιμη η φωτογραφική μηχανή μου;	*po*·te tha *i*·ne e·ti·mi i fo·to·ghra·fi·*ki* mi·kha·*ni* mu

When will my backpack be ready?

Πότε θα είναι έτοιμος ο σάκος μου;	*po*·te tha *i*·ne e·ti·mos o *sa*·kos mu

SOUVENIRS

backgammon board	τάβλι **n**	*tav*·li
baskets	καλάθια **n pl**	ka·*la*·thia
bouzouki	μπουζούκι **n**	bu·*zu*·ki
bronzeware	μπρούτζινα **n pl**	*bru*·dzi·na
carpets	χαλιά **n pl**	kha·*lia*
ceramics	κεραμικά **n pl**	ke·ra·mi·*ka*
copperware	χάλκινα **n pl**	*khal*·ki·na
cushion covers	μαξιλαροθήκες **f pl**	mak·si·la·ro·*thi*·kes
evil eye (blue eye warding off evil spirits)	φυλαχτό **n**	fi·lakh·*to*
icons	εικόνες **f pl**	i·*ko*·nes
lace	δαντέλλα **f**	ţhan·*te*·la
leather work	δερμάτινα **n pl**	ţher·*ma*·ti·na
pottery	είδη αγγειοπλαστικής **n pl**	*i*·ţhi a·gi·o·pla·sti·*kis*
rugs	τάπητες **m pl**	*ta*·pi·tes
sculptures	γλυπτά **n pl**	ghlip·*ta*
worry beads	κομπολόγια **n pl**	ko·bo·*lo*·yia
woven shoulder bag	υφαντή τσάντα ώμου **f**	i·fa·*di tsa*·da *o*·mu
... jewellery	… κοσμήματα **n pl**	... koz·*mi*·ma·ta
filigree	φιλιγκράν	fi·li·*gran*
gold	χρυσά	khri·sa
silver	ασημένια	a·si·*me*·nia

Communications

ΕΠΙΚΟΙΝΩΝΙΕΣ

POST OFFICE

ταχυδρομείο

I want to send a ...	Θέλω να στείλω ...	*the*·lo na *sti*·lo ...
letter	ένα γράμμα	e·na *ghra*·ma
parcel	ένα δέμα	e·na *ţhe*·ma
postcard	μια κάρτα	mia *kar*·ta
I want to buy a/an ...	Θέλω να αγοράσω ένα ...	*the*·lo na a·gho·*ra*·so e·na ...
envelope	φάκελο	*fa*·ke·lo
stamp	γραμματόσημο	ghra·ma·*to*·si·mo
customs declaration	δήλωση τελωνείου f	*ţhi*·lo·si te·lo·*ni*·u
domestic	εσωτερικό	e·so·te·ri·*ko*
fragile	εύθραυστο	*ef*·thraf·sto
international	διεθνές	ţhi·eth·*nes*
mail	αλληλογραφία f	a·li·lo·ghra·*fi*·a
mailbox	ταχυδρομικό κουτί n	ta·hi·ţhro·mi·*ko* ku·*ti*
postcode	ταχυδρομικός τομέας m	ta·hi·ţhro·mi·*kos* to·*me*·as

SNAIL MAIL

airmail	αεροπορικώς	a·e·ro·po·ri·*kos*
express mail	εξπρές	eks·*pres*
registered mail	συστημένο	si·sti·*me*·no
sea mail	ατμοπλοϊκώς	at·mo·plo·i·*kos*
surface mail	δια ξηράς	ţhi·*a* ksi·*ras*

Please send it by airmail to (Australia).

Παρακαλώ στείλτε το αεροπορικώς στην (Αυστραλία). — pa·ra·ka·*lo* *stil*·te to a·e·ro·po·ri·*kos* stin (af·stra·*li*·a)

Please send it by surface mail to (New Zealand).

Παρακαλώ στείλτε το δια ξηράς στην (Νέα Ζηλανδία). — pa·ra·ka·*lo* *stil*·te to ţhi·*a* ksi·*ras* stin (*ne*·a zi·lan·*thi*·a)

It contains (souvenirs).

Περιέχει (σουβενίρ). — pe·ri·e·hi (su·ve·*nir*)

Where's the poste restante section?

Πού είναι το ποστ ρεστάντ; — pu *i*·ne to post re·*stant*

Is there any mail for me?

Υπάρχουν γράμματα για μένα; — i·*par*·khun *ghra*·ma·ta yia *me*·na

I'd like to collect a parcel.

Θα ήθελα να παραλάβω ένα δέμα. — tha *i*·the·la na pa·ra·*la*·vo e·na *ţhe*·ma

Do you have internet services?

Έχετε υπηρεσία Διαδικτύου; — e·he·te i·pi·re·*si*·a ţhi·a·ţhik·*ti*·u

MEDUSA

Medusa, famous for turning mortals to stone, had hair much like the tentacles of a jellyfish. In fact the jellyfish is named after her in Greek (μέδουσα *me*·ţhu·sa), French (*méduse* me·*dooz*) and Spanish (*medusa* me·*doo*·sa), to name just a few languages.

PHONE

τηλέφωνο

What's your phone number?
Τι αριθμό τηλεφώνου έχεις; ti a·rith·*mo* ti·le·*fo*·nu e·his

I want to ...	Θέλω να ...	*the*·lo na ...
call (Singapore)	τηλεφωνήσω (στη Σιγκαπούρη)	ti·le·fo·*ni*·so (sti sing·ga·*pu*·ri)

LISTEN FOR

Ποιος μιλάει; pios mi·*la*·i	**Who's calling?**
Σε ποιον θέλετε να μιλήσετε; se pion *the*·le·te na mi·*li*·se·te	**Who do you want to speak to?**
Μια στιγμή. mia stigh·*mi*	**One moment.**
Δεν είναι εδώ. ţhen *i*·ne e·*ţho*	**He's/She's not here.**
Λάθος αριθμός. *la*·thos a·rith·*mos*	**Wrong number.**

The number is ...
Ο αριθμός είναι ... o a·rith·*mos* *i*·ne ...

What's the code for (New Zealand)?
Ποιος είναι ο κωδικός αριθμός για (τη Νέα Ζηλανδία); — pios *i*·ne o ko·ţhi·*kos* a·rith·*mos* yia (ti *ne*·a zi·lan·*ţhi*·a)

It's engaged.
Είναι κατειλημμένη. — *i*·ne ka·ti·li·*me*·ni

I've been cut off.
Με διέκοψαν. — me ţhi·*e*·kop·san

The connection's bad.
Η σύνδεση είναι κακή. — i *sin*·ţhe·si *i*·ne ka·*ki*

Hello.
Εμπρός. — e·*bros*

It's ...
Είμαι ... — *i*·me ...

Is ... there?
Είναι ... εκεί; — *i*·ne ... e·*ki*

Can I speak to ...?
Μπορώ να μιλήσω με ...; — bo·*ro* na mi·*li*·so me ...

Can I leave a message?
Μπορώ να αφήσω ένα μήνυμα; — bo·*ro* na a·*fi*·so e·na *mi*·ni·ma

Please tell him/her I called.
Παρακαλώ πες του/της ότι τηλεφώνησα. — pa·ra·ka·*lo* pes tu/tis o·ti ti·le·*fo*·ni·sa

My number is ...
Ο αριθμός μου είναι ... — o a·rith·*mos* mu *i*·ne ...

I don't have a contact number.
Δεν έχω αριθμό για επικοινωνία. — ţhen e·kho a·rith·*mo* yia e·pi·ki·no·*ni*·a

I'll call back later.
Θα τηλεφωνήσω αργότερα. — tha ti·le·fo·*ni*·so ar·*gho*·te·ra

MOBILE/CELL PHONE

κινητό τηλέφωνο

I'd like a ...	Θα ήθελα ...	tha *i*·the·la ...
charger for my phone	ένα φορτιστή για το τηλέφωνό μου	e·na for·ti·*sti* yia to ti·*le*·fo·*no* mu
SIM card for your network	μια κάρτα SIM για το δίκτυό σας	mia *kar*·ta sim yia to *ţhik*·ti·*o* sas

What are the rates?
Ποιες είναι οι τιμές; — pies *i*·ne i ti·*mes*

INTERNET

διαδίκτυο

I'd like to ...	Θα ήθελα να ...	tha *i*·the·la na ...
check my email	ελέγξω την ηλεκτρονική αλληλογραφία μου	e·*leng*·so tin i·lek·tro·ni·*ki* a·li·lo·ghra·*fi*·a mu
get internet access	έχω πρόσβαση στο Διαδίκτυο	e·kho *pros*·va·si sto ţhi·a·*ţhik*·ti·o
use a printer	χρησιμοποιήσω έναν εκτυπωτή	khri·si·mo·pi·*i*·so e·nan ek·ti·po·*ti*
use a scanner	χρησιμοποιήσω ένα σκάνερ	khri·si·mo·pi·*i*·so e·na *ska*·ner

Do you have ...?	Έχετε ...;	e·he·te ...
Macs	Κομπιούτερ Mac	kom·*piu*·ter mak
PCs	Κομπιούτερ PC	kom·*piu*·ter pi si
a Zip drive	Zip drive	zip *dra*·iv

How much per ...?	Πόσο κοστίζει κάθε ...;	*po*·so ko·*sti*·zi *ka*·the ...
hour	ώρα	*o*·ra
page	σελίδα	se·*li*·ţha

How do I log on?
Πώς μπαίνω μέσα; — pos *be*·no *me*·sa

Please change it to the (English)-language setting.
Παρακαλώ άλλαξέ το στην (αγγλική) γλώσσα. — pa·ra·ka·*lo* a·lak·se to stin (ang·gli·*ki*) *glo*·sa

Do you have (English) keyboards?
έχεις (Αγγλικό) πληκτρολόγιο; — e·his (ang·gli·*ko)* plik·tro·*lo*·yi·o

It's crashed.
κατέρρευσε. — ka·*te*·ref·se

I've finished.
Τελείωσα. — te·*li*·o·sa

Banking

ΣΥΝΑΛΛΑΓΗ ΜΕ ΤΡΑΠΕΖΑ

What time does the bank open?
Τι ώρα ανοίγει η τράπεζα; — ti *o*·ra a·*ni*·yi i *tra*·pe·za

Where's a/an ...?	Πού είναι ...;	pu *i*·ne ...
automated teller machine	μια αυτόματη μηχανή χρημάτων	mia af·*to*·ma·ti mi·kha·*ni* khri·*ma*·ton
foreign exchange office	ένα γραφείο αλλαγής χρημάτων	*e*·na ghra·*fi*·o a·la·*yis* khri·*ma*·ton
Where can I ...?	Πού μπορώ να ...;	pu bo·*ro* na ...
I'd like to ...	Θα ήθελα να ...	tha *i*·the·la na ...
change money	αλλάξω χρήματα	a·*lak*·so *khri*·ma·ta
get a cash advance	κάνω μια ανάληψη σε μετρητά	*ka*·no mia a·*na*·lip·si se me·tri·*ta*
withdraw money	αποσύρω χρήματα	a·po·*si*·ro *khri*·ma·ta
What's the ...?	Ποια είναι ... ;	pia *i*·ne ...
exchange rate	η τιμή συναλλάγματος	i ti·*mi* si·na·*lagh*·ma·tos
charge for that	η χρέωση για αυτό	i *khre*·o·si yia af·*to*

Has my money arrived yet?
Έχουν φτάσει τα χρήματά μου; — e·khun *fta*·si ta *khri*·ma·*ta* mu

How long will it take to arrive?
Σε πόσο καιρό θα φτάσουν; — se *po*·so ke·*ro* tha *fta*·sun

The automated teller machine took my card.
Η αυτόματη μηχανή χρημάτων κράτησε την κάρτα μου. — i af·*to*·ma·ti mi·kha·*ni* khri·*ma*·ton *kra*·ti·se tin *kar*·ta mu

I've forgotten my PIN.
Ξέχασα τον κωδικό ΠΙΝ μου. — *kse*·ha·sa ton ko·ţhi·*ko* pin mu

Can I use my credit card to withdraw money?
Μπορώ να χρησιμοποιήσω την πιστωτική μου κάρτα για να βγάλω χρήματα; — bo·*ro* na khri·si·mo·pi·*i*·so tin pi·sto·ti·*ki* mu *kar*·ta yia na *vga*·lo *khri*·ma·ta

LISTEN FOR

διαβατήριο n	ţhia·va·*ti*·ri·o	**passport**
ταυτότητα f	taf·*to*·ti·ta	**identification**

Δεν μπορούμε να το κάνουμε αυτό.
ţhen bo·*ru*·me na to *ka*·nu·me af·*to* — **We can't do that.**

Τελείωσαν τα χρήματά σας.
te·*li*·o·san ta *khri*·ma·*ta* sas — **You have no funds left.**

Υπάρχει ένα πρόβλημα.
i·*par*·hi e·na *prov*·li·ma — **There's a problem.**

Υπογράψτε εδώ.
i·po·*ghrap*·ste e·*ţho* — **Sign here.**

Sightseeing

ΠΕΡΙΗΓΗΣΗ ΣΕ ΑΞΙΟΘΕΑΤΑ

I'd like a/an ...	Θα ήθελα ...	tha *i*·the·la ...
audio set	ακουστικά	a·ku·sti·*ka*
catalogue	ένα κατάλογο	e·na ka·*ta*·lo·gho
guide	έναν οδηγό	e·nan o·ţhi·*gho*
guidebook in (English)	έναν οδηγό στα (Αγγλικά)	e·nan o·ţhi·*gho* sta (ang·gli·*ka*)
(local) map	ένα (τοπικό) χάρτη	e·na (to·pi·*ko*) *khar*·ti

Do you have information on ... sights?	Έχετε πληροφορίες για ... χώρους;	e·he·te pli·ro·fo·*ri*·es yia ... *kho*·rus
ancient	αρχαίους	ar·*he*·us
archaic	αρχαϊκούς	ar·kha·i·*kus*
archaeological	αρχαιολογικούς	ar·he·o·lo·yi·*kus*
architectural	αρχιτεκτονικούς	ar·hi·tek·to·ni·*kus*
Byzantine	Βυζαντινούς	vi·za·di·*nus*
classical	κλασσικούς	kla·si·*kus*
cultural	πολιτιστικούς	po·li·ti·sti·*kus*
Hellenistic	Ελληνιστικούς	e·li·ni·sti·*kus*
historical	ιστορικούς	i·sto·ri·*kus*
neoclassical	νεοκλασσικούς	ne·o·kla·si·*kus*
Orthodox	Ορθόδοξους	or·*tho*·dok·sus
Ottoman	Οθωμανικούς	o·tho·ma·ni·*kus*
religious	θρησκευτικούς	thris·kef·ti·*kus*
Roman	Ρωμαικούς	ro·ma·i·*kus*

LOOK FOR

Ανδρών	an·*ţhron*	**Men**
Είσοδος	*i*·so·ţhos	**Entrance**
Έξοδος	*ek*·so·ţhos	**Exit**
Τουαλέτες	tu·a·*le*·tes	**Toilets**
Γυναικών	yi·ne·*kon*	**Women**

I'd like to see (the) ...	Θα ήθελα να δω ...	tha *i*·the·la na ţho ...
Acropolis	την Ακρόπολη	tin ak·*ro*·po·li
amphitheatre	το αμφιθέατρο	to am·fi·*the*·a·tro
Archaeological Museum	το Αρχαιολογικό Μουσείο	to ar·he·o·lo·yi·*ko* mu·*si*·o
Byzantine frescoes	Βυζαντινά φρέσκο	vi·za·di·*na* *fres*·ko
labyrinth	τον λαβύρινθο	ton la·*vi*·rin·tho
mosaics	τα μωσαϊκά	ta mo·sa·i·*ka*
Mt Athos monasteries	τα μοναστήρια του Αγίου Όρους	ta mo·na·*sti*·ria tu a·*yi*·u *o*·rus
Mycenaean tombs	Μυκηναϊκούς τάφους	mi·ki·na·i·*kus* *ta*·fus
oracle of Delphi	το μαντείο των Δελφών	to ma·*di*·o ton ţhel·*fon*
palace	το παλάτι	to pa·*la*·ti
ruins	τα ερείπια	ta e·*ri*·pi·a
sculptures	τα γλυπτά	ta ghlip·*ta*
statues	τα αγάλματα	ta a·*ghal*·ma·ta
temple	το ναό	to na·*o*

What's that?
Τι είναι εκείνο; — ti *i*·ne e·*ki*·no

Who made it?
Ποιος το έκανε; — pios to e·ka·ne

How old is it?
Πόσο χρονώ είναι; — *po*·so khro·*no* *i*·ne

When was this discovered?
Πότε ανακαλύφτηκε αυτό; — *po*·te a·na·ka·*lif*·ti·ke af·*to*

When were the excavations done?
Πότε έγιναν οι ανασκαφές; — *po*·te e·yi·nan i a·nas·ka·*fes*

Could you take a photograph of me?
Μπορείς να μου βγάλεις μια φωτογραφία; — bo·*ris* na mu *vgha*·lis mia fo·to·ghra·*fi*·a

Can I take a photo (of you)?
Μπορώ να (σου) βγάλω μια φωτογραφία; — bo·*ro* na (su) *vgha*·lo mia fo·to·ghra·*fi*·a

GETTING IN

είσοδος

What time does it open?
Τι ώρα ανοίγει; — ti *o*·ra a·*ni*·yi

What time does it close?
Τι ώρα κλείνει; — ti *o*·ra *kli*·ni

Is it open every day?
Είναι ανοιχτό κάθε μέρα; — *i*·ne a·nikh·*to* *ka*·the *me*·ra

What's the admission charge?
Πόσο κοστίζει η είσοδος; — *po*·so ko·*sti*·zi i *i*·so·ţhos

Can I go in wearing these clothes?
Μπορώ να μπω με αυτά τα ρούχα; — bo·*ro* na bo me af·*ta* ta *ru*·kha

Is there a discount for ...?	Υπάρχει έκπτωση για ...;	i·*par*·hi *ek*·pto·si yia ...
children	παιδιά	pe·*ţhia*
families	οικογένειες	i·ko·*ye*·ni·es
groups	γκρουπ	grup
older people	υπερήλικους	i·pe·*ri*·li·kus
pensioners	συνταξιούχους	si·dak·si·*u*·khus
students	σπουδαστές	spu·ţha·*stes*

TOURS

περιηγήσεις

Can you recommend a tour?
Μπορείς να προτείνεις κάποια περιήγηση;
bo·*ris* na pro·*ti*·nis *ka*·pia pe·ri·*i*·yi·si

When's the next tour?
Πότε είναι η επόμενη περιήγηση;
po·te *i*·ne i e·*po*·me·ni pe·ri·*i*·yi·si

How long is the tour?
Πόσην ώρα διαρκεί η περιήγηση;
po·sin *o*·ra ţhi·ar·*ki* i pe·ri·*i*·yi·si

The guide will pay.
Ο/Η οδηγός θα πληρώσει. m/f
o / i o·ţhi·*ghos* tha pli·*ro*·si

The guide has paid.
Ο/Η οδηγός έχει πληρώσει. m/f
o / i o·ţhi·*ghos* *e*·hi pli·*ro*·si

What time should we be back?
Τι ώρα πρέπει να επιστρέψουμε;
ti *o*·ra *pre*·pi na e·pi·*strep*·su·me

I'm with them.
Είμαι με αυτούς.
i·me me af·*tus*

I've lost my group.
Έχασα την ομάδα μου.
e·kha·sa tin o·*ma*·ţha mu

Business

ΕΠΙΧΕΙΡΗΣΕΙΣ

DOING BUSINESS

επιχειρήσεις

I'm attending a ...	Παρακολουθώ ...	pa·ra·ko·lu·*tho* ...
conference	ένα συνέδριο	e·na sin·e·ţhri·o
course	μια σειρά μαθημάτων	mia si·*ra* ma·thi·*ma*·ton
meeting	μια συνεδρίαση	mia sin·e·*ţhri*·a·si
trade fair	μια εμπορική έκθεση	mia e·bo·ri·*ki* *ek*·the·si
I'm with ...	Είμαι με ...	*i*·me me ...
(Olympiaki)	(την Ολυμπιακή)	(tin o·li·bi·a·*ki*)
my colleague	τον συνάδελφό μου m	ton sin·*a*·ţhel·*fo* mu
	την συναδέλφισσά μου f	tin sin·a·*ţhel*·fi·sa mu
my colleagues	τους συναδέλφους μου	tus sin·a·*ţhel*·fus mu

I'm alone.
Είμαι μόνος/μόνη. m/f — *i*·me *mo*·nos / *mo*·ni

I have an appointment with ...
Έχω ένα ραντεβού με ... — e·kho e·na ra·de·*vu* me ...

I'm staying at (the Xenia), room (10).
Μένω στο (Ξενία), δωμάτιο (10). — *me*·no sto (kse·*ni*·a) ţho·*ma*·ti·o (*ţhe*·ka)

I'm here for (two) days/weeks.
Είμαι εδώ για (δύο) μέρες/εβδομάδες. — *i*·me e·*ţho* yia (*ţhi*·o) *me*·res / ev·ţho·*ma*·ţhes

Here's my business card.
Ορίστε η κάρτα μου. — o·*ri*·ste i *kar*·ta mu

Can I have your business card?
Μπορώ να έχω την κάρτα σου; — bo·*ro* na *e*·kho tin *kar*·ta su

Here's my ...	Ορίστε ... μου.	o·*ri*·ste ... mu
What's your ...?	Ποια είναι η δική σου η ...;	pia *i*·ne i ţhi·*ki* su i ...
address	διεύθυνση	ţhi·*ef*·thin·si
email address	ηλεκτρονική διεύθυνση	i·lek·tro·ni·*ki* ţhi·*ef*·thin·si
Here's my ... number.	Εδώ είναι ο αριθμός ... μου.	e·*ţho i*·ne o a·rith·*mos* ... mu
What's your ... number?	Ποιος είναι ο δικός σου ο αριθμός ...;	pios *i*·ne o ţhi·*kos* su o a·rith·*mos* ...
mobile	του κινητού	tu ki·ni·*tu*
work	της δουλειάς	tis ţhu·*lias*
Where's the ...?	Πού είναι ...;	pu *i*·ne ...
business centre	ο χώρος εργασίας	o *kho*·ros er·gha·*si*·as
conference	το συνέδριο	to sin·e·ţhri·o
meeting	η συνεδρίαση	i sin·e·*ţhri*·a·si
I need (a/an) ...	Χρειάζομαι ...	khri·a·zo·me ...
computer	ένα κομπιούτερ	e·na kom·*piu*·ter
internet connection	σύνδεση στο διαδίκτυο	*sin*·ţhe·si sto ţhi·a·*ţhik*·ti·o
interpreter	διερμηνέα	ţhi·er·mi·*ne*·a
more business cards	περισσότερες κάρτες	pe·ri·*so*·te·res *kar*·tes
some space to set up	χώρο να τοποθετήσω τα πράγματα	*kho*·ro na to·po·the·*ti*·so ta *pragh*·ma·ta

Thank you for your time.
Ευχαριστώ για το χρόνο σου. ef·kha·ri·*sto* yia to *khro*·no su

That went very well.
Πήγε πολύ καλά. *pi*·ye po·*li* ka·*la*

Shall we go for a drink/meal?
Πάμε για ποτό/φαγητό; *pa*·me yia po·*to*/fa·yi·*to*

LOOKING FOR A JOB

ψάχνοντας για δουλειά

Where are jobs advertised?
Πού διαφημίζονται οι δουλειές; — pu ţhi·a·fi·*mi*·zo·de i ţhu·*lies*

I'm enquiring about the position advertised.
ζητώ πληροφορίες για τη θέση που διαφημίστηκε. — zi·*to* pli·ro·fo·*ri*·es yia ti *the*·si pu ţhi·a·fi·*mi*·sti·ke

I have experience.
Έχω πείρα. — e·kho *pi*·ra

What's the wage?
Τι μισθό έχει; — ti mi·*stho* e·hi

I'm looking for ... work.	Ψάχνω για δουλειά ...	*psakh*·no yia ţhu·*lia* ...
bar	σε μπαρ	se bar
casual	προσωρινή	pro·so·ri·*ni*
English-teaching	να διδάσκω αγγλικά	na ţhi·*ţha*·sko ang·gli·*ka*
fruit-picking	να μαζεύω φρούτα	na ma·*ze*·vo *fru*·ta
full-time	με πλήρη απασχόληση	me *pli*·ri a·pa·*skho*·li·si
labouring	χειρωνακτική	hi·ro·nak·ti·*ki*
office	γραφείου	ghra·*fi*·u
part-time	μερικής απασχόλησης	me·ri·*kis* a·pa·*skho*·li·sis
waitering	γκαρσόν	gar·*son*

Do I need (a/an)...?	Χρειάζομαι ...;	khri·*a*·zo·me ...
contract	συμβόλαιο	sim·*vo*·le·o
experience	πείρα	*pi*·ra
insurance	ασφάλεια	as·*fa*·li·a
my own transport	δικό μου μεταφορικό μέσο	ţhi·*ko* mu me·ta·fo·ri·*ko* *me*·so
paperwork	ντοκουμέντα	do·ku·*men*·ta
uniform	στολή	sto·*li*
work permit	άδεια εργασίας	a·ţhi·a er·gha·*si*·as

Here is/are my ...	Ορίστε ...	o·*ri*·ste ...
bank account details	ο τραπεζικός μου λογαριασμός	o tra·pe·zi·*kos* mu lo·gha·riaz·*mos*
CV/résumé	το βιογραφικό μου σημείωμα	to vi·o·ghra·fi·*ko* mu si·*mi*·o·ma
residency permit	η άδεια παραμονής μου	i *a*·ţhi·a pa·ra·mo·*nis* mu
visa	η βίζα μου	i *vi*·za mu
work permit	η άδεια εργασίας μου	i *a*·ţhi·a er·gha·*si*·as mu
What time do I ...?	Τι ώρα ...;	ti *o*·ra ...
finish	τελειώνω	te·li·*o*·no
have a break	έχω διάλειμμα	e·kho *ţhia*·li·ma
start	αρχίζω	ar·*hi*·zo
I can start ...	Μπορώ να αρχίσω ...	bo·*ro* na ar·*hi*·so ...
Can you start ...?	Μπορείς να αρχίσεις ...;	bo·*ris* na ar·*hi*·sis ...
at (eight) o'clock	στις (οχτώ)	stis (okh·*to*)
next week	την επόμενη εβδομάδα	tin e·*po*·me·ni ev·tho·*ma*·ţha
today	σήμερα	*si*·me·ra
tomorrow	αύριο	*av*·ri·o
advertisement	διαφήμιση **f**	ţhi·a·*fi*·mi·si
contract	συμβόλαιο **n**	sim·*vo*·le·o
employee	υπάλληλος **m&f**	i·*pa*·li·los
employer	εργοδότης **m** εργοδότρια **f**	er·gho·*ţho*·tis er·gho·*ţho*·tri·a
job	δουλειά **f**	ţhu·*lia*
work experience	πείρα στη δουλειά **f**	*pi*·ra sti ţhu·*lia*

Seniors & Travellers with Disabilities

ΥΠΕΡΗΛΙΚΟΙ ΚΑΙ ΑΝΑΠΗΡΟΙ ΤΑΞΙΔΙΩΤΕΣ

I have a disability.

Έχω μια αναπηρία. — e·kho mia a·na·pi·*ri*·a

I need assistance.

Χρειάζομαι βοήθεια. — khri·a·zo·me vo·*i*·thi·a

What services do you have for people with a disability?

Τι υπηρεσίες έχετε για άτομα με αναπηρίες; — ti i·pi·re·*si*·es e·he·te yia a·to·ma me a·na·pi·*ri*·es

Are there accessible toilets?

Υπάρχουν τουαλέτες για άτομα με αναπηρίες; — i·*par*·khun tu·a·*le*·tes yia a·to·ma me a·na·pi·*ri*·es

Are there parking spaces for disabled visitors?

Υπάρχει πάρκνιγκ για άτομα με αναπηρίες; — i·*par*·hi *par*·king yia a·to·ma me a·na·pi·*ri*·es

Is there wheelchair access?

Υπάρχει δρόμος για αναπηρικά αμαξίδια; — i·*par*·hi *ţhro*·mos yia a·na·pi·ri·*ka* a·ma·*xi*·di·a

How wide is the entrance?

Πόσο πλατιά είναι η είσοδος; — *po*·so pla·*tia* *i*·ne i *i*·so·ţhos

Is there somewhere I can sit down?

Υπάρχει κάπου να καθίσω; — i·*par*·hi *ka*·pu na ka·*thi*·so

I'm deaf.

Είμαι κωφός. — *i*·me ko·*fos*

I have a hearing aid.

Έχω ακουστικά βαρηκοΐας. — e·kho a·ku·sti·*ka* va·ri·ko·*i*·as

Are guide dogs permitted?

Επιτρέπεται στα σκυλιά για τυφλούς; — e·pi·*tre*·pe·te sta ski·*lia* yia ti·*flus*

How many steps are there?

Πόσα σκαλοπάτια υπάρχουν; — *po*·sa ska·lo·*pa*·tia i·*par*·khun

Is there a lift/elevator?

Υπάρχει ασανσέρ; — i·*par*·khi a·san·*ser*

Are there rails in the bathroom?

Υπάρχουν στηρίγματα στο μπάνιο;	i·*par*·khun sti·*righ*·ma·ta sto *ba*·nio

Could you call me an accessible taxi?

Μπορείς να καλέσεις ένα ταξί για άτομα με αναπηρίες;	bo·*ris* na ka·*le*·sis e·na tak·*si* yia *a*·to·ma me a·na·pi·*ri*·es

Could you help me cross the street safely?

Μπορείς να με βοηθήσεις να περάσω το δρόμο με ασφάλεια;	bo·*ris* na me vo·i·*thi*·sis na pe·*ra*·so to *ţhro*·mo me as·*fa*·li·a

guide dog	σκύλος-οδηγού τυφλών n	*ski*·los o·di·*gou* ti·*flon*
older person	υπερήλικος m υπερήλικη f	i·pe·*ri*·li·kos i·pe·*ri*·li·ki
person with a disability	άτομο με αναπηρίες n	*a*·to·mo me a·na·pi·*ri*·es
ramp	ράμπα f	*ram*·pa
walking frame	περιπατητής n	pe·ri·pa·ti·*tis*
walking stick	μπαστούνι n	ba·*stu*·ni
wheelchair	αναπηρικό αμαξίδιο n	a·na·pi·ri·*ko* a·ma·*xi*·di·o

Children

ΠΑΙΔΙΑ

TRAVELLING WITH CHILDREN

ταξιδεύοντας με παιδιά

Is there a ...?	Υπάρχει ...;	i·*par*·hi ...
baby change room	δωμάτιο για άλλαγμα μωρών	ţho·*ma*·ti·o yia a·lagh·ma mo·*ron*
child-minding service	υπηρεσία διαφύλαξης παιδιών	i·pi·re·*si*·a ţhi·a·*fi*·lak·sis pe·*ţhion*
children's menu	παιδικό μενού	pe·ţhi·*ko* me·*nu*
child's portion	παιδική μερίδα	pe·ţhi·*ki* me·*ri*·ţha
creche	παιδικός σταθμός	pe·di·*kos* stath·*mos*
discount for children	έκπτωση για παιδιά	*ek*·pto·si yia pe·*ţhia*
family ticket	οικογενειακό εισιτήριο	i·ko·ye·ni·a·*ko* i·si·*ti*·ri·o
I need a/an ...	Χρειάζομαι ...	khri·a·zo·me ...
baby seat	κάθισμα μωρού	*ka*·thiz·ma mo·*ru*
(English-speaking) babysitter	(αγγλομαθή) μπέημπι σίτερ	(ang·glo·ma·*thi*) *be*·i·bi *si*·ter
booster seat	ανυψωμένο κάθισμα	a·nip·so·*me*·no *ka*·thiz·ma
cot	παιδικό κρεβάτι	pe·ţhi·*ko* kre·*va*·ti
highchair	παιδική καρέκλα	pe·ţhi·*ki* ka·*re*·kla
plastic sheet	πλαστικό σεντόνι	pla·sti·*ko* se·*do*·ni
plastic bag	πλαστική σακούλα	pla·sti·*ki* sa·*ku*·la
potty	γιογιό	yio·*yio*
pram	παιδικό καροτσάκι	pe·ţhi·*ko* ka·rot·*sa*·ki
sick bag	σακούλα εμετού	sa·*ku*·la e·me·*tu*
stroller	καροτσάκι	ka·rot·*sa*·ki

Where's the nearest ...?	Πού είναι το πιο κοντινό ...;	pu *i*·ne to pio ko·di·*no* ...
park	πάρκο	*par*·ko
playground	παιδική χαρά	pe·di·*ki* kha·*ra*
toy shop	κατάστημα παιχνιδιών	ka·*ta*·sti·ma pekh·ni·*ţhion*
Where's the nearest ...?	Πού είναι η πιο κοντινή ...;	pu *i*·ne i pio ko·di·*ni* ...
drinking fountain	βρύση με πόσιμο νερό	*vri*·si me *po*·si·mo ne·*ro*
swimming pool	πισίνα	pi·*si*·na
tap/faucet	βρύση	*vri*·si
theme park	θεματικό πάρκο	the·ma·ti·*kho* *par*·kho
Do you sell ...?	Πουλάτε ...;	pu·*la*·te ...
baby wipes	μωρομάντηλα	mo·ro·*ma*·di·la
painkillers for infants	παυσίπονα για μωρά	paf·*si*·po·na yia mo·*ra*
disposable nappies/diapers	πάνες μιας χρήσης	*pa*·nes mias *khri*·sis
tissues	χαρτομάντηλα	khar·to·*ma*·di·la
Do you hire out ...?	Νοικιάζετε ...;	ni·*kia*·ze·te ...
prams	παιδικά καροτσάκια	pe·ţhi·*ka* ka·rot·*sa*·kia
strollers	καροτσάκια	ka·rot·*sa*·kia

Are there any good places to take children around here?
Υπάρχουν καλά μέρη εδώ κοντά για τα παιδιά; — i·*par*·khun ka·*la* me·ri e·*ţho* ko·*da* yia ta pe·*ţhia*

Is there space for a pram?
Υπάρχει χώρος για το παιδικό καροτσάκι; — i·*par*·hi *kho*·ros yia to pe·ţhi·*ko* ka·rot·*sa*·ki

Are children allowed?
Επιτρέπεται στα παιδιά; — e·pi·*tre*·pe·te sta pe·*ţhia*

Where can I change a nappy/diaper?
Πού μπορώ να αλλάξω την πάνα; — pu bo·*ro* na a·*lak*·so tin *pa*·na

Do you mind if I breast-feed here?

Σε πειράζει αν θηλάσω εδώ το μωρό;	se pi·*ra*·zi an thi·*la*·so e·*ţho* to mo·*ro*

Could I have some paper and pencils, please?

Μπορώ να έχω λίγο χαρτί και μολύβια, παρακαλώ.	bo·*ro* na e·kho *li*·gho khar·*ti* ke mo·*li*·via pa·ra·ka·*lo*

Is this suitable for (five)-year-old children?

Είναι αυτό κατάλληλο για παιδιά (πέντε) χρονών;	*i*·ne af·*to* ka·*ta*·li·lo yia pe·*ţhia* (*pe*·de) khro·*non*

Do you know a dentist / doctor who is good with children?

Ξέρεις ένα οδοντίατρο/ γιατρό που είναι καλός με τα παιδιά;	*kse*·ris *e*·na o·ţho·*di*·a·tro / yia·*tro* pu *i*·ne ka·*los* me ta pe·*ţhia*

If your child is sick, see **health**, p195.

TALKING WITH CHILDREN

μιλώντας με τα παιδιά

What's your name?

Πώς σε λένε;	pos se *le*·ne

How old are you?

Πόσο χρονών είσαι;	*po*·so khro·*non i*·se

When's your birthday?

Πότε είναι τα γενέθλιά σου;	*po*·te *i*·ne ta ye·*neth*·li·a su

Do you go to school / kindergarten?

Πηγαίνεις στο σχολείο/ νηπιαγωγείο;	pi·*ye*·nis sto skho·*li*·o / ni·pi·a·gho·*yi*·o

What grade are you in?

Σε ποια τάξη είσαι;	se pia *tak*·si *i*·se

Do you like ...?	Σου αρέσει ...;	su a·*re*·si ...
music	η μουσική	i mu·si·*ki*
school	το σχολείο	to skho·*li*·o
your teacher	ο δάσκαλός σου m	o ţha·ska·*los* su
	η δασκάλα σου f	i ţha·*ska*·la su

Do you like sport?
Σου αρέσουν τα σπορ; — su a·*re*·sun ta spor

What do you do after school?
Τι κάνεις μετά το σχολείο; — ti *ka*·nis me·*ta* to skho·*li*·o

Do you learn English?
Μαθαίνεις αγγλικά; — ma·*the*·nis ang·gli·*ka*

TALKING ABOUT CHILDREN

μιλώντας για παιδιά

When's the baby due?
Πότε είναι να γεννηθεί το μωρό; — *po*·te *i*·ne na ye·ni·*thi* to mo·*ro*

What are you going to call the baby?
Πώς θα το ονομάσεις το μωρό; — pos tha to·o·no·*ma*·sis to mo·*ro*

Is this your first child?
Είναι το πρώτο σου παιδί; — *i*·ne to *pro*·to su pe·*ţhi*

How many children do you have?
Πόσα παιδιά έχεις; — *po*·sa pe·*ţhia* *e*·his

What a beautiful child!
Τι όμορφο παιδί! — ti *o*·mor·fo pe·*ţhi*

Is it a boy or a girl?
Είναι αγόρι ή κορίτσι; — *i*·ne a·*gho*·ri i ko·*rit*·si

How old is he/she?
Πόσο χρονών είναι; — *po*·so khro·*non* *i*·ne

Does he/she go to school?
Πηγαίνει στο σχολείο; — pi·*ye*·ni sto skho·*li*·o

What's his/her name?
Πώς τον/την λένε; — pos ton/tin *le*·ne

Is he/she well-behaved?
Είναι καλό παιδί; — *i*·ne ka·*lo* pe·*ţhi*

He/She has your eyes.
Έχει τα μάτια σου. — *e*·hi ta *ma*·tia su

He/She looks like you.
Σου μοιάζει. — su *mia*·zi

SOCIAL

Meeting People

ΣΥΝΑΝΤΩΝΤΑΣ ΚΟΣΜΟ

BASICS

βασικά

Yes.	Ναι.	ne
No.	Όχι.	o·hi
Please.	Παρακαλώ.	pa·ra·ka·*lo*
Thank you (very much).	Ευχαριστώ (πολύ).	ef·kha·ri·*sto* (po·*li*)
You're welcome.	Παρακαλώ.	pa·ra·ka·*lo*
Sorry.	Συγνώμη.	si·*ghno*·mi
Excuse me.	Με συγχωρείτε.	me sing·kho·*ri*·te
I beg your pardon?	Ορίστε;/Συγνώμη;	o·*ri*·ste / si·*ghno*·mi
Here you are.	Ορίστε.	o·*ri*·ste

GREETINGS & GOODBYES

χαιρετισμοί και **αποχαιρετισμοί**

Greeks shake hands when greeting each other and saying goodbye. When greeting friends, male or female, they often kiss each other on both cheeks.

Hello / Hi.	Γεια σου.	yia su
Good afternoon.	Χαίρετε.	*he*·re·te
Good morning.	Καλημέρα.	ka·li·*me*·ra
Good evening.	Καλησπέρα.	ka·li·*spe*·ra

WHEN IN GREECE...

Be sure not to turn up empty-handed when you visit a Greek friend's house. It's customary to bring ένα κουτί γλυκά e · na ku · *ti* ghli · *ka* (a box of sweets) or μια ανθοδέσμη mia an · tho · *ţhes* · mi (a bunch of flowers).

How are you?
Τι κάνεις; — ti *ka*·nis

So-so.
Έτσι και έτσι. — *et*·si ke *et*·si

Fine. And you?
Καλά. Εσύ; — ka·*la* e·*si*

What's your name?
Πώς σε λένε; — pos se *le*·ne

My name is ...
Με λένε ... — me *le*·ne ...

I'm pleased to meet you.
Χαίρω πολύ. — *he*·ro po·*li*

I'd like to introduce you to ... (a man).
Θα ήθελα να σε συστήσω στον ... — tha *i*·the·la na se si·*sti*·so ston ...

I'd like to introduce you to ... (a woman).
Θα ήθελα να σε συστήσω στην ... — tha *i*·the·la na se si·*sti*·so stin ...

This is my ...	Από εδώ ...	a·*po* e·*ţho* ...
child	το παιδί μου	to pe·*ţhi* mu
colleague	ο συνάδελφός μου m	o sin·a·ţhel·*fos* mu
	η συναδέλφισσά μου f	i sin·a·*ţhel*·fi·sa mu
friend	ο φίλος μου m	o *fi*·los mu
	η φίλη μου f	i *fi*·li mu
husband	ο σύζυγός μου	o *si*·zi·*ghos* mu
partner (intimate)	ο σύντροφός μου m	o *si*·dro·*fos* mu
	η σύντροφός μου f	i *si*·dro·*fos* mu
wife	η σύζυγός μου	i *si*·zi·*ghos* mu

For other family members, see **family**, p114.

See you later / Goodbye / Bye.
Αντίο. a·*di*·o

Good night.
Καλήνύχτα. ka·li·*nikh*·ta

Bon voyage!
Καλό ταξίδι! ka·*lo* tak·*si*·ţhi

ADDRESSING PEOPLE

απευθυνόμενος σε ανθρώπους

The Greek language has two forms of the word 'you'. Use the polite form εσείς e · *sis* with adult strangers, elders or those in a position of authority. In all other cases, you can use the informal form εσύ e · *si*. The polite form is simply the plural form of 'you', and you use it even when addressing one person. In this book we've chosen the appropriate form for the situation that the phrase is used in. For phrases where either form might be suitable, we've given both.

Also note that when speaking to older people you know well, their first name comes after Κύριε *ki* · ri · e (Sir), or Κυρία ki · *ri* · a (Madam).

Mr / Sir	Κύριε	*ki*·ri·e
Ms / Mrs	Κα	ki·*ri*·a
Miss	Δις	ţhes·pi·*nis*
Madam	Κυρία	ki·*ri*·a

ON FRIENDLY TERMS

People will indicate when you can use the informal form of the word 'you' (εσύ e · *si*). If you want to initiate a more informal conversation with a Greek acquaintance, say:

Please speak to me in the singular.
Μίλα μου στον ενικό. *mi*·la mu ston e·ni·*ko*

And here are a few casual terms to address your Greek pals:

friend	φίλε/φίλη m/f	*fi*·le / *fi*·li
dude	ρε μάγκα	re *ma*·ga
mate (Cyprus only)	κουμπάρε	ku·*ba*·re

MAKING CONVERSATION

κάνοντας συζήτηση

How are you going?		
	Πώς πάμε;	pos *pa*·me
What's happening?		
	Τι γίνεται;	ti *yi*·ne·te
What's new?		
	Τι νέα;	ti *ne*·a
What a beautiful day!		
	Τι όμορφη μέρα!	ti *o*·mor·fi *me*·ra
Nice / Awful weather, isn't it?		
	Καλός/απαίσιος καιρός, έτσι δεν είναι;	ka·*los* / a·*pe*·si·os ke·*ros* *et*·si ţhen i·*ne*
Where are you going?		
	Πού πηγαίνεις;	pu pi·*ye*·nis
What are you doing?		
	Τι κάνεις;	ti *ka*·nis
What's this called?		
	Πώς το λένε αυτό;	pos to *le*·ne af·*to*
That's (beautiful), isn't it!		
	Είναι (όμορφο), έτσι δεν είναι!	*i*·ne (*o*·mor·fo) *et*·si ţhen *i*·ne

☑ DON'T MENTION THE WAR

These topics are usually best avoided:

- anything linked to Το Μακεδονικό to ma·ke·ţho·ni·*ko* (the Macedonian issue). A northern region of Greece is called Macedonia, and many Greek patriots object to the country of North Macedonia usurping 'their' name.
- any mention of Το Κυπριακό to kip·ri·a·*ko* (the Cyprus issue). Displaced Greek Cypriots object to the Turkish occupation of Northern Cyprus.

Can I take a photo (of you)?
Μπορώ να (σου) βγάλω μια φωτογραφία; — bo·*ro* na (su) *vgha*·lo mia fo·to·ghra·*fi*·a

Do you live here?
Μένεις εδώ; — *me*·nis e·*ţho*

Are you here on holiday?
Είσαι εδώ για διακοπές; — *i*·se e·*ţho* yia ţhia·ko·*pes*

I'm here ...	Είμαι εδώ για ...	*i*·me e·*ţho* yia ...
for a holiday	διακοπές	ţhia·ko·*pes*
on business	δουλειά	ţhu·*lia*
to study	σπουδές	spu·*ţhes*

How long are you here for?
Πόσο καιρό θα είσαι εδώ; — *po*·so ke·*ro* tha *i*·se e·*ţho*

I'm here for (four) weeks/days.
Θα είμαι εδώ για (τέσσερις) εβδομάδες/μέρες. — tha *i*·me e·*ţho* yia (*te*·se·ris) ev·tho·*ma*·ţhes/*me*·res

Do you like it here?
Σου αρέσει εδώ; — su a·*re*·si e·*ţho*

I love it here.
Μου αρέσει εδώ. — mu a·*re*·si e·*ţho*

NATIONALITIES

εθνικότητες

Where are you from?
Από πού είσαι; — a·*po* pu *i*·se

I'm from ...	Είμαι από ...	*i*·me a·*po* ...
Australia	την Αυστραλία	tin af·stra·*li*·a
Canada	τον Καναδά	ton ka·na·*ţha*
Singapore	τη Σιγκαπούρη	ti si·ga·*pu*·ri

AGE

ηλικία

How old ...?	Πόσο χρονών ...;	*po*·so khro·*non* ...
are you	είσαι	*i*·se
is your son	είναι ο γιος σου	*i*·ne o yios su
is your daughter	είναι η κόρη σου	*i*·ne i *ko*·ri su

I'm ... years old.
Είμαι ... χρονών. — *i*·me ... khro·*non*

He / She is ... years old.
Αυτός/αυτή είναι ... χρονών. — af·*tos* / af·*ti* *i*·ne ... khro·*non*

I'm younger than I look.
Είμαι νεώτερος/νεώτερη από ό,τι φαίνομαι. **m/f** — *i*·me ne·o·te·ros / ne·o·te·ri a·*po* o·ti *fe*·no·me

For your age, see **numbers & amounts**, p35.

LOCAL TALK

Absolutely!	Απολύτως!	a·po·*li*·tos
Don't stress!	Μην κάνεις έτσι!	min *ka*·nis *et*·si
Enough!	Αρκετά!	ar·ke·*ta*
Exactly!	Ακριβώς!	a·kri·*vos*
Great!	Απίθανο!	a·*pi*·tha·no
Hey!	Εε!	e·e
I don't care.	Δεν με νοιάζει.	ţhen me *nia*·zi
I don't give a stuff.	Δεν δίνω δεκάρα.	ţhen *ţhi*·no ţhe·*ka*·ra
It's OK.	Είναι εντάξει.	*i*·ne e·*dak*·si
Just a minute.	Μισό λεπτό.	mi·*so* lep·*to*
Just joking.	Αστειεύομαι.	a·sti·e·vo·me
Maybe.	Ίσως.	*i*·sos
No problem.	Δεν υπάρχει πρόβλημα.	ţhen i·*par*·hi *prov*·li·ma
No way!	Αποκλείεται!	a·po·*kli*·e·te
Rubbish!	Σαχλαμάρες!	sakh·la·*ma*·res
Sure.	Σίγουρα.	*si*·ghu·ra
Well now ...	Λοιπόν ...	li·*pon* ...
You're wrong.	Κάνεις λάθος.	*ka*·nis *la*·thos

THE CALL OF THE WILD...AND THE DOMESTICATED

Dogs in Greece don't 'woof' – instead, they say ghav. Greek cows, on the other hand, seem to speak English. Here are some animal noises as they sound to Greek ears:

bird	τσίου-τσίου	*tsi*·u *tsi*·u
cat	νιάου	*nia*·ou
chick	κο-κο-κο	ko·ko·*ko*
cow	μου	mu
crow	κρα	kra
dog	γαβ	ghav
hen	κα-κα-κα	ka·ka·*ka*
rooster	κι-κιρίκου	ki·ki·*ri*·ku

OCCUPATIONS & STUDIES

επαγγέλματα και σπουδές

What's your occupation?
Τι δουλειά κάνεις; — ti ţhu·*lia ka*·nis

I'm a ...	Είμαι ...	*i*·me ...
businessperson	επιχειρηματίας m&f	e·pi·hi·ri·ma·*ti*·as
journalist	δημοσιογράφος m&f	ţhi·mo·si·o·*ghra*·fos
salesperson	πωλητής m	po·li·*tis*
	πωλήτρια f	po·*li*·tri·a
student	σπουδαστής m	spu·ţha·*stis*
	σπουδάστρια f	spu·*ţha*·stri·a
teacher	δάσκαλος m	*ţha*·ska·los
	δασκάλα f	ţha·*ska*·la
waiter	σερβιτόρος	ser·vi·*to*·ros
waitress	σερβιτόρα	ser·vi·*to*·ra

I work in ...	Δουλεύω ...	ţhu·*le*·vo ...
administration	στη διοίκηση	sti ţhi·*i*·ki·si
health	στην υγεία	stin i·*yi*·a
sales & marketing	στις πωλήσεις και μάρκετινγκ	stis po·*li*·sis ke *mar*·ke·ting

I'm ...	Είμαι ...	*i*·me ...
retired	συνταξιούχος m/f	si·dak·si·*u*·khos
employee	ιδιωτικός/ιδιωτική	i·ţhi·o·ti·*kos*/i·ţhi·o·ti·*ki*
	υπάλληλος m/f	i·*pa*·li·los
unemployed	άνεργος/άνεργη m/f	*an*·er·ghos/*an*·er·yi
What are you studying?	Τι σπουδάζεις;	ti spu·*ţha*·zis
I'm studying ...	Σπουδάζω ...	spu·*ţha*·zo ...
Greek	Ελληνικά	e·li·ni·*ka*
languages	γλώσσες	*ghlo*·ses
science	θετικές επιστήμες	the·ti·*kes* e·pi·*sti*·mes

FAMILY

οικογένεια

Are you married? (to a man)
Είσαι παντρεμένος; — *i*·se pa·dre·*me*·nos

Are you married? (to a woman)
Είσαι παντρεμένη; — *i*·se pa·dre·*me*·ni

I live with someone. (with a woman)
Ζω με κάποια. — zo me *ka*·pia

I live with someone. (with a man)
Ζω με κάποιον. — zo me *ka*·pion

I'm ...	Είμαι ...	i·*me* ...
married	παντρεμένος m	pa·dre·*me*·nos
	παντρεμένη f	pa·dre·*me*·ni
separated	χωρισμένος m	kho·riz·*me*·nos
	χωρισμένη f	kho·riz·*me*·ni
single	ανύπαντρος m	a·*ni*·pa·dros
	ανύπαντρη f	a·*ni*·pa·dri

Do you have a/an ...?
Έχεις ...; — *e*·his ...

I (don't) have a/an ...
(Δεν) έχω ... — (ţhen) *e*·kho ...

aunt	θεία f	*thi*·a
brother	αδερφό m	a·ţher·*fo*
brother-in-law	γαμπρό m	gha·*bro*
cousin	ξάδερφο m	*ksa*·ţher·fo
	ξαδέρφη f	ksa·*ţher*·fi
daughter	κόρη f	*ko*·ri
daughter-in-law	νύφη f	*ni*·fi
family	οικογένεια f	i·ko·*ye*·ni·a
father	πατέρα m	pa·*te*·ra
father-in-law	πεθερό m	pe·the·*ro*
granddaughter	εγγονή f	e·go·*ni*
grandfather	παππού m	pa·*pu*
grandmother	γιαγιά f	yia·*yia*
grandson	εγγονό m	e·go·*no*
husband	σύζυγο m	*si*·zi·gho
mother	μητέρα f	mi·*te*·ra
mother-in-law	πεθερά f	pe·the·*ra*
nephew	ανιψιό m	a·nip·*sio*
niece	ανιψιά f	a·nip·*sia*
partner (intimate)	σύντροφο m&f	*si*·dro·fo
sister	αδερφή f	a·ţher·*fi*
sister-in-law	νύφη f	*ni*·fi
son	γιο m	yio
son-in-law	γαμπρό m	gha·*bro*
uncle	θείο m	*thi*·o
spouse	σύζυγο f	*si*·zi·gho

FAREWELLS

αποχαιρετισμοί

Tomorrow is my last day here.

Αύριο είναι η τελευταία μέρα μου εδώ. — *av*·ri·o *i*·ne i te·*lef*·te·a *me*·ra mu e·*ţho*

It's been great meeting you.

Χάρηκα πολύ για τη γνωριμία. — *kha*·ri·ka po·*li* yia ti ghno·ri·*mi*·a

If you come to (Scotland) you can stay with me.
Αν έρθεις (στη Σκωτία) μπορείς να μείνεις μαζί μου. — an *er*·this (sti sko·*ti*·a) bo·*ris* na *mi*·nis ma·*zi* mu

Here's my address.
Εδώ είναι η διεύθυνσή μου. — e·*ţho* *i*·ne i ţhi·*ef*·thin·*si* mu

What's your address?
Ποια είναι η δική σου διεύθυνση; — pia *i*·ne i ţhi·*ki* su ţhi·*ef*·thin·si

What's your ...?	Ποιο είναι το … σου;	pio *i*·ne to ... su
Here's my ...	Εδώ είναι το … μου.	e·*ţho* *i*·ne to ... mu
phone number	τηλέφωνό	ti·*le*·fo·*no*
email address	ημέιλ	i·*me*·il

Keep in touch!
Μη χαθούμε! — mi kha·*thu*·me

We'll talk again soon.
Θα τα πούμε σύντομα. — tha ta *pu*·me *sin*·do·ma

Farewell.
Γεια χαρά. — yia ha·*ra*

Adieu.
Αντίο. — a·*di*·o

WELL-WISHING

Bless you!	Ο Θεός να σε φυλάει!	o the·*os* na se fi·*la*·i
Bon voyage!	Καλό ταξίδι!	ka·*lo* tak·*si*·ţhi
Congratulations!	Συγχαρητήρια!	sing·kha·ri·*ti*·ri·a
Good luck!	Καλή τύχη!	ka·*li* *ti*·hi
Happy Birthday!	Χαρούμενα γενέθλια!	kha·*ru*·me·na ye·*ne*·thli·a
Have a nice/ good time!	Καλά/Ωραία να περάσεις!	ka·*la* / or·*e*·a na pe·*ra*·sis
Merry Christmas!	Καλά Χριστούγεννα!	ka·*la* khri·*stu*·ye·na

If you're lost for words on a special occasion, just wish people Χρόνια πολλά! *khro*·nia po·*la* (Many years!) – this works for just about any festive occasion.

Interests

ΕΝΔΙΑΦΕΡΟΝΤΑ

COMMON INTERESTS

κοινά ενδιαφέροντα

What do you do in your spare time?
Τι κάνεις τον ελεύθερο χρόνο σου; — ti *ka*·nis ton e·*lef*·the·ro *khro*·no su

Do you like ...?	Σου αρέσει ...;	su a·*re*·si ...
I (don't) like ...	(Δεν) μου αρέσει ...	(ţhen) mu a·*re*·si ...
billiards	το μπιλιάρδο	to bi·*liar*·ţho
chess	το σκάκι	to *ska*·ki
cooking	η μαγειρική	i ma·yi·ri·*ki*
dancing	ο χορός	o kho·*ros*
dominoes	το ντόμινο	to *do*·mi·no
drawing	το σχέδιο	to *she*·ţhi·o
gardening	η κηπουρική	i ki·pu·ri·*ki*
music	η μουσική	i mu·si·*ki*
painting	η ζωγραφική	i zo·ghra·fi·*ki*
reading	το διάβασμα	to *ţhia*·vaz·ma
Do you like ...?	Σου αρέσουν ...;	su a·*re*·sun ...
I (don't) like ...	(Δεν) μου αρέσουν τα ...	(ţhen) mu a·*re*·sun ta ...
films	φιλμ	film
sport	σπορ	spor
Do you like ...?	Σου αρέσει να ...;	su a·*re*·si na ...
shopping	ψωνίζεις	pso·*ni*·zis
travelling	ταξιδεύεις	tak·si·*ţhe*·vis
I (don't) like ...	(Δεν) μου αρέσει να ...	(ţhen) mu a·*re*·si na ...
shopping	ψωνίζω	pso·*ni*·zo
travelling	ταξιδεύω	tak·si·*ţhe*·vo

For sporting activities, see **sport**, p141.

astrology	αστρολογία **f**	a·stro·lo·*yi*·a
backgammon	τάβλι **n**	*tav*·li
***bouzouki* (instrument)**	μπουζούκι **n**	bu·*zu*·ki
current affairs	επίκαιρα θέματα **n pl**	e·*pi*·ke·ra *the*·ma·ta
playing cards	χαρτιά **n pl**	khar·*tia*
politics	πολιτική **f**	po·li·ti·*ki*
***sirtaki* (Greek dancing)**	συρτάκι **n**	sir·*ta*·ki

MUSIC

μουσική

What music do you like?

Τι μουσική σου αρέσει; — ti mu·si·*ki* su a·*re*·si

Which bands / singers do you like?

Τι/Ποιοι μπάντες/τραγουδιστές σου αρέσουν; — ti / *pi*·i *ba*·des / tra·ghu·ţhi·*stes* su a·*re*·sun

TRADITIONAL GREEK DANCES

Many traditional dances are specific to certain regions of Greece, while others are popular throughout the country. The most common ones are the Ζεϊμπέκικο ze · i · *be* · ki · ko (Zeibekiko), the Τσάμικο *tsa* · mi · ko (Tsamiko), Καλαματιανό ka · la · ma · tia · *no* (Kalamatiano) – also called the Συρτό sir · *to* (Sirto) – and the Χασαποσέρβικο ha · sa · po · *ser* · vi · ko.

In most of these dances, the participants hold hands to form a semicircle and, moving in repetitive steps, they follow the lead dancer in an anticlockwise direction. The one exception is the Zeibekiko, which is danced by individuals – although sometimes called the 'drunken sailor's dance' for its seeming clumsiness, and actually takes great skill to perform.

Other popular dances are the Κότσαρι *kot* · sa · ri (Kotsari), the Κρητικός kri · ti · *kos* (Kritikos) and the Ποντιακός po · di · a · *kos* (Pontiakos).

Do you ...?		
dance	Χορεύεις;	kho·*re*·vis
go to concerts	Πηγαίνεις σε συναυλίες;	pi·*ye*·nis se si·na·*vli*·es
listen to music	Ακούς μουσική;	a·*kus* mu·si·*ki*
play an instrument	Παίζεις κάποιο όργανο;	*pe*·zis *kha*·pio *or*·gha·no
sing	Τραγουδάς;	tra·ghu·*ţhas*

blues	μπλουζ **n**	bluz
classical music	κλασσική μουσική **f**	kla·si·*ki* mu·si·*ki*
electronic music	ηλεκτρονική μουσική **f**	i·lek·tro·ni·*ki* mu·si·*ki*
Greek folk music	Ελληνική παραδοσιακή μουσική **f**	e·li·ni·*ki* pa·ra·ţho·si·a·*ki* mu·si·*ki*
jazz	τζαζ **f**	tzaz
pop music	ποπ **f**	pop
rembetika	ρεμπέτικα **n pl**	re·*be*·ti·ka
rock music	μουσική ροκ **f**	mu·si·*ki* rok
traditional music	παραδοσιακή μουσική **f**	pa·ra·ţho·si·a·*ki* mu·si·*ki*

Planning to go to a concert? See **tickets**, p46, and **going out**, p127.

CINEMA & THEATRE

Σινεμά και θέατρο

I feel like going to a ...	Θέλω να πάω σε ...	*the*·lo na *pa*·o se ...
ballet	μπαλέτο	ba·*le*·to
film	ταινία	te·*ni*·a
play	θέατρο	*the*·a·tro

What's showing at the cinema / theatre tonight?
Τι παίζει στο σινεμά/ θέατρο απόψε; — ti *pe*·zi sto si·ne·*ma* / *the*·a·tro a·*pop*·se

Is it in English / Greek?
Είναι στα Αγγλικά/Ελληνικά; — *i*·ne sta ang·gli·*ka* / e·li·ni·*ka*

Does it have (English) subtitles?
Έχει (Αγγλικούς) υπότιτλους; — e·hi (ang·gli·*kus*) i·*po*·tit·lus

Is this seat taken?
Είναι αυτή η θέση πιασμένη; — *i*·ne af·*ti* i *the*·si piaz·*me*·ni

Have you seen ...?
Έχεις δει ...; — e·his ţhi ...

Who's in it?
Ποιος παίζει σ' αυτό; — pios *pe*·zi saf·*to*

Did you like the film?
Σου άρεσε η ταινία; — su a·re·se i te·*ni*·a

I thought it was ...	Νομίζω ότι ήταν ...	no·*ni*·zo o·ti *i*·tan ...
excellent	εξαιρετικό	ek·se·re·ti·*ko*
long	μεγάλο	me·*gha*·lo
OK	εντάξει	e·*dak*·si

I (don't) like ...	(Δεν) μου αρέσουν ...	(ţhen) mu a·*re*·sun ...
action movies	οι ταινίες δράσης	i te·*ni*·es *ţhra*·sis
animated films	οι ταινίες κινουμένων σχεδίων	i te·*ni*·es ki·nu·*me*·non she·*ţhi*·on
comedies	οι κωμωδίες	i ko·mo·*ţhi*·es
documentaries	τα ντοκιμαντέρ	ta do·ki·man·*ter*
drama	οι δραματικές ταινίες	i dra·ma·ti·*kes* te·*ni*·es
Greek cinema	ελληνικό σινεμά	e·li·ni·*kho* si·ne·*ma*
horror movies	οι ταινίες τρόμου	i te·*ni*·es *tro*·mu
sci-fi	οι ταινίες επιστημονικής φαντασίας	i te·*ni*·es e·pi·sti·mo·ni·*kis* fa·da·*si*·as
short films	ταινίες μικρού μήκους	te·*ni*·es mi·*khru* *mi*·kus
thrillers	τα θρίλερ	ta *thri*·ler
war movies	πολεμικές ταινίες	po·le·mi·*khes* te·*ni*·es

Feelings & Opinions

ΑΙΣΘΗΜΑΤΑ ΚΑΙ ΓΝΩΜΕΣ

FEELINGS

αισθήματα

Are you ...?	Είσαι ...;	*i*·se ...
I'm (not) ...	(Δεν) Είμαι ...	(ţhen) *i*·me ...
annoyed	ενοχλημένος m	e·no·khli·*me*·nos
	ενοχλημένη f	e·no·khli·*me*·ni
disappointed	απογοητευμένος m	a·po·gho·i·tev·*me*·nos
	απογοητευμένη f	a·po·gho·i·tev·*me*·ni
embarrassed	αμήχανος m	a·*mi*·kha·nos
	αμήχανη f	a·*mi*·kha·ni
happy	ευτυχισμένος m	ef·ti·hiz·*me*·nos
	ευτυχισμένη f	ef·ti·hiz·*me*·ni
hot	ζεστός m	ze·*stos*
	ζεστή f	ze·*sti*
hungry	πεινασμένος m	pi·naz·*me*·nos
	πεινασμένη f	pi·naz·*me*·ni
in a hurry	βιαστικός m	via·sti·*kos*
	βιαστική f	via·sti·*ki*
sad	στενοχωρημένος m	ste·no·kho·ri·*me*·nos
	στενοχωρημένη f	ste·no·kho·ri·*me*·ni
surprised	έκπληκτος m	*ek*·plik·tos
	εκπληκτη f	*ek*·plik·ti
thirsty	διψασμένος m	ţhip·saz·*me*·nos
	διψασμένη f	ţhip·saz·*me*·ni
tired	κουρασμένος m	ku·raz·*me*·nos
	κουρασμένη f	ku·raz·*me*·ni
worried	ανήσυχος m	a·*ni*·si·khos
	ανήσυχη f	a·*ni*·si·hi
I'm (not) cold.	(Δεν) Κρυώνω.	(ţhen) kri·*o*·no

If you're not feeling well, see **health**, p195.

MIXED FEELINGS

a little	λίγο	*li*·gho
I'm a little sad.	Είμαι λίγο στενοχωρημένος/ στενοχωρημένη. **m/f**	*i*·me *li*·gho ste·no·kho·ri·*me*·nos ste·no·kho·ri·*me*·ni
very	πολύ	po·*li*
I feel very lucky.	Αισθάνομαι πολύ τυχερός/τυχερή. **m/f**	es·*tha*·no·me po·*li* ti·he·*ros*/ti·he·*ri*
extremely	πάρα πολύ	*pa*·ra po·*li*
I'm extremely sorry.	Λυπάμαι πάρα πολύ.	li·*pa*·me *pa*·ra po·*li*

OPINIONS

γνώμες

Did you like it?
Σου άρεσε; — su *a*·re·se

What do you think of it?
Ποια είναι η γνώμη σου για αυτό; — pia *i*·ne i *ghno*·mi su yia af·*to*

I thought it was ...	Νομίζω ήταν ...	no·*mi*·zo *i*·tan ...
It's ...	Είναι ...	*i*·ne ...
awful	απαίσιο	a·*pe*·si·o
beautiful	όμορφο	*o*·mor·fo
boring	βαρετό	va·re·*to*
great	καταπληκτικό	ka·ta·plik·ti·*ko*
interesting	ενδιαφέρον	en·ţhia·*fe*·ron
OK	εντάξει	e·*dak*·si
strange	παράξενο	pa·*rak*·se·no
too expensive	πάρα πολύ ακριβό	*pa*·ra po·*li* a·kri·*vo*

POLITICS & SOCIAL ISSUES

πολιτική και κοινωνικά θέματα

Who do you vote for?	Ποιον ψηφίζεις;	pion psi·*fi*·zis
I support the ... party.	Εγώ υποστηρίζω το κόμμα ...	e·*gho* i·po·sti·*ri*·zo to *ko*·ma ...
I'm a member of the ... party.	Είμαι μέλος του κόμματος ...	*i*·me *me*·los tu *ko*·ma·tos ...
coalition	συνασπισμός	si·nas·piz·*mos*
communist	κομμουνιστικό	ko·mu·ni·sti·*ko*
conservative	συντηρητικό	si·di·ri·ti·*ko*
democratic	δημοκρατικό	ţhi·mo·kra·ti·*ko*
green	οικολογικό	i·ko·lo·yi·*ko*
liberal	φιλελεύθεροι	fil·e·*lef*·the·ri
republican	ρεπουμπλικανικό	re·pu·bli·ka·ni·*ko*
social democratic	κοινωνικό δημοκρατικό	ki·no·ni·*ko* ţhi·mo·kra·ti·*ko*
socialist	σοσιαλιστικό	so·si·a·li·sti·*ko*

Did you hear about ...?
Άκουσες για ...; — a·ku·ses yia ...

Do you agree with it?
Συμφωνείς με αυτό ...; — sim·fo·*nis* me af·*to* ...

I (don't) agree with ...
(Δεν) Συμφωνώ με ... — (ţhen) sim·fo·*no* me ...

How do people feel about ...?
Πώς αισθάνονται οι άνθρωποι για ...; — pos es·*tha*·no·de i *an*·thro·pi yia ...

How can we support ...?
Πώς μπορούμε να υποστηρίξουμε ...; — pos bo·*ru*·me na i·po·sti·*rik*·su·me ...

How can we protest against ...?
Πώς μπορούμε να διαμαρτυρηθούμε για ...; — pos bo·*ru*·me na ţhi·a·mar·ti·ri·*thu*·me yia ...

☑ 'NO' MEANS 'YES'

Although it may sound like 'no', remember that ναι ne really means 'yes'.

abortion	εκτρώσεις f	ek·*tro*·sis
animal rights	δικαιώματα των ζώων n	ţhi·ke·*o*·ma·ta ton *zo*·on
civil servants	δημοσίους υπαλλήλους m	tus ţhi·mo·*si*·us i·pa·*li*·lus
crime	έγκλημα n	*eng*·li·ma
democracy	δημοκρατία f	ţhi·mo·kra·*ti*·a
diaspora	διασπορά f	ţhi·a·spo·*ra*
discrimination	διακρίσεις f	ţhi·a·*kri*·sis
drugs	ναρκωτικά n	nar·ko·ti·*ka*
the economy	οικονομία f	i·ko·no·*mi*·a
education	εκπαίδευση f	ek·*pe*·ţhef·si
the environment	περιβάλλον n	pe·ri·*va*·lon
equal opportunity	ίσες ευκαιρίες f	*i*·ses ef·ke·*ri*·es
euthanasia	ευθανασία f	ef·tha·na·*si*·a
the European Union	Ευρωπαϊκή Ένωση f	ev·ro·pa·i·*ki* *e*·no·si
gay rights	δικαιώματα των γκέι n	ţhi·ke·*o*·ma·ta ton *ge*·i
globalisation	παγκοσμιοποίηση f	pa·goz·mi·o·*pi*·i·si
human rights	ανθρώπινα δικαιώματα n	an·*thro*·pi·na ţhi·ke·*o*·ma·ta
immigration	μετανάστευση f	me·ta·*na*·stef·si
inequality	ανισότητα f	a·ni·*so*·ti·ta
inflation	πληθωρισμό m	pli·tho·riz·*mo*
the military junta	στρατιωτική χούντα f	stra·ti·o·ti·*ki* *khu*·da
the Macedonian question	Μακεδονικό ζήτημα n	ma·ke·ţho·ni·*ko* *zi*·ti·ma
the monarchy	μοναρχία f	mo·nar·*hi*·a

NATO	ΝΑΤΟ n	*na*·to
parliament	κοινοβούλιο n	ki·no·*vu*·li·o
the partition of Cyprus	διχοτόμηση της Κύπρου f	ţhi·kho·*to*·mi·si tis *ki*·pru
party politics	πολιτική του κόμματος f	po·li·ti·*ki* tu *ko*·ma·tos
privatisation	ιδιοτικοποίηση f	i·ţhi·o·ti·ko·*pi*·i·si
poverty	φτώχεια f	*fto*·hia
racism	ρατσισμό n	rat·siz·*mo*
refugees	πρόσφυγες m	*pros*·fi·yes
relations with Turkey	σχέσεις με την Τουρκία f	*she*·sis me tin tur·*ki*·a
sexism	σεξισμό m	sek·siz·*mo*
social welfare	κοινωνική πρόνοια f	ki·no·ni·*ki* *pro*·ni·a
strikes	απεργίες f	ap·er·*yi*·es
terrorism	τρομοκρατία f	tro·mo·kra·*ti*·a
traffic restrictions	περιορισμό της κυκλοφορίας m	pe·ri·o·riz·*mo* tis ki·klo·fo·*ri*·as
unemployment	ανεργία f	an·er·*yi*·a
US military bases	στρατιωτικές βάσεις των ΗΠΑ f	stra·ti·o·ti·*kes* *va*·sis ton *i*·pa

THE ENVIRONMENT

το περιβάλλον

Is there a ... problem here?

Υπάρχει κάποιο πρόβλημα εδώ με ...; — i·*par*·hi *ka*·pio *pro*·vli·ma e·*ţho* me ...

What should be done about ...?

Τι θα πρέπει να γίνει με ...; — ti tha *pre*·pi na *yi*·ni me ...

beach cleaning	καθαρισμό των ακτών m	ka·tha·riz·*mo* ton ak·*ton*
conservation	προστασία του περιβάλλοντος f	pro·sta·*si*·a tu pe·ri·*va*·lo·dos
deforestation	αποδάσωση f	a·po·*ţha*·so·si
drought	ανομβρία f	a·nom·*vri*·a
earthquakes	σεισμούς m	siz·*mus*
ecosystem	οικοσύστημα n	i·ko·*si*·sti·ma
endangered species	είδη υπό εξαφάνιση n	*i*·ţhi i·*po* ek·sa·*fa*·ni·si
erosion	διάβρωση f	ţhi·*av*·ro·si
forest fires	φωτιές στα δάση f	fo·*tyes* sta *ţha*·si
genetically modified food	γενετικά μεταλλαγμένο φαγητό n	ye·ne·ti·*ka* me·ta·lagh·*me*·no fa·yi·*to*
hunting	κυνήγι n	ki·*ni*·yi
hydroelectricity	υδροηλεκτρισμό m	i·ţhro·i·lek·triz·*mo*
irrigation	άρδευση f	*ar*·ţhef·si
marine reserves	θαλάσσια πάρκα f	tha·*la*·si·a *par*·kha
national parks	εθνικά πάρκα n	eth·ni·*ka* *par*·ka
nuclear energy	πυρηνική ενέργεια f	pi·ri·ni·*ki* e·*ner*·yi·a
nuclear testing	πυρηνικές δοκιμές f	pi·ri·ni·*kes* ţho·ki·*mes*
ozone layer	στρώμα του όζοντος n	*stro*·ma tu o·zo·dos
pesticides	φυτοφάρμακα n	fi·to·*far*·ma·ka
pollution	μόλυνση f	*mo*·lin·si
recycling programme	πρόγραμμα ανακύκλωσης n	*pro*·ghra·ma a·na·*ki*·klo·sis
smog	νέφος n	*ne*·fos
toxic waste	τοξικά απόβλητα n	tok·si·*ka* a·*pov*·li·ta
urban encroachment	αστική εξάπλωση f	a·sti·*ki* ek·sa·plo·si
water supply	ύδρευση f	*id*·ref·si

Is this a protected ...?	Είναι αυτό προστατευόμενο ...;	*i*·ne af·*to* pro·sta·te·*vo*·me·no
forest	δάσος	*ţha*·sos
park	πάρκο	*par*·ko
species	είδος	*i*·ţhos

Going Out

ΒΓΑΙΝΟΥΜΕ ΕΞΩ

WHERE TO GO

πού να πάμε

What's there to do in the evenings?

Τι μπορούμε να κάνουμε το βράδυ;	ti bo·*ru*·me na *ka*·nu·me to *vra*·ţhi

What's on ...?	Τι γίνεται ...;	ti *yi*·ne·te ...
locally	εδώ γύρω	e·*ţho yi*·ro
this weekend	αυτό το Σαββατοκύριακο	af·*to* to sa·va·to·*ki*·ria·ko
today	σήμερα	*si*·me·ra
tonight	απόψε	a·*pop*·se

Where can I find ...?	Πού μπορώ να βρω ...;	pu bo·*ro* na vro ...
a *bouzouki* joint (venue with live Greek music)	ταβέρνα με μπουζούκια	ta·*ver*·na me bu·*zu*·kia
clubs	κλαμπ	klab
gay venues	γκέι κλαμπ και μπαρ	*ge*·i klab ke bar
an open-air cinema	θερινό κινηματογράφο	the·ri·*no* ki·ni·ma·to·*ghra*·fo
places to eat	εστιατόρια	e·sti·a·*to*·ri·a
pubs	μπιραρίες	bi·ra·*ri*·es

Is there a local ... guide?	Υπάρχει τοπικός οδηγός για ...;	i·*par*·hi to·pi·*kos* o·ţhi·*ghos* yia ...
entertainment	διασκέδαση	ţhias·*ke*·tha·si
film	ταινία	te·*ni*·a
gay	γκέη	*ge*·i
music	μουσική	mu·si·*ki*

I feel like going to a ...	Έχω όρεξη να πάω σε ...	e·kho o·rek·si na *pa*·o se ...
ballet	μπαλέτο	ba·*le*·to
bar	μπαρ	bar
cafe	καφενείο	ka·fe·*ni*·o
concert	συναυλία	si·na·*vli*·a
film	ταινία	te·*ni*·a
karaoke bar	καραόκε μπαρ	ka·ra·o·ke bar
nightclub	νυχτερινό κέντρο	nikh·te·ri·*no* *ke*·dro
party	πάρτυ	*par*·ti
performance	θέαμα	the·a·ma
play	έργο	*er*·gho
pub	μπιραρία	bi·ra·*ri*·a
***rebetiko* club**	ρεμπετάδικο	re·be·*ta*·di·ko
restaurant	εστιατόριο	e·sti·a·*to*·ri·o
sports match	αθλητικός αγώνας	ath·li·ti·*kos* a·*gho*·nas

For more on bars and drinks, see **romance**, p131, and **eating out**, from p166.

INVITATIONS

προσκλήσεις

What are you doing ...?	Τι κάνεις ...;	ti *ka*·nis ...
now	τώρα	*to*·ra
this weekend	το Σαββατοκύριακο	to sa·va·to·*ki*·ria·ko
tonight	απόψε	a·*pop*·se

Do you know a good restaurant?
Ξέρεις κανένα καλό εστιατόριο; — *kse*·ris ka·*ne*·na ka·*lo* e·sti·a·*to*·ri·o

My round.
Η σειρά μου. — i si·*ra* mu

We're having a party.
Κάνουμε πάρτι. — *kha*·nu·me *par*·ti

Would you like to go (for a) ...?	Θέλεις να πάμε να πας ...;	*the*·lis na *pa*·me na pas ...
coffee	για καφέ	yia ka·*fe*
dancing	για χορό	yia kho·*ro*
drink	για ποτό	yia po·*to*
meal	για φαγητό	yia fa·yi·*to*
out somewhere	κάπου έξω	*ka*·pu *ek*·so
walk	βόλτα	*vol*·ta

RESPONDING TO INVITATIONS

απαντώντας σε προσκλήσεις

Sure!
Βέβαια! — *ve*·ve·a

Yes, I'd love to.
Ναι, θα το ήθελα πολύ. — ne tha to *i*·the·la po·*li*

That's very kind of you.
Πολύ ευγενικό εκ μέρους σου. — po·*li* ev·ye·ni·*ko* ek *me*·rus su

No, I'm afraid I can't.
Όχι, δυστυχώς πως δεν . μπορώ — *o*·hi di·sti·*khos* ţhen bo·*ro*

What about tomorrow?
Τι θα έλεγες για αύριο; — ti tha *e*·le·yes yia *av*·ri·o

Where shall we go?
Πού να πάμε; — pu na *pa*·me

ARRANGING TO MEET

κανονίζοντας μια συνάντηση

What time will we meet?
Τι ώρα θα συναντηθούμε; — ti *o*·ra tha si·na·di·*thu*·me

Where will we meet?
Πού θα συναντηθούμε; — pu tha si·na·di·*thu*·me

Let's meet at ...	Ας συναντηθούμε ...	as si·na·di·*thu*·me ...
(eight) o'clock	στις (οχτώ)	stis (okh·*to*)
the entrance	στην είσοδο	stin *i*·so·ţho

I'll pick you up.
Θα σε πάρω εγώ. — tha se *pa*·ro e·*gho*

Are you ready?
Είσαι έτοιμος/έτοιμη; m/f — *i*·se e·ti·mos / e·ti·mi

I'm ready.
Είμαι έτοιμος/έτοιμη. m/f — *i*·me e·ti·mos / e·ti·mi

Where will you be?
Πού θα είσαι; — pu tha *i*·se

If I'm not there by (nine), don't wait for me.
Αν δεν είμαι εκεί μέχρι (τις εννέα), μή με περιμένεις. — an ţhen *i*·me e·*ki* *me*·khri (tis e·*ne*·a) mi me pe·ri·*me*·nis

I'm looking forward to it.
Το περιμένω πώς και πώς. — to pe·ri·*me*·no pos ke pos

OK!	Εντάξει!	e·*dak*·si
I'll see you then.	Θα σε δω τότε.	tha se ţho *to*·te
Sorry I'm late.	Συγνώμη που άργησα.	sigh·*no*·mi pu *ar*·yi·sa

DRUGS

ναρκωτικά

Do you have a light?
Έχεις φωτιά; — e·his fo·*tia*

Do you want to have a smoke?
Θέλεις να καπνίσεις; — *the*·lis na kap·*ni*·sis

I don't take drugs.
Δεν παίρνω ναρκωτικά. — ţhen *per*·no nar·ko·ti·*ka*

I take ... occasionally.
Παίρνω ... καμιά φορά. — *per*·no ... ka·*mia* fo·*ra*

Romance

ΕΙΔΥΛΛΙΟ

ASKING SOMEONE OUT

Κλείνω ραντεβού

Where would you like to go (tonight)?
Πού θα ήθελες να πάμε (απόψε); — pu tha *the*·lis na *pa*·me (a·*pop*·se)

Would you like to do something (tomorrow)?
Θα ήθελες να κάνουμε κάτι (αύριο); — tha *i*·the·les na *ka*·nu·me *ka*·ti (*av*·ri·o)

Yes, I'd love to.
Ναι, θα το ήθελα πολύ. — ne tha to *i*·the·la po·*li*

Sorry, I can't.
Συγνώμη, δεν μπορώ. — sigh·*no*·mi ţhen bo·*ro*

PICK-UP LINES

Ατάκες φλερτ

Would you like a drink?
Θα ήθελες ένα ποτό; — tha *i*·the·les e·na po·*to*

You look like someone I know. (to a man)
Μοιάζεις με κάποιον που ξέρω. — *mia*·zis me *ka*·pion pu *kse*·ro

You look like someone I know. (to a woman)
Μοιάζεις με κάποια που ξερω. — *mia*·zis me *ka*·pia pu *kse*·ro

You're a fantastic dancer. (to a man)
Είσαι απίθανος χορευτής. — *i*·se a·*pi*·tha·nos kho·ref·*tis*

You're a fantastic dancer. (to a woman)
Είσαι απίθανη χορεύτρια. — *i*·se a·*pi*·tha·ni kho·*ref*·tria

Can I ...?	Μπορώ να ...;	bo·*ro* na ...
dance with you	χορέψω μαζί σου	kho·*rep*·so ma·*zi* su
sit here	καθίσω εδώ	ka·*thi*·so e·*ţho*
take you home	σε πάω στο σπίτι	se *pa*·o sto *spi*·ti

REJECTIONS

απόρριψη

No, thank you.
Όχι, ευχαριστώ. — *o*·hi ef·kha·ri·*sto*

I'd rather not.
Νομίζω πως όχι. — no·*mi*·zo pos *o*·hi

I'm here with my boyfriend.
Είμαι εδώ με τον φίλο μου. — *i*·me e·*ţho* me ton *fi*·lo mu

I'm here with my girlfriend.
Είμαι εδώ με τη φίλη μου. — *i*·me e·*ţho* me tin *fi*·li mu

Excuse me, I have to go now.
Συγνώμη, πρέπει να πηγαίνω τώρα. — sigh·*no*·mi *pre*·pi na pi·*ye*·no *to*·ra

Leave me alone! (a man)
Άσε με ήσυχο! — *a*·se me *i*·si·kho

Leave me alone! (a woman)
Άσε με ήσυχη! — *a*·se me *i*·si·khi

Get lost!
Άντε από δω, ρε! — *a*·de a·*po* ţho re

LOCAL TALK

He's a babe.
Είναι κούκλος. — *i*·ne *ku*·klos

She's a babe.
Είναι κούκλα. — *i*·ne *ku*·kla

He's hot.
Είναι πολύ ωραίος. — *i*·ne po·*li* o·*re*·os

She's hot.
Είναι πολύ ωραία. — *i*·ne po·*li* o·*re*·a

GETTING CLOSER

έρχοντας πιο κοντά

I like you very much.
Μου αρέσεις πολύ. — mu a·*re*·sis po·*li*

You're great.
Είσαι φοβερός/φοβερή m/f — *i*·se fo·ve·*ros*/fo·ve·*ri*

Can I kiss you?
Μπορώ να σε φιλήσω; — bo·*ro* na se fi·*li*·so

Do you want to come inside for a while?
Θέλεις να έρθεις μέσα, για λίγάκι; — *the*·lis na *er*·this *me*·sa yia *li*·gh·a·ki

Do you want a massage?
Θέλεις ένα μασάζ; — *the*·lis e·na ma·*saz*

Can I stay over?
Μπορώ να μείνω τη νύχτα; — bo·*ro* na *mi*·no ti *nikh*·ta

SEX

έρωτας

Kiss me.	Φίλα με.	*fi*·la me
I want you.	Σε θέλω.	se *the*·lo
Touch me here.	Ακούμπησε με εδώ.	a·*khu*·bi·se me e·*ţho*
Let's go to bed.	Πάμε στο κρεβάτι.	*pa*·me sto kre·*va*·ti

Do you like this?
Σου αρέσει αυτό; — su a·*re*·si af·*to*

I (don't) like that.
(Δεν) Μου αρέσει αυτό. — (ţhen) mu a·*re*·si af·*to*

I think we should stop now.
Νομίζω πως πρέπει να σταματήσουμε τώρα. — no·*mi*·zo pos *pre*·pi na sta·ma·*ti*·su·me *to*·ra

Do you have a condom?
Έχεις προφυλακτικό; — e·his pro·fi·lak·ti·*ko*

Let's use a condom.
Ας χρησιμοποιήσουμε προφυλακτικό. — as khri·si·mo·pi·*i*·su·me pro·fi·lak·ti·*ko*

I won't do it without protection.
Δεν το κάνω χωρίς προφύλαξη. — ţhen to *ka*·no kho·*ris* pro·*fi*·lak·si

It's my first time.
Είναι η πρώτη μου φορά. — *i*·ne i *pro*·ti mu fo·*ra*

It helps to have a sense of humour.
Καλό είναι να έχεις λίγο χιούμορ. — ka·*lo* *i*·ne na e·his *li*·gho *hiu*·mor

Oh my god!
Ω, θεέ μου! — o the·e mu

That's great.
Ωραίο είναι αυτό. — o·*re*·o *i*·ne af·*to*

Easy tiger!
Κούλαρε! *ku*·la·re

That was ...	Ήταν …	*i*·tan ...
amazing	καταπληκτικό	ka·ta·plik·ti·*ko*
romantic	ρομαντικό	ro·ma·di·*ko*
wild	άγριο	*a*·ghri·o

LOVE

αγάπη

I think we're good together.
Νομίζω ταιριάζουμε. no·*mi*·zo te·*ria*·zu·me

I love you.
Σ'αγαπώ. sa·gha·*po*

Will you ...?	Θα …;	tha ...
go out with me	ήθελες να γίνουμε ζευγάρι	*i*·thel·es na *ghi*·nu·me *zev*·ghar·i
marry me	με παντρευτείς	me pa·dref·*tis*
meet my parents	συναντήσεις τους γονείς μου	si·na·*di*·sis tus gho·*nis* mu

SWEET TALK

my baby	μωρό μου	mo·*ro* mu
my darling	γλυκιά f μου	ghli·*ki*·a mu
my doll	κούκλα μου	*ku*·kla mu
my hunk	κούκλος μου	*ku*·klos mu
my soul	ψυχούλα μου	psi·*hu*·la mu
my treasure	χρυσό μου	khri·*so* mu
sweetheart	καρδούλα μου	kar·*thu*·la mu

PROBLEMS

προβλήματα

Are you seeing someone else? (to a woman)
βλέπεις κάποιον άλλον; — *vle*·pis *ka*·pion a·lon

Are you seeing someone else? (to a man)
βλέπεις κάποια άλλη; — *vle*·pis ka·pia a·li

He/She is just a friend.
Είναι απλά φίλος/φίλη. — *i*·ne a·*pla fi*·los / *fi*·li

You're just using me for sex.
Με θέλεις μόνο για σεξ. — me *the*·lis *mo*·no yia seks

I never want to see you again.
Δεν θέλω να σε ξαναδώ. — ţhen *the*·lo na se ksa·na·*ţho*

I don't think it's working out.
Δεν νομίζω ότι πάνε καλά τα πράγματα. — ţhen no·*mi*·zo o·ti *pa*·ne ka·*la* ta *pragh*·ma·ta

We'll work it out.
Θα τα βρούμε. — tha ta *vru*·me

LEAVING

φεύγοντας

I have to leave (tomorrow).
Πρέπει να φύγω (αύριο). — *pre*·pi na *fi*·gho (*av*·ri·o)

I'll ...	Θα ...	tha ...
keep in touch	μείνω σε επαφή	*mi*·no se e·pa·*fi*
miss you	μου λείψεις	mu *lip*·sis
visit you	σε επισκεφτώ	se e·pis·kef·*to*

IT'S A TRAGEDY

The poet Thespis (Θέσπις *thes*·pis) was one of the founders of the theatrical tragedy genre during the 6th century BCE. His name survives in the English word 'Thespian', meaning 'actor' or 'relating to drama or theatre'.

Beliefs & Cultural Differences

ΠΙΣΤΗ ΚΑΙ ΠΟΛΙΤΙΣΤΙΚΕΣ ΔΙΑΦΟΡΕΣ

RELIGION

θρησκεία

What's your religion?

Ποια είναι η θρησκεία σου; — pia *i*·ne i thris·*ki*·a su

I'm not religious.

Δεν είμαι θρήσκος. — ţhen *i*·me *thris*·kos

I'm ...	Είμαι ...	*i*·me ...
agnostic	αγνωστικιστής m	agh·no·sti·ki·*stis*
	αγνωστικίστρια f	agh·no·sti·*ki*·stri·a
Buddhist	Βουδιστής m	vu·ţhi·*stis*
	Βουδίστρια f	vu·*ţhi*·stri·a
Catholic	Καθολικός m	ka·tho·li·*kos*
	Καθολική f	ka·tho·li·*ki*
Christian	Χριστιανός m	khri·stia·*nos*
	Χριστιανή f	khri·stia·*ni*
Hindu	Ινδουιστής m	in·ţhu·i·*stis*
	Ινδουίστρια f	in·ţhu·*i*·stri·a
Jewish	Ιουδαίος m	i·u·*ţhe*·os
	Ιουδαία f	i·u·*ţhe*·a
Muslim	Μουσουλμάνος m	mu·sul·*ma*·nos
	Μουσουλμάνα f	mu·sul·*ma*·na
Orthodox	Ορθόδοξος m	or·*tho*·ţhok·sos
	Ορθόδοξη f	or·*tho*·ţhok·si

I (don't) believe in ...	(Δεν) Πιστεύω ...	(ţhen) pi·*ste*·vo ...
astrology	στην αστρολογία	stin a·stro·lo·*yi*·a
fate	στη μοίρα	sti *mi*·ra
God	στο Θεό	sto the·*o*

Can I ... here?	Μπορώ να … εδώ;	bo·*ro* na ... e·*ţho*
Where can I ...?	Πού μπορώ να …;	pu bo·*ro* na ...
attend mass	παρακολουθήσω τη λειτουργία	pa·ra·ko·lu·*thi*·so ti li·tur·*yi*·a
attend a service	παρακολουθήσω την ακολουθία	pa·ra·ko·lu·*thi*·so tin a·ko·lu·*thi*·a
pray	προσευχηθώ	pro·sef·hi·*tho*
worship	προσκυνήσω	pros·ki·*ni*·so

CULTURAL DIFFERENCES

πολιτιστικές διαφορές

Is this a local or national custom?
Είναι αυτό τοπικό ή εθνικό έθιμο; — *i*·ne af·*to* to·pi·*ko* i eth·ni·*ko* e·thi·mo

I'm not used to this.
Δεν είμαι συνηθισμένος σ'αυτό. — ţhen *i*·me si·ni·thiz·*me*·nos saf·*to*

I'd rather not join in.
Θα προτιμούσα να μη λάβω μέρος. — tha pro·ti·*mu*·sa na mi *la*·vo *me*·ros

I'll try it.
Θα το δοκιμάσω. — tha to ţho·ki·*ma*·so

I didn't mean to do anything wrong.
Δεν ήθελα να κάνω κάτι που δεν έπρεπε. — ţhen *i*·the·la na *ka*·no *ka*·ti pu ţhen e·pre·pe

I didn't mean to say anything wrong.
Δεν ήθελα να πω κάτι που δεν έπρεπε. — ţhen *i*·the·la na po *ka*·ti pu ţhen e·pre·pe

I don't want to offend you.
Δεν θέλω να σε προσβάλω. — ţhen *the*·lo na se proz·*va*·lo

I'm sorry, it's against my ...	Συγνώμη, είναι αντίθετο με … μου.	sigh·*no*·mi *i*·ne a·*di*·the·to me ... mu
beliefs	την πίστη	tin *pi*·sti
religion	τη θρησκεία	ti thris·*ki*·a

Art

ΤΕΧΝΗ

When's the museum open?
Πότε είναι ανοιχτό το μουσείο; — *po*·te *i*·ne a·nikh·*to* to mu·*si*·o

When's the gallery open?
Πότε είναι ανοιχτή η πινακοθήκη; — *po*·te *i*·ne a·nikh·*ti* i pi·na·ko·*thi*·ki

What kind of art are you interested in?
Τι είδους τέχνη σε ενδιαφέρει; — ti *i*·ţhus *tekh*·ni se en·ţhia·*fe*·ri

I'm interested in ...
Με ενδιαφέρει ... — me en·ţhia·*fe*·ri ...

What's in the collection?
Τι υπάρχει στη συλλογή; — ti i·*par*·hi sti si·lo·*yi*

It's an exhibition of ...
Είναι μια έκθεση ... — *i*·ne mia *ek*·the·si ...

Where are the exhibits from (Knossos)?
Πού είναι τα εκθέματα από την (Κνωσσό); — pu *i*·ne ta ek·*the*·ma·ta a·*po* tin (kno·*so*)

What style is this?
Τι στυλ είναι αυτό; — ti stil *i*·ne af·*to*

Is it an original or a copy?
Είναι αυθεντικό ή αντίγραφο; — *i*·ne af·the·di·*ko* i a·*di*·ghra·fo

What do you think of ...?
Πώς σου φαίνεται ...; — pos su *fe*·ne·te ...

I like the works of ...
Μου αρέσουν τα έργα ... — mu a·*re*·sun ta *er*·gha

It reminds me of ...
Μου θυμίζει ... — mu thi·*mi*·zi ...

Byzantine	Βυζαντινός	vi·za·di·*nos*
classical	κλασσικός	kla·si·*kos*
Hellenistic	Ελληνιστικός	e·li·ni·sti·*kos*
modern	μοντέρνος	mo·*der*·nos
Roman	Ρωμαϊκός	ro·ma·i·*kos*

ART SOCIAL

... civilisation	... πολιτισμός m	... po·li·tiz·*mos*
Cycladic	Κυκλαδικός	ki·kla·ţhi·*kos*
Minoan	Μινωικός	mi·no·i·*kos*
Mycenaean	Μυκηναϊκός	mi·ki·na·i·*kos*
... style	... ρυθμός m	... rith·*mos*
Corinthian	Κορινθιακός	ko·rin·thi·a·*kos*
Doric	Δωρικός	ţho·ri·*kos*
Ionic	Ιωνικός	i·o·ni·*kos*
architecture	αρχιτεκτονική f	ar·hi·tek·to·ni·*ki*
artwork	έργο τέχνης n	*er*·gho *tekh*·nis
column	κολόνα f	ko·*lo*·na
decorative arts	διακοσμητικές τέχνες f pl	ţhi·a·koz·mi·ti·*kes* *tekh*·nes
etching	χαλκογραφία f	khal·ko·ghra·*fi*·a
exhibit	έκθεση f	*ek*·the·si
exhibition hall	αίθουσα έκθεσης f	e·thu·sa *ek*·the·sis
fresco	φρέσκο n	*fres*·ko
metalwork	μεταλλοτεχνία f	me·ta·lo·tekh·*ni*·a
mosaic	μωσαϊκό n	mo·sa·i·*ko*
museum curator	έφορος μουσείου m	e·fo·ros mu·*si*·u
painter	ζωγράφος m	zo·*ghra*·fos
painting (artwork)	πίνακας m	*pi*·na·kas
painting (the art)	ζωγραφική f	zo·ghra·fi·*ki*
period	περίοδος f	pe·*ri*·o·ţhos
permanent collection	μόνιμη συλλογή f	*mo*·ni·mi si·lo·*yi*
print	αντίγραφο n	a·*di*·ghra·fo
sculptor	γλύπτης m	*ghlip*·tis
sculpture	γλυπτική f	ghlip·ti·*ki*
shield	ασπίδα f	a·*spi*·ţha
spear	δόρυ n	*ţho*·ri
sword	σπαθί n	spa·*thi*
statue	άγαλμα n	a·ghal·ma
terracotta pot	αγγείο τερακότα n	a·*gi*·o te·ra·*ko*·ta
tunic	χιτώνας m	hi·*to*·nas
vessel	αγγείο n	a·*gi*·o

Sport

ΣΠΟΡ

SPORTING INTERESTS

αθλητικά ενδιαφέροντα

What sport do you follow/play?
Τι σπορ ακολουθείς/παίζεις; — ti spor a·ko·lu·*this*/*pe*·zis

I follow (basketball).
Παρακολουθώ (μπάσκετ). — pa·ra·ko·lu·*tho* (*ba*·sket)

I play (football/soccer).
Παίζω (ποδόσφαιρο). — *pe*·zo (po·*ţhos*·fe·ro)

I do ...	Κάνω ...	*kha*·no ...
athletics	στίβο	*sti*·vo
hiking	πεζοπορία	pe·zo·po·*ri*·a
sailing	ιστιοπλοΐα	i·sti·o·plo·*i*·a
scuba diving	κατάδυση	ka·ta·*ţhi*·si
windsurfing	γουιντσέρφινγκ	windsurfing
water-skiing	θαλάσσιο σκι	tha·*la*·si·o ski

For more sports, see the **dictionary**, p207.

TOP SPORTS

football/soccer	ποδόσφαιρο n	po·*ţhos*·fe·ro
basketball	μπάσκετ n	*bas*·ket
volleyball	βόλεϋ n	*vo*·le·i
gymnastics	γυμναστική m	yim·na·sti·*khi*
swimming	κολύμπι n	ko·*lim*·bi

To exercise your brain, try Greece's favourite nonphysical pastime:

backgammon	τάβλι n	*tav*·li

I ...	Εγώ ...	e·*gho* ...
cycle	κάνω ποδήλατο	*ka*·no po·ţhi·la·to
run	τρέχω	*tre*·kho
walk	βαδίζω	va·ţhi·zo

Do you like (football/soccer)?
Σου αρέσει (το ποδόσφαιρο); — su a·*re*·si (to po·ţhos·fe·ro)

Yes, very much.
Ναι, πάρα πολύ. — ne *pa*·ra po·*li*

Not really.
Όχι ιδιαίτερα. — o·hi i·di·e·te·ra

I like watching it.
Μου αρέσει να το παρακολουθώ. — mu a·*re*·si na to pa·ra·kho·lu·*tho*

What's your favourite team?
Ποια ομάδα υποστηρίζεις; — pia o·*ma*·ţha i·po·sti·*ri*·zis

Who's your favourite athlete?
Ποιος είναι ο αγαπημένος σου αθλητής; — pios *i*·ne o a·gha·pi·*me*·nos ath·li·*this*

GOING TO A GAME

πηγαίνοντας σε έναν αγώνα

Would you like to go to a game?
Θα ήθελες να πας σε έναν αγώνα; — tha *i*·the·les na pas se e·nan a·*gho*·na

Who do you support?
Ποιον υποστηρίζεις; — pion i·po·sti·*ri*·zis

Who's playing/winning?
Ποιος παίζει/κερδίζει; — pios *pe*·zi / ker·ţhi·zi

SCORING

What's the score?	Ποιο είναι το σκορ;	pio *i*·ne to skor
draw/even	ισοπαλία	i·so·pa·*li*·a
love/zero/nil	μηδέν	mi·*ţhen*
match-point	ματς πόιντ	mats *point*

SPORTS TALK

What a ...!	Τι ...!	ti ...
goal	γκολ	gol
hit	χτύπημα	*khti*·pi·ma
kick	σουτ	soot
pass	πάσα	*pa*·sa
performance	απόδοση	a·*po*·ţho·si
That was a ... game!	Ήταν ... παιχνίδι!	*i*·tan ... peh·*ni*·ţhi
bad	άσχημο	a·shi·mo
boring	βαρετό	va·re·*to*
great	υπέροχο	i·*pe*·ro·kho

PLAYING SPORT

παίζοντας σπορ

Do you want to play?
Θέλεις να παίξεις; *the*·lis na *pek*·sis

Can I join in?
Να παίξω και εγώ; na *pek*·so ke e·*gho*

That would be great.
Αυτό θα ήταν υπέροχο. af·*to* tha *i*·tan i·*pe*·ro·kho

I can't.
Δεν μπορώ. ţhen bo·*ro*

I have an injury.
Έχω ένα τραύμα. e·kho e·na *trav*·ma

Your / My point.
Δικός σου/μου πόντος. ţhi·*kos* su / mu *po*·dos

Kick it to me!
κλώτσα τη σε μένα! — *klot*·sa ti se *me*·na

Pass it to me!
ρίξ'τη σε μένα! — *riks*·ti se *me*·na

You're a good player.
Είσαι καλός παίχτης. — *i*·se ka·*los pekh*·tis

Thanks for the game.
Ευχαριστώ για το παιχνίδι. — ef·kha·ri·*sto* yia to peh·*ni*·ţhi

Where's a good place to ...?	Πού είναι ένα καλό μέρος για να ...;	pu *i*·ne e·na ka·*lo me*·ros yia na ...
fish	ψαρέψεις	psa·*rep*·sis
go horse riding	κάνεις ιππασία	*ka*·nis i·pa·*si*·a
run	τρέξεις	*trek*·sis
snorkel	κάνεις σνόρκελινγκ	*ka*·nis *snor*·ke·ling
surf	σερφάρεις	ser·*fa*·ris

SOCIAL SPORT

Where's the nearest ...?	Πού είναι το πιο κοντινό ...;	pu *i*·ne to pio ko·*di*·*no* ...
golf course	γήπεδο του γκολφ	*yi*·pe·ţho tu golf
gym	γυμναστήριο	yim·na·*sti*·ri·o
tennis court	γήπεδο του τένις	*yi*·pe·ţho tu *te*·nis

Where's the nearest swimming pool?
Πού είναι η πιο κοντινή πισίνα; pu *i*·ne i pio ko·di·*ni* pi·*si*·na

Do I have to be a member to attend?
Πρέπει να είμαι μέλος για να πάω; *pre*·pi na *i*·me *me*·los yia na *pa*·o

Is there a women-only session?
Υπάρχει ορισμένη ώρα μόνο για γυναίκες; i·*par*·hi o·riz·*me*·ni *o*·ra *mo*·no yia yi·*ne*·kes

Can I book a lesson?
Μπορώ να κλείσω ένα μάθημα; bo·*ro* na *kli*·so e·na *ma*·thi·ma

Where are the changing rooms?
Πού είναι τα αποδυτήρια; pu *i*·ne ta a·po·ţhi·*ti*·ri·a

What's the charge per ...?	Πόσο κοστίζει ...;	*po*·so ko·*sti*·zi ...
day	την ημέρα	tin i·*me*·ra
game	το παιχνίδι	to peh·*ni*·ţhi
hour	την ώρα	tin *o*·ra
visit	την επίσκεψη	tin e·*pis*·kep·si

Can I hire a ...?	Μπορώ να νοικιάσω ...;	bo·*ro* na ni·*kia*·so ...
ball	μια μπάλα	mia *ba*·la
bicycle	ένα ποδήλατο	e·na po·*ţhi*·la·to
court	το γήπεδο	to *yi*·pe·ţho
racquet	μια ρακέτα	mia ra·*ke*·ta

FISHING

ψάρεμα

Where are the good spots?
Πού είναι τα καλά μέρη; — pu *i*·ne ta ka·*la* *me*·ri

Do I need a fishing permit?
Χρειάζομαι άδεια για ψάρεμα; — khri·a·zo·me *a*·ţhi·a yia *psa*·re·ma

Do you do fishing tours?
Κάνετε εκδρομές για ψάρεμα; — *ka*·ne·te ek·ţhro·*mes* yia *psa*·re·ma

What's the best bait?
Ποιο είναι το καλύτερο δόλωμα; — pio *i*·ne to ka·*li*·te·ro *ţho*·lo·ma

Are they biting?
Τσιμπάνε; — tsi·*ba*·ne

What kind of fish are you landing?
Τι ψάρι βγάζεις; — ti *psa*·ri *vgha*·zis

How much does it weigh?
Πόσο ζυγίζει; — *po*·so zi·*yi*·zi

bait	δόλωμα n	*ţho*·lo·ma
fishing line	πετονιά f	pe·to·*nia*
flare	φανάρι n	fa·*na*·ri
float	φελλός f	fe·*los*
hooks	αγκίστρια n pl	a·*gi*·stri·a
life jacket	σωσίβιο n	so·*si*·vi·o
lure	δόλωμα n	*ţho*·lo·ma
rod	καλάμι n	ka·*la*·mi
sinkers	βαρίδια n pl	va·*ri*·ţhia

☑ NOT BITING?

Fishing with dynamite used to be quite common in Greece, but this 'sport' has been outlawed because of its environmental impact. Look out for signs warning Απαγορεύεται η χρήση δυναμίτη (No Dynamite).

HORSE RIDING

ιππασία

How much is a (one-)hour ride?

Πόσο κοστίζει η ιππασία (την) ώρα;	*po*·so kos·*ti*·zi i i·pa·*si*·a (tin) *o*·ra

How long is the ride?

πόση ώρα διαρκεί η διαδρομή με το άλογο;	*po*·si *o*·ra ţhi·ar·*ki* i ţhi·a·ţhro·*mi* me to *a*·lo·gho

I'm (not) an experienced rider.

(Δεν) Είμαι έμπειρος αναβάτης.	(ţhen) *i*·me *em*·bi·ros a·na·*va*·tis

Can I rent a hat and boots?

Μπορώ να νοικιάσω ένα καπέλο και μπότες;	bo·*ro* na ni·*kia*·so e·na ka·*pe*·lo ke *bo*·tes

bit	στομίδα f	sto·*mi*·ţha
bridle	χαλινάρι n	kha·li·*na*·ri
canter	τριποδισμός m	tri·po·ţhiz·*mos*
crop	μαστίγιο ιππασίας n	mas·*ti*·yi·o i·pa·*si*·as
gallop	καλπασμός m	kal·paz·*mos*
groom	ιπποκόμος m	i·po·*ko*·mos
horse	άλογο n	*a*·lo·gho
pony	πόνυ n	*po*·ni
race	κούρσα f	*kur*·sa
reins	γκέμια n pl	*ge*·mia
saddle	σέλα f	*se*·la
stable	στάβλος m	*stav*·los
stirrup	αναβολέα m	a·na·vo·*le*·as
trot	τροχασμός m	tro·khaz·*mos*
walk	βάδισμα n	*va*·ţhiz·ma

FOOTBALL/SOCCER

ποδόσφαιρο

Who plays for (Iraklis)?
Ποιος παίζει στον (Ηρακλή); — pios *pe*·zi ston (i·ra·*kli*)

He's a great (player).
Είναι μεγάλος (παίχτης). — *i*·ne me·*gha*·los (*pekh*·tis)

He played brilliantly in the match against (Italy).
Έπαιξε υπέροχα στο ματς εναντίον (της Ιταλίας). — e·pek·se i·*pe*·ro·kha sto mats e·na·*di*·on (tis i·ta·*li*·as)

Which team is at the top of the league?
Ποια ομάδα είναι στην κορυφή της πρώτης εθνικής; — pia o·*ma*·ţha *i*·ne stin ko·ri·*fi* tis *pro*·tis eth·ni·*kis*

What a great/terrible team!
Τι μεγάλη/χάλια ομάδα! — ti me·*gha*·li / *ha*·lia o·*ma*·ţha

ball	μπάλα f	*ba*·la
coach	προπονητής m	pro·po·ni·*tis*
corner (kick)	κόρνερ n	*kor*·ner
expulsion	αποβολή n	a·po·vo·*li*
fan	οπαδός m	o·pa·*ţhos*
foul	φάουλ n	*fa*·ul
free kick	φρί κικ n	fri kik
goal (structure)	γκολπόστ n	gol·*post*
goalkeeper	γκολκήπερ m	gol·*ki*·per
manager	μάνατζερ m	*ma*·na·dzer
offside	οφσάιντ n	of·*sa*·id
penalty	πέναλτι n	*pe*·nal·ti
player	παίχτης m	*pekh*·tis
red card	κόκκινη κάρτα f	*ko*·ki·ni *kar*·ta
referee	διαιτητής m	ţhi·e·ti·*tis*
substitute	αναπληρωματικός m	a·na·pli·ro·ma·ti·*kos*
yellow card	κίτρινη κάρτα n	*ki*·tri·ni *kar*·ta

TENNIS & TABLE TENNIS

τένις και πινγκ πονγκ

I'd like to ...	Θα ήθελα να ...	tha *i*·the·la na ...
book a time to play	κλείσω ώρα να παίξω	*kli*·so *o*·ra na *pek*·so
play table tennis	παίξω πινγκ πονγκ	*pek*·so ping pong
play tennis	παίξω τένις	*pek*·so *te*·nis

Can we play at night?
Μπορούμε να παίξουμε τη νύχτα;
bo·*ru*·me na *pek*·su·me ti *nikh*·ta

I need my racquet restrung.
Η ρακέτα μου χρειάζεται επισκευή.
i ra·*ke*·ta mu khri·*a*·ze·te e·pis·ke·*vi*

ace	άσος m	*a*·sos
advantage	πλεονέκτημα n	ple·o·*nek*·ti·ma
bat	μπαστούνι n	ba·*stu*·ni
clay court	χωμάτινο γήπεδο τένις n	ho·*ma*·ti·no *yi*·pe·tho *te*·nis
fault	σφάλμα n	*sfal*·ma
game, set, match	γκέιμ, σετ, ματς n	game set mats
grass	γρασίδι n	ghra·*si*·ţhi
hard court	σκληρό γήπεδο n	skli·*ro* *yi*·pe·ţho
net	δίχτυ n	*ţhikh*·ti
ping-pong ball	μπαλάκι του πινγκ πονγκ n	ba·*la*·ki tu ping pong
play doubles	παίζουμε διπλό	*pe*·zu·me ţhi·*plo*
racket	ρακέτα f	ra·*ke*·ta
serve v	σερβίς	ser·*vis*
tennis ball	μπαλάκι του τένις n	ba·*la*·ki tu *te*·nis
table-tennis table	τραπέζι του πινγκ πονγκ n	tra·*pe*·zi tu ping pong

WATER SPORTS

θαλάσσια σπορ

Can I hire (a) ...?	Μπορώ να νοικιάσω ...;	bo·*ro* na ni·*kia*·so ...
boat	μια βάρκα	mia *var*·ka
canoe	ένα κανό	e·na ka·*no*
kayak	ένα καγιάκ	e·na ka·*yiak*
life jacket	ένα σωσίβιο	e·na so·*si*·vi·o
scuba diving gear	μια στολή κατάδυσης	mia sto·*li* ka·*ta*·ţhi·sis
water-skis	θαλάσσια σκι	tha·*la*·si·a ski
wetsuit	αδιάβροχη στολή	a·*ţhiav*·ro·hi sto·*li*
Are there any ...?	Υπάρχουν ...;	i·*par*·khun ...
reefs	ξέρες	*kse*·res
rips	δυνατό ρεύμα	ţhi·na·*to rev*·ma
water hazards	υδάτινοι κίνδυνοι	i·*ţha*·ti·ni *kin*·ţhi·ni
guide	οδηγός **m&f**	o·ţhi·*ghos*
motorboat	βάρκα με μηχανή **f**	*var*·ka me mi·kha·*ni*
oars	κουπιά **n pl**	ku·*pia*
windsurfing	γουιντσέρφινγκ **n**	windsurfing
sailboat	ιστιοπλοϊκό **n**	is·ti·o·plo·i·*kho*
surfboard	σανίδα σερφ **f**	sa·*ni*·da serf
surfing	σέρφινγκ **n**	*ser*·fing
wave	κύμα **n**	*ki*·ma

☑ DIVING IN

During the summer months, ask around for diving lessons:

Is there a diving school here?

Υπάρχει σχολή καταδύσεων εδώ; — i·*par*·hi skho·*li* ka·ta·*ţhi*·se·on e·*ţho*

Do you offer diving lessons (in English)?

Προσφέρετε μαθήματα καταδύσεων (στα αγγλικά); — pros·*fe*·re·te ma·*thi*·ma·ta ka·ta·*thi*·se·on (sta ang·gli·*ka*)

Outdoors

ΥΠΑΙΘΡΟ

HIKING

πεζοπορία

Where can I ...?	Πού μπορώ να ...;	pu bo·*ro* na ...
buy supplies	αγοράσω προμήθειες	a·gho·*ra*·so pro·*mi*·thi·es
find someone who knows this area	βρω κάποιον που ξέρει αυτή την περιοχή	vro *ka*·pion pu *kse*·ri af·*ti* tin pe·ri·o·*hi*
get a map	πάρω ένα χάρτη	*pa*·ro e·na *khar*·ti
hire hiking gear	νοικιάσω εξοπλισμό για πεζοπορία	ni·*kia*·so ek·so·pliz·*mo* yia pe·zo·po·*ri*·a
How ...?	Πόσο ...;	*po*·so ...
high is the climb	ψηλό είναι το ανέβασμα	psi·*lo* *i*·ne to a·*ne*·vaz·ma
long is the trail	μακρύ είναι το μονοπάτι	ma·*kri* *i*·ne to mo·no·*pa*·ti
Do we need to take ...?	Χρειάζεται να πάρουμε ...;	khri·a·ze·te na *pa*·ru·me ...
bedding	σκεπάσματα	ske·*paz*·*ma*·ta
food	φαγητό	fa·yi·*to*
water	νερό	ne·*ro*

Do we need a guide?
Χρειαζόμαστε οδηγό; — khri·a·*zo*·ma·ste o·thi·*gho*

Are there waymarked trails?
Υπάρχουν μονοπάτια με σήματα; — i·*par*·khun mo·no·*pa*·tia me *si*·ma·ta

Is there a path to (Profitis Ilias)?
Υπάρχει μονοπάτι για (τον Προφήτη Ηλία); — i·*par*·hi mo·no·*pa*·ti yia (ton pro·*fi*·ti i·*li*·a)

Is it safe?
Είναι ασφαλές; — *i*·ne as·fa·*les*

Is it steep?
Είναι απότομο; — *i*·ne a·*po*·to·mo

Are there any rockfalls?
Πέφτουν πουθενά πέτρες; — *pef*·tun pu·the·*na* *pet*·res

Is there a hut?
Υπάρχει κανένα καλύβι; — i·*par*·hi ka·*ne*·na ka·*li*·vi

When does it get dark?
Πότε σκοτεινιάζει; — *po*·te sko·ti·*nia*·zi

Is the track ...?	Είναι ο δρόμος ...;	*i*·ne o ţ*hro*·mos ...
(well-) marked	σημαδεμένος (καλά)	si·ma·ţhe·*me*·nos (ka·*la*)
open	ανοιχτός	a·nikh·*tos*
scenic	γραφικός	ghra·fi·*kos*

Which is the ... route?	Ποια είναι η πιο ... διαδρομή;	pia *i*·ne i pio ... ţhi·a·ţhro·*mi*
easiest	εύκολη	*ef*·ko·li
most interesting	ενδιαφέρουσα	en·ţhia·*fe*·ru·sa
shortest	κοντινή	ko·di·*ni*

Where can I find the ...?	Πού μπορώ να βρω το ...	pu bo·*ro* na vro to ...
camping ground	χώρο του κάμπινγκ	*kho*·ro tu *kam*·ping
nearest village	πιο κοντινό χωριό	pio ko·di·*no* kho·*rio*
showers	ντουζ	duz
toilets	την τουαλέτα	tin tu·a·*le*·ta

Where have you come from?
Από πού ήρθες; — a·*po* pu *ir*·thes

How long did it take?
Πόση ώρα σου πήρε; — *po*·si o·ra su *pi*·re

Does this path go to ...?
Πηγαίνει αυτό το μονοπάτι στο ...; — pi·*ye*·ni af·*to* to mo·no·*pa*·ti sto ...

Can I go through here?

Μπορώ να πάω μέσα από εδώ; — bo·*ro* na *pa*·o *me*·sa a·*po* e·*ţho*

Is the water OK to drink?

Είναι εντάξει το νερό για να πιω; — *i*·ne e·*dak*·si to ne·*ro* yia na pio

I'm lost.

Χάθηκα. — *kha*·thi·ka

BEACH

παραλία

Where's the ... beach?	Πού είναι η ... παραλία;	pu *i*·ne i ... pa·ra·*li*·a
best	καλύτερη	ka·*li*·te·ri
nearest	κοντινότερη	ko·di·*no*·te·ri
public	δημόσια	ţhi·*mo*·si·a

Where's the nudist beach?

Πού είναι η πλαζ γυμνιστών; — pu *i*·ne i plaz yim·ni·*ston*

Do we have to pay?

Πρέπει να πληρώσουμε; — *pre*·pi na pli·*ro*·su·me

What time is high/low tide?

Τι ώρα είναι η παλίρροια/άμπωτις; — ti *o*·ra *i*·ne i pa·*li*·ri·a/ *a*·bo·tis

Is it safe to dive/swim here?

Είναι ασφαλές να κάνω βουτιές/κολυμπήσω εδώ; — *i*·ne as·fa·*les* na *ka*·no vu·*ties*/ko·li·*bi*·so e·*ţho*

LISTEN FOR

Είναι επικίνδυνο!
i·ne e·pi·*kin*·ţhi·no — **It's dangerous!**

Πρόσεχε το υπόγειο ρεύμα!
pro·se·he to i·*po*·yi·o *rev*·ma — **Be careful of the undertow!**

LOOK FOR

Απαγορεύεται το κολύμπι	a·pa·gho·*re*·ve·te to ko·*li*·bi	**No Swimming**
Απαγορεύονται οι βουτιές	a·pa·gho·*re*·vo·de i vu·*ties*	**No Diving**

Are there any ...?	Υπάρχουν ...;	i·*par*·khun ...
currents	ρεύματα	*rev*·ma·ta
jellyfish	μέδουσες	*me*·ţhu·ses
rocks	βράχια	*vra*·hia
sea urchins	αχινοί	a·hi·*ni*

How much for a/an ...?	Πόσο για μια ...;	*po*·so yia mia ...
cabana bed	καμπάνα	ka·*ba*·na
sun lounger	ξαπλώστρα	xa·*plo*·stra
umbrella	ομπρέλα	o·*bre*·la

WEATHER

καιρός

What's the weather like?

Πώς είναι ο καιρός; — pos *i*·ne o ke·*ros*

What will the weather be like tomorrow?

Πώς θα είναι ο καιρός αύριο; — pos tha *i*·ne o ke·*ros* *av*·ri·o

It's ...	Έχει ...	e·hi ...
cloudy	συννεφιά	si·ne·*fia*
dry	ξηρασία	ksi·ra·*si*·a
fine	καλός καιρός	ka·*los* ke·*ros*
freezing	παγωνιά	pa·gho·*nia*
humid	υγρασία	i·ghra·*si*·a
mild	μαλακός καιρός	ma·la·*kos* ke·*ros*
sunny	λιακάδα	lia·*ka*·ţha

It's ...		
raining	Βρέχει.	*vre*·hi
snowing	Χιονίζει.	hio·*ni*·zi
windy	Φυσάει.	fi·*sa*·i
drizzling	Ψιχαλίζει.	psi·kha·*li*·zi
It's ...	Κάνει ...	*ka*·ni ...
cold	κρύο	*kri*·o
hot	πολλή ζέστη	po·*li* *ze*·sti
warm	ζέστη	*ze*·sti
Where can I buy a/an ...?	Πού μπορώ να αγοράσω ...;	pu bo·*ro* na a·gho·*ra*·so ...
rain jacket	ένα αδιάβροχο	e·na a·ţhiav·ro·kho
umbrella	μια ομπρέλα	mia o·*bre*·la

WEATHERING THE LOCAL STORMS

heatwave	καύσωνας m	*kaf*·so·nas
strong northerly wind	μελτέμι n	mel·*te*·mi
strong cold wind	βοριάς m	vo·*rias*
thunderstorm	καταιγίδα f	ka·te·*yi*·ţha

FLORA & FAUNA

χλωρίδα και πανίδα

What ... is that?	Τι ... είναι εκείνο;	ti ... *i*·ne e·*ki*·no
animal	ζώο	*zo*·o
flower	λουλούδι	lu·*lu*·ţhi
plant	φυτό	fi·*to*
tree	δέντρο	*ţhe*·dro

What's it used for?
Σε τι χρησιμοποιείται; se ti khri·si·mo·pi·*i*·te

Can you eat the fruit?
Μπορείς να φας τον καρπό; bo·*ris* na fas ton kar·*po*

Is it ...?	Είναι ...;	*i*·ne ...
common	κοινό	ki·*no*
dangerous	επικίνδυνο	e·pi·*kin*·ţhi·no
endangered	υπό εξαφάνιση	i·*po* ek·sa·*fa*·ni·si
poisonous	δηλητηριώδες	ţhi·li·ti·ri·*o*·ţhes
protected	προστατευόμενο	pro·sta·te·*vo*·me·no

LOCAL PLANTS & ANIMALS

basil	βασιλικός **m**	va·si·li·*kos*
carnation	γαρύφαλο **n**	gha·*ri*·fa·lo
carob	χαρούπι **n**	kha·*ru*·pi
Dalmatian pelican	Δαλματικός πελεκάνος **m**	ţhal·ma·ti·*kos* pe·le·*ka*·nos
dolphin	δελφίνι **n**	ţhel·*fi*·ni
falcon	γεράκι **n**	ye·*ra*·ki
fig	σύκο **n**	*si*·ko
iris	κρίνος **m**	*kri*·nos
lizard	σαύρα **f**	*sav*·ra
monk seal	φώκια μοναχός **f**	fo·kia mo·na·*hos*
olive	ελιά **f**	e·*lia*
orchid	ορχιδέα **f**	or·hi·*ţhe*·a
pine	πεύκο **n**	*pef*·ko
rose	τριαντάφυλλο **n**	tri·a·*da*·fi·lo
seagull	γλάρος **m**	*gla*·ros
sea turtle	θαλάσσια χελώνα **f**	tha·*la*·si·a khe·*lo*·na
snake	φίδι **n**	*fi*·ţhi
swallow	χελιδόνι **n**	he·li·*ţho*·ni
wildflowers	αγριολούλουδα **n pl**	a·ghri·o·*lu*·lu·ţha

FOOD

Eating Out

ΤΡΩΓΟΝΤΑΣ ΕΞΩ

BASICS

βασικά

breakfast	πρωινό n	pro·i·*no*
lunch	μεσημεριανό n	me·si·me·ri·a·*no*
dinner	βραδινό n	vra·di·*no*
snack	κολατσιό n	ko·la·*tsio*
eat	τρώω	*tro*·o
drink v	πίνω	*pi*·no
I'd like ...	Θα ήθελα ...	tha *i*·the·la ...
Please.	Παρακαλώ.	pa·ra·ka·*lo*
Thank you.	Ευχαριστώ.	ef·kha·ri·*sto*
I'm starving!	Πεθαίνω της πείνας	pe·*the*·no tis *pi*·nas
Enjoy your meal.	Καλή όρεξη.	ka·*li* o·rek·si

☑ FOOD GLORIOUS FOOD

For **breakfast**, Greeks usually have a hot cup of milk, tea or coffee with φρυγανιά fri·gha·*nia* (crispbread). If eating out, a typical order is a τυρόπιτα ti·*ro*·pi·ta (cheese pie) or σπανακόπιτα spa·na·*ko*·pi·ta (spinach pie).

Lunch is an early afternoon affair. A typical lunch will be a salad or a sandwich.

Dinner is the the main meal of the day, eaten no earlier than eight o'clock. A typical dinner will be a meat dish with rice, pasta or potatoes, or fish with a side salad. Legume dishes such as φακές fa·*kes* (lentil broth) and φασολάδα fa·so·*la*·ţha (bean broth) are especially popular in winter.

After **Dessert**, seasonal fresh fruit frequently finishes off a meal.

FINDING A PLACE TO EAT

βρίσκοντας κάπου για φαγητό

Can you recommend a ...?	Μπορείς να προτείνεις ένα ...;	bo·*ris* na pro·*ti*·nis e·na ...
bar	μπαρ	bar
cafe	καφέ	ka·*fe*
restaurant	εστιατόριο	e·sti·a·*to*·ri·o
Where would you go for (a) ...?	Πού θα πήγαινες για ...;	pu tha *pi*·ye·nes yia ...
celebration	ένα πάρτυ	e·na *par*·ti
cheap meal	ένα οικονομικό γεύμα	e·na i·ko·no·mi·*ko* *yev*·ma
local specialities	τοπικές λιχουδιές	to·pi·*kes* li·hu·*ţhies*
I'd like to reserve a table for ...	Θα ήθελα να κάνω κράτηση για ένα τραπέζι για ...	tha *i*·the·la na *ka*·no *kra*·ti·si yia e·na tra·*pe*·zi yia ...
(two) people	(δύο) άτομα	(*ţhi*·o) a·to·ma
(eight) o'clock	στις (οχτώ)	stis (okh·*to*)

LISTEN FOR

Δεν υπάρχει άδειο τραπέζι. ţhen i·*par*·hi a·ţhio tra·*pe*·zi	**We're full.**
Κλείσαμε. *kli*·sa·me	**We're closed.**
Μια στιγμή. mia stigh·*mi*	**One moment.**
Πού θα θέλατε να καθίσετε; pu tha *the*·la·te na ka·*thi*·se·te	**Where would you like to sit?**
Τι μπορώ να σας φέρω; ti bo·*ro* na sas *fe*·ro	**What can I get for you?**
Ορίστε! o·*ri*·ste	**Here you go!**

I'd like (a/the) ..., please.	Θα ήθελα ..., παρακαλώ.	tha *i*·thela ... pa·ra·ka·*lo*
children's menu	ένα μενού για παιδιά	e·na me·*nu* yia pe·*ţhia*
drink list	τον κατάλογο με τα ποτά	ton ka·*ta*·lo·gho me ta po·*ta*
half portion	μισή μερίδα	mi·*si* me·*ri*·ţha
menu (in English)	ένα μενού (στα αγγλικά)	e·na me·*nu* (sta ang·gli·*ka*)
mixed plate	μια ποικιλία	mia pi·ki·*li*·a
nonsmoking	στους μη καπνίζοντες	stus mi kap·*ni*·zo·des
smoking	στους καπνίζοντες	stus kap·*ni*·zo·des
table for (five)	ένα τραπέζι για (πέντε)	e·na tra·*pe*·zi yia (*pe*·de)
table outside	ένα τραπέζι έξω	e·na tra·*pe*·zi *ek*·so

Are you still serving food?
Σερβίρετε ακόμη φαγητό; ser·*vi*·re·te a·*ko*·mi fa·ghi·*to*

How long is the wait?
Πόση ώρα θα περιμένουμε; *po*·si *o*·ra tha pe·ri·*me*·nu·me

EATERIES

In the past, locals would order some μερικά παξιμάδια me·ri·*ka* pak·si·*ma*·ţhia (dried bread) for dunking in their coffee or other hot drinks in one of these eateries, but this is now mostly done at home:

καφέ f	ka·*fe*	cafe
καφενείο n	ka·fe·*ni*·o	traditional coffee shop
γαλακτοπωλείο n	gha·lak·to·po·*li*·o	dairy shop
φαστφουντάδικο n	fast·fun·*da*·ţhi·ko	fast-food eatery
ουζερί n	u·ze·*ri*	ouzeri
οινοπωλείο n	i·no·po·*li*·o	wine shop
ταβέρνα f	ta·*ver*·na	taverna

AT THE RESTAURANT

στο εστιατόριο

What would you recommend?
Τι προτείνεις; — ti pro·*ti*·nis

What are you serving today?
Τι έχετε σήμερα; — ti e·he·te s*i*·me·ra

What's that called?
Πώς το λένε αυτό; — pos to *le*·ne af·*to*

What's in that dish?
Τι περιέχει αυτό το φαγητό; — ti pe·ri·e·hi af·*to* to fa·ghi·*to*

I'll have that.
Θα πάρω αυτό. — tha *pa*·ro af·*to*

LISTEN FOR

Πώς θα το θέλατε ψημένο; pos tha to *the*·la·te psi·*me*·no	**How would you like that cooked?**
Σας αρέσει …; sas a·*re*·si …	**Do you like …?**
Συνιστώ … si·ni·*sto* …	**I suggest the …**

Is it savoury or sweet?
Είναι αλμυρό ή γλυκό; — *i*·ne al·mi·*ro* i ghli·*ko*

I'd like it hot, please.
Θα το ήθελα ζεστό, παρακαλώ. — tha to *i*·the·la ze·*sto* pa·ra·ka·*lo*

Does it take long to prepare?
Θέλει πολύ χρόνο να ετοιμαστεί; — *the*·li po·*li* *khro*·no na e·ti·ma·*sti*

Is it self-serve?
Είναι σελφ σέρβις; — *i*·ne self *ser*·vis

Is there a cover charge?
Υπάρχει κουβέρ; — i·*par*·hi ku·*ver*

Is service included in the bill?
Συμπεριλαμβάνεται και πουρμπουάρ στο λογαριασμό; — si·be·ri·lam·*va*·ne·te ke pur·bu·*ar* sto lo·gha·riaz·*mo*

Are these complimentary?
Είναι αυτά δωρεάν; — *i*·ne af·*ta* ţho·re·*an*

How much is that?
Πόσο κάνει αυτό; — *po*·so *ka*·ni af·*to*

I'd like (a/the) ...	Θα ήθελα ...	tha *i*·the·la ...
chicken	το κοτόπουλο	to ko·*to*·pu·lo
local speciality	τοπικό πιάτο	to·pi·*ko pia*·to
meal fit for a king	ένα λουκούλλειο γεύμα	e·na lu·*ku*·li·o *yev*·ma
menu	το μενού	to me·*nu*
sandwich	ένα σάντουιτς	e·na *sa*·du·its
that dish	εκείνο το φαγητό	e·*ki*·no to fa·yi·*to*

LOOK FOR

Ορεκτικά	o·rek·ti·*ka*	Appetisers
Σούπες	*su*·pes	Soups
Πρώτα	*pro*·ta	Starters
Σαλάτες	sa·*la*·tes	Salads
Κύρια φαγητά	*ki*·ri·a fa·yi·*ta*	Main Courses
Ψητά της ώρας	psi·*ta* tis *o*·ras	Freshly Grilled Dishes
Μαγειρευτά	ma·yi·re·*fta*	Casseroles/oven-baked dishes
Σαλάτες	sa·*la*·tes	Salads
Μακαρόνια	ma·ka·*ro*·nia	Pasta
Ψάρια	*psa*·ria	Fish
Θαλασσινά	tha·la·si·*na*	Seafood
Επιδόρπια	e·pi·*ţhor*·pi·a	Desserts
Ποτά	po·*ta*	Drinks
Απεριτίφ	a·pe·ri·*tif*	Apéritifs
Αναψυκτικά	a·nap·sik·ti·*ka*	Soft Drinks
Οινοπνευματώδη ποτά	i·nop·nev·ma·*to*·ţhi po·*ta*	Spirits
Μπύρες	*bi*·res	Beers
Σαμπάνια	sam·*pa*·nia	Sparkling Wines and Champagne
Λευκό κρασί	lef·*ko* kra·*si*	White Wine
Κόκκινο κρασί	*ko*·ki·no kra·*si*	Red Wine
Επιδόρπια κρασιά	e·pi·*ţhor*·pi·a kra·*sia*	Dessert Wines
Ρετσίνα	ret·*si*·na	Retsina
Χωνευτικά	kho·nef·ti·*ka*	Digestifs

STREET FOOD

If you've got the munchies, try one of these snacks:

κουλούρι n	ku·*lu*·ri	crisp sesame-coated bread rings
γύρος m	*yi*·ros	spit-roasted meat (usually pork or chicken)
πασατέμπο n	pa·sa·*tem*·po	pumpkin seeds
σουβλάκι n	suv·la·ki	meat-filled pita wrap
σπανακόπιτα f	spa·na·*ko*·pi·ta	spinach pie
τυρόπιτα f	ti·*ro*·pi·ta	cheese pie
ψημένα κάστανα n pl	psi·*me*·na *ka*·sta·na	roasted chestnuts
ψημένο καλαμπόκι n	psi·*me*·no ka·la·*bo*·ki	roasted corn

I'd like it with/without ...	Θα το ήθελα με/χωρίς ...	tha to *i*·the·la me/kho·*ris* ...
cheese	τυρί	ti·*ri*
chili	τσίλι	*tsi*·li
chili sauce	σάλτσα τσίλι	*salt*·sa *tsi*·li
garlic	σκόρδο	*skor*·ţho
ketchup	κέτσαπ	*ke*·tsap
oil	λάδι	*la*·ţhi
pepper	πιπέρι	pi·*pe*·ri
salt	αλάτι	a·*la*·ti
tomato sauce	σάλτσα ντομάτας	*salt*·sa do·*ma*·tas
vinegar	ξύδι	*ksi*·ţhi
walnuts	καρύδια	ka·*ri*·ţhia

For additional items, see the **menu decoder**, p175. For other specific meal requests, see **vegetarian & special meals**, p173.

AT THE TABLE

στο τραπέζι

Please bring (a/the) ...	Παρακαλώ φέρε ...	pa·ra·ka·*lo* *fe*·re ...
bill	το λογαριασμό	to lo·gha·riaz·*mo*
tablecloth	ένα τραπεζομάντηλο	e·na tra·pe·zo·*ma*·di·lo
glass	ένα ποτήρι	e·na po·*ti*·ri
napkin	μια χαρτοπετσέτα	mia har·to·pe·*tse*·ta
wineglass	ένα ποτήρι κρασιού	e·na po·*ti*·ri kra·*siu*

This is ...	Αυτό είναι ...	af·*to* *i*·ne ...
(too) cold	(πολύ) κρύο	(po·*li*) *kri*·o
spicy	καυτερό	ka·fte·*ro*
superb	καταπληκτικό	ka·ta·plik·ti·*ko*

There's a mistake in the bill.
Υπάρχει κάποιο λάθος στο λογαριασμό.
i·*par*·hi *ka*·pio *la*·thos sto lo·gha·riaz·*mo*

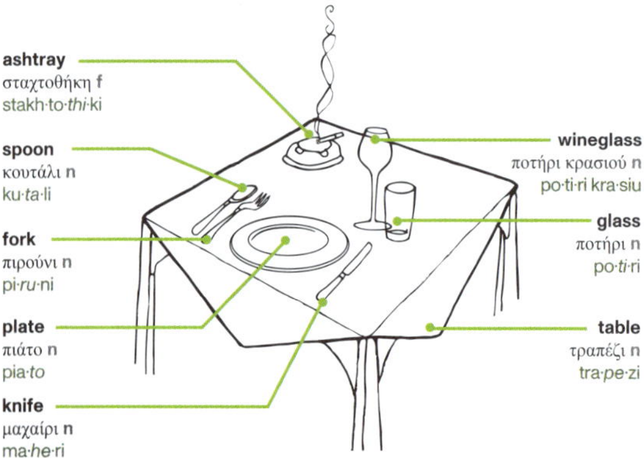

TALKING FOOD

μιλώντας για φαγητό

I love this dish.
Μου αρέσει πολύ αυτό το φαγητό. — mu a·*re*·si po·*li* af·*to* to fa·yi·*to*

I love the local cuisine.
Μου αρέσει η τοπική κουζίνα. — mu a·*re*·si i to·pi·*ki* ku·*zi*·na

That was delicious!
Ήταν νοστιμότατο! — *i*·tan no·sti·*mo*·ta·to

My compliments to the chef.
Τα συγχαρητήριά μου στο σεφ. — ta sing·kha·ri·*ti*·ri·a mu sto sef

METHODS OF PREPARATION

μέθοδοι παρασκευής

I'd like it ...	Θα το ήθελα ...	tha to *i*·the·la ...
I don't want it ...	Δεν το θέλω ...	ţhen to *the*·lo ...
boiled	βρασμένο	vraz·*me*·no
broiled	ψημένο στο γκριλ	psi·*me*·no sto grill
deep-fried	τηγανισμένο σε πολύ λάδι	ti·gha·niz·*me*·no se po·*li la*·di
fried	τηγανητό	ti·gha·ni·*to*
grilled	στο γκριλ	sto grill
mashed	πουρέ	pu·*re*
reheated	ξαναζεσταμένο	ksa·na·ze·sta·*me*·no
steamed	βρασμένο στον ατμό	vraz·*me*·no ston at·*mo*

HOW WOULD YOU LIKE THAT?

medium	Μέτριο	*me*·tri·o
rare	σενιάν	se·*nian*
well-done	καλοψημένο	ka·lop·si·*me*·no

NONALCOHOLIC DRINKS

μη αλκοολούχο ποτά

... mineral water	... μεταλλικό νερό n	... me·ta·li·*ko* ne·*ro*
sparkling	γκαζόζα	gha·*zo*·za
still	χωρίς ανθρακικό	kho·*ris* an·thra·ki·*ko*
(hot) water	(ζεστό) νερό n	(ze·*sto*) ne·*ro*
bottled water	εμφιαλωμένο νερό n	em·fi·a·lo·*me*·no ne·*ro*
tap water	νερό βρύσης n	ne·*ro* *vri*·sis
apple juice	χυμός μήλου m	hi·*mos* *mi*·lu
hot chocolate	ζεστή σοκολάτα n	ze·*sti* so·ko·*la*·ta
herbal tea	τσάι από βότανα n	*tsa*·i a·*po* *vo*·ta·na
sour cherry juice	βυσσινάδα f	vi·si·*na*·ţha
orange juice	χυμός πορτοκάλι m	hi·*mos* por·to·*ka*·li
soft drink	αναψυκτικό n	a·nap·sik·ti·*ko*
(cup of) tea	(ένα φλυτζάνι) τσάι n	(e·na fli·*dza*·ni) *tsa*·i
(cup of) coffee	(ένα φλυτζάνι) καφέ m	(e·na fli·*dza*·ni) ka·*fe*
with milk	με γάλα	me *gha*·la
with lemon	με λεμόνι	me le·*mo*·ni
sweetened	με ζάχαρη	me *za*·kha·ri
unsweetened	χωρίς ζάχαρη	kho·*ris* *za*·kha·ri

COFFEE TIME

black	χωρίς γάλα	kho·*ris* *gha*·la
decaffeinated	ντεκαφεϊνέ	de·ka·fe·i·*ne*
Espresso	εσπρέσο	es·*pres*·o
Espresso freddo	εσπρέσο φρέντο	es·*pres*·o *fre*·do
Greek	ελληνικός	e·li·ni·*kos*
Frappe	φραπέ	fra·*pe*
instant	στιγμιαίος	stigh·*mi*·e·os
medium	μέτριος	*me*·tri·os
plain (no sugar)	σκέτος	*ske*·tos
strong	δυνατός	ţhi·na·*tos*
sweet	γλυκός	ghli·*kos*
weak	ελαφρύς	e·la·*fris*
with milk	με γάλα	me *gha*·la

LOCAL LIQUORS

κουμανταρία f	ku·ma·da·*ri*·a	traditional Cypriot wine
ζιβανία f	zi·va·*ni*·a	a clear Cypriot apéritif made from grapes
ούζο n	*u*·zo	aniseed-flavoured spirit
ρετσίνα f	ret·*si*·na	pine-resinated wine, served chilled
τσίπουρο n	*tsi*·pu·ro	spirit made from grapes, high in alcohol
τσικουδιά f	tsi·ku·*ţhia*	Crete's version of τσίπουρο

ALCOHOLIC DRINKS

Αλκοολούχα ποτά

To get drinks at a bar in Greece, you don't have to memorise numerous measurements – standard serves are ordered using 'one'. For example: μία μπύρα *mi*·a *bi*·ra (one beer) or ένα ούζο *e*·na *u*·zo (one ouzo). See also **numbers & amounts** (p35).

beer	μπύρα f	*bi*·ra
brandy	μπράντι n	*bran*·di
Champagne	σαμπάνια f	sam·*pa*·nia
cocktail	κοκτέηλ n	kok·*te*·il
a glass of ...	ένα ... m	e·na ...
gin	τζιν	dzin
rum	ρούμι	*ru*·mi
whisky	ουίσκι	u·*i*·ski

a shot of ...	μία ... **f**	mia ...
tequila	τεκίλα	te·*ki*·la
vodka	βότκα	*vot*·ka
a bottle/glass of ... wine	ένα μπουκάλι/ ποτήρι ... κρασί **n**	e·na bu·*ka*·li / po·*ti*·ri ... kra·*si*
dessert	επιδόρπιο	e·pi·*ţhor*·pi·o
dry	ξηρό	ksi·*ro*
red	κόκκινο	*ko*·ki·no
rosé	ροζέ	ro·*ze*
sparkling	αφρώδες κρασί	af·*ro*·ţhes kra·*si*
sweet	γλυκό	ghli·*ko*
white	λευκό	lef·*ko*
a ... of beer	ένα ... μπύρα **n**	e·na ... *bi*·ra
glass	ποτήρι	po·*ti*·ri
pint	μεγάλο ποτήρι	me·*gha*·lo po·*ti*·ri
small bottle	μικρό μπουκάλι	mi·*kro* bu·*ka*·li
large bottle	μεγάλο μπουκάλι	me·*gha*·lo bu·*ka*·li
a ... of beer	μια ... μπύρα **f**	mia ... *bi*·ra
carafe	καράφα	ka·*ra*·fa
jug	κανάτα	ka·*na*·ta

GIVE IT A GO

Try more traditional Greek delicacies from these eating options:

αρτοποιείο n	ar·to·pi·*i*·o	bakery
ζαχαροπλαστείο n	za·kha·ro·pla·*sti*·o	patisserie or sweet shop
γαλακτοπωλείο n	gha·lak·to·po·li·o	dairy shop
καντίνα f	kan·*ti*·na	canteen or food van
μεζεδοπωλείο f	me·ze·ţho·po·*li*·o	meze restaurant
σουβλατζίδικο n	suv·lat·*zi*·ţhi·ko	kebab and souvlaki shop
τυροπωλείο n	ti·ro·po·*li*·o	cheese shop
ψαροταβέρνα f	psa·ro·ta·*ver*·na	fish taverna
ψητοπωλείο n	psi·to·po·*li*·o	eatery serving spit-roasted and barbecue-style meat

IN THE BAR

στο μπαρ

Excuse me!
Συγνώμη! — sigh·*no*·mi

I'm next.
Είναι η δική μου σειρά. — *i*·ne i ţhi·*ki* mu si·*ra*

I'll have ...
Θα πάρω … — tha *pa*·ro ...

Same again, please.
Μία Από τα ίδια, παρακαλώ. — *mi*·a a·*po* ta *i*·ţhia pa·ra·ka·*lo*

No ice, thanks.
Όχι πάγο, ευχαριστώ. — o·hi *pa*·gho ef·kha·ri·*sto*

I'll buy you a drink.
Θα σε κεράσω εγώ. — tha se ke·*ra*·so e·*gho*

What would you like?
Τι θα ήθελες; — ti tha *i*·the·les

I don't drink alcohol.
Δεν πίνω αλκοόλ. — ţhen *pi*·no al·ko·*ol*

It's my round.
Κερνάω εγώ. — ker·*na*·o e·*go*

How much is that?
Πόσο κάνει αυτό; — *po*·so *ka*·ni af·*to*

Do you serve meals here?
Σερβίρετε φαγητό εδώ; — ser·*vi*·re·te fa·yi·*to* e·*ţho*

LISTEN FOR

Τι θα παρεις;
ti tha *pa*·ris — **What are you having?**

Νομίζω ήπιες αρκετά.
no·*mi*·zo *i*·ples ar·ke·*ta* — **I think you've had enough.**

Τελευταίς παραγγελίες.
te·lef·*te*·es pa·ra·ghe·*li*·es — **Last orders.**

Τα ποτά τα κερνάει το κατάστημα.
ta po·*ta* ta ker·*na*·i to ka·*ta*·sti·ma — **Drinks are on the house.**

DRINKING UP

τα πίνουμε

Cheers!
Στην υγειά μας! — stin i·*yia*·mas

I feel fantastic!
Είμαι στα κέφια μου! — *i*·me sta *ke*·fia mu

I think I've had one too many.
Νομίζω ήπια παραπάνω. — no·*mi*·zo *i*·pia pa·ra·*pa*·no

I'm feeling drunk.
Μέθυσα. — *me*·thi·sa

I feel ill.
Δεν αισθάνομαι καλά. — ţhen es·*tha*·no·me ka·*la*

Where's the toilet?
Πού είναι η τουαλέτα; — pu *i*·ne i tu·a·*le*·ta

I'm tired, I'd better go home.
Είμαι κουρασμένος/κουρασμένη, καλύτερα να πάω σπίτι. **m/f** — *i*·me ku·raz·*me*·nos / ku·raz·*me*·ni ka·*li*·te·ra na *pa*·o *spi*·ti

Can you call a taxi for me?
Μπορείς να μου καλέσεις ένα ταξί; — bo·*ris* na mu ka·*le*·sis e·na tak·*si*

I don't think you should drive.
Νομίζω ότι δεν πρέπει να οδηγήσεις. — no·*mi*·zo o·ti ţhen *pre*·pi na o·ţhi·*yi*·sis

POT PLANT

When you're in Greece, you shouldn't necessarily eat the decoration – βασιλικός va · si · li · *kos* (basil) is often used as an ornamental plant.

Self-catering

ΦΡΟΝΤΙΖΟΝΤΑΣ ΓΙΑ ΤΟΝ ΕΑΥΤΟ ΣΟΥ

What's the local speciality?
Ποιες είναι οι τοπικές λιχουδιές; — pies *i*·ne i to·pi·*kes* li·khu·*ţhies*

What's that?
Τι είναι εκείνο; — ti *i*·ne e·*ki*·no

Can I taste it?
Μπορώ να το δοκιμάσω; — bo·*ro* na to ţho·ki·*ma*·so

Can I have a bag, please?
Μπορώ να έχω μια σακούλα, παρακαλώ; — bo·*ro* na e·kho mia sa·*ku*·la pa·ra·ka·*lo*

How much is (a kilo of cheese)?
Πόσο κάνει (ένα κιλό τυρί); — *po*·so *ka*·ni (e·na ki·*lo* ti·*ri*)

I'd like ...	Θα ήθελα ...	tha *i*·the·la ...
(three) pieces	(τρία) κομμάτια	(*tri*·a) ko·*ma*·tia
(six) slices	(έξι) φέτες	(*ek*·si) *fe*·tes
that one	εκείνο	e·*ki*·no
this one	αυτό	af·*to*

Less.	Πιο λίγο.	pio *li*·gho
A bit more.	Λιγάκι πιο πολύ.	li·*gha*·ki pio po·*li*
Enough.	Αρκετά.	ar·ke·*ta*

For more on quantities, see **numbers & amounts**, p35.

LISTEN FOR

Δεν υπάρχει άλλο.
ţhen i·*par*·hi *a*·lo — **There's none left.**

Μπορώ να σας βοηθήσω;
bo·*ro* na sas vo·i·*thi*·so — **Can I help you?**

Τι θα θέλατε;
ti tha *the*·la·te — **What would you like?**

Τίποτε άλλο;
ti·po·te a·lo — **Anything else?**

FOOD STUFF

cooked	μαγειρεμένο	ma·yi·re·*me*·no
cured	παστό	pa·*sto*
dried	ξηρό	ksi·*ro*
fresh	φρέσκο	*fre*·sko
frozen	κατεψυγμένο	ka·tep·sigh·*me*·no
grilled	στο γκριλ	sto grill
raw	ωμό	o·*mo*
roasted	ψητό	psi·*to*
savoury	αλμυρό	al·mi·*ro*
smoked	καπνιστό	kap·ni·*sto*
sweet	γλυκό	ghli·*ko*

Do you have ...?	Έχετε κάτι ...;	e·he·te *ka*·ti ...
anything cheaper	πιο οικονομικό	pio i·ko·no·mi·*ko*
other kinds	διαφορετικό	ţhia·fo·re·ti·*ko*

Where can I find the ... section?	Πού μπορώ να βρω το τμήμα με ...;	pu bo·*ro* na vro to *tmi*·ma me ...
bread	το ψωμί	to pso·*mi*
dairy	τα γαλακτοκομικά	ta gha·lak·to·mi·*ka*
fish	τα ψάρια	ta *psa*·ria
frozen goods	τα κατεψυγμένα	ta ka·tep·sigh·*me*·na
fruit and vegetable	τα φρούτα και τα λαχανικά	ta *fru*·ta ke ta la·kha·ni·*ka*
meat	το κρέας	to *kre*·as
poultry	τα πουλερικά	ta pu·le·ri·*ka*
seafood	τα θαλασσινά	ta tha·la·si·*na*

Could I please borrow a ...?	Μπορώ παρακαλώ να δανειστώ ...;	bo·*ro* pa·ra·ka·*lo* na ţha·ni·*sto* ...
I need a ...	Χρειάζομαι ...	khri·*a*·zo·me ...
chopping board	μια σανίδα κοπής	mia sa·*ni*·ţha ko·*pis*
frying pan	ένα τηγάνι	e·na ti·*gha*·ni
knife	ένα μαχαίρι	e·na ma·*he*·ri
saucepan	μια κατσαρόλα	mia kat·sa·*ro*·la

For more cooking implements, see the **dictionary**, p207.

Vegetarian & Special Meals

ΦΑΓΗΤΑ ΓΙΑ ΧΟΡΤΟΦΑΓΟΥΣ ΚΑΙ ΕΙΔΙΚΑ ΠΙΑΤΑ

ORDERING FOOD

παραγγέλλοντας φαγητό

Do you have ... food?	Έχετε φαγητό ...;	e·he·te fa·yi·*to* ...
halal	χαλάλ	kha·*lal*
kosher	κοσέρ	ko·*ser*
Lent	Σαρακοστιανό	sa·ra·ko·stia·*no*
pulse-based	με όσπρια	me *os*·pri·a
vegetarian	για χορτοφάγους	yia khor·to·*fa*·ghus

Is there a ... restaurant near here?
Υπάρχει ένα εστιατόριο ... εδώ κοντά; — i·*par*·hi e·na e·sti·a·*to*·ri·o ... e·*ţho* ko·*da*

Is it cooked in / with ...?
Είναι μαγειρεμένο σε/με ...; — *i*·ne ma·yi·re·*me*·no se / me ...

Could you prepare a meal without ...?
Μπορείτε να φτιάξετε φαγητό χωρίς ...; — bo·*ri*·te na *ftia*·xe·te fa·yi·*to* kho·*ris* ...

I don't eat ...	Δεν τρώω ...	ţhen *tro*·o ...
butter	βούτυρο	*vu*·ti·ro
eggs	αβγά	av·*gha*
fish	ψάρι	*psa*·ri
fish stock	ζωμός ψαριού	zo·*mos* psa·*riou*
lamb	αρνί	ar·*ni*
(red) meat	(κόκκινο) κρέας	(*ko*·ki·no) *kre*·as
meat stock	ζωμός κρέατος	zo·*mos* *kre*·a·tos
oil	λάδι	*la*·ţhi
olives	ελιές	e·*lies*
pork	χοιρινό	hi·ri·*no*
poultry	πουλερικά	pu·le·ri·*ka*

Is this ...?	Είναι αυτό ...;	*i*·ne af·*to* ...
decaffeinated	χωρίς καφεΐνη	kho·*ris* ka·fe·*i*·ni
gluten-free	χωρίς γλουτένη	kho·*ris* ghlu·*te*·ni
low in fat	χαμηλό σε λιπαρά	kha·mi·*lo* se li·pa·*ra*
low in sugar	χαμηλό σε ζάχαρη	kha·mi·*lo* se *za*·kha·ri
organic	βιολογικό	vi·o·lo·ghi·*ko*
salt-free	χωρίς αλάτι	kho·*ris* a·*la*·ti

SPECIAL DIETS & ALLERGIES

ειδικές δίαιτες και αλλεργίες

I'm on a special diet.
Ακολουθώ ειδική δίαιτα. a·ko·lu·*tho* i·ţhi·*ki* *ţhi*·e·ta

I'm allergic to ...	Είμαι αλλεργικός/αλλεργική ... **m/f**	*i*·me a·ler·yi·*kos*/a·ler·yi·*ki* ...
dairy produce	στα γαλακτοκομικά	sta gha·lak·to·mi·*ka*
eggs	στα αβγά	sta av·*gha*
gluten	στη γλουτένη	sti ghlu·*te*·ni
honey	στο μέλι	sto *me*·li
MSG	στο MSG	sto em s dzi
nuts	στους ξηρούς καρπούς	stus ksi·*rus* kar·*pus*
seafood	στα θαλασσινά	sta tha·la·si·*na*
shellfish	στα οστρακοειδή	sta os·tra·ko·i·*ţhi*

I'm (a) ...	Είμαι ...	*i*·me ...
Buddhist	Βουδιστής **m** Βουδίστρια **f**	vu·ţhi·*stis* vu·*ţhi*·stri·a
Hindu	Ινδουιστής **m** Ινδουίστρια **f**	in·ţhu·i·*stis* in·ţhu·*i*·stri·a
Jewish	Ιουδαίος **m** Ιουδαία **f**	i·u·*ţhe*·os i·u·*ţhe*·a
Muslim	Μουσουλμάνος **m** Μουσουλμάνα **f**	mu·sul·*ma*·nos mu·sul·*ma*·na
vegan	βίγκαν **m&f**	*ve*·gan
vegetarian	χορτοφάγος **m&f**	khor·to·*fa*·ghos

Menu Decoder

ΟΔΗΓΟΣ ΓΑΣΤΡΟΝΟΜΙΑΣ

This miniguide lists dishes and ingredients used in Greek cuisine. It's designed to help you get the most out of your gastronomic experience by providing you with food terms that you may see on menus. For certain dishes we've marked the region or city where they're most popular.

The **menu decoder** has been ordered according to the Greek alphabet:

Α α Β β Γ γ Δ δ Ε ε Ζ ζ Η η Θ θ Ι ι Κ κ Λ λ Μ μ
Ν ν Ξ ξ Ο ο Π π Ρ ρ Σ σ/ς Τ τ Υ υ Φ φ Χ χ Ψ ψ Ω ω

Α α

αβγολέμονο ⓝ av·gho·*le*·mo·no egg and lemon sauce added to meat, chicken or fish soup and other dishes

αβγοτάραχο ⓝ av·gho·*ta*·ra·kho salted, cured grey mullet roe, coated in beeswax

αγκινάρες ⓕ pl a·gi·*na*·res globe artichokes

— **αλαπολίτα** a·la·po·*li*·ta 'Constantinople-style artichokes' – artichokes, carrots & potatoes in dill-spiked chicken stock

— **καλόγριες** ka·*lo*·ghri·es 'nuns' – artichoke hearts braised in creamy onion broth (Crete)

αγγουροντομάτα σαλάτα ⓕ ang·gu·ro·do·*ma*·ta sa·*la*·ta cucumber slices, tomato wedges with oil & salt

αγγουροσαλάτα ⓕ ang·gu·ro·sa·*la*·ta sliced cucumbers sprinkled with salt & served with oil & vinegar

άγρια χόρτα ⓝ pl *a*·ghri·a *khor*·ta seasonal wild greens

άγρια σπαράγγια ⓝ pl *a*·ghri·a spa·*rang*·gi·a wild asparagus

άγριες αγκινάρες ⓕ pl *a*·ghri·es ang·gi·*na*·res small prickly artichokes, eaten raw with salt & lemon juice

αμελέτητα ⓝ pl a·me·*le*·ti·ta beef or lamb testicles

αμπελοφάσουλα ⓝ pl am·be·lo·*fa*·su·la green beans

αρμπαρόριζα ⓕ ar·ba·*ro*·ri·za rose geranium (leaves are used as a flavouring for cakes, pastries & preserved fruits)

αμύγδαλα ⓝ pl *migh*·ţha·la almonds

αμυγδαλωτά ⓝ pl a·migh·ţha·lo·*ta* almond shortbread sprinkled with icing sugar & chopped almonds

αμυγδαλωτό γλύκισμα ⓝ a·migh·ţha·lo·*to* *ghli*·kiz·ma nougat

αναρή ⓕ a·na·*ri* soft ricotta-like cheese from goat's or sheep's milk (Cyprus)

αρακάς ⓜ a·ra·*kas* fresh peas

— **λαδερός** la·*ţhe*·ros peas stewed with carrots, garlic bulbs & herbs in oil & paprika (Corfu)

αρνάκι ⓝ ar·*na*·ki milk-lamb (very young lamb)

— **γεμιστό** ye·mi·*sto* Easter dish of stuffed roast lamb (Dodecanese Islands)

αρνί ⓝ ar·*ni* lamb

— **βραστό** vra·*sto* slow-boiled mutton served with mutton-stock soup (Crete)

— **γιαχνί** yiakh·*ni* lamb stewed with tomatoes, onions, carrots & celery

— **γιουβέτσι με κριθαράκι** yiu·*vet*·si me kri·tha·*ra*·ki lamb baked with tomatoes & barley-shaped pasta in an earthenware pot

— **εξοχικό** ek·so·hi·*ko* 'country-style lamb' – baked filo parcels of lamb, potato, feta & **κεφαλοτύρι**

— **φρικασέ με μαρούλι** fri·ka·se me ma·*ru*·li poached lamb with shredded lettuce, egg & lemon sauce
— **κεφαλάκι ριγανάτο** ke·fa·*la*·ki ri·gha·*na*·to lamb's head (generally roasted) complete with tongue, cheek, brains & eyes
— **κοκκινιστό** ko·ki·ni·*sto* lamb braised in white wine with onions & bay leaves
— **οφτό** of·*to* roast lamb on the spit
— **στη σούβλα** sti *suv*·la spit-roast lamb basted with olive oil, lemon juice & garlic – a traditional Easter dish
— **στο φούρνο** sto *fur*·no roasted leg or shoulder of lamb

αρνίσια παϊδάκια ⓝ pl ar·*ni*·sia pa·i·*ţha*·kia marinated & chargrilled lamb cutlets

αστακός a·sta·*kos* ⓜ lobster, usually boiled or chargrilled

αφέλια ⓝ pl a·*fe*·lia pork braised with potato & mushrooms in red wine

αχηβάδα ⓕ a·hi·*va*·ţha clam

αχινοί ⓜ pl a·hi·*ni* sea urchins
— **σαλάτα** sa·*la*·ta sea urchin salad
— **γεμιστοί** ye·mi·*sti* sea urchin stuffed with rice, onions & tomatoes

Β β

βασιλόπιτα ⓕ va·si·*lo*·pi·ta New Year loaf decorated with almonds – whoever finds the coin in the bread is blessed with good luck for the year ahead

βατόμουρο ⓝ va·*to*·mu·ro blackberry

βατραχοπόδαρα τηγανητά ⓝ pl va·tra·kho·*po*·ţha·ra ti·gha·ni·*ta* fried frog's legs (Western Greece)

βυσσινάδα ⓕ vi·si·*na*·ţha syrup of morello cherries – mixed with cold water for summer-time cordials

βύσσινο ⓝ *vi*·si·no morello cherry • sour black cherry
— **γλυκό** ghli·*ko* morello cherry preserve

βλίτο ⓝ *vli*·to amaranth – its sweet nutty flavour & soft texture make it popular for warm salads

βοδινό ⓝ vo·ţhi·*no* beef
— **καπαμά** ka·pa·*ma* beef stewed with tomatoes, red wine, cinnamon & cloves
— **με λαχανικά** me la·kha·ni·*ka* beef braised with carrots, potatoes & celery

βολβοί ⓜ pl vol·*vi* grape hyacinth bulbs
— **βραστοί** vra·*sti* bulbs boiled, dressed with dill vinaigrette & accompanied by **σκορδαλιά** garlic dip

βρούβα ⓕ *vru*·va charlock • field green with sharp peppery taste

Γ γ

γαϊδουρελιά ⓕ gha·i·ţhu·re·*lia* 'donkey olive' – named so because of its large size

γαλακτομπούρεκο ⓝ gha·lak·to·*bu*·re·ko baked custard-cream filo pie sprinkled with a lemony syrup

γαλοπούλα ⓕ gha·lo·*pu*·la turkey
— **γεμιστή** ye·mi·*sti* stuffed roast turkey

γαλύπες ⓕ pl gha·*li*·pes a sea anemone
— **τηγανητές** ti·gha·ni·*tes* lightly battered & fried sea anemone

γαλυποκεφτέδες ⓜ pl gha·li·po·kef·*te*·ţhes sea anemone rissoles

γαρδούμια ⓝ pl ghar·*ţhu*·mia small offal rolls made from strips of lamb's stomach, bound with intestines then roasted

γαρίδες ⓕ pl gha·*ri*·ţhes prawns • shrimps
— **σαγανάκι** sa·gha·*na*·ki prawns fried with tomatoes & red wine, topped with feta & baked
— **τηγανητές** ti·gha·ni·*tes* fried prawns
— **βραστές** vra·*stes* boiled prawns accompanied by **λαδολέμονο**
— **γιουβετσάκι** yiu·vet·*sa*·ki prawns with tomatoes, parsley, oregano & feta chunks baked in earthenware pots

γαριδοσαλάτα ⓕ gha·ri·ţho·sa·*la*·ta prawn salad

γαύρος ⓜ *ghav*·ros fresh anchovy

γεμιστά ⓝ pl ye·mi·*sta* stuffed vegetables

γεμιστός ye·mi·*stos* method of stuffing meat, fish or vegetables prior to cooking

γιαούρτι ⓝ yia·*ur*·ti thick, heavy yoghurt with a tangy bite, made from sheep's, goat's or cow's milk
— **αγελάδος** a·ye·*la*·ţhos cow's milk yoghurt
— **φρούτων** *fru*·ton fruit yoghurt
— **με μέλι** me *me*·li yoghurt with honey
— **πρόβειο** *pro*·vio sheep's milk yoghurt

γιαουρτλού ⓕ yia·ur·*tlu* pie cooked with finely sliced grilled meat, topped with a yoghurt sauce
γιαουρτόπιτα ⓕ yia·ur·*to*·pi·ta light moist cake made with yoghurt, sugar, lemon rind & lots of eggs
γίδα βραστή ⓕ *yi*·tha vra·*sti* aromatic dish of boiled goat
γύρος *yi*·ros 'to spin' – seasoned lamb packed onto a spit & rotisseried upright, carved for meat platters or served in **πίτα** with tomatoes, onions & **τζατζίκι**
γιορτή ⓕ yior·*ti* small pieces of pork & goat boiled with corn, topped with melted butter, cinnamon & pepper (Samos)
γιουβαρλάκια ⓝ pl *yiu*·var·*la*·kia egg-shaped rissoles of minced beef or lamb simmered in a light stock
γιουβέτσι ⓝ yiu·*vet*·si casserole of meat & seafood with tomatoes & barley pasta
— **με θαλασσινά** me tha·la·si·*na* casserole of seafood, barley pasta, tomatoes & chicken stock (Ionian Islands)
γιουσλεμέδες ⓜ pl yiuz·le·*me*·thes golden pies filled with eggs & **κεφαλοτύρι**, deep-fried then served with grated cheese (Lesvos)
γλιστρίδα ⓕ ghli·*stri*·tha purslane – small-leafed plant with lemony flavour & crisp texture used mainly in salads
— **με καπαρόφυλλα σαλάτα** me ka·pa·*ro*·fi·la sa·*la*·ta purslane leaves, sliced tomatoes, black olives & caper leaves with oil & lemon dressing
— **με γιαούρτι** me yia·*ur*·ti chopped purslane beaten with strained yoghurt, garlic, lemon, salt & oil (Crete)
γλυκά κουταλιού ⓝ pl ghli·*ka* ku·ta·*liu* 'spoon sweets' – preserved fruits
γλυκάνισο ⓝ ghli·*ka*·ni·so aniseed
γλυκά ταψιού ⓝ pl ghli·*ka* tap·*siu* sweets made with filo pastry
γλύκισμα ⓝ pl *ghli*·kiz·ma sweet pastry • cake
γλυκοκολοκύθα ⓕ ghli·ko·ko·lo·*ki*·tha marrow • pumpkin • squash
γλώσσα ⓕ *ghlo*·sa tongue (fish) • generic name for any flat fish
— **μοσχαρίσια κρασάτη** mo·sha·*ri*·sia kra·*sa*·ti tongue (fish) fried in butter, then poached in white wine
γουρουνάκι (του γάλακτος) ⓝ ghu·ru·*na*·ki (tu *gha*·lak·tos) piglet • suckling pig
— **στη σούβλα** sti *suv*·la whole suckling pig spit-roasted until tender
— **γεμιστό με φέτα** ye·mi·*sto* me *fe*·ta suckling pig stuffed with feta & roasted
γυαλιστερές ⓕ pl yia·li·ste·*res* shellfish eaten fresh with a squeeze of lemon juice (Dodecanese Islands)

Δ δ

δάχτυλα ⓝ pl *thakh*·ti·la 'fingers' – deep-fried, nut-filled pastries (Cyprus)
δίπλες ⓕ pl *thi*·ples sweet pastry, deep-fried & drizzled with honey & sesame seeds
— **Δράμας** *thra*·mas yoghurt pie with vine leaves
δρύλοι αλευρολέμονο ⓜ pl *thri*·li a·lev·ro·*le*·mo·no wild greens in lemon

Ε ε

ελαιόλαδο ⓝ e·le·*o*·la·tho olive oil
ελαιόπιτες ⓕ pl e·le·*o*·pi·tes small olive & leek pies (Cyprus)
ελαιότη ⓕ e·le·*o*·ti bread with a layer of chopped black olives & onions (Cyprus)
ελαιόψωμο ⓝ e·le·*op*·so·mo olive bread
ελιές ⓕ pl e·*lies* olives
— **Αμφίσσης** am·*fi*·sis large blue-black olives with nutty flavour
— **Αταλάντης** a·ta·*lan*·dis big fruity greenish-purple or purple olives
— **χαμούρες** ha·*mu*·res dried newly fallen olives
— **Ιονίων πράσινες** i·o·*ni*·on *pra*·si·nes mild green olives (Ionian Islands)
— **Καλαμάτας** ka·la·*ma*·tas large black olives with pungent flavour
— **μαύρες** *mav*·res black olives
— **Ναυπλίου** naf·*pli*·u nutty flavoured green olives (Nafplio)
— **παστές** pa·*stes* dried salted olives
— **πελτέ** pel·*te* olive paste
— **πράσινες** *pra*·si·nes green olives

— **τσακιστές** tsa·ki·*stes* cracked green olives marinated in oil, lemon & herbs
— **τουρσί** tur·*si* pickled olives
ελίτσες ⓕ pl e·*lit*·ses tiny sweet black olives
εντόσθια ⓝ pl en·*do*·sthi·a offal • innards (usually lamb)
— **κοκκινιστά** ko·ki·ni·*sta* chicken giblets in a rich gravy
— **πουλιών** pu·*lion* giblets

Ζ ζ

ζαχαροπούλια ⓝ pl za·kha·ro·*pu*·lia marzipan sweets (Lesvos)
ζαχαρωτό με αμύγδαλο ⓝ za·kha·ro·*to* me a·*migh*·ţha·lo marzipan
ζαμπόν ⓝ zam·*bon* ham
ζαργάνα ⓕ zar·*gha*·na garfish
ζύμη ⓕ *zi*·mi pastry
— **με γιαούρτι** me yia·*ur*·ti baked pasta dish consisting of homemade macaroni, strained yoghurt & onions (Kos)

Θ θ

θαλασσινά ⓝ pl tha·la·si·*na* seafood
— **του Αιγαίου** tu e·*ye*·u paella-style rice dish cooked with seafood (Hydra)
θρούμπες ⓕ pl *thru*·mbes ripe black olives
θυμάρι ⓝ thi·*ma*·ri thyme

Ι ι

ιμάμ-μπαϊλντί ⓝ i·*mam*·ba·il·*di* Turkish-inspired dish of aubergine/eggplant stuffed with aubergine/eggplant pulp, tomato, garlic, onion, parsley, then baked

Κ κ

καβούρι ⓝ ka·*vu*·ri crab
— **βραστό** vra·*sto* crab boiled & dressed with **λαδολέμονο**
καϊμάκι ⓝ to ka·i·*ma*·ki froth that forms on top of Greek coffee while it brews
— **πηγμένο** pigh·*me*·no clotted cream
κακαβιά ⓕ ka·ka·*via* saltwater fish soup
καλαμαράκια ⓝ pl ka·la·ma·*ra*·kia baby squid
καλαμάρι ⓝ ka·la·*ma*·ri squid
— **γεμιστό** ye·mi·*sto* squid stuffed with rice & baked in a lemony broth
— **Λεβριανά** lev·ria·*na* squid stewed in dry red wine with green olives, tomatoes, onions & parsley
— **με ρύζι** me *ri*·zi fried squid with onions simmered with water, crushed tomatoes, rice & cinnamon
— **τηγανητό** ti·gha·ni·*to* squid cut in rings or strips, lightly battered & fried
καλιτσούνια ⓝ pl ka·lit·*su*·nia small cheese pies
καπαμάς ⓜ ka·pa·*mas* method of stewing meat with tomatoes, wine, cinnamon & sometimes red pepper/capsicum & cloves
κάππαρη ⓕ *ka*·pa·ri capers, usually pickled & eaten as an appetiser
κάπρος ⓜ *ka*·pros wild boar
καραμέλα ⓕ ka·ra·*me*·la sweets • candy • caramel
καραβίδα ⓕ ka·ra·*vi*·ţha crayfish
καρύδια ⓝ pl ka·*ri*·ţhia walnuts
— **γεμιστά** ye·mi·*sta* walnuts & roasted almonds preserved in syrup (Cyprus)
καρυδόπιτα ⓕ ka·ri·*ţho*·pi·ta rich moist walnut cake
κάσιου ⓝ *ka*·siu cashews
καταΐφι ⓝ ka·ta·*i*·fi 'angel hair' pastry – syrupy nest-like nut-filled rolls
κατσικάκι ⓝ kat·si·*ka*·ki goat • kid
— **πατούδο** pa·*tu*·ţho roast kid stuffed with liver, rice, breadcrumbs, feta & raisins or **κεφαλοτύρι**, bacon, rice & dill (Cyclades)
— **ψητό** psi·*to* roast kid, sometimes served with a spicy red wine sauce
καφές ⓜ ka·*fes* coffee
— **ελληνικός** e·li·ni·*kos* freshly brewed Greek coffee
— **γλυκός** ghli·*kos* sweet coffee
— **μέτριος** *me*·tri·os medium-strength coffee with a little sugar
— **πολλά βαρύς** po·*la* va·*ris* strong coffee
— **σκέτος** *ske*·tos sugarless coffee
— **βαρύγλυκος** va·*ri*·ghli·kos strong & sweet coffee
κεφαλάκι ⓝ ke·fa·*la*·ki head – usually refers specifically to lamb's head

κεφτεδάκια (n) pl kef·te·*ţha*·kia miniature meat rissoles served at parties
κεφαλοτύρι (n) ke·fa·lo·*ti*·ri 'head cheese' – known as 'kefalotiri', a hard, pale yellow cheese made from sheep and goat's milk
κεφτέδες (m) pl kef·*te*·ţhes small tasty rissoles, often made with minced lamb, pork or veal
— **στη σχάρα** sti *skha*·ra chargrilled meat rissoles
κιχώρι (n) ki·*kho*·ri chicory • green leaves
κιμαδόπιτα (f) ki·ma·*ţho*·pi·ta mincemeat pie
κιμάς ki·*mas* (m) sauce made from mincemeat, onions & tomatoes served with pasta or rice
κληματόφυλλο (n) kli·ma·*to*·fi·lo vine leaf
κοφίσι (n) ko·*fi*·si pie made from boiled & shredded dried fish mixed with onion, garlic, rice & tomatoes (Kefallonia)
κόκκοι καφέ (m) pl *ko*·ki ka·*fe* coffee beans
κοκκινέλι (n) ko·ki·*ne*·li red resinated wine
κόκκινη πιπεριά (f) *ko*·ki·ni pi·pe·*ria* red pepper / capsicum
κοκκινιστό (n) ko·ki·ni·*sto* 'reddened' – method of simmering meat, chicken or rice with tomatoes
κόκκινο φασόλι (n) *ko*·ki·no fa·*so*·li red kidney bean
— **λάχανο** *la*·kha·no red cabbage
κοκκινοπίπερο (n) ko·ki·no·*pi*·pe·ro cayenne (spice)
κόκορας (m) *ko*·ko·ras rooster
— **κρασάτος** kra·*sa*·tos lightly floured rooster fried with onions & spices, then cooked in red wine sauce
κοκορέτσι (n) ko·ko·*ret*·si chopped lamb offal wrapped in lamb's intestines & grilled
κοκορόζουμο (n) ko·ko·*ro*·zu·mo lemony rooster broth used as a post-party pick-me-up (Cyclades)
κολιός (m) ko·li·*os* mackerel
— **λαδορίγανη** la·ţho·*ri*·gha·ni mackerel baked with oil, lemon, oregano, garlic & parsley
— **σε κληματόφυλλα** kli·ma·*to*·fi·la mackerel in vine leaves
κολιτσάνοι (m) pl ko·lit·*sa*·ni a sea anemone
κολοκέτα (n) pl ko·lo·*ke*·ta pastries stuffed with red pumpkin, raisins & cracked wheat (Cyprus)
κολοκύθα (f) ko·lo·*ki*·tha marrow • pumpkin • squash
κολοκυθάκια (n) pl ko·lo·ki·*tha*·kia courgette • zucchini
— **με αβγά** me av·*gha* courgette / zucchini & egg omelette
— **τηγανητά** ti·gha·ni·*ta* courgette / zucchini battered & deep-fried, served with lemon & **σκορδαλιά**
— **βραστά** vra·*sta* boiled baby courgette / zucchini with oil & lemon dressing
κολοκύθι (n) ko·lo·*ki*·thi marrow • pumpkin • squash
κολοκυθόανθοι (m) pl ko·lo·ki·*tho*·an·thi courgette / zucchini flowers
— **τηγανητοί** ti·gha·ni·*ti* courgette / zucchini flowers & cheese fritters (Andros)
— **γεμιστοί** ye·mi·*sti* courgette / zucchini flower **ντολμάδες** stuffed with rice, tomato & parsley & simmered until tender
κολοκυθοκεφτέδες ko·lo·ki·tho·kef·*te*·ţhes rissoles of puréed courgette / zucchini, parsley, onion, mint & garlic
κολοκυθόπιτα (f) ko·lo·ki·*tho*·pi·ta courgette / zucchini pie
κόλυβα (n) pl *ko*·li·va wheat mixed with fruit, pomegranate seeds, sugar & nuts – eaten after the death of a family member & on the anniversary of their death
κομπόστα (f) ko·*bo*·sta compote • stewed fruit
κονσερβολιά (f) kon·ser·vo·*lia* common type of olive from the central mainland
κοντοσούβλι (n) kon·do·*suv*·li spit-roast pieces of lamb or pork seasoned with onions, oregano, salt & pepper
κορωναίικη (f) ko·ro·*ne*·i·ki a smaller, oil-bearing variety of the kalamata olive
κοτόπιτα (f) ko·*to*·pi·ta chicken filo pastry
κοτόπουλο (n) ko·*to*·pu·lo chicken
— **χυλοπίτες** hi·lo·*pi*·tes whole chicken & noodles simmered in tomato, onion & cinnamon broth until liquid is absorbed
— **λεμονάτο** le·mo·*na*·to roast chicken basted with butter & lemon juice
— **με μπάμιες** me *ba*·mies chicken & okra braised in tomato & onion gravy

κοτόσουπα ⓕ ko·to·su·pa
soup made from boiled whole chicken
κρασί ⓝ kra·si wine
— **άσπρο** a·spro white wine
— **κόκκινο** ko·ki·no red wine
— **λευκό** lef·ko white wine
— **ροζέ** ro·ze rosé wine
κρέας ⓝ kre·as meat
— **ελαφιού** e·la·fiu venison
— **στη στάμνα** sti stam·na
meat cooked in a pot
— **στο φούρνο με πατάτες** sto fur·no me pa·ta·tes roast meat with potatoes
κρεατικά ⓝ pl kre·a·ti·ka
meat dishes, mostly stewed or roasted
κρεατόπιτα ⓕ kre·a·to·pi·ta
lamb or veal pie, usually with cinnamon
— **Κεφαλλονίτικη** ke·fa·lo·ni·ti·ki
meat pie cooked with onions, eggs, rice, potatoes, tomatoes & spices (Kefalonia)
— **της Κρήτης** tis kri·tis
pie of alternating layers of cubed lamb (or goat) & **μυζήθρα** covered in butter & baked in shortcrust pastry (Crete)
κρεατόσουπα ⓕ kre·a·to·su·pa nourishing broth made from boiled meat – sometimes thickened with rice & **αβγολέμονο**
κρεμμυδόπιτα ⓕ kre·mi·ţho·pi·ta
pie with a filling of **μυζήθρα**, grated onion, eggs & dill (Mykonos)
Κρητική κρεατόπιτα ⓕ
kri·ti·ki kre·a·to·pi·ta
see **κρεατόπιτα της Κρήτης**
κριθαράκι ⓝ kri·tha·ra·ki
tiny spindle-shaped barley pasta used for pasta dishes, soups & casseroles
— **με βούτυρο και τυρί** me vu·ti·ro ke ti·ri pasta baked with brown butter, cheese, lemon juice & herbs
κουκουβάγια ⓕ ku·ku·va·yia
see **παξιμάδια σαλάτα**
κουκιά ⓝ pl ku·kia broad beans
— **ξερά βραστά** kse·ra vra·sta broad beans boiled in water & lemon juice & served with oil, dill & onion rings
— **με αγριαγκινάρες**
me a·ghri·ang·gi·na·res
broad beans with artichokes
κουλουκόψωμο ⓝ ku·lu·kop·so·mo
see **παξιμάδια με ντομάτες και φέτα**
κουλουράκια ⓝ pl ku·lu·ra·kia
cookies • biscuits • buns
— **με πετιμέζι** me pe·ti·me·zi sweet buns made with syrup, cinnamon & spices
κουλούρι ⓝ ku·lu·ri crisp sesame-coated bread rings sold on streets • generic name for circular rolls, buns & biscuits
κουλούρια αστυπαλίτικα ⓝ pl ku·lu·ri·a a·sti·pa·li·ti·ka saffron biscuits (Astypalea)
κουμκουάτ ⓝ kum·ku·at cumquat
— **λικέρ** li·ker cumquat liqueur (Corfu)
Κουμμανταρία ⓕ ku·man·da·ri·a
heavy dessert wine originally made during the Crusades by the Knights of the Order of St John (Cyprus)
κουνέλι ⓝ ku·ne·li rabbit
— **κρασάτο** kra·sa·to rabbit casserole with red wine, garlic & bay leaves
— **με καρύδι** me ka·ri·ţhi marinated rabbit, fried & simmered in white wine infused with coarsely ground walnuts
— **με γιαούρτι** me yia·ur·ti
rabbit marinated in lemon juice & black pepper, then baked with a creamy egg & yoghurt sauce
— **στιφάδο** sti·fa·ţho rabbit ragout spiced with cloves, cinnamon & cumin
κουπέπια ⓝ pl ku·pe·pia **ντολμάδες** made with minced lamb & veal, served hot with **αβγολέμονο** sauce (Cyprus)
κούπες ⓕ pl ku·pes deep-fried pastries of mincemeat, onion & spices (Cyprus)
κουραμπιέδες ⓜ pl ku·ra·bie·ţhes
buttery almond shortbread
κυδώνι ⓝ ki·ţho·ni quince
— **μπελτές** bel·tes quince jelly
— **γλυκό** ghli·ko quince preserve flavoured with rose geranium
— **στο φούρνο** sto fur·no buttered quince baked in a water & sugar solution until liquid has caramelised
— **γεμιστό** ye·mi·sto arge quince stuffed with minced beef, rice, onions, raisins, cloves & nutmeg
κυδωνόπαστο ⓝ ki·ţho·no·pa·sto dark-red quince paste dried until firm, cut in small diamonds & dusted with sugar

Λ λ

λαβράκι ⓝ lav·*ra*·ki sea bass
— **στο αλάτι** sto a·*la*·ti whole sea bass buried in salt & baked – the salt-encrusted skin is slit & the flesh is eaten from the bone with an oil & lemon dressing

λαγάνα ⓕ la·*gha*·na bread sprinkled with sesame seeds baked on the first day of Lent

λαγός ⓜ la·*ghos* hare
— **στιφάδο** sti·*fa*·ţho hare ragout spiced with cumin & cloves, usually marinated in vinegar prior to cooking

λαγωτό ⓝ la·gho·*to* hare ragout (Kefallonia)

λαδόξιδο ⓝ la·*ţhok*·si·ţho vinaigrette of oil, vinegar, parsley, salt & pepper

λαδολέμονο ⓝ la·ţho·*le*·mo·no thick dressing of oil beaten with lemon juice, salt & pepper

λάχανα ⓝ pl *la*·kha·na seasonal wild greens
— **με λαρδί** me lar·*ţhi* casserole of seasonal greens & fatty bacon (Mykonos)

λαχανικά ⓝ pl la·kha·ni·*ka* vegetables
— **της θάλασσας** tis *tha*·la·sas sea vegetables

λάχανο ⓝ *la*·kha·no cabbage
— **κοκκινιστό** ko·ki·ni·*sto* cabbage stewed with tomatoes, onions, parsley, dill & paprika (Corfu)
— **με κιμά** me ki·*ma* cabbage braised with onions, mincemeat & tomatoes, finished with fresh butter (Chios)

λαχανοσαλάτα ⓕ la·kha·no·sa·*la*·ta shredded white cabbage sprinkled with oil, lemon juice & salt

λεμονάτος ⓜ le·mo·*na*·tos method of cooking with oil & lemon juice

λιθρίνι ⓝ li·*thri*·ni sea bream

λουκάνικα ⓝ pl lu·*ka*·ni·ka pork sausages seasoned with coriander & orange peel • generic word for sausages & frankfurters

λουκανόπιτες ⓕ pl lu·ka·*no*·pi·tes filo-wrapped sausages

λουκουμάδες ⓜ pl lu·ku·*ma*·ţhes rosette-shaped, light-as-air doughnuts served hot with honey & cinnamon

λουκούμι ⓝ lu·*ku*·mi Turkish delight

λουκούμια ⓝ pl lu·*ku*·mia wedding shortbread (Cyprus)

λούντζα ⓕ *lun*·dza spicy ham made from cured smoked pork fillet (Cyprus, Cyclades)
— **με χαλούμι** me kha·*lu*·mi grilled ham topped with melted **χαλούμι** (Cyprus)

λουβιά ⓝ pl lu·*via* black-eyed peas
— **με λάχανα** me *la*·kha·na warm salad of black-eyed peas & seasonal greens with oil & lemon dressing (Cyprus)

λουζές ⓜ lu·*zes* salted fillet of pork stuffed into thick pig's intestine & sun-dried (Mykonos)

λιαστός ⓜ lia·*stos* sun-dried

Μ μ

μαγειρίτσα ⓕ ma·yi·*rit*·sa lamb's offal soup thickened with rice & **αβγολέμονο**, eaten to celebrate the end of Lent

μακαρόνια ⓝ pl ma·ka·*ro*·nia macaroni • spaghetti
— **με κιμά** me ki·*ma* pasta with a sauce of mincemeat, tomatoes, onions & red wine
— **με σάλτσα** me *sal*·tsa pasta with tomato, onion & oregano sauce
— **με βούτυρο και τυρί** me *vu*·ti·ro ke ti·*ri* pasta with butter sauce & cheese
— **στο φούρνο** sto *fur*·no pasta baked in cheese & butter sauce

μαντί ⓝ man·*di* small pasta pockets filled with mincemeat, cooked in meat broth seasoned with pepper / capsicum & served with a yoghurt & garlic sauce (Northern Greece)

μάραθο ⓝ *ma*·ra·tho fennel
— **με ούζο σούπα** me *u*·zo *su*·pa ouzo & fennel soup

μαχαλεπί ⓝ ma·kha·le·*pi* creamy custard pudding in rose-water syrup (Cyprus)

μαχλέπι ⓝ ma·*khle*·pi pungent bitter-sweet black cherry pips used for spicing breads & stuffings

μαρίδα πικάντικη ⓕ ma·*ri*·ţha pi·*kan*·di·ki whitebait, tomato & mint fritters (Rhodes)

μαρίδες ⓕ pl ma·*ri*·ţhes whitebait
— **λιαστές** lia·*stes* whitebait seasoned with oregano & strung out to dry then chargrilled & served with oil & lemon juice

— **τηγανητές** ti·gha·ni·*tes* whitebait rolled in flour & deep fried until crisp, served with lemon wedges

μαστίχα ⓕ ma·*sti*·kha mastic • crystallised resin from the mastic bush, eaten as chewing gum & used as a flavouring (Chios)

μαυρομάτικα φασόλια ⓝ pl mav·ro·*ma*·ti·ka fa·*so*·lia black-eyed peas

— **με χόρτα** me *khor*·ta black-eyed peas stewed with greens, onions, tomatoes, parsley, mint & garlic (Crete)

μεγαρίτικη ⓕ me·gha·*ri*·ti·ki olives grown in Attica, near Athens, named after the city of Megara

μελανούρι ⓝ me·la·*nu*·ri sea bream

μεζές ⓜ me·*zes* snack

μεζεδάκι ⓝ me·ze·*ţha*·ki tasty morsels served with ouzo – favourites include olives, salted cucumber slices, feta, salted anchovies, mackerel & mini-meat rissoles

μέλι ⓝ *me*·li honey

— **με ξηρούς καρπούς** me ksi·*rus* kar·*pus* honey poured over walnuts or almonds

μελιτζάνες ⓕ pl me·li·*dza*·nes aubergine / eggplant

— **στο φούρνο** sto *fur*·no sliced aubergine / eggplant fried with potatoes, & baked with tomatoes, cumin, parsley & feta

— **τηγανητές** ti·gha·ni·*tes* see **κολοκυθάκια τηγανητά**

μελιτζανοσαλάτα ⓕ me·li·dza·no·sa·*la*·ta smoky purée of grilled mashed aubergine / eggplant, onion, garlic, oil & lemon

μελιτίνι ⓝ me·li·*ti*·ni golden pastry tarts filled with fresh cheese, eggs & sugar, traditionally eaten at Easter

μελόπιτα ⓕ me·*lo*·pi·ta cheesecake made with **μυζήθρα** & clear honey

μηλοπιτάκια ⓝ pl mi·lo·pi·*ta*·kia crescent-shaped apple & walnut pies

μοσχάρι ⓝ mo·*sha*·ri veal

— **κατσαρόλας με αρακά** kat·sa·*ro*·las me a·ra·*ka* veal stewed with fresh peas in white wine & thyme

— **κοκκινιστό με μακαρόνια** ko·ki·ni·*sto* me ma·ka·*ro*·nia veal stewed with tomatoes, served with spaghetti

— **ψητό** psi·*to* rolled veal rubbed with lemon juice, pepper & salt, pot-roasted with onion, tomatoes & wine

— **στιφάδο** sti·*fa*·ţho veal ragout with garlic, peppercorns & bay leaves

μουσακάς ⓜ mu·sa·*kas* thick-sliced aubergine / eggplant & mincemeat arranged in layers, topped with béchamel & baked

— **με αγγινάρες** me ang·gi·*na*·res alternating layers of minced veal & artichoke hearts

μουσταλευριά ⓕ mu·sta·lev·ri·*a* dark gelatinous pudding made from boiled grape must, thickened with flour & sprinkled with cinnamon, seeds & nuts

μούστος ⓜ *mu*·stos grape must collected from crushed wine grapes

— **κουλούρα** ku·*lu*·ra hard, turban-shaped grape must buns

μπακαλιάρος ⓜ ba·ka·*lia*·ros dried salt cod soaked for several hours prior to cooking

μπουρδέτο ⓝ bur·*ţhe*·to salt cod stew

— **κροκετάκια** kro·ke·*ta*·kia deep-fried salt cod mashed with potato & nutmeg

— **πλακί** pla·*ki* salt cod simmered with onions, potatoes, celery, carrots & garlic in a tomato-based sauce

— **τηγανητός** ti·gha·ni·*tos* salt cod fried in crisp, golden batter, traditionally accompanied with **σκορδαλιά**

μπακλαβάς ⓜ pl ba·kla·*vas* nut-filled layers of filo bathed in honey syrup

μπάμιες ⓕ pl *ba*·mies okra

— **λαδερές** la·ţhe·*res* okra stewed in oil

— **γιαχνί** yia·*khni* okra braised with pulped tomatoes & onions

μπαρμπούνια ⓝ pl bar·*bu*·nia small, sweet-fleshed red mullet

— **ψητά στον άνιθο** psi·*ta* ston a·ni·tho red mullet on a bed of dill

— **στη σκάρα** sti *ska*·ra red mullet basted with oil & lemon & chargrilled

— **τηγανητά** ti·gha·ni·*ta* red mullet rolled in seasoned flour & fried

μπεκάτσα ⓕ be·*kat*·sa woodcock

— **κρασάτη** kra·*sa*·ti woodcock casserole with dry red wine, tomatoes & spices, served on fried bread

μπεκρή μεζέ ⓜ be·*kri* me·*ze* 'drunken **μεζέ**' – meat cooked in tomato & wine sauce

μπομπότα ⓕ bo·*bo*·ta
sweet corn bread studded with raisins, walnuts, cloves & flavoured with cinnamon & orange juice (Zakynthos)
μπισκότα ⓝ pl bi·*sko*·ta biscuits • cookies
μπιζελόσουπα ⓕ bi·ze·*lo*·su·pa
fragrant pea soup loaded with dill
μπόλια *bo*·li·a ⓕ lacy caul of fat encasing lamb's stomach
μπριάμ ⓝ bri·*am* casserole of sliced potatoes, courgette / zucchini, peppers / capsicums, tomatoes & herbs • roast vegetables
μπριζόλες ⓕ pl bri·*zo*·les chops • steak
μπουγάτσα ⓕ bu·*ghat*·sa creamy semolina pudding wrapped in pastry & baked
μπουρδέτο ⓝ bur·*ţhe*·to
hot fish casserole spiked with paprika
μπουρεκάκια ⓝ pl bu·re·*ka*·kia little filo pies in cigar, cigarette & envelope shapes
μπουρέκια ⓝ pl bu·*re*·kia filo pies shaped into thin long rolls, batons & pinwheels
— **με ανερί** me a·ne·*ri* deep-fried pastry pouches stuffed with cheese (Cyprus)
μυαλά ⓝ pl mia·*la* brains
— **αρνίσια λαδολέμονο** ar·*ni*·si·a la·ţho·*le*·mo·no poached lamb's brains
— **τηγανητά** ti·gha·ni·*ta* fried brains
μύδια ⓝ pl *mi*·ţhia mussels
— **κρασάτα** kra·*sa*·ta poached mussels in a white wine sauce
— **τηγανητά** ti·gha·ni·*ta* mussels shucked, lightly battered, fried in hot oil & served with a garlic yoghurt sauce
— **γεμιστά** ye·mi·*sta* mussels stuffed with rice, onions & parsley, slow-simmered in fish stock, tomato purée & white wine
μυζήθρα ⓕ mi·*zi*·thra soft mild ricotta-like cheese made from sheep's or goat's milk (sweet or savoury)
μυζηθρόπιτες ⓕ pl mi·zi·*thro*·pi·tes delicate deep-fried pies with **μυζήθρα** (Crete)

νουμπουλό ⓝ num·bu·*lo*
bacon-flavoured sausage (Corfu)
ντολμάδες dol·*ma*·ţhes ⓜ pl
dolmades – parcels of rice-wrapped leaves (usually vine leaves) & cooked in water, oil & lemon juice
— **φυλλιανές** fi·lia·*nes* Christmas & New Year dish of onion sleeves stuffed with minced veal, pork & rice (Lesvos)
— **με αυγολέμονο** me av·gho·*le*·mo·no dolmades with rice, minced lamb, tomatoes, mint & cumin, served hot with **αλευρολέμονο**
— **με κουκιά** me ku·*kia*
dolmades with boiled & sliced broad beans & dried ox meat, cooked on a bed of beef bones (Northern Greece)
— **με λαχανόφυλλα** me la·kha·*no*·fi·la stuffed cabbage leaves, served hot with **αβγολέμονο**
— **γιαλαντζί** yia·lan·*dzi*
'fraud' – stuffed meatless dolmades
— **Σμυρναίικα** zmir·*ne*·i·ka
dolmades stuffed with sautéed onions, rice, aubergine / eggplant, oregano, dill, garlic & cooked in tomato broth
ντομάτες ⓕ pl do·*ma*·tes tomatoes
— **λιαστές** lia·*stes* sun-dried tomatoes
— **γεμιστές** ye·mi·*stes*
large tomatoes stuffed with rice, tomato pulp, onion, garlic & herbs
ντοματοκεφτέδες ⓜ pl
do·ma·to·kef·*te*·ţhes
deep-fried tomato rissoles
ντοματομπελτές ⓜ do·ma·to·pel·*tes*
tomato paste
ντοματόσουπα ⓕ do·ma·*to*·su·pa soup made with tomatoes & sometimes pasta
νυχάκι ⓝ ni·*kha*·ki kalamata table olive (Messenia & Laconia)

Ν ν

νεγκόσκα ⓕ ne·*go*·ska variety of red grape
νεραντζάκι γλυκό ⓝ ne·ran·*dza*·ki ghli·*ko*
preserved small bitter green oranges
νεράτη ⓕ ne·*ra*·ti
variety of cheese pie (Crete)

Ξ ξ

ξεροτήγανα ⓝ pl kse·ro·*ti*·gha·na see **δίπλες**
ξινόχοντρος ⓜ ksi·*no*·khon·dros ground wheat cooked in sour milk & dried
ξινομυζήθρα ⓕ ksi·no·mi·*zi*·thra
savoury **μυζήθρα**

O o

οινοπνευματώδη ⓝ pl i·nop·nev·ma·*to*·ţhi alcoholic spirits
οστρακοειδή ⓝ pl o·stra·ko·i·*ţhi* shellfish
ούζο ⓝ *u*·zo clear spirit distilled from grape seeds, stems & skins with a strong aniseed flavour
οφτή σαλάτα ⓕ of·*ti* sa·*la*·ta grilled salad of potatoes, onions & **σταφιδολιές**, foil-wrapped & chargrilled (Crete)
οφτό ⓝ of·*to* sausage made from pig's intestines, rice, walnuts, pistachios, raisins, cinnamon & orange peel (Crete)
ουρά βοδιού ⓕ u·*ra* vo·*ţhiu* oxtail

Π π

παϊδάκια ⓝ pl pa·i·*ţha*·kia chops • cutlets
παξιμάδια ⓝ pl pak·si·*ma*·ţhia hard wheat or barley rusks eaten slightly moistened with water at meal times (both wheat & barley varieties are common)
— **με ντομάτες και φέτα** me do·*ma*·tes ke *fe*·ta **παξιμάδια** moistened with water or tomato juice & topped with sliced tomatoes, feta, oregano, oil, salt & pepper – very popular snack or light lunch
— **σαλάτα** sa·*la*·ta **παξιμάδια** broken into pieces, moistened with water & sprinkled with diced tomatoes, crumbled feta or oregano, oil, salt & pepper
παλαμίδα ⓕ pa·la·*mi*·ţha bonito • tunny fish (a variety of tuna)
— **ψητή με χόρτα** psi·*ti* me *khor*·ta marinated bonito steaks
παλικάρια ⓝ pl pa·li·*ka*·ri·a mix of legumes & grains boiled & tossed with oil, onions & dill
πανέ pa·*ne* crumbed & fried
παντρεμένοι ⓜ pl pan·dre·*me*·ni beans with other foods (rice, meat, tomatoes)
παντζάρι ⓝ pan·*dza*·ri beetroot • beet
— **σαλάτα** sa·*la*·ta boiled thickly sliced beetroot dressed with vinaigrette & served with **σκορδαλιά**
παντσέττα ⓕ pan·*tse*·ta pancetta
— **γεμιστή στο φούρνο** ye·mi·*sti* sto *fur*·no pig's stomach stuffed with parmesan, garlic, onions & oregano, basted with oil, wine & lemon juice & baked with potatoes (Zakynthos)
πάπια ⓕ *pa*·pia duck
— **με σάλτσα ροδιού** me *sal*·tsa ro·*ţhiu* fried duck breast served with sauce made from pomegranate seeds, lemon juice, duck stock & walnuts (Northern Greece)
— **σαλμί** sal·*mi* whole duck seared in oil, then jointed & cooked in its own juices, wine, orange juice & onions
πάπρικα ⓕ *pa*·pri·ka paprika
παπουτσάκι ⓝ pa·put·*sa*·ki 'little shoe' – stuffed baby aubergine / eggplant topped with béchamel sauce & baked
παρμεζάνα ⓕ par·me·*za*·na parmesan
πασατέμπος ⓜ pa·sa·*te*·bos 'pass the time' – roasted pumpkin seeds sold as a snack
πάστα ⓕ *pa*·sta gateau
παστέλι ⓝ pa·*ste*·li sweet honey & sesame seed wafers
παστιτσάδα ⓕ pa·stit·*sa*·ţha pot-roasted veal with tomato, red wine, cloves, cinnamon & paprika (Corfu)
παστίτσιο ⓝ pa·*stit*·si·o baked layers of buttery macaroni & minced lamb topped with white sauce & grated **κεφαλοτύρι**
παστός pa·*stos* salted & dried
παστουρμάς ⓜ pa·stur·*mas* spicy dried ox meat
πατάτες ⓕ pl pa·*ta*·tes potatoes
— **γιαχνί** yia·*khni* potatoes stewed with tomatoes, onions & oregano
— **κεφτέδες** kef·*te*·ţhes fried potato, feta & parsley rissoles
— **λεμονάτες** le·mo·*na*·tes potatoes roasted with oil, lemon juice, oregano, salt & pepper
— **πουρέ** pu·*re* mashed potatoes
— **στο φούρνο** sto *fur*·no potatoes baked or roasted with oil, salt & oregano
— **τηγανητές** ti·gha·ni·*tes* fried potato slices
πατατοσαλάτα ⓕ pa·ta·to·sa·*la*·ta potato salad
πατατού ⓕ pa·ta·*tu* baked mashed potato pie (Cyclades)

πατσάς pat·*sas* Ⓜ tripe • rich-textured & surprisingly delicate-flavoured soup made with the stomach of a young lamb & finished with **αβγολέμονο**
πατούδα Ⓕ pa·*tu*·ţha pastries filled with walnuts, almonds & cinnamon, baked, sprinkled with orange flower water & dredged in icing sugar (Crete)
πεϊνιρλί Ⓝ pe·i·nir·*li* savoury pastries with a variety of fillings such as mincemeat, feta, ham & egg, & dried ox meat
πέρδικες Ⓕ pl *per*·ţhi·kes partridges
— **με ελιές και σέλινο** me e·*lies* ke *se*·li·no partridges browned in butter & simmered in their own juices with green olives, sliced celery & tomatoes
πέρκα Ⓕ *per*·ka sea perch
πέστροφα Ⓕ *pe*·stro·fa trout
πεταλίδες Ⓕ pl pe·ta·*li*·ţhes limpets
— **με θαλασσινούς χοχλιούς** me tha·la·si·*nus* kho·khli·*us* limpets & sea snails stewed with ripe tomatoes, onions & black pepper (Lesvos)
πετιμέζι Ⓝ pe·ti·*me*·zi syrup made from unfermented grape juice, used to flavour rolls, cakes & sweets – when mixed with cold water makes a refreshing drink
πιλάφι Ⓝ pi·*la*·fi pilau – rice & stock cooked to a creamy consistency – served to complement boiled meat or chicken
— **με ντομάτες** me do·*ma*·tes pilau with the addition of tomatoes, meat stock, garlic, parsley, salt & pepper
— **με γαρίδες** me gha·*ri*·ţhes pilau with prawns, onions & oregano
— **με μύδια** me *mi*·ţhia pilau with fresh mussels, onions & white wine
— **με περδίκια** me per·*ţhi*·ki·a pilau with partridge, tomato & cloves (Kefallonia)
πιπέρι Ⓝ pi·*pe*·ri black pepper
πιροσκί Ⓝ pi·ro·*ski* deep-fried, dough-wrapped sausage roll
πίτα Ⓕ *pi*·ta pie – filo is the most common pastry used • flat doughy circular bread seared on grill until golden, mainly used for wrapping **σουβλάκι** & **γύρος**
πιτσούνια Ⓝ pl pit·*su*·nia squab • love-bird • any tiny bird used for cooking
— **κρασάτα** kra·*sa*·ta baby squabs doused in red wine, tomato pulp, cinnamon & cloves then braised
— **με κουκουνάρια** me ku·ku·*na*·ria squab ignited with brandy, splashed with retsina & dressed with a garlic cream sauce (Northern Greece)
— **με κουκιά** me ku·*kia* stewed squab & fresh broad beans cooked in chicken stock, white wine, dill, garlic & lots of black pepper
πλακί pla·*ki* method of baking or braising with tomatoes, onion, garlic & parsley
ποδαράκια Ⓝ pl po·ţha·*ra*·kia trotters
— **αρνίσια** ar·*ni*·si·a boiled lamb's trotters browned in butter & garlic, roasted, then finished with egg & lemon sauce
πόρτο Ⓝ *por*·to port
πορτοκάλι Ⓝ por·to·*ka*·li orange
— **γλυκό** ghli·*ko* preserved orange
ποτό Ⓝ po·*to* drinks • spirits (on menus)
πράσα Ⓝ pl *pra*·sa leeks
— **αλευρολέμονο** a·lev·ro·*le*·mo·no braised leeks in lemony sauce
— **με δαμάσκηνα** me ţha·*ma*·ski·na leeks & prunes sprinkled with cinnamon & nutmeg
— **με ρύζι** me *ri*·zi leeks & celery simmered with rice & crushed tomatoes
πρασάκια με πατάτες Ⓝ pl pra·sa·ki·a me pa·*ta*·tes leeks & sliced potatoes cooked in butter, chicken stock, onions, oregano & parsley
πρασόπιτα Ⓕ pra·*so*·pi·ta pie made with braised leeks, feta, **μυζήθρα** & skimmed milk (Western Greece)

Ρ ρ

ραβιόλες Ⓕ pl ra·vi·*o*·les pasta envelopes stuffed with a mixture of cheese & mint, served with melted butter & grated cheese (Cyprus)
ραδίκι Ⓝ ra·*ţhi*·ki chicory • term used for common varieties of **χόρτα**
— **σαλάτα** sa·*la*·ta spring salad of young dandelion leaves splashed with oil & lemon

ρακί ⓝ ra·*ki* fiery village spirit made from grapes, like ouzo but without the aniseed taste, high in alcohol
ραφιόλια ⓝ pl ra·fi·o·li·a sweet half-moon filo pastries stuffed with cheese, eggs, cinnamon, orange rind & ouzo (Cyclades)
ρεβανί ⓝ re·va·*ni* very sweet semolina sponge, flavoured with vanilla & orange juice & smothered with honey syrup
ρεβίθια ⓝ pl re·*vi*·thia chickpeas
— **αλευρολέμονο** a·lev·ro·*le*·mo·no chickpeas simmered in a rich lemony broth
— **στο φούρνο** sto *fur*·no casserole of chickpeas, onions, garlic & bay leaves – favourite fasting food during Lent
— **σούπα** *su*·pa chickpea soup
ρεβιθοκεφτέδες ⓜ pl re·vi·tho·kef·*te*·ţhes rissoles of mashed chickpeas, potatoes, onion, parsley & black pepper
ρέγγα ⓕ *reng*·ga smoked herrings, eaten plain or grilled with oil & lemon
ρέσσι ⓝ *re*·si pilau made with bulgur & lamb (including the tail) & served at weddings (Cyprus)
ρετσίνα ⓕ ret·*si*·na retsina – pine-resinated wine, often served chilled
ριγανάτος ⓜ ri·gha·*na*·tos seasoned with oregano, salt & pepper
ρίγανη ⓕ *ri*·gha·ni pungent Greek oregano
ριζάδα ⓕ ri·*za*·ţha thick soup made with rice & shellfish or tiny game birds (Corfu)
ριζόγαλο ⓝ ri·*zo*·gha·lo vanilla-flavoured rice pudding sprinkled with cinnamon
ρόδι ⓝ *ro*·ţhi pomegranate – used to flavour sweets, syrups, cakes & salads
ροδόνερο ⓝ ro·*ţho*·ne·ro fragrant rosewater used to flavour cakes, pies & sweets
ροφός ⓜ ro·*fos* grouper • blackfish
ρολό από κιμά ⓝ ro·*lo* a·*po* ki·*ma* baked mincemeat roll with hard-boiled eggs cuddled in the middle
ρύζι ⓝ *ri*·zi rice

Σ σ

σαλάχι ⓝ sa·*la*·hi ray fish • skate
— **σαλάτα** sa·*la*·ta boiled ray fish salad dressed with **λαδολέμονο**
σαλιγκάρια ⓝ pl sa·ling·*ga*·ri·a snails – cooked in the shell & eaten with a fork
— **φρικασέ** fri·ka·*se* large snails sautéed in oil & stewed with courgette/zucchini, onions, fresh dill & finished with **αβγολέμονο**
— **με σάλτσα** me *sal*·tsa snails cooked with crushed tomatoes, tomato paste, onions & oregano
— **συμπεθεριό** sim·be·the·*rio* 'in-laws' – snails cooked with sliced aubergine/eggplant, tomato pulp & **ξινόχοντρος**
— **στα κάρβουνα** sta *kar*·vu·na live snails chargrilled & doused with **λαδολέμονο** & bay leaves (Cyclades)
— **στιφάδο** sti·*fa*·ţho snail ragout with bay leaves (Crete)
σαλμί ⓝ sal·*mi* method of casseroling game with red wine, vegetables & herbs
σάλτσα ⓕ *sal*·tsa sauce • generic term for tomato sauce
— **από ζωμό κρέατος** a·*po* zo·*mo* *kre*·a·tos gravy
— **άσπρη** *a*·spri béchamel sauce with egg
— **άσπρη ξινή** *a*·spri ksi·*ni* 'sharp white sauce' – made with butter, flour, meat stock, eggs & lemon
— **αυγολέμονο** av·gho·*le*·mo·no see **αβγολέμονο**
— **ντομάτα** do·*ma*·ta tomato sauce with bay leaves
— **ντομάτα με κιμά** do·*ma*·ta me ki·*ma* tomato & mincemeat sauce
— **μαρινάτα** ma·ri·*na*·ta marinade
— **μουστάρδα** mu·*star*·ţha mustard & garlic beaten with lemon juice
— **ταρτάρ** tar·*tar* tartare sauce
Σάμος sa·mos rich golden dessert wine (Samos)
σαρακοστιανά ⓝ pl sa·ra·ko·sti·a·*na* see **νηστήσιμα**
σαρδέλες ⓕ pl sar·*ţhe*·les sardines
— **παστές** pa·*stes* salted sardines
— **στο φούρνο** sto *fur*·no sardines baked with oil, lemon, garlic & oregano
σαρμάς ⓜ sar·*mas* pie-like offal dish (Northern Greece)
σβίγγοι ⓜ pl *zving*·gi deep-fried fritters served with honey, cinnamon & cognac syrup

σελινόριζα ⓕ se·li·*no*·ri·za celeriac
— **με αυγολέμονο** me av·gho·*le*·mo·no creamy dish of celeriac in chicken stock & finished with egg & lemon sauce
— **με πράσα** me *pra*·sa braised celeriac wedges & leek strips thickened with **αβγολέμονο**

σέσκουλο ⓝ *se*·sku·lo swiss chard, type of **χόρτα**
— **με κιμά** me ki·*ma* silverbeet sautéed with chopped onion in butter & cooked with minced lamb, rice, dill, lemon juice & salt

σεσκουλόρυζο ⓝ se·sku·*lo*·ri·zo see **σπανακόρυζο**

σεφταλιά ⓕ sef·ta·*lia* pork rissoles wrapped in sheep's caul & chargrilled (Cyprus)

σκαλτσοτσέτα ⓝ pl skal·tsot·*se*·ta paper-thin slices of fillet steak skewered & simmered in oil, water & tomatoes

σκορδαλιά ⓕ skor·ţha·*lia* thick paste of walnuts, bread, potatoes, olive oil, lemon & garlic

σκόρδο ⓝ *skor*·ţho garlic
— **στούμπι** *stu*·bi vinegar bottled with a garlic bulb, used for dressing vegetable dishes & salads (Ionian Islands)
— **τσιγαριστά** tsi·gha·ri·*sta* fried whole garlic bulbs • peeled & sliced garlic cloves fried & simmered in white wine, tomato paste, salt & pepper (Ithaca)

σκουμπρί ⓝ sku·*bri* mackerel

σνακς ⓝ pl snaks snacks

σοφρίτο ⓝ so·*fri*·to fried veal slices braised in a sauce of crushed garlic, wine vinegar, parsley, mint & brandy (Corfu)

σοκολάτα ⓕ so·ko·*la*·ta chocolate
γάλα *gha*·la hot chocolate

σουσάμι ⓝ su·*sa*·mi sesame seed

σούβλα ⓕ *suv*·la spit-roasted • skewers • method of chargrilling meat or fish

σουβλάκι ⓝ suv·*la*·ki souvlaki – tender chunks of seasoned or marinated meat (or fish) skewered & chargrilled
— **με πίτα** me *pi*·ta souvlaki with **πίτα**

σούγλι ⓝ *sugh*·li sun-dried baby bogue fish coated in batter & fried (Cyclades)

σούπα ⓕ *su*·pa soup
— **ξιδάτη** ksi·*ţha*·ti sour soup of lentils, parsley & vinegar
— **με τσουκνίδες** me tsuk·*ni*·ţhes electric-green soup of stinging nettles & diced potatoes cooked in chicken stock & thickened with milk

σουπιές ⓕ pl su·*pies* cuttlefish
— **κρασάτες** kra·*sa*·tes cuttlefish cooked in wine
— **με σάλτσα μελάνης** me *sal*·tsa me·*la*·nis cuttlefish cooked in a rich sauce made from its own black ink & wine (Crete)
— **με σπανάκι** me spa·*na*·ki cuttlefish cooked with spinach, onions, dill & mint

σουτζουκάκια ⓝ pl su·dzu·*ka*·kia rissoles of minced lamb, veal or pork braised in a very spicy tomato gravy

σουτζούκι ⓝ su·*dzu*·ki strings of almonds dipped in syrup & sun-dried

σπάλα ⓕ *spa*·la shoulder of meat
— **μοσχαρίσια** mos·kha·*ri*·si·a silverside

σπανακόπιτα ⓕ spa·na·*ko*·pi·ta spinach filo pie, often includes feta or **κεφαλοτύρι**, eggs & herbs

σπανακόρυζο ⓝ spa·na·*ko*·ri·zo sautéed spinach, rice, spring onions & dill simmered in water until liquid is absorbed

σπετζοφάι ⓝ spe·dzo·*fa*·i sliced pork sausages stewed with sweet green peppers, aubergine/eggplant, tomatoes & oregano

σπλήνα ⓕ *spli*·na spleen
— **γεμιστή** ye·mi·*sti* calf's spleen stuffed with chopped sautéed liver, onion, garlic & herbs, then roasted

σπληνάντερο ⓝ spli·*nan*·de·ro spit-roast sausage made from intestine stuffed with sliced spleen & garlic

σταφίδες ⓕ pl sta·*fi*·ţhes raisins • currants

σταφιδολιές ⓕ pl sta·fi·ţho·*lies* type of olive sun-dried until wrinkled, lightly salted & packed, or immersed in oil

σταφιδωτά ⓝ pl sta·fi·ţho·*ta* *oval short-bread biscuits with chewy raisin centres*

σταφύλια ⓝ pl sta·*fi*·li·a grapes

στάκα ⓕ *sta*·ka creamy butter made from fresh goat's or sheep's milk, used to flavour pies, stuffed vegetables & pilau
— **με αβγά** me av·*gha* omelette with **στάκα** (Crete)

στάμνα ⓕ stam·na method of cooking meat & potatoes in a pot sealed with wet clay & baked in charcoal embers
στιφάδο ⓝ sti·fa·ţho meat, game or seafood ragout
στραγάλια ⓝ pl stra·gha·lia roasted chickpeas for snacking
σύκο ⓝ si·ko fig
— **αποστολιάτικο** a·po·sto·lia·ti·ko young green fig
— **γλυκό** ghli·ko green fig preserve
— **στο φούρνο** sto fur·no figs baked in a syrup of honey, vanilla, orange juice & orange flower water
συκόπιτα ⓕ si·ko·pi·ta fig cake (Corfu)
συκόψωμο ⓝ si·kop·so·mo heavy aromatic fig cake • dried green figs minced & mixed with ouzo shaped into balls, flattened, dried & wrapped in vine leaves
συκωταριά ⓕ si·ko·ta·ria innards • offal
συκώτι ⓝ si·ko·ti liver
— **κρασάτα** kra·sa·ta chopped liver marinated in red wine
— **λαδορίγανη** la·ţho·ri·gha·ni grilled liver with oil, lemon & oregano
— **μαρινάτα** ma·ri·na·ta thinly sliced livers fried & finished with vinegar, white wine & rosemary
— **με κρεμμυδάκια** me kre·mi·ţha·kia livers fried with spring onions & cloves in a sauce of white wine & tomato juice
σφακιανόπιτες ⓕ pl sfa·ki·a·no·pi·tes pies consisting of balls of cheese wrapped in dough, then fried & served with a dollop of honey
σφουγγάτο ⓝ sfung·ga·to Spanish-style omelette made with more vegetables than eggs, fried or baked (Rhodes)

Τ τ

ταβάς ⓜ ta·vas casserole of seasoned beef or lamb, fried onions, diced tomatoes, oil, vinegar & cinnamon
ταλαττούρι ⓝ ta·la·tu·ri **τζατζίκι** flavoured with mint (Cyprus)
ταραμάς ⓜ ta·ra·mas salted pressed roe of the grey mullet or cod
ταράξακο ⓝ ta·rak·sa·ko dandelion
ταχίνι ⓝ ta·hi·ni sesame seed paste
ταχινόσουπα ⓕ ta·hi·no·su·pa creamy lemony soup made from sesame paste (popular during Lent)
τελεμές ⓜ te·le·mes heavily salted feta-style cheese
τηγανόψωμο ⓝ ti·gha·nop·so·mo fried tomato & spring onion bread (Santorini)
τίλιο ⓝ ti·li·o infusion of lime leaves
τζατζίκι ⓝ dza·dzi·ki refreshing purée of grated cucumber, yoghurt & garlic
τσόχος ⓜ tso·khos milk thistle – mild sweet-tasting green used in warm salads, pies & stews • type of **χόρτα**
της ώρας tis o·ras dishes cooked to order, such as steaks or chops
τσουρέκι ⓝ tot·su·re·ki braided Easter bread spiced with lemon rind & cherry pips, sprinkled with almonds & crushed **μαστίχα**
τραχανόσουπα ⓕ tra·kha·no·su·pa thick gruel of granulated pasta cooked in chicken broth with butter, lemon juice
τριαντάφυλλο γλυκό ⓝ tri·an·da·fi·lo ghli·ko delicate soft jam made from dark red rose petals
τσικουδιά ⓕ tsi·ku·ţhia see **ρακί**
τσιπούρα ⓕ tsi·pu·ra gilt head bream • snapper
τσίπουρο ⓝ tsi·pu·ro see **ρακί**
τσίρος ⓜ tsi·ros small dried mackerel
τσουκνίδες ⓕ pl tsu·kni·ţhes stinging nettles used in salads & soups
τουρσί ⓝ tur·si pickles • pickled
τούρτα ⓕ tur·ta cake • gateau • tart
τυρί ⓝ ti·ri cheese
— **μπλε** ble blue cheese
— **ημίσκληρο** i·mi·skli·ro semi-firm cheese
— **κατσικίσιο** kat·si·ki·si·o goat's cheese
— **κρεμώδες** kre·mo·ţhes cream cheese
— **μαλακή μυζήθρα** ma·la·ki mi·zi·thra cottage cheese
— **μαλακό** ma·la·ko soft cheese
— **σαγανάκι** sa·gha·na·ki sharp, hard cheese fried until crispy on the outside & soft in the centre, served with a squeeze of lemon juice
— **σκληρό** skli·ro hard cheese
τυρόπηγμα ⓝ ti·ro·pigh·ma curd

τυρόπιτα (f) ti·*ro*·pi·ta cheese pies, the classic mixture is feta & **κεφαλοτύρι** wrapped in flaky filo pastry & baked
τυροβολιά (f) ti·ro·vo·*lia* cheese variety

Φ φ

φάβα (f) *fa*·va yellow split pea purée served with raw onion rings
— **παντρεμένη** pan·dre·*me*·ni 'married' – leftover **φάβα** served as a hot dish with the addition of tomatoes & cumin
φαγκρί (n) fa·*ghri* sea bream
φακές (f) pl fa·*kes* lentils
— **με μακαρόνια** me ma·ka·*ro*·nia lentils simmered in water & vinegar with mint, garlic & pearl pasta (Astypalea)
— **σούπα** *su*·pa lentil soup
Φανουρόπιτα (f) fa·nu·*ro*·pi·ta cake spiced with dried fruit, brandy & cinnamon – served on Saint Fanourios Day
φασκόμηλο (n) fa·*sko*·mi·lo sage
φασολάδα (f) fa·so·*la*·ţha thick fragrant soup of beans, tomatoes, tomato paste, carrots, celery, garlic & parsley
φασολάκια (n) pl fa·so·*la*·kia green beans
— **λαδερά** la·ţhe·*ra* green beans cooked in oil with tomatoes & onions
— **σαλάτα** sa·*la*·ta boiled fresh green beans with **λαδολέμονο** or **λαδόξιδο**
φασόλια (n) pl fa·*so*·li·a dried beans – usually refers to white haricot / lima beans
— **μάραθο** *ma*·ra·tho dried beans browned in oil & onions, simmered with tomato pulp & fennel leaves
— **σαλάτα** sa·*la*·ta bean salad
φέτα (f) *fe*·ta
feta – white, crumbly, salty cheese
— **σχάρας** *skha*·ras grilled feta
φέτες ψαριού με ντομάτα και σταφίδες (f) pl *fe*·tes psa·*riu* me do·*ma*·ta ke sta·*fi*·ţhes fish with tomato & currants
φιλέτο (n) fi·*le*·to fillet • steak
φιρίκια (n) pl fi·*ri*·ki·a
small crisp apples (Northern Greece)
— **με αμύγδαλα** me a·*migh*·ţha·la baked **φιρίκια** stuffed with almonds
— **γεμιστά** ye·mi·*sta* **φιρίκια** stuffed with minced veal, coriander & cumin
φιστίκια (n) pl fi·*sti*·kia peanuts
— **Αιγίνης** e·*yi*·nis pistachios

φλαούνες (f) pl fla·*u*·nes baked savoury tarts (Cyprus)
φοινίκια (n) pl fi·*ni*·ki·a honey-dipped shortbread sprinkled with cinnamon & marked with a criss-cross design
φρικασέ (n) fri·ka·*se* meat or vegetable stew thickened & flavoured with **αβγολέμονο**
φρουταλιά (f) fru·ta·*lia* omelette-type dish consisting of eggs, potatoes, parsley & sliced smoked pork sausages (Andros)
φρυγαδέλια (n) pl fri·gha·*ţhe*·lia liver parcels in lamb's caul, fried or skewered & chargrilled (Northern Greece, Thessaly)
φύλλο (n) *fi*·lo flaky tissue-thin pastry used for pies & sweet pastries

Χ χ

χαβιάρι (n) kha·*via*·ri caviar
χαλβάς (m) khal·*vas* rich creamy sweet made from sesame seeds & honey, flavoured with pistachio, chocolate or almonds
— **σιμιγδαλένιος** si·migh·ţha·*le*·nios moist cake of semolina & honey, decorated with almonds & cinnamon
— **της Ρίνας** tis *ri*·nas baked semolina & almond cake served hot with sugar syrup
χαλορίνι (n) kha·lo·*ri*·ni pouch-shaped cheese filled with crushed coriander (Cyprus)
χαλούμι (n) kha·*lu*·mi
firm, white, sheep's milk cheese with elastic texture & salty taste (Cyprus)
χαλουμόπιτες (f) pl kha·lu·*mo*·pi·tes savoury cake made with **χαλούμι**, eggs, mint, sultanas & **μαστίχα** (Cyprus)
χαλουμόψωμο (n) kha·lu·*mop*·so·mo bread baked with chunks of **χαλούμι** (Cyprus)
χαμομήλι (n) kha·mo·*mi*·li chamomile
χαμψιά (f) kham·*psia* fresh anchovy
χαμψοπίλαφο (n) kham·pso·*pi*·la·fo onion & anchovy pilau seasoned with oregano
χείλη της χανούμισσας (n) pl *hi*·li tis kha·*nu*·mi·sas 'the Turkish lady's lips' – crunchy honey cakes (Rhodes)
χέλι (n) *he*·li eel
— **πλακί** pla·*ki* eel baked with tomatoes, onions, potatoes & herbs (Corfu)

χοιρινές ⓕ pl hi·ri·*nes* pork chops
— **κρασάτες** kra·*sa*·tes pork chops simmered in red wine
— **στη σχάρα** sti *skha*·ra pork chops chargrilled with salt, pepper & lemon juice
— **τηγανητές** ti·gha·ni·*tes* fried pork chops
χοιρινό ⓝ hi·ri·*no* pork
— **με κυδώνια** me ki·*ţho*·nia pork & quinces simmered in red wine spiced with orange peel & cinnamon
— **με πράσα** me *pra*·sa pork & leek casserole
— **με σέλινο αυγολέμενο** me *se*·li·no av·gho·*le*·mo·no pork & celery in egg & lemon sauce
— **μπούτι ψητό** *bu*·ti psi·*to* crispy, roast leg of pork
— **παστό** pa·*sto* salted pork
χοιρομέρι ⓝ hi·ro·*me*·ri cured leg of ham (Cyprus, Zakynthos)
χόντρος ⓜ *khon*·dros hand-milled wheat used in soups, dolmades, snail dishes & stews (see also **ξινόχοντρος**)
χόρτα ⓝ pl *khor*·ta wild or cultivated greens used in salads, pie fillings, casseroles or boiled & served hot with an oil & lemon dressing
— **τσιγάρι** tsi·*gha*·ri lightly fried wild greens
χορτόπιτα ⓕ khor·*to*·pi·ta pies made from seasonal greens
χορτοσαλάτα ⓕ khor·to·sa·*la*·ta warm salad of greens dressed with salt, oil & lemon
χορτόσουπα ⓕ khor·*to*·su·pa vegetable soup
χουρμάδες ⓜ pl khur·*ma*·ţhes dates
χοχλιοί ⓜ pl kho·khli·*i* snails
— **μπουμπουριστοί** bu·bu·ri·*sti* 'upside-down' – live snails deep-fried & doused with vinegar & rosemary
χριστόψωμο ⓝ khri·*stop*·so·mo sweet Christmas bread baked in the shape of a cross
χταπόδι ⓝ khta·*po*·ţhi octopus
— **βραστό** vra·*sto* boiled octopus coated with oil & lemon sauce
— **κεφτέδες** kef·*te*·ţhes rissoles of minced octopus, onion, mint & cheese
— **κρασάτο** kra·*sa*·to octopus cooked in red wine sauce
— **λιαστό** lia·*sto* sun-dried, chargrilled octopus sprinkled with oil & lemon juice
— **με μακαρόνι κοφτό** me ma·ka·*ro*·ni kof·*to* casserole of octopus, tomatoes, macaroni & red wine
— **στα κάρβουνα** sta *kar*·vu·na grilled octopus
— **στιφάδο** sti·*fa*·ţho octopus ragout
— **τουρσί** tur·*si* pickled octopus
χυλόφτα ⓝ pl hi·*lof*·ta macaroni served with hot butter & grated cheese (Crete)
χωριάτικη σαλάτα ⓕ kho·ri·a·ti·ki sa·*la*·ta 'village salad' – tomatoes, cucumber, olives & feta (known outside Greece as 'Greek salad')

Ψ ψ

ψάρι ⓝ *psa*·ri fish
— **μαρινάτο** ma·ri·*na*·to fish fried until golden, served with a piquant sauce of garlic, rosemary & vinegar (also called **ψάρι σαβόρι**)
— **πλακί** pla·*ki* whole fish basted with oil, lemon & parsley, baked on a bed of chopped tomatoes & onions
— **σαβόρι** sa·*vo*·ri see **ψάρι μαρινάτο**
— **Σπετσιώτο** spet·si·o·*to* fish baked with bread crumbs & white wine (Spetses)
— **στη σχάρα** sti *skha*·ra chargrilled fish
— **στο φούρνο λαδορίγανη** sto *fur*·no la·ţho·*ri*·gha·ni sliced fish & potato wedges baked in a broth of oil, water & lemon juice
— **τηγανητό** ti·gha·ni·*to* battered fish
— **βραστό με λαχανικά** vra·*sto* me la·kha·ni·*ka* poached fish with vegetables – the broth is often strained, thickened with **αβγολέμονο**
ψαροκεφτέδες ⓜ pl psa·ro·kef·*te*·ţhes fried fish rissoles
ψαρονέφρι ⓝ psa·ro·*ne*·fri pork fillet steak
ψαρόσουπα ⓕ psa·*ro*·su·pa fish soup thickened with rice & **αβγολέμονο**
ψητός psi·*tos* an all-purpose term for grilling, baking & barbecuing
ψωμιά με ανάγλυφες διακοσμήσεις ⓕ pl pso·*mia* me a·*na*·ghli·fes ţhi·a·koz·*mi*·sis decorated bread (usually made with doughs of different colours) eaten at festivals, baptisms & weddings

SAFE TRAVEL

Essentials

ΤΑ ΑΠΑΡΑΙΤΗΤΑ

EMERGENCIES

έκτακτη ανάγκη

Help!	Βοήθεια!	vo·*i*·thia
Stop!	Σταμάτα!	sta·*ma*·ta
Go away!	Φύγε!	*fi*·ye
Thief!	Κλέφτης!	*klef*·tis
Fire!	Φωτιά!	fo·*tia*
Watch out!	Πρόσεχε!	*pro*·se·he

Call an ambulance!
Κάλεσε ασθενοφόρο. — *ka*·le·se as·the·no·*fo*·ro

Call the doctor!
Κάλεσε έναν γιατρό. — *ka*·le·se e·nan yia·*tro*

Call the police!
Κάλεσε την αστυνομία. — *ka*·le·se tin a·sti·no·*mi*·a

It's an emergency.
Είναι επείγουσα ανάγκη. — *i*·ne e·*pi*·gou·sa a·*na*·gi

There's been an accident.
Έγινε ατύχημα. — e·yi·ne a·*ti*·hi·ma

Could you please help?
Μπορείς να βοηθήσεις, παρακαλώ; — bo·*ris* na vo·i·*thi*·sis pa·ra·ka·*lo*

Is it safe ...?	Είναι ασφαλές ...;	*i*·ne as·fa·*les* ...
at night	τη νύχτα	ti *nikh*·ta
for gay people	για γκέι	yia *ge*·i
for travellers	για ταξιδιώτες	yia tak·si·*ţhio*·tes
for women	για γυναίκες	yia yi·*ne*·kes
on your own	χωρίς παρέα	kho·*ris* pa·*re*·a

LOOK FOR

Αστυνομία	a·sti·no·*mi*·a	**Police**
Αστυνομικός Σταθμός	a·sti·no·mi·*kos* stath·*mos*	**Police Station**
Νοσοκομείο	no·so·ko·*mi*·o	**Hospital**
Σταθμός Πρώτων Βοηθειών	stath·*mos pro*·ton vo·i·thi·*on*	**Emergency Department**

I'm lost.
Έχω χαθεί. — e·kho kha·*thi*

Where are the toilets?
Πού είναι η τουαλέτα; — pu *i*·ne i tu·a·*le*·ta

Are there military bases in this region?
Υπάρχουν στρατιωτικές βάσεις σ' αυτή την περιοχή; — i·*par*·khun stra·ti·o·ti·*kes* *va*·sis saf·*ti* tin pe·ri·o·*hi*

POLICE

αστυνομία

Where's the police station?
Πού είναι ο αστυνομικός σταθμός; — pu *i*·ne o a·sti·no·mi·*kos* stath·*mos*

Please telephone the Tourist Police.
Παρακαλώ τηλεφώνα την τουριστική αστυνομία. — pa·ra·ka·*lo* ti·le·*fo*·na tin tu·ri·sti·*ki* a·sti·no·*mi*·a

I want to report an offence.
Θέλω να αναφέρω μια παρανομία. — *the*·lo na a·na·*fe*·ro mia pa·ra·no·*mi*·a

It was him/her.
Ήταν αυτός/αυτή. — *i*·tan af·*tos* / af·*ti*

I have insurance.
Έχω ασφάλεια. e·kho as·*fa*·li·a

I've been ...	Με έχουν ...	me e·khun ...
He/She has been ...	Τον/Την έχουν ...	ton/tin e·khun ...
assaulted	κακοποιήσει	ka·ko·pi·*i*·si
raped	βιάσει	vi·a·si
robbed	ληστέψει	li·*step*·si

THE POLICE MAY SAY...

Κατηγορείσαι για ... ka·ti·gho·*ri*·se yia ...	**You're charged with ...**
Αυτός κατηγορείται για ... af·*ti* ka·ti·gho·*ri*·te yia ...	**He's charged with ...**
Αυτή κατηγορείται για ... af·*tos* ka·ti·gho·*ri*·te yia ...	**She's charged with ...**

διατάραξη ησυχίας	ţhi·a·*ta*·rak·si i·si·*hi*·as	**disturbing the peace**
εξαγωγή αρχαιοτήτων χωρίς άδεια	ek·sa·gho·*yi* ar·he·o·*ti*·ton kho·*ris* a·ţhi·a	**exporting antiquities without a permit**
κακοποίηση	ka·ko·*pi*·i·si	**assault**
κλοπή από κατάστημα	klo·*pi* a·*po* ka·*ta*·sti·ma	**shoplifting**
κλοπή	klo·*pi*	**theft**
μετακίνηση αρχαιοτήτων	me·ta·*ki*·ni·si ar·he·o·*ti*·ton	**removing antiquities**
μη κατοχή βίζας	mi ka·to·*hi* *vi*·zas	**not having a visa**
κατοχή (παράνομων ουσιών)	ka·to·*hi* (pa·*ra*·no·mon u·si·*on*)	**possession (of illegal substances)**
υπέρβαση της βίζας	i·*per*·va·si tis *vi*·zas	**overstaying a visa**

Είναι πρόστιμο για ...	*i*·ne *pro*·sti·mo yia ...	**It's a ... fine.**
πάρκινγκ	*par*·king	**parking**
ταχύτητα	ta·*hi*·ti·ta	**speeding**

I've lost my ...	Έχασα ... μου.	e·kha·sa ... mu
My ... was/were stolen.	Έκλεψαν ... μου.	e·klep·san ... mu
luggage	τις βαλίτσες	tis va·*lit*·ses
money	τα χρήματα	ta *khri*·ma·ta
passport	το διαβατήριό	to ţhia·va·*ti*·rio

What am I accused of?
Για ποιο πράγμα κατηγορούμαι; — yia pio *pra*·ghma ka·ti·gho·*ru*·me

I didn't realise I was doing anything wrong.
Δεν κατάλαβα ότι έκανα κάτι λάθος. — ţhen ka·*ta*·la·va *o*·ti *e*·ka·na *ka*·ti *la*·thos

I didn't do it.
Δεν το έκανα. — ţhen to *e*·ka·na

I'm sorry.
Συγνώμη. — sigh·*no*·mi

Can I pay an on-the-spot fine?
Μπορώ να πληρώσω ένα πρόστιμο επί τόπου; — bo·*ro* na pli·*ro*·so *e*·na *pro*·sti·mo e·*pi* *to*·pu

I want to contact my embassy.
Θέλω να έρθω σε επαφή με την πρεσβεία μου. — *the*·lo na *er*·tho se e·pa·*fi* me tin prez·*vi*·a mu

Can I make a phone call?
Μπορώ να κάνω ένα τηλεφώνημα; — bo·*ro* na *ka*·no *e*·na ti·le·*fo*·ni·ma

Can I have a lawyer (who speaks English)?
Μπορώ να έχω έναν δικηγόρο (που μιλάει αγγλικά); — bo·*ro* na *e*·kho *e*·nan ţhi·ki·*gho*·ro (pu mi·*la*·i ang·gli·*ka*)

This medication is for personal use.
Αυτό το φάρμακο είναι για προσωπική χρήση. — af·*to* to *far*·ma·ko *i*·ne yia pro·so·pi·*ki* *hri*·si

I have a prescription for this medication.
Έχω συνταγή για αυτό το φάρμακο. — *e*·kho si·da·*yi* yia af·*to* to *far*·ma·ko

I (don't) understand.
(Δεν) καταλαβαίνω. — (ţhen) ka·ta·la·*ve*·no

Health

ΥΓΕΙΑ

DOCTOR

γιατρός

Where's the nearest ...?	Πού είναι το πιο κοντινό...;	pu *i*·ne to pio ko·di·*no* ...
emergency department	πρώτων βοηθειών	*pro*·ton vo·i·thi·*on*
hospital	νοσοκομείο	no·so·ko·*mi*·o
medical centre (after hours)	ιατρικό κέντρο (εφημερεύον)	i·a·tri·*ko ke*·dro (e·fi·me·*re*·von)
pharmacy	φαρμακείο	far·ma·*ki*·o
Where's the nearest ...?	Πού είναι ο πιο κοντινός ...;	pu *i*·ne o pio ko·di·*nos* ...
dentist	οδοντίατρος	o·ţho·di·a·*tros*
doctor	γιατρός	yia·*tros*
optometrist	οφθαλμίατρος	of·thal·*mi*·a·tros

I need a doctor (who speaks English).
Χρειάζομαι έναν γιατρό (που μιλάει αγγλικά). — khri·a·zo·me e·nan yia·*tro* (pu mi·*la*·i ang·gli·*ka*)

Could I see a female doctor?
Μπορώ να δω μια γυναίκα γιατρό; — bo·*ro* na ţho mia yi·*ne*·ka yia·*tro*

Could the doctor come here?
Μπορεί ο γιατρός να έρθει εδώ; — bo·*ri* o yia·*tros* na *er*·thi e·*ţho*

Is there an after-hours emergency number?
Υπάρχει τηλεφωνικός αριθμός για επείγουσες ανάγκες εκτός ωραρίου; — i·*par*·hi ti·le·fo·ni·*kos* a·rith·*mos* yia e·*pi*·ghu·ses a·*na*·ges ek·*tos* o·ra·*ri*·u

I've run out of my medication.
Μου έχουν τελειώσει τα φάρμακά. — mu e·khun te·li·*o*·si ta *far*·ma·*ka*

This is my usual medicine.
Αυτά είναι τα συνηθισμένα μου φάρμακα. — af·*ta* *i*·ne ta si·ni·thiz·*me*·na mu *far*·ma·ka

What's the correct dosage?
Ποια είναι η σωστή δόση; — pia *i*·ne i so·*sti* *ţho*·si

I don't want a blood transfusion.
Δεν θέλω μετάγγιση αίματος. — ţhen *the*·lo me·*ta*·gi·si *e*·ma·tos

Please use a new syringe.
Παρακαλώ χρησιμοποίησε καινούργια σύριγγα. — pa·ra·ka·*lo* khri·si·mo·*pi*·i·se ke·*nur*·yia *si*·ri·ga

I have my own syringe.
Έχω δική μου σύριγγα. — *e*·kho ţhi·*ki* mu *si*·ri·ga

I've been vaccinated against ...
Έχω κάνει εμβόλιο για ... — *e*·kho *ka*·ni em·*vo*·li·o yia

He/She has been vaccinated against ...	Αυτός/Αυτή έχει κάνει εμβόλιο για ...	af·*tos*/af·*ti* *e*·khi *ka*·ni em·*vo*·li·o yia ...
hepatitis A/B/C	ηπατίτιδα A/B/C	i·pa·*ti*·ti·ţha e·i/bi/si
tetanus	τέτανο	*te*·ta·no
typhoid	τύφο	*ti*·fo

I need new ...	Χρειάζομαι ...	khri·a·zo·me ...
contact lenses	καινούργιους φακούς επαφής	ke·*nur*·yius fa·*kus* e·pa·*fis*
glasses	καινούργια γυαλιά	ke·*nur*·yia yia·*lia*

My prescription is ...
Η συνταγή μου είναι ... — i si·da·*yi* mu *i*·ne ...

How much will it cost?
Πόσο θα κοστίσει; — *po*·so tha ko·*sti*·si

Can I have a receipt for my insurance?
Μπορώ να έχω μια απόδειξη για την ασφάλειά μου; — bo·*ro* na *e*·kho mia a·*po*·ţhik·si yia tin as·*fa*·li·*a* mu

THE DOCTOR MAY SAY...

Ποιο είναι το πρόβλημα;
pio *i*·ne to *prov*·li·ma — **What's the problem?**

Πού πονάει;
pu po·*na*·i — **Where does it hurt?**

Έχετε πυρετό;
e·he·te pi·re·*to* — **Do you have a temperature?**

Πόσον καιρό είστε έτσι;
po·son ke·*ro* *i*·ste *et*·si — **How long have you been like this?**

Το είχατε αυτό πριν;
to *i*·kha·te af·*to* prin — **Have you had this before?**

Έχετε σεξουαλικές σχέσεις;
e·he·te sek·su·a·li·*kes she*·sis — **Are you sexually active?**

Μήπως είχατε σεξ χωρίς προφύλαξη;
mi·pos *i*·kha·te seks kho·*ris* pro·*fi*·lak·si — **Have you had unprotected sex?**

Πίνετε;/Καπνίζετε;
pi·ne·te / ka·*pni*·ze·te — **Do you drink / smoke?**

Παίρνετε ναρκωτικά;
per·ne·te nar·ko·ti·*ka* — **Do you take drugs?**

Είστε αλλεργικός σε κάτι;
i·ste a·ler·yi·*kos* se *ka*·ti — **Are you allergic to anything?**

Παίρνετε φάρμακα;
per·ne·te *far*·ma·ka — **Are you on medication?**

Πόσον καιρό ταξιδεύετε;
po·son ke·*ro* tak·si·*the*·ve·te — **How long have you been travelling for?**

Πρέπει να μπείτε στο νοσοκομείο.
pre·pi na *bi*·te sto no·so·ko·*mi*·o — **You need to be admitted to hospital.**

Πρέπει να το ελέγξετε όταν επιστρέψετε στη χώρα σας.
pre·pi na to e *leng*·kse·te o·tan e·pi·*strep*·se·te sti *kho*·ra sas — **You should have it checked when you go home.**

THE DOCTOR MAY SAY...

Πρέπει να επιστρέψετε στη χώρα σας για θεραπεία. *pre*·pi na e·pi·*strep*·se·te sti *kho*·ra sas yia the·ra·*pi*·a	**You should return home for treatment.**
Είστε υποχονδριακός/υποχονδριακή. m/f *i*·ste i·po·khon·ţhri·a·*kos*/ po·khon·ţhri·a·*ki*	**You're a hypochondriac.**

SYMPTOMS & CONDITIONS

συμπτώματα και καταστάσεις

I'm sick.	
Είμαι άρρωστος.	i·*me* a·ro·stos
My friend is (very) sick. (about a man)	
Ο φίλος μου είναι (πολύ) άρρωστος.	o *fi*·los mu *i*·ne (po·*li*) a·ro·stos
My friend is (very) sick. (about a woman)	
Η φίλη μου είναι (πολύ) άρρωστη.	i *fi*·li mu *i*·ne (po·*li*) a·ro·sti
My child is (very) sick.	
Το παιδί μου είναι (πολύ) άρρωστο.	to pe·*ţhi* mu *i*·ne (po·*li*) a·ro·sto

He/She is having a/an ...	Αυτός/Αυτή έχει ...	af·*tos*/af·*ti* e·hi ...
allergic reaction	αλλεργική αντίδραση	a·ler·yi·*ki* a·*di*·ţhra·si
asthma attack	κρίση άσθματος	*KRI*·si as·thma·tos
epileptic fit	επιληπτική κρίση	e·pi·lip·ti·*ki* *kri*·si
heart attack	καρδιακή προσβολή	kar·ţhi·a·*ki* pros·vo·*li*

He/She has been ...	Αυτός/Αυτή ...	af·*tos*/af·*ti* ...
injured	έχει τραυματιστεί	e·hi trav·ma·ti·*sti*
vomiting	κάνει εμετό	*ka*·ni e·me·*to*

I've been ...		
injured	Έχω τραυματιστεί.	e·kho trav·ma·ti·*sti*
vomiting	Κάνω εμετό.	*ka*·no e·me·*to*
I've been bitten/ stung by a ...	Με έχει δαγκώσει/ τσιμπήσει ...	me e·hi ţha·*go*·si/ tsi·*bi*·si ...
bee	μέλισσα	*me*·li·sa
jellyfish	μέδουσα	*me*·ţhu·sa
sea urchin	αχινός	a·hi·*nos*
snake	φίδι	*fi*·ţhi
wasp	σφήκα	*sfi*·ka
weever fish	δράκαινα	*ţhra*·ke·na
I feel ...	Αισθάνομαι ...	es·*tha*·no·me ...
anxious	αγχωμένος/η m/f	an·ho·*me*·nos/i
better	καλύτερα m&f	ka·*li*·te·ra
depressed	θλιμμένος/η m/f	thli·*me*·nos/i
dizzy	ζαλάδα m&f	za·*la*·ţha
hot and cold	ζέστη και κρύο m&f	*ze*·sti ke *kri*·o
nauseous	ναυτία m&f	naf·*ti*·a
shivery	ρίγος m&f	*ri*·ghos
strange	παράξενα m&f	pa·*rak*·se·na
weak	αδύναμος/η m/f	a·*ţhi*·na·mos/i
worse	χειρότερα m&f	hi·*ro*·te·ra

It hurts here.
Πονάει εδώ. — po·*na*·i e·*ţho*

I can't sleep.
Δεν μπορώ να κοιμηθώ. — ţhen bo·*ro* na ki·mi·*tho*

I think it's the medication I'm on.
Νομίζω είναι τα φάρμακα που παίρνω. — no·*mi*·zo *i*·ne ta *far*·ma·ka pu *per*·no

I'm on medication for ...
Παίρνω φάρμακα για ... — *per*·no *far*·ma·ka yia ...

He/She is on medication for ...
Αυτός/αυτή παίρνει φάρμακα για ... — af·*tos*/af·*ti* *per*·ni *far*·ma·ka yia ...

I have (a/an) ...
Έχω ... — e·kho ...

He/She has (a/an) ...
Αυτός/αυτή έχει ... — af·*tos*/af·*ti* e·hi ...

I've recently had (a/an) ...
Είχα πρόσφατα ... — *i*·kha *pros*·fa·ta ...

He/She has recently had (a/an) ...
Αυτός/αυτή είχε πρόσφατα ... — af·*tos*/af·*ti* *i*·he *pros*·fa·ta ...

AIDS	Έηντς n	e·idz
asthma	άσθμα n	as·thma
burn	έγκαυμα n	e·gav·ma
cold	κρύωμα n	*kri*·o·ma
constipation	δυσκοιλιότητα f	ţhis·ki·li·*o*·ti·ta
cough	βήχα m	*vi*·kha
dehydration	αφυδάτωση f	a·fi·*ţha*·to·si
diabetes	διαβήτη m	ţhia·*vi*·ti
diarrhoea	διάρροια f	ţhi·a·ri·a
encephalitis	εγκεφαλίτιδα f	e·ge·fa·*li*·ti·ţha
fever	πυρετό m	pi·re·*to*
headache	πονοκέφαλο m	po·no·*ke*·fa·lo
heatstroke	θερμοπληξία	ther·mo·pli·*xi*·a
indigestion	δυσπεψία f	ţhis·pep·*si*·a
(fungal) infection	(μυκητώδη) μόλυνση f	(mi·ki·*to*·ţhi) *mo*·lin·si
insect bite	τσίμπημα από έντομο n	*tsi*·bi·ma a·*po* e·do·mo
Lyme disease	νόσο του lyme f	*no*·so tu *la*·im
nausea	ναυτία f	naf·*ti*·a
pain	πόνο m	*po*·no
rabies	λύσσα f	*li*·sa
rash	εξάνθημα n	ek·san·thi·ma
sea sickness	ναυτία f	naf·*ti*·a
sore throat	πονόλαιμο m	po·*no*·le·mo
sprain	στραμπούληγμα n	stra·*bu*·ligh·ma
stomachache	στομαχόπονο m	sto·ma·*kho*·po·no
sunburn	ηλιακό έγκαυμα n	i·li·a·*ko* e·gav·ma
tick typhus	τσιμπούρι τύφου n	tsi·*bu*·ri *ti*·fu

WOMEN'S HEALTH

γυναικεία υγεία

(I think) I'm pregnant.
(Νομίζω) Είμαι έγγυος. — (no·*mi*·zo) *i*·me e·gi·os

I'm on the Pill.
Παίρνω το Χάπι. — *per*·no to *kha*·pi

I haven't had my period for (six) weeks.
Δεν έχω περίοδο για (έξι) εβδομάδες. — ţhen e·kho pe·*ri*·o·ţho yia (*ek*·si) ev·ţho·*ma*·ţhes

I've noticed a lump here.
Παρατήρησα ένα εξόγκωμα εδώ. — pa·ra·*ti*·ri·sa e·na ek·so·go·ma e·*ţho*

Do you have something for (period pain)?
Έχετε κάτι για (πόνους περιόδου); — e·he·te *ka*·ti yia (*po*·nus pe·ri·*o*·ţhou)

I have a ...	Έχω ...	e·kho ...
urinary tract infection	ουρολοίμωξη	u·ro·*li*·mo·xi
yeast infection	κολπική μυκητίαση	kol·pi·*ki* mik·*ti*·a·ʒi

THE DOCTOR MAY SAY...

Χρησιμοποιείτε αντισυλληπτικά;
khri·si·mo·pi·*i*·te a·di·si·lip·ti·*ka* — **Are you using contraception?**

Έχετε περίοδο;
e·he·te pe·*ri*·o·ţho — **Are you menstruating?**

Είστε έγγυος;
i·ste e·gi·os — **Are you pregnant?**

Πότε είχατε περίοδο τελευταία;
po·te *i*·kha·te pe·*ri*·o·ţho te·lef·*te*·a — **When did you last have your period?**

Είστε έγγυος.
i·ste e·gi·os — **You're pregnant.**

I need (a/the) ...	Χρειάζομαι ...	khri·a·zo·me ...
contraception	αντισυλληπτικό	a·di·si·lip·ti·*ko*
morning-after pill	το χάπι της επόμενης ημέρας	to *kha*·pi tis e·*po*·me·nis *me*·ras
pregnancy test	τεστ εγκυμοσύνης	test e·gi·mo·*si*·nis

ALLERGIES

αλλεργίες

I have a skin allergy.
Έχω δερματική αλλεργία. e·kho ţher·ma·ti·ki a·ler·*yi*·a

I'm allergic to ...	Είμαι αλλεργικός/ αλλεργική ... m/f	*i*·me a·ler·yi·*kos* a·ler·yi·*ki*
He's allergic to ...	Αυτός είναι αλλεργικός ...	af·*tos i*·ne a·ler·yi·*kos* ...
She's allergic to ...	Αυτή είναι αλλεργική ...	af·*ti i*·ne a·ler·yi·*ki* ...
antibiotics	στα αντιβιωτικά	sta a·di·vi·o·ti·*ka*
anti-inflammatories	στα αντιφλεγμονώδη	sta a·di·flegh·mo·*no*·ţhi
aspirin	στην ασπιρίνη	stin as·pi·*ri*·ni
bees	στις μέλισσες	stis *me*·li·ses
codeine	στην κωδεΐνη	stin ko·ţhe·*i*·ni
penicillin	στην πενικιλλίνη	stin pe·ni·ki·*li*·ni
pollen	στη γύρη	sti *yi*·ri
sulphur-based drugs	στα φάρμακα με θείο	sta *far*·ma·ka me *thi*·o
wasps	στις σφήκες	stis *sfi*·kes

inhaler	εισπνευστήρας m	is·nap·nef·*sti*·ras
injection	ένεση f	e·ne·si
antihistamines	αντιισταμινικά n	a·di·i·sta·mi·ni·*KA*

For food-related allergies, see **vegetarian & special meals**, p173.

PARTS OF THE BODY

μέρη του σώματος

My ... hurts.
Πονάει … po·*na*·i ...

I can't move my ...
Δεν μπορώ να κουνήσω … ţhen bo·*ro* na ku·*ni*·so ...

I have a cramp in my ...
Έχω κράμπα … e·kho *kra*·ba ...

My ... is swollen.
Είναι πρησμένο … *i*·ne priz·*me*·no ...

It hurts when you touch it.
Πονάει όταν το αγγίζεις. po·*ne* *o*·tan to a·*gi*·zis

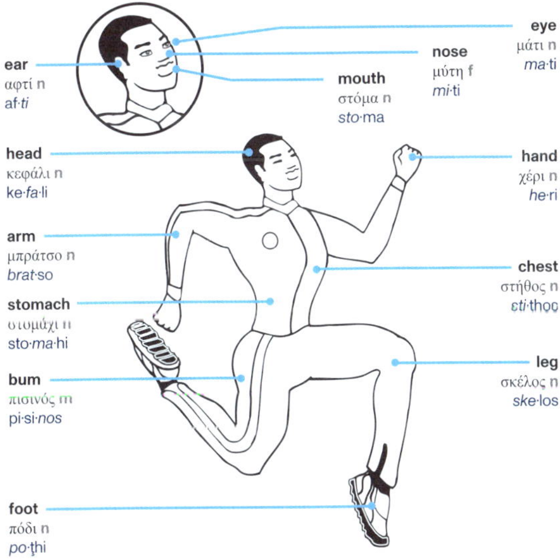

ALTERNATIVE TREATMENTS

εναλλακτικές θεραπείες

I don't subscribe to (Western medicine).
Δεν συμφωνώ με (συμβατική ιατρική). — ţhen sim·fo·*no* me (sim·va·ti·*ki* i·a·tri·*ki*)

I prefer ...	Προτιμώ ...	pro·ti·*mo* ...
Can I see someone who practises ...?	Μπορώ να δω κάποιον που ασκεί ...;	bo·*ro* na ţho *ka*·pion pu a·*ski* ...
acupuncture	βελονισμό	ve·lo·niz·*mo*
naturopathy	φυσιοπαθητική	fi·si·o·pa·thi·ti·*ki*
reflexology	ρεφλεξολογία	re·fle·xo·lo·*ghi*·a

CHEMIST/PHARMACIST

φαρμακοποιός

I need something for (a headache).
Χρειάζομαι κάτι για (πονοκέφαλο). — khri·*a*·zo·me *ka*·ti yia (po·no·*ke*·fa·lo)

Do I need a prescription for (antihistamines)?
Χρειάζομαι συνταγή για (αντιισταμινικά); — khri·*a*·zo·me si·da·*yi* yia (a·di·i·sta·mi·ni·*ka*)

I have a prescription.
Έχω συνταγή. — e·kho si·da·*yi*

☑ COME AGAIN?

If you need something repeated in a consultation or conversation, say Ορίστε; o·*ris*·te (Sorry?). Use Συγνώμη sigh·*no*·mi (Sorry) when you need to apologise.

How many times a day?
Πόσες φορές την ημέρα; — *po*·ses fo·*res* tin i·*me*·ra

Will it make me drowsy?
Θα με κάνει να νυστάζω; — tha me *ka*·ni na ni·*sta*·zo

antiseptic	αντισηπτικό n	a·di·sip·ti·*ko*
condoms	προφυλακτικά n pl	pro·fi·lakh·ti·*ka*
contraceptives	αντισυλληπτικά n pl	a·di·si·lip·ti·*ka*
insect repellent	εντομοαπωθητικό n	e·do·mo·a·po·thi·ti·*ko*
laxative	καθαρτικό n	ka·thar·ti·*ko*
painkillers (for infants)	παυσίπονα (για μωρά) n pl	paf·*si*·po·na (yia mo·*ra*)
rehydration salts	άλατα ενυδάτωσης n pl	a·la·ta e·ni·*ţha*·to·sis
spray for insect bites	σπρέι για τσιμπήματα εντόμων n	*spre*·i yia tsi·*bi*·ma·ta en·*do*·mon
sunburn lotion	λοσιόν για ηλιακό έγκαυμα n	lo·*sion* yia i·li·a·*ko* e·gav·ma
sunscreen	αντιηλιακό n	a·di·i·li·a·*ko*
talcum powder	ταλκ n	talk
thermometer	θερμόμετρο n	ther·*mo*·me·tro
zinc cream	αλοιφή ψευδαργύρου f	a·li·*fi* psev·ţhar·*yi*·ru

THE CHEMIST/PHARMACIST MAY SAY...

Δυο φορές την ημέρα (με φαγητό).
ţhio fo·*res* tin i·*me*·ra (me fa·yi·*to*) — **Twice a day (with food).**

Το έχετε ξαναπάρει;
to e·he·te ksa·na·*pa*·ri — **Have you taken this before?**

Πρέπει να τελειώσετε όλη τη σειρά.
pre·pi na te·li·o·se·te o·li ti si·*ra* — **You must complete the course.**

DENTIST

οδοντίατρος

I have a ...	Έχω ...	e·ho ...
broken tooth	ένα σπασμένο δόντι	e·na spaz·*me*·no *ţho*·di
cavity	ένα τρύπιο δόντι	e·na *tri*·*pio* *ţho*·di
toothache	πονόδοντο	po·*no*·ţho·do

I've lost a filling.
Έχασα ένα σφράγισμα. — e·kha·sa e·na *sfra*·yiz·ma

My dentures are broken.
Η μασέλα μου έσπασε. — i ma·se·la mu e·spa·se

My gums hurt.
Πονούν τα ούλα μου. — po·*nun* ta *u*·la mu

I need an anaesthetic/a filling.
Χρειάζομαι αναισθητικό/σφράγισμα. — khri·a·zo·me a·nes·thi·ti·*ko*/*sfra*·yiz·ma

I don't want it extracted.
Δεν θέλω να το βγάλω. — ţhen *the*·lo na to *vgha*·lo

Ouch!
Όου! — *o*·u

THE DENTIST MAY SAY...

Ανοίξτε καλά το στόμα
a·*nik*·ste kala to *sto*·ma. — **Open wide.**

Δεν θα πονέσει καθόλου.
ţhen tha po·*ne*·si ka·*tho*·lu — **This won't hurt a bit.**

Δαγκώστε αυτό.
ţha·*go*·ste af·*to* — **Bite down on this.**

Μην κουνηθείτε.
min ku·ni·thi·te — **Don't move.**

Ξεβγάλτε!
ksev·*ghal*·te — **Rinse!**

Γυρίστε πίσω, δεν τελείωσα.
yi·*ri*·ste *pi*·so ţhen te·*li*·o·sa — **Come back, I haven't finished.**

Dictionary

ENGLISH – GREEK

Greek nouns in the **dictionary** have their gender indicated by ⓜ masculine, ⓕ feminine or ⓝ neuter. If it's a plural noun you'll also see pl. When a word that could be either a noun or a verb has no gender indicated, it's a verb. Adjectives are given in the masculine form only – see **adjectives & adverbs** (p17) in the **phrasebuilder** for more on how to form feminine and neuter adjectives. Both nouns and adjectives are provided in the nominative case only – refer to p19 in the **phrasebuilder** for more information on **case**. Note that we've also added the abbreviations a adjective and v verb for added clarity where required.

A

aboard επάνω e·*pa*·no
abortion έκτρωση ⓕ *ek*·tro·si
about περίπου pe·*ri*·pu
above από πάνω a·*po pa*·no
abroad στο εξωτερικό sto ek·so·te·ri·*ko*
accident ατύχημα ⓝ a·*ti*·hi·ma
accommodation κατάλυμα ⓝ ka·*ta*·li·ma
account λογαριασμός ⓜ lo·gha·riaz·*mos*
across απέναντι a·*pe*·nan·di
activist ακτιβιστής/ακτιβίστρια ⓜ/ⓕ a·kti·vi·*stis* / a·kti·*vi*·stri·a
actor ηθοποιός ⓜ&ⓕ i·tho·pi·*os*
acupuncture βελονισμός ⓜ ve·lo·niz·*mos*
adaptor μετασχηματιστής ⓜ me·ta·shi·ma·ti·*stis*
addiction εθισμός ⓜ e·thiz·*mos*
address διεύθυνση ⓕ ţhi·*ef*·thin·si
administration διοίκηση ⓕ ţhi·*i*·ki·si
admission (price) τιμή εισόδου ⓜ ti·*mi* i·so·ţhu
admit δέχομαι *ţhe*·kho·me
adult ενήλικος/ενήλικη ⓜ/ⓕ e·*ni*·li·kos / e·*ni*·li·ki
advertisement διαφήμιση ⓕ ţhi·a·*fi*·mi·si
advice συμβουλή ⓕ sim·vu·*li*
Aegean Αιγαίο ⓝ e·*ye*·o
aerobics αερόμπικς ⓝ pl a·e·*ro*·biks
aeroplane αεροπλάνο ⓝ a·e·ro·*pla*·no
Africa Αφρική ⓕ a·fri·*ki*
after μετά me·*ta*
(this) afternoon (το) απόγευμα ⓝ (to) a·*po*·yev·ma
aftershave λοσιόν ξυρίσματος ⓕ lo·si·*on* ksi·*riz*·ma·tos
again πάλι *pa*·li
age ηλικία ⓕ i·li·*ki*·a
(three days) ago (τρεις μέρες) πριν (tris *me*·res) prin
agree συμφωνώ sim·fo·*no*
agriculture γεωργία ⓕ ye·or·*yi*·a
ahead μπροστά bros·*ta*
AIDS Έηντς ⓝ *e*·idz
air αέρας ⓜ a·*e*·ras
air-conditioned με ερκοντίσιον me er·kon·*di*·si·on
air conditioning έρκοντίσιον ⓝ er kon·*di*·si·on
airline αεροπορική εταιρεία ⓕ a·e·ro·po·ri·*ki* e·te·*ri*·a
airmail αεροπορικό ταχυδρομείο ⓝ a·e·ro·po·ri·*ko* ta·hi·ţhro·*mi*·o
airplane αεροπλάνο ⓝ a·e·ro·*pla*·no
airport αεροδρόμιο ⓝ a·e·ro·*ţhro*·mi·o
airport tax τέλος αεροδρομίου ⓜ *te*·los a·e·ro·ţhro·*mi*·u
aisle (on plane) διάδρομος (αεροπλάνου) ⓜ ţhi·*a*·ţhro·mos (a·e·ro·*pla*·nu)
alarm clock ξυπνητήρι ⓝ ksi·pni·*ti*·ri
Albania Αλβανία ⓕ al·va·*ni*·a
alcohol αλκοόλ ⓝ al·ko·*ol*
all όλοι ⓜ *o*·li
allergy αλλεργία ⓕ a·ler·*yi*·a
almond αμύγδαλο ⓝ a·*migh*·ţha·lo
almost σχεδόν she·*ţhon*
alone μόνος *mo*·nos
already ήδη *i*·ţhi
also επίσης e·*pi*·sis

altar βωμός ⓜ vo·*mos*
altitude ύψος ⓝ *ip*·sos
always πάντα *pa*·da
ambassador πρέσβης/πρέσβειρα ⓜ/ⓕ *prez*·vis / *prez*·vi·ra
ambulance ασθενοφόρο ⓝ a·sthe·no·*fo*·ro
America Αμερική ⓕ a·me·ri·*ki*
American football Αμερικανικό ποδόσφαιρο ⓝ a·me·ri·ka·ni·*ko* po·*thos*·fe·ro
amphitheatre αμφιθέατρο ⓝ am·fi·*the*·a·tro
anaemia αναιμία ⓕ a·ne·*mi*·a
anarchist αναρχικός/αναρχική ⓜ/ⓕ a·nar·hi·*kos* / a·nar·hi·*ki*
ancient a αρχαίος ar·*he*·os
and και ke
angry θυμωμένος thi·mo·*me*·nos
animal ζώο ⓝ *zo*·o
ankle αστράγαλος ⓜ a·*stra*·gha·los
another ένας άλλος *e*·nas *a*·los
answer απάντηση ⓕ a·*pa*·di·si
ant μυρμήγκι ⓝ mir·*mi*·gi
antibiotics αντιβιοτικά ⓝ pl a·di·vi·o·ti·*ka*
antinuclear αντιπυρηνικό ⓝ a·di·pi·ri·ni·*ko*
antique αντίκα ⓕ an·*ti*·ka
antiseptic αντισηπτικό ⓝ a·di·si·lip·ti·*ko*
any καθόλου ka·*tho*·lu
anxious αγχωμένος/αγχωμένη ⓜ/ⓕ an·ho·*me*·nos / an·ho·*me*·ni
apartment διαμέρισμα ⓝ thi·a·*me*·riz·ma
appendix (body) σκωληκοειδής απόφυση ⓜ sko·li·ko·i·*this* a·*po*·fi·si
apple μήλο ⓝ *mi*·lo
appointment ⓝ ραντεβού ra·de·*vu*
apricot βερύκοκο ⓝ ve·*ri*·ko·ko
April Απρίλιος ⓜ a·*pri*·li·os
archaic αρχαϊκός ar·kha·i·*kos*
archaeological αρχαιολογικός ar·he·o·lo·yi·*kos*
architect αρχιτέκτονας ⓜ&ⓕ ar·hi·*tek*·to·nas
architecture αρχιτεκτονική ⓕ ar·hi·tek·to·ni·*ki*
argue λογομαχώ lo·gho·ma·*ho*
arm χέρι ⓝ *he*·ri
aromatherapy αρωματοθεραπεία ⓕ a·ro·ma·to·the·ra·*pi*·a
arrest v συλλαμβάνω si·lam·*va*·no
arrivals αφίξεις ⓕ pl a·*fik*·sis
arrive φτάνω *fta*·no
art τέχνη ⓕ *tekh*·ni
art gallery πινακοθήκη ⓕ pi·na·ko·*thi*·ki
artist καλλιτέχνης ⓜ ka·li·*tekh*·nis
ashtray σταχτοθήκη ⓕ stakh·to·*thi*·ki
Asia Ασία ⓕ a·*si*·a
ask (a question) ρωτάω ro·*ta*·o
ask (for something) ζητάω zi·*ta*·o
asparagus σπαράγγι ⓝ spa·*ra*·gi
aspirin ασπιρίνη ⓕ a·spi·*ri*·ni
asthma άσθμα ⓝ *asth*·ma
astrology αστρολογία ⓕ a·stro·lo·*yi*·a
at σε se
athletics στίβος ⓜ pl *sti*·vos
atmosphere ατμόσφαιρα ⓕ at·*mos*·fe·ra
aubergine μελιτζάνα ⓕ me·li·*dza*·na
August Αύγουστος ⓜ *av*·ghu·stos
aunt θεία ⓕ *thi*·a
Australia Αυστραλία ⓕ af·stra·*li*·a
Australian Rules Football Αυστραλιανό ποδόσφαιρο ⓝ af·stra·li·a·*no* po·*thos*·fe·ro
automated teller machine (ATM) αυτόματη μηχανή χρημάτων ⓕ af·*to*·ma·ti mi·kha·*ni* khri·*ma*·ton
autumn φθινόπωρο ⓝ fthi·*no*·po·ro
avenue λεωφόρος ⓕ le·o·*fo*·ros
avocado αβοκάντο ⓝ a·vo·*ka*·do
awful απαίσιος a·*pe*·si·os

B

B&W (movie) ασπρόμαυρο (ταινία) ⓝ as·*pro*·ma·vro (te·*ni*·a)
baby μωρό ⓝ mo·*ro*
baby food φαγητό για μωρά ⓝ fa·yi·*to* yia mo·*ra*
baby powder ταλκ ⓝ talk
babysitter μπέιμπι σίτερ ⓕ *be*·i·bi *si*·ter
back (body) πλάτη ⓕ *pla*·ti
back (position) πίσω *pi*·so
backgammon τάβλι ⓝ *tav*·li
backpack σακίδιο ⓝ sa·*ki*·thi·o
bacon μπέικον ⓝ *be*·i·kon
bad κακός ka·*kos*
bag σάκος ⓜ *sa*·kos

baggage αποσκευές (f) pl a·po·ske·ves
baggage allowance επιτρεπόμενες αποσκευές (f) pl e·pi·tre·po·me·nes a·po·ske·ves
baggage claim παραλαβή αποσκευών (f) pa·ra·la·vi a·po·ske·von
bakery φούρνος (m) fur·nos
balance (account) υπόλοιπο (λογαριασμού) (n) i·po·li·po (lo·gha·riaz·mu)
Balkans Βαλκάνια (n) pl val·ka·ni·a
balcony μπαλκόνι (n) bal·ko·ni
ball (sport) μπάλα (f) ba·la
ballet μπαλέτο (n) ba·le·to
banana μπανάνα (f) ba·na·na
band (music) μπάντα (f) ba·da
bandage επίδεσμος (m) e·pi·ţhez·mos
Band-Aid τσιρότο (n) tsi·ro·to
bank τράπεζα (f) tra·pe·za
bank account τραπεζικός λογαριασμός (m) tra·pe·zi·kos lo·gha·riaz·mos
banknote χαρτονόμισμα (n) khar·to·no·miz·ma
baptism βάπτιση (f) vap·ti·si
bar μπαρ (n) bar
barber κουρέας (m) ku·re·as
bar work δουλειά σε μπαρ (f) ţhu·lia se bar
baseball μπέιζμπολ (n) be·iz·bol
basket καλάθι (n) ka·la·thi
basketball μπάσκετ (n) ba·sket
bath μπάνιο (n) ba·nio
bathing suit μαγιό (n) ma·yio
bathroom μπάνιο (n) ba·nio
battery μπαταρία (f) ba·ta·ri·a
be είμαι i·me
beach παραλία (f) pa·ra·li·a
beach volleyball μπιτς βόλεϊ (n) bits vo·le·i
bean φασόλι (n) fa·so·li
beansprouts φυτρα φασολιών (f) fit·ra fa·so·lion
beautiful όμορφος (m) / όμορφη (f) o·mor·fos / o·mor·fi
beauty salon ινστιτούτο αισθητικής (n) in·sti·tu·to es·thi·ti·kis
because επειδή e·pi·ţhi
bed κρεβάτι (n) kre·va·ti
bedding σκεπάσματα (n) pl ske·paz·ma·ta
bed linen σεντόνια (n) pl se·do·nia
bedroom υπνοδωμάτιο (n) ip·no·ţho·ma·ti·o
bee μέλισσα (f) me·li·sa
beef βοδινό (n) vo·ţhi·no
beer μπύρα (f) bi·ra
beet / beetroot πατζάρι (n) pat·za·ri
before πριν prin
beggar ζητιάνος/ζητιάνα (m)/(f) zi·tia·nos / zi·tia·na
behind πίσω pi·so
Belgium Βέλγιο (n) vel·yi·o
below κάτω ka·to
beside δίπλα ţhi·pla
best a καλύτερος ka·li·te·ros
bet στοίχημα (n) sti·hi·ma
better καλύτερος/καλύτερη (m)/(f) ka·li·te·ros / ka·li·te·ri
between ανάμεσα a·na·me·sa
bible Βίβλος (f) viv·los
bicycle ποδήλατο (n) po·ţhi·la·to
big μεγάλος me·gha·los
bigger μεγαλύτερος me·gha·li·te·ros
biggest ο μεγαλύτερος o me·gha·li·te·ros
bike ποδήλατο (n) po·ţhi·la·to
bike chain αλυσίδα ποδηλάτου (f) a·li·si·ţha po·ţhi·la·tu
bike lock κλειδαριά ποδηλάτου (f) kli·ţha·ria po·ţhi·la·tu
bike path ποδολατόδρομος (m) po·thi·la·to ţhro·mos
bike shop κατάστημα ποδηλάτου (n) ka·ta·sti·ma po·ţhi·la·tu
bill (restaurant etc) λογαριασμός (m) lo·gha·riaz·mos
billiards μπιλιάρδο (n) bi·liar·ţho
binoculars κιάλια (n) pl kia·lia
bird πουλί (n) pu·li
birthday γενέθλια (n) pl ye·ne·thli·a
birth certificate πιστοποιητικό γεννήσεως (n) pi·sto·pi·i·ti·ko ye·ni·se·os
biscuit μπισκότο (n) bi·sko·to
bite (dog) δάγκωμα (f) [illegible]
bite (insect) τσίμπημα (n) tsi·bi·ma
bitter πικρός pi·kros
black a μαύρος mav·ros
bladder κύστη (f) ki·sti
blanket κουβέρτα (f) ku·ver·ta
blind a τυφλός ti·flos
blister φουσκάλα (f) fu·ska·la
blocked μπλοκαρισμένος blo·ka·riz·me·nos
blood αίμα (n) e·ma
blood group ομάδα αίματος (f) o·ma·ţha e·ma·tos

blood pressure πίεση αίματος ⓕ *pi*·e·si e·ma·tos
blood test εξέταση αίματος ⓕ ek·se·ta·si *e*·ma·tos
blue a μπλε ble
board (transport) v ανεβαίνω a·ne·*ve*·no
boarding house πανσιόν ⓕ pan·*sion*
boarding pass κάρτα επιβίβασης ⓕ *kar*·ta e·pi·*vi*·va·sis
boat βάρκα ⓕ *var*·ka
body σώμα ⓝ *so*·ma
boiled βρασμένος vraz·*me*·nos
bone κόκαλο ⓝ *ko*·ka·lo
book βιβλίο ⓝ viv·*li*·o
book (reserve) v κλείνω θέση *kli*·no *the*·si
booked out πλήρες *pli*·res
bookshop βιβλιοπωλείο ⓝ viv·li·o·po·*li*·o
boot (footwear) μπότα ⓕ *bo*·ta
boots (footwear) μπότες ⓕ pl *bo*·tes
border σύνορο ⓝ *si*·no·ro
bored βαριεστημένος va·ri·e·sti·*me*·nos
boring βαρετός va·re·*tos*
borrow δανείζομαι tha·*ni*·zo·me
botanical garden βοτανικός κήπος ⓜ vo·ta·ni·*kos* *ki*·pos
both και οι δύο ke i *thi*·o
bottle μπουκάλι ⓝ bu·*ka*·li
bottle opener ανοιχτήρι ⓝ a·nikh·*ti*·ri
bottle shop κάβα ⓕ *ka*·va
bottom (body) πισινός ⓜ pi·si·*nos*
bottom (position) κάτω *ka*·to
bouzouki (traditional music) μπουζούκι ⓝ bu·*zu*·ki
bouzouki place μπουζουκτσίδικο ⓝ bu·zuk·*tsi*·thi·ko
bowl μπωλ ⓝ bol
box κουτί ⓝ ku·*ti*
boxer shorts μποξεράκι ⓝ box·e·*ra*·ki
boxing μποξ ⓝ boks
boy αγόρι ⓝ a·*gho*·ri
boyfriend φίλος ⓜ *fi*·los
bra σουτιέν ⓝ su·ti·*en*
brakes φρένα ⓝ pl *fre*·na
brandy κονιάκ ⓝ ko·*niak*
brave γενναίος ye·*ne*·os
bread ψωμί ⓝ pso·*mi*
bread rolls ψωμάκια ⓝ pl pso·*ma*·kia
break v σπάω *spa*·o
break down χαλάω ha·*la*·o
breakfast πρωινό ⓝ pro·i·*no*
breast (body) στήθος ⓝ *sti*·thos
breathe αναπνέω a·nap·*ne*·o
bribe v δωροδοκώ tho·ro·tho·*ko*
bridge γεφύρι ⓝ ye·*fi*·ri
briefcase ⓜ χαρτοφύλακας khar·to·*fi*·la·kas
brilliant λαμπρός la·*bros*
bring φέρνω *fer*·no
broccoli μπρόκολο ⓝ *bro*·ko·lo
brochure μπροσούρα ⓕ bro·*su*·ra
broken σπασμένος spaz·*me*·nos
broken down χαλασμένος kha·laz·*me*·nos
bronchitis βρογχίτιδα ⓕ vro·*hi*·ti·tha
bronze μπρούτζος ⓜ *bru*·dzos
brother αδερφός ⓜ a·ther·*fos*
brown καφέ ka·*fe*
bruise μελανιά ⓕ me·la·ni·*a*
brush βούρτσα ⓕ *vur*·tsa
bucket κουβάς ⓜ ku·*vas*
Buddhist Βουδιστής/Βουδίστρια vu·thi·*stis* / vu·*thi*·stri·a ⓜ/ⓕ
budget προϋπολογισμός ⓜ pro·i·po·lo·yiz·*mos*
buffet μπουφές ⓜ bu·*fes*
bug κοριός ⓜ ko·*rios*
build v χτίζω *khti*·zo
builder χτίστης ⓜ *khti*·stis
building κτήριο ⓝ *kti*·ri·o
Bulgaria Βουλγαρία ⓕ vul·gha·*ri*·a
bumbag μπανάνα ⓝ ba·*na*·na
burn έγκαυμα ⓝ *e*·gav·ma
burnt καμένος ka·*me*·nos
bus (city) αστικό λεωφορείο ⓝ a·sti·*ko* le·o·fo·*ri*·o
bus (intercity) υπεραστικό λεωφορείο ⓝ i·per·as·ti·*ko* le·o·fo·*ri*·o
bus station σταθμός λεωφορείου ⓜ stath·*mos* le·o·fo·*ri*·u
bus stop σταση λεωφορείου ⓕ *sta*·si le·o·fo·*ri*·u
business επιχείρηση ⓕ e·pi·*hi*·ri·si
business class μπιζνες κλασ *biz*·nes klas
businessperson επιχειρηματίας ⓜ&ⓕ e·pi·hi·ri·ma·*ti*·as
business trip επαγγελματικό ταξίδι ⓝ e·pal·ghe·ma·ti·*ko* tak·*si*·thi
busker πλανόδιος μουσικός ⓜ pla·*no*·thi·os mu·si·*kos*

busy απασχολημένος a·pa·skho·li·*me*·nos
but αλλά a·*la*
butcher χασάπης ⓜ kha·*sa*·pis
butcher's shop κρεοπωλείο ⓝ kre·o·po·*li*·o
butter βούτυρο ⓝ *vu*·ti·ro
butterfly πεταλούδα ⓕ pe·ta·*lu*·ţha
button κουμπί ⓝ ku·*bi*
buy v αγοράζω a·gho·*ra*·zo
Byzantine Βυζαντινός vi·za·di·*nos*

C

cabin καμπίνα ⓕ ka·*bi*·na
cabbage λάχανο ⓕ *la*·ha·no
cable car τελεφερίκ ⓝ te·le·fe·*rik*
cafe καφέ ⓝ ka·fe·sti·a·*to*·ri·o
cafeteria καφετηρία ⓕ ka·*fe*
cake γλυκό ⓜ ghli·*ko*
cake shop ζαχαροπλαστείο ⓝ za·kha·ro·pla·*sti*·o
calculator αριθμομηχανή ⓕ a·rith·mo·mi·kha·*ni*
calendar ημερολόγιο ⓝ i·me·ro·*lo*·yi·o
call v καλώ ka·*lo*
camera φωτογραφική μηχανή ⓕ fo·to·ghra·fi·*ki* mi·kha·*ni*
camera shop κατάστημα φωτογραφικών ειδών ⓝ ka·*ta*·sti·ma fo·to·ghra·fi·*kon* i·*ţhon*
camp v κατασκηνώνω ka·ta·ski·*no*·no
camping ground χώρος για κάμπινγκ ⓜ *kho*·ros yia *kam*·ping
camping store κατάστημα ειδών κατασκήνωσης ⓝ ka·*ta*·sti·ma i·*ţhon* ka·ta·*ski*·no·sis
campsite χώρος για κάμπινγκ ⓜ *kho*·ros yia *kam*·ping
can (be able) v μπορώ bo·*ro*
can (tin) κουτί ⓝ ku·*ti*
can opener ανοιχτήρι ⓝ a·nikh·*ti*·ri
Canada Καναδάς ⓜ ka·na·*ţhas*
cancel ακυρώνω a·ki·*ro*·no
cancer καρκίνος ⓜ kar·*ki*·nos
candle κερί ⓝ ke·*ri*
candy καραμέλα ⓕ ka·ra·*me*·la
cantaloupe πεπόνι ⓝ pe·*po*·ni
capsicum πιπεριά ⓕ pi·pe·*ria*
car αυτοκίνητο ⓝ af·to·*ki*·ni·to
caravan τροχόσπιτο ⓝ tro·*kho*·spi·to

cardiac arrest καρδιακή προσβολή ⓕ kar·ţhi·a·*ki* proz·vo·*li*
cards (playing) χαρτιά ⓝ pl khar·*tia*
care (for someone) φροντίζω fro·*di*·zo
car hire ενοικίαση αυτοκινήτου ⓕ e·ni·*ki*·a·si af·to·ki·*ni*·tu
carob χαρούπι ⓝ kha·*ru*·pi
car owner's title άδεια κυκλοφορίας ⓜ a·di·a kik·lo·fo·*ri*·as
car park χώρος στάθμευσης αυτοκινήτων ⓜ *kho*·ros *stath*·mef·sis af·to·ki·*ni*·ton
carpenter μαραγκός ⓜ ma·ra·*gos*
car registration άδεια κυκλοφορίας αυτοκινήτου ⓕ a·ţhia ki·klo·fo·*ri*·as af·to·ki·*ni*·tu
carrot καρότο ⓝ ka·*ro*·to
carry μεταφέρω me·ta·*fe*·ro
carton χαρτοκιβώτιο ⓝ khar·to·ki·*vo*·ti·o
cash μετρητά ⓝ pl me·tri·*ta*
cash (a cheque) v εξαργυρώνω ek·sar·yi·*ro*·no
cash register ταμείο ⓝ ta·*mi*·o
cashew κάσιου ⓝ *ka*·si·u
cashier ταμίας ⓜ&ⓕ ta·*mi*·as
casino καζίνο ⓝ ka·*zi*·no
castle κάστρο ⓝ *ka*·stro
casual work ημερομίσθια εργασία ⓕ i·me·ro·*mi*·sthi·a er·gha·*si*·a
cat γάτα ⓕ *gha*·ta
catamaran καταμαράν ⓝ ka·ta·ma·*ran*
cathedral μητρόπολη ⓕ mi·*tro*·po·li
Catholic Καθολικός/Καθολική ⓜ/ⓕ ka·tho·li·*kos* / ka·tho·li·*ki*
cauliflower κουνουπίδι ⓝ ku·nu·*pi*·ţhi
cave σπηλιά ⓕ spi·*lia*
celebration γιορτή ⓕ yior·*ti*
cellphone κινητό ⓝ ki·ni·*to*
cemetery κοιμητήριο ⓝ ki·mi·*ti*·ri·o
cent σεντ ⓝ sent
centimetre εκατοστό ⓝ e·ka·to·*sto*
centre κέντρο ⓝ *ke*·dro
ceramics κεραμικά ⓝ pl ke·ra·mi·*ka*
cereal δημητριακά ⓝ pl ţhi·mi·tri·a·*ka*
certificate πιστοποιητικό ⓝ pi·sto·pi·i·ti·*ko*
chain αλυσίδα ⓕ a·li·*si*·ţha
chair καρέκλα ⓕ ka·*re*·kla
chairlift (skiing) τελεφερίκ ⓝ te·le·fe·*rik*
Champagne σαμπάνια ⓕ sam·*pa*·nia

championships πρωτάθλημα ⓝ pro·*ta*·thli·ma
chance πιθανότητα ⓕ pi·tha·*no*·ti·ta
change αλλαγή ⓕ a·la·*yi*
change (coins) ψιλά ⓝ pl psi·*la*
change (from sale) ρέστα ⓝ pl *re*·sta
change (money) v αλλάζω a·*la*·zo
changing room (in shop) δοκιμαστήριο ⓝ ţho·ki·ma·*sti*·ri·o
charming χαριτωμένος kha·ri·to·*me*·nos
charter flight πτήση τσάρτερ ⓕ *pti*·si *tsar*·ter
chat up (somebody) v ψήνω *psi*·no
cheap φτηνός fti·*nos*
cheat απατεώνας/απατεώνισσα ⓜ/ⓕ a·pa·te·o·nas / a·pa·te·o·ni·sa
check v ελέγχω e·*leng*·kho
check (banking) επιταγή ⓕ e·pi·ta·*yi*
check (bill) λογαριασμός ⓜ lo·gha·riaz·*mos*
check-in (desk) ρεσεψιόν ⓕ re·sep·*sion*
checkpoint σημείο ελέγχου ⓝ si·*mi*·o e·*leng*·khu
cheese τυρί ⓝ ti·*ri*
cheese shop τυροπωλείο ⓝ ti·ro·po·*li*·o
chef ⓜ σεφ sef
chemist (shop) φαρμακείο ⓝ far·ma·*ki*·o
chemist (pharmacist) φαρμακοποιός ⓜ&ⓕ far·ma·ko·pi·*os*
cheque επιταγή ⓕ e·pi·ta·*yi*
cherry κεράσι ⓝ ke·*ra*·si
chess σκάκι ⓝ *ska*·ki
chessboard σκακιέρα ⓕ ska·*kie*·ra
chest (body) στήθος ⓝ *sti*·thos
chestnut κάστανο ⓝ *ka*·sta·no
chewing gum μαστίχα ⓕ ma·*sti*·kha
chicken κοτόπουλο ⓝ ko·*to*·pu·lo
chicken pox ανεμοβλογιά ⓕ a·ne·mov·lo·*yia*
chickpea στραγάλι ⓝ stra·*gha*·li
child παιδί ⓝ pe·*ţhi*
childminding φύλαξη παιδιών ⓕ *fi*·la·ksi pe·*ţhion*
children παιδιά ⓝ pl pe·*ţhia*
child seat παιδικό κάθισμα ⓝ pe·ţhi·*ko* *ka*·thiz·ma
chili πιπεριά ⓕ pi·pe·*ria*
chili sauce σάλτσα τσίλι ⓕ *sal*·tsa *tsi*·li
chipura τσίπουρο ⓝ *tsi*·pu·ro
chiropractor χειροπράκτης ⓜ&ⓕ hi·ro·*prak*·tis
chocolate σοκολάτα ⓕ so·ko·*la*·ta
choose διαλέγω ţhia·*le*·gho
chopping board σανίδα κοπής ⓕ sa·*ni*·ţha ko·*pis*
chopsticks τσοπ στικς ⓝ pl tsop stiks
Christian Χριστιανός/Χριστιανή ⓜ/ⓕ khri·sti·a·*nos* / khri·sti·a·*ni*
Christian name μικρό όνομα ⓝ mi·*kro* *o*·no·ma
Christmas Χριστούγεννα ⓝ pl khri·*stu*·ye·na
Christmas Day ημέρα Χριστουγέννων ⓕ i·*me*·ra khri·stu·*ye*·non
Christmas Eve παραμονή Χριστουγέννων ⓕ pa·ra·mo·*ni* khri·stu·*ye*·non
church εκκλησία ⓕ e·kli·*si*·a
cider μηλίτης ⓜ mi·*li*·tis
cigar πούρο ⓝ *pu*·ro
cigarette τσιγάρο ⓝ tsi·*gha*·ro
cigarette lighter αναπτήρας ⓜ a·nap·*ti*·ras
cinema σινεμά ⓝ si·ne·*ma*
circus τσίρκο ⓝ *tsir*·ko
citizenship ιθαγένεια ⓕ i·tha·*ye*·ni·a
city πόλη ⓕ *po*·li
city centre κέντρο της πόλης ⓝ *ke*·dro tis *po*·lis
civil rights ατομικά δικαιώματα ⓝ pl a·to·mi·*ka* ţhi·ke·*o*·ma·ta
civil servant δημόσιος υπάλληλος ⓜ&ⓕ ţhi·*mo*·si·os i·*pa*·li·los
class (category) τάξη ⓕ *tak*·si
classical κλασικός kla·si·*kos*
class system ταξικό σύστημα ⓝ tak·si·*ko* *si*·sti·ma
clean a καθαρός ka·tha·*ros*
clean v καθαρίζω ka·tha·*ri*·zo
cleaning καθάρισμα ⓝ ka·*tha*·riz·ma
client πελάτης/πελάτισσα ⓜ/ⓕ pe·*la*·tis / pe·*la*·ti·sa
cliff γκρεμός ⓜ gre·*mos*
climb v σκαρφαλώνω skar·fa·*lo*·no
cloakroom γκαρνταρόμπα ⓕ gar·da·*ro*·ba
clock ρολόι ⓝ ro·*lo*·i
close a κοντινός ko·di·*nos*
close v κλείνω *kli*·no
closed κλεισμένος kliz·*me*·nos

clothesline σχοινί απλώματος ⓝ skhi·ni ap·lo·ma·tos
clothing ρούχα ⓝ pl ru·kha
clothing store κατάστημα ρούχων ⓝ ka·ta·sti·ma ru·khon
cloud σύννεφο ⓝ si·ne·fo
cloudy συννεφιασμένος si·ne·fiaz·me·nos
clutch (car) συμπλέκτης ⓜ si·ble·ktis
coach (sport) προπονητής/προπονήτρια ⓜ/ⓕ pro·po·ni·tis / pro·po·ni·tri·a
coalition συνασπισμός ⓜ sin·as·piz·mos
coast ακτή ⓕ ak·ti
coat παλτό ⓝ pal·to
cocaine κοκαΐνη ⓕ ko·ka·i·ni
cockroach κοριός ⓜ ko·rios
cocktail κοκτέιλ ⓝ kok·te·il
cocoa κακάο ⓝ ka·ka·o
coconut ινδική καρύδα ⓕ in·ţhi·ki ka·ri·ţha
coffee καφές ⓜ ka·fes
coffee shop καφέ ⓝ ka·fe
coins κέρματα ⓝ pl ker·ma·ta
cold κρύο ⓝ kri·o
cold a κρυωμένος kri·o·me·nos
colleague συνάδελφος/συναδέλφισσα ⓜ/ⓕ si·na·ţhel·fos / si·na·ţhel·fi·sa
college κολέγιο ⓝ ko·le·yi·o
colour χρώμα ⓝ khro·ma
column κολόνα ⓕ ko·lo·na
comb χτένα ⓕ khte·na
come έρχομαι er·kho·me
comedy κωμωδία ⓕ ko·mo·ţhi·a
comfortable άνετος a·ne·tos
commission προμήθεια ⓕ pro·mi·thi·a
communications (profession) επικοινωνίες ⓕ pl e·pi·ki·no·ni·es
communion κοινωνία ⓕ ki·no·ni·a
communist κομμουνιστής/κομμουνίστρια ⓜ/ⓕ ko·mu·ni·stis / ko·mu·ni·stri·a
companion συντροφος/συντροφισσα ⓜ/ⓕ si·dro·fos / si·dro·fi·sa
company (firm) εταιρεία ⓕ e·te·ri·a
company (friends) συντροφιά ⓕ si·dro·fia
compass πυξίδα ⓕ pik·si·ţha
complain παραπονούμαι pa·ra·po·nu·me
complaint παράπονο ⓝ pa·ra·po·no
complimentary (free) δωρεάν ţho·re·an
computer υπολογιστής ⓜ i·po·lo·ghi·stis
computer game παιχνίδι στο κομπιούτερ ⓝ peh·ni·ţhi sto kom·piu·ter
concert κονσέρτο/συναυλία ⓝ kon·ser·to / si·na·vli·a
concussion κλονισμός ⓜ klo·niz·mos
conditioner (hair) κοντίσιονερ ⓝ kon·di·si·o·ner
condom προφυλακτικό ⓝ pro·fi·lak·ti·ko
conference συνέδριο ⓝ si·ne·ţhri·o
confession εξομολόγηση ⓕ ek·so·mo·lo·ghi·si
confirm (a booking) επιβεβαιώνω e·pi·ve·ve·o·no
conjunctivitis επιπεφυκίτιδα ⓜ e·pi·pe·fi·ki·ti·ţha
connection σύνδεσμος ⓜ sin·ţhez·mos
conservative a συντηρητικός si·di·ri·ti·kos
constipation δυσκοίλια ⓕ ţhis·ki·li·a
consulate προξενείο ⓝ prok·se·ni·o
contact lenses φακοί επαφής ⓜ pl fa·ki e·pa·fis
contact lens solution υγρό φακών επαφής ⓝ i·ghro fa·kon e·pa·fis
contraceptives αντισυλληπτικά ⓝ pl a·di·si·lip·ti·ka
contract συμβόλαιο ⓝ sim·vo·le·o
convenience store μίνι μάρκετ ⓝ mi·ni mar·ket
convent μονή ⓕ mo·ni
cook μάγειρας/μαγείρισσα ⓜ/ⓕ ma·yi·ras / ma·yi·ri·sa
cook v μαγειρεύω ma·yi·re·vo
cookie μπισκότο ⓝ bis·ko·to
cooking μαγείρεμα ⓝ ma·yi·re·ma
cool (temperature) δροσερό ţhro·se·ro
copper χαλκός ⓜ khal·kos
copy αντίγραφο ⓝ a·di·ghra·fo
Corinthian Κορινθιακός ko·rin·thi·a·kos
corkscrew ανοιχτήρι ⓝ a·nikh·ti·ri
corn καλαμπόκι ⓝ ka·la·bo·ki
corner γωνία ⓕ gho·ni·a
cornflakes κορν φλέικς ⓝ pl korn fle·iks
corrupt διεφθαρμένος ţhi·ef·thar·me·nos
cost v κοστίζω ko·sti·zo
cotton βαμβάκι ⓝ va·va·ki
cotton balls μπάλες από βαμβάκι ⓝ pl ba·les a·po va·va·ki
cotton buds μπατονέτες ⓝ ba·to·ne·tes

cough v βήχω vi·kho
cough medicine αντιβηχικό φάρμακο ⓝ an·di·vi·hi·ko far·ma·ko
count v μετράω me·tra·o
counter (at bar) πάγκος ⓜ pa·gos
country χώρα ⓕ kho·ra
countryside εξοχή ⓕ ek·so·hi
coupon κουπόνι ⓝ ku·po·ni
courgette κολοκυθάκι ⓝ ko·lo·ki·tha·ki
court (legal) δικαστήριο ⓝ ţhi·ka·sti·ri·o
court (tennis) γήπεδο ⓝ yi·pe·ţho
couscous κουσκούς ⓝ kus·kus
cover charge κουβέρ ⓕ ku·ver
cow αγελάδα ⓕ a·ye·la·ţha
cracker (biscuit) κράκερ ⓕ kra·ker
craft τέχνη ⓕ tekh·ni
crash ⓜ σύγκρουση si·ghru·si
crazy τρελός tre·los
cream κρέμα ⓕ kre·ma
creche παιδικός σταθμός ⓜ pe·ţhi·kos stath·mos
credit πίστωση ⓕ pi·sto·si
credit card πιστωτική κάρτα ⓕ pi·sto·ti·ki kar·ta
cricket (sport) κρίκετ ⓝ kri·ket
crop σοδειά ⓕ so·ţhia
cross (religious) σταυρός ⓜ stav·ros
crowded γεμάτο (κόσμο) ye·ma·to (koz·mo)
cruise κρουαζιέρα ⓕ kru·a·zi·e·ra
cucumber αγγούρι ⓝ a·gu·ri
cup φλυτζάνι ⓝ fli·dza·ni
cupboard ντουλάπι ⓝ du·la·pi
currency exchange υπηρεσία συναλλάγματος ⓕ i·pi·re·si·a si·na·lagh·ma·tos
current (electricity) ρεύμα ⓝ rev·ma
current affairs επικαιρότητα ⓕ e·pi·ke·ro·ti·ta
curry κάρι ⓝ ka·ri
cushion cover μαξιλαροθήκη ⓕ mak·si·la·ro·thi·ki
custom έθιμο ⓝ e·thi·mo
customs τελωνείο ⓝ te·lo·ni·o
cut v κόβω ko·vo
cutlery μαχαιροπήρουνα ⓝ pl ma·he·ro·pi·ru·na
CV βιογραφικό σημείωμα ⓝ vi·o·ghra·fi·ko si·mi·o·ma
Cycladic Κυκλαδικός ki·kla·ţhi·kos
cycle v κάνω ποδήλατο ka·no po·ţhi·la·to
cycling ποδηλασία ⓕ po·ţhi·la·si·a
cyclist ποδηλάτης/ποδηλάτισσα ⓜ/ⓕ po·ţhi·la·tis / po·ţhi·la·ti·sa
Cypriot (person) Κύπριος/Κύπρια ⓜ/ⓕ ki·pri·os / ki·pri·a
Cypriot (wine etc) κυπριακός/κυπριακή ⓜ/ⓕ ki·pri·a·kos / ki·pri·a·ki
Cyprus Κύπρος ⓕ ki·pros
cystitis κυστίτιδα ⓕ kis·ti·ti·ţha

D

dad μπαμπάς ⓜ ba·bas
daily καθημερινός ka·thi·me·ri·nos
dairy shop γαλακτοπωλείο ⓝ gha·lak·to·po·li·o
dance v χορεύω kho·re·vo
dancing χορός kho·ros
dangerous επικίνδυνος e·pi·kin·ţhi·nos
dark (night) a σκοτεινός sko·ti·nos
dark (colour) a σκούρος sku·ros
date (a person) v βγαίνω (με κάποιον) vye·no (me ka·pion)
date (appointment) ραντεβού ⓝ ra·de·vu
date (day) ημερομηνία ⓕ i·me·ro·mi·ni·a
date (fruit) χουρμάς ⓜ khur·mas
date of birth ημερομηνία γεννήσεως ⓕ i·me·ro·mi·ni·a ye·ni·se·os
daughter κόρη ⓕ ko·ri
dawn αυγή ⓕ av·yi
day ημέρα ⓕ i·me·ra
day after tomorrow μεθαύριο me·thav·ri·o
day before yesterday προχθές prokh·tes
dead a νεκρός ne·kros
deaf a κουφός ku·fos
deal (cards) μοιράζω (χαρτιά) mi·ra·zo (khar·tia)
December Δεκέμβριος ⓜ de·kem·vri·os
decide αποφασίζω a·po·fa·si·zo
deck κατάστρωμα ⓝ ka·ta·stro·ma
deep βαθύς va·this
deforestation αποδάσωση ⓕ a·po·ţha·so·si
degrees (temperature) βαθμοί ⓜ pl vath·mi

dehydration αφυδάτωση ⓕ a·fi·*ţha*·to·si

delay καθυστέρηση ⓕ ka·thi·*ste*·ri·si

delicatessen ντελικατέσεν ⓝ de·li·ka·*te*·sen

delineation line διαχωριστική γραμμή ⓕ ţhi·a·kho·ri·sti·*ki* ghra·*mi*

deliver παραδίνω pa·ra·*ţhi*·no

democracy δημοκρατία ⓕ ţhi·mo·kra·*ti*·a

demonstration διαδήλωση ⓕ ţhi·a·*ţhi*·lo·si

Denmark Δανία ⓕ ţha·*ni*·a

dental floss οδοντιατρική κλωστή ⓕ o·ţho·di·a·tri·*ki* klo·*sti*

dentist οδοντίατρος ⓜ&ⓕ o·ţho·*di*·a·tros

deodorant αποσμητικό ⓝ a·poz·mi·ti·*ko*

depart (leave) αναχωρώ a·na·kho·*ro*

department store πολυκατάστημα ⓝ po·li·ka·*ta*·sti·ma

departure αναχώρηση ⓕ a·na·*kho*·ri·si

departure gate πύλη αναχώρησης ⓕ *pi*·li a·na·*kho*·ri·sis

deposit (bank) κατάθεση ⓕ ka·*ta*·the·si

deposit (on house etc) προκαταβολή ⓕ pro·ka·ta·vo·*li*

depressed θλιμμένος/θλιμμένη ⓜ/ⓕ thli·*me*·nos / thli·*me*·ni

derailleur ντεραγέ ⓜ de·ra·*ye*

descendent απόγονος ⓜ a·*po*·gho·nos

desert έρημος ⓕ *e*·ri·mos

design σχέδιο ⓝ *skhe*·ţhi·o

dessert επιδόρπιο ⓝ e·pi·*ţhor*·pi·o

destination προορισμός ⓜ pro·o·riz·*mos*

details λεπτομέρειες ⓕ pl lep·to·*me*·ri·es

diabetes διαβήτης ⓜ ţhi·a·*vi*·tis

dial tone ήχος κλήσης ⓜ *i*·khos *kli*·sis

diaper πάνα ⓕ *pa*·na

diaphragm διάφραγμα ⓝ ţhi·*a*·fragh·ma

diarrhoea διάρροια ⓕ ţhi·*a*·ri·a

diary ημερολόγιο ⓝ i·me·ro·*lo*·yi·o

diaspora διασπορά ⓕ ţhi·a·spo·*ra*

dice ζάρια ⓝ pl *za*·ria

dictionary λεξικό ⓝ lek·si·*ko*

die v πεθαίνω pe·*the*·no

diet δίαιτα ⓕ *ţhi*·e·ta

different διαφορετικός ţhia·fo·re·ti·*kos*

difficult δύσκολος *ţhi*·sku·los

digital a ψηφιακός psi·fi·a·*kos*

dining car βαγόνι εστιατορίου ⓝ va·*gho* e·sti·a·to·*ri*·u

dinner δείπνο ⓝ *ţhip*·no

direct a άμεσος *a*·me·sos

direction κατεύθυνση ⓕ ka·*tef*·thin·si

director διευθυντής/διευθύντρια ⓜ/ⓕ ţhi·ef·thi·*dis* / ţhi·ef·*thi*·dri·a

dirty a βρώμικος *vro*·mi·kos

disabled a ανάπηρος a·*na*·pi·ros

disco ντισκοτέκ ⓕ di·sko·*tek*

discount έκπτωση ⓕ *ek*·pto·si

discrimination διάκριση ⓕ ţhi·*a*·kri·si

disease ασθένεια ⓕ a·*sthe*·ni·a

dish πιάτο ⓝ *pia*·to

diving κατάδυση ⓕ ka·*ta*·ţhi·si

diving gear εξοπλισμός κατάδυσης ⓜ e·kso·plis·*mos* ka·*ta*·ţhi·sis

divorced a διαζευγμένος/διαζευγμένη ⓜ/ⓕ ţhi·a·zev·*ghme*·nos / ţhi·a·zev·*ghme*·ni

dizzy ζαλισμένος/ζαλισμένη ⓜ/ⓕ za·liz·*me*·nos / za·liz·*me*·ni

do v κάνω *ka*·no

doctor γιατρός ⓜ&ⓕ yia·*tros*

documentary ντοκιμαντέρ ⓝ do·ki·man·*ter*

dog σκυλί ⓝ ski·*li*

dole επίδομα ανεργίας ⓝ e·*pi*·ţho·ma an·er·*yi*·as

doll κούκλα ⓕ *ku*·kla

dollar δολάριο ⓝ ţho·*la*·ri·o

dolphin δελφίνι ⓝ ţhel·*fi*·ni

dhomatia (room for rent) δωμάτια (για ενοικίαση) ⓝ pl ţho·*ma*·ti·a (yia e·ni·*ki*·a·si)

dominoes ντόμινο ⓝ *do*·mi·no

door πόρτα ⓕ *por*·ta

dope (drugs) ναρκωτικά ⓝ pl nar·ko·ti·*ka*

Doric Δωρικός ţho·ri·*kos*

double a διπλός ţhi·*plos*

double bed διπλό κρεβάτι ⓝ ţhi·*plo* kre·*va*·ti

double room διπλό δωμάτιο ⓝ ţhi·*plo* ţho·*ma*·ti·o

down κάτω *ka*·to

downhill κατηφορικός ka·ti·fo·ri·*kos*

dozen ντουζίνα ⓕ du·*zi*·na

drama δράμα ⓝ *ţhra*·ma

dream όνειρο ⓝ *o*·ni·ro

dress ⓝ φόρεμα ⓝ *fo*·re·ma

dried ξηρός ksi·ros
dried fruit αποξηραμένα φρούτα ⓝ pl a·po·ksi·ra·me·na fru·ta
drink ποτό ⓝ po·to
drink v πίνω pi·no
drink (alcoholic) ποτό (αλκοολούχο) ⓝ po·to (al·ko·o·lu·ho)
drive v οδηγώ o·thi·gho
drivers licence άδεια οδήγησης ⓕ a·thi·a o·thi·yi·sis
drizzle ψιχάλα ⓕ psi·kha·la
drug (illegal) ναρκωτικό ⓝ nar·ko·ti·ko
drug addict ναρκομανής ⓜ&ⓕ nar·ko·ma·nis
drug addiction εθισμός στα ναρκωτικά ⓜ e·thiz·mos sta nar·ko·ti·ka
drug dealer έμπορος ναρκωτικών ⓜ&ⓕ e·bo·ros nar·ko·ti·kon
drug trafficking εμπόριο ναρκωτικών ⓕ em·bo·ri·o nar·ko·ti·kon
drugs (illicit) ναρκωτικά ⓝ pl nar·ko·ti·ka
drum τύμπανο ⓝ ti·ba·no
drunk μεθυσμένος me·thiz·me·nos
dry a στεγνός stegh·nos
dry v στεγνώνω stegh·no·no
duck πάπια ⓕ pa·pia
dummy (pacifier) πιπίλα ⓕ pi·pi·la

E

each καθένας ka·the·nas
ear αφτί ⓝ af·ti
early νωρίς no·ris
earn κερδίζω ker·thi·zo
earplugs ωτοασπίδες ⓕ pl o·to·a·spi·thes
earrings σκουλαρίκια ⓝ pl sku·la·ri·kia
Earth Γη ⓕ yi
earthquake σεισμός ⓜ siz·mos
east ανατολή ⓕ a·na·to·li
Easter Πάσχα ⓝ pas·kha
easy εύκολο ef·ko·lo
eat τρώγω tro·gho
economy class τουριστική θέση ⓕ tu·ri·sti·ki the·si
ecstacy (drug) έκσταση ⓕ ek·sta·si
eczema έκζεμα ⓝ ek·ze·ma
education εκπαίδευση ⓕ ek·pe·thef·si
egg αβγό ⓝ av·gho
eggplant μελιτζάνα ⓕ me·li·dza·na
election εκλογή ⓕ ek·lo·yi
electrical store κατάστημα ηλεκτρικών ειδών ⓝ ka·ta·sti·ma i·lek·tri·kon i·thon
electricity ηλεκτρισμός ⓜ i·lek·triz·mos
elevator ασανσέρ ⓝ a·san·ser
email ημέιλ ⓝ i·me·il
embarrassed αμήχανος a·mi·kha·nos
embassy πρεσβεία ⓕ pre·zvi·a
embroidery κέντημα ⓝ ke·di·ma
emergency έκτακτη ανάγκη ⓕ ek·tak·ti a·na·gi
emotional συναισθηματικός si·ne·sthi·ma·ti·kos
employee υπάλληλος ⓜ&ⓕ i·pa·li·los
employer εργοδότης/εργοδότρια ⓜ/ⓕ er·gho·tho·tis / er·gho·tho·tri·a
empty a άδειο a·thi·o
end τέλος ⓝ te·los
endangered species είδη υπό εξαφάνιση ⓝ pl i·thi i·po ek·sa·fa·ni·si
engaged (to marry) αρραβωνιασμένος/αρραβωνιασμένη ⓜ/ⓕ a·ra·vo·niaz·me·nos / a·ra·vo·niaz·me·ni
engagement (undertaking) υποχρέωση ⓕ i·po·khre·o·si
engine μηχανή ⓕ mi·kha·ni
engineer μηχανικός ⓜ&ⓕ mi·kha·ni·kos
engineering μηχανική ⓕ mi·kha·ni·ki
England Αγγλία ⓕ ang·gli·a
English (language) Αγγλικά ⓝ pl ang·gli·ka
enjoy oneself απολαμβάνω a·po·lam·va·no
enough αρκετά ar·ke·ta
enter μπαίνω be·no
entertainment guide οδηγός διασκέδασης ⓜ o·thi·ghos thia·ske·tha·sis
entry είσοδος ⓕ i·so·thos
envelope φάκελος ⓜ fa·ke·los
environment περιβάλλον ⓝ pe·ri·va·lon
epilepsy επιληψία ⓕ e·pi·lip·si·a
erosion διάβρωση ⓕ thi·av·ro·si
equal opportunity ίσες ευκαιρίες ⓕ pl i·ses ef·ke·ri·es
equality ισότητα ⓕ i·so·ti·ta
equipment εξοπλισμός ⓜ ek·so·pliz·mos
escalator κυλιόμενες σκάλες ⓕ pl ki·li·o·me·nes ska·les
estate agency κτηματομεσιτικό γραφείο ⓝ kti·ma·to·me·si·ti·ko ghra·fi·o
euro ευρώ ⓝ ev·ro

Europe Ευρώπη ⓕ ev·*ro*·pi
European Union Ευρωπαϊκή Ένωση ⓕ ev·ro·pa·i·*ki* *e*·no·si
euthanasia ευθανασία ⓕ ef·tha·na·*si*·a
evening βράδυ ⓝ *vra*·ţhi
every κάθε *ka*·the
everyone όλοι ⓜ *o*·li
everything όλα ⓝ *o*·la
exactly ακριβώς a·kri·*vos*
example παράδειγμα ⓝ pa·*ra*·ţhigh·ma
excavation ανασκαφή ⓕ a·na·ska·*fi*
excellent εξαιρετικός ek·se·re·ti·*kos*
excess baggage υπέρβαρες αποσκευές ⓝ i·*per*·va·res a·po·ske·*ves*
exchange συνάλλαγμα ⓝ si·*na*·lagh·ma
exchange v ανταλλάζω a·da·*la*·zo
exchange rate τιμή συναλλάγματος ⓕ ti·*mi* si·na·*lagh*·ma·tos
excluded εξαιρούμενος ek·se·*ru*·me·nos
exhaust (car) εξάτμιση ⓕ ek·*sat*·mi·si
exhibition έκθεση ⓕ *ek*·the·si
exhibit έκθεμα ⓝ *ek*·the·ma
exit έξοδος ⓕ *ek*·so·ţhos
expensive ακριβός a·kri·*vos*
experience εμπειρία ⓕ e·bi·*ri*·a
exploitation εκμετάλλευση ⓕ ek·me·*ta*·lef·si
export permit άδεια εξαγωγής ⓕ *a*·ţhi·a ek·sa·gho·*yis*
(by) express mail επείγον (ταχυδρομείο) ⓝ e·*pi*·ghon (ta·hi·ţhro·*mi*·o)
extension (visa) παράταση ⓕ pa·*ra*·ta·si
eye μάτι ⓝ *ma*·ti
eye drops σταγόνες ματιών ⓕ pl sta·*gho*·nes ma·ti·*on*
eyes μάτια ⓝ pl *ma*·tia

F

fabric ύφασμα ⓝ *i*·faz·ma
face πρόσωπο ⓝ *pro*·so·po
face cloth πετσέτα προσώπου ⓕ pet·*se*·ta pro·*so*·pu
factory εργοστάσιο ⓝ er·gho·*sta*·si·o
factory worker εργάτης εργοστασίου ⓜ er·*gha*·tis er·gho·sta·*si*·u
εργάτρια εργοστασίου ⓕ er·*gha*·tri·a er·gho·sta·*si*·u
falcon γεράκι ⓝ ye·*ra*·ki
fall (autumn) φθινόπωρο ⓝ fthi·*no*·po·ro
fall (down) πτώση ⓕ *pto*·si
family οικογένεια ⓕ i·ko·*ye*·ni·a
family name επώνυμο ⓝ e·*po*·ni·mo
famous a φημισμένος fi·miz·*me*·nos
fan (machine) ανεμιστήρας ⓜ a·ne·mi·*sti*·ras
fan (of sport) οπαδός ⓜ o·pa·*ţhos*
fan belt ιμάντας ανεμιστήρα ⓜ i·*man*·das a·ne·mi·*stira*
far μακριά ma·kri·*a*
fare εισιτήριο ⓝ i·si·*ti*·ri·o
farm φάρμα ⓕ *far*·ma
farmer αγρότης ⓜ&ⓕ agh·*ro*·tis
fashion μόδα ⓕ *mo*·ţha
fast a γρήγορος *ghri*·gho·ros
fat a παχύς pa·*his*
father πατέρας ⓜ pa·*te*·ras
father-in-law πεθερός ⓜ pe·the·*ros*
faucet βρύση ⓕ *vri*·si
fault (someone's) λάθος ⓝ *la*·thos
faulty ελαττωματικός e·la·to·ma·ti·*kos*
fax machine μηχανή φαξ ⓕ mi·kha·*ni* faks
February Φεβρουάριος ⓜ fev·ru·*a*·ri·os
feed v ταΐζω ta·*i*·zo
feel (touch) v αγγίζω a·*gi*·zo
feeling (physical) αφή ⓕ a·*fi*
feelings αισθήματα ⓝ pl es·*thi*·ma·ta
female a θηλυκός thi·li·*kos*
fence φράχτης ⓜ *frakh*·tis
fencing (sport) ξιφομαχία ⓕ ksi·fo·ma·*hi*·a
ferry φέρυ ⓝ *fe*·ri
festival φεστιβάλ ⓝ fe·sti·*val*
fever πυρετός ⓜ pi·re·*tos*
few λίγοι *li*·yi
fiancé αρραβωνιαστικός ⓜ a·ra·vo·nia·sti·*kos*
fiancée αρραβωνιαστικιά ⓕ a·ra·vo·nia·sti·*kia*
fiction μυθιστόρημα ⓝ mi·tho·*sto*·ri·ma
fig σύκο ⓝ *si*·ko
fight πάλη ⓕ *pa*·li
filigree (jewellery) φιλιγκράν ⓝ fi·li·*gran*
fill γεμίζω ye·*mi*·zo
fillet φιλέτο ⓝ fi·*le*·to
film (camera / cinema) φιλμ ⓝ film
filtered φιλτραρισμένος fil·tra·riz·*me*·nos
find βρίσκω *vri*·sko
fine (penalty) πρόστιμο ⓝ *pros*·ti·mo
fine (weather) a ωραίος o·*re*·os

finger δάκτυλο ⓝ *thak*·ti·lo
finish τελείωμα ⓝ te·*li*·o·ma
finish v τελειώνω te·li·*o*·no
Finland Φινλανδία ⓕ fin·lan·*thi*·a
fire φωτιά ⓕ fo·*tia*
firewood καυσόξυλα ⓝ pl kaf·*sok*·si·la
first a πρώτος *pro*·tos
first class πρώτη θέση ⓕ *pro*·ti *the*·si
first-aid kit κουτί πρώτων βοηθειών ⓝ ku·*ti pro*·ton vo·i·thi·*on*
first name μικρό όνομα ⓝ mi·*kro* o·no·ma
fish ψάρι ⓝ *psa*·ri
fishing ψάρεμα ⓝ *psa*·re·ma
fish monger ιχθυοπώλης/ιχθυοπώλισσα ⓜ/ⓕ ikh·thi·o·*po*·lis / ikh·thi·o·*po*·li·sa
fish shop ιχθυοπωλείο ⓝ ikh·thi·o·po·*li*·o
flag σημαία ⓕ si·*me*·a
flannel φανέλα (ύφασμα) ⓕ fa·*ne*·la (*i*·faz·ma)
flashlight φακός ⓜ fa·*kos*
flat a επίπεδος e·*pi*·pe·thos
flat (apartment) διαμέρισμα ⓝ thi·a·*me*·riz·ma
flea ψύλλος ⓜ *psi*·los
fleamarket παζάρι ⓝ pa·*za*·ri
flight πτήση ⓕ *pti*·si
flood πλημμύρα ⓕ pli·*mi*·ra
floor πάτωμα ⓝ *pa*·to·ma
floor (storey) όροφος ⓜ *o*·ro·fos
florist ανθοπώλης/ανθοπώλισσα ⓜ/ⓕ an·tho·*po*·lis / an·tho·*po*·li·sa
flour αλεύρι ⓝ a·*lev*·ri
flower λουλούδι ⓝ lu·*lu*·thi
flu γρίπη ⓕ *ghri*·pi
fly πετάω v pe·*ta*·o
foggy έχει ομίχλη e·*khi* o·*mi*·kli
folk (art) a λαϊκός la·i·*kos*
follow ακολουθώ a·ko·lu·*tho*
food φαγητό ⓝ fa·yi·*to*
food supplies προμήθειες φαγητού ⓕ pl pro·*mi*·thi·es fa·yi·*tu*
foot πόδι ⓝ *po*·thi
football (soccer) ποδόσφαιρο ⓝ po·*thos*·fe·ro
footpath πεζοδρόμιο ⓝ pe·zo·*thro*·mi·o
foreign ξένος *kse*·nos
forest δάσος ⓝ *tha*·sos
forever πάντα *pa*·da
forget ξεχνώ ksekh·*no*
forgive συγχωρώ sing·kho·*ro*
fork πιρούνι ⓝ pi·*ru*·ni
fortnight δεκαπενθήμερο ⓝ da·ka·pen·*thi*·me·ro
fortune teller μάντης/μάντισσα ⓜ/ⓕ *ma*·dis / *ma*·di·sa
foul φάουλ ⓝ *fa*·ul
foyer φουαγιέ ⓝ fu·a·*ye*
fragile εύθραυστος *ef*·thraf·stos
France Γαλλία ⓕ gha·*li*·a
free (available) διαθέσιμος thi·a·*the*·si·mos
free (gratis) δωρεάν tho·re·*an*
free (not bound) ελεύθερος e·*lef*·the·ros
freeze παγώνω pa·*gho*·no
fresco φρέσκο ⓝ *fre*·sko
fresh φρέσκος *fre*·skos
Friday Παρασκευή ⓕ pa·ra·ske·*vi*
fridge ψυγείο ⓝ psi·*yi*·o
fried τηγανισμένος ti·gha·niz·*me*·nos
friend φίλος/φίλη ⓜ/ⓕ *fi*·los / *fi*·li
from από a·*po*
frost παγωνιά ⓕ pa·gho·*nia*
frozen παγωμένος pa·gho·*me*·nos
fruit φρούτα ⓝ pl *fru*·ta
fruit picking μάζεμα φρούτων ⓝ *ma*·ze·ma *fru*·ton
fry v τηγανίζω ti·gha·*ni*·zo
frying pan τηγάνι ⓝ ti·*gha*·ni
full γεμάτο ye·*ma*·to
full-time πλήρους απασχόλησης *pli*·rus a·pa·*skho*·li·sis
fun a διασκεδαστικό thia·ske·tha·sti·*ko*
funeral κηδεία ⓕ ki·*thi*·a
funny αστείος a·*sti*·os
furniture έπιπλα ⓝ pl e·pi·pla
future μέλλον ⓝ *me*·lon

G

game (football) ματς ⓝ mats
game (sport) αγώνας ⓜ a·*gho*·nas
garage γκαράζ ⓝ ga·*raz*
garbage σκουπίδια ⓝ pl sku·*pi*·thia
garbage can σκουπιδοτενεκές ⓜ sku·pi·tho·te·ne·*kes*
garden κήπος ⓜ *ki*·pos
gardener κηπουρός ⓜ&ⓕ ki·pu·*ros*
gardening κηπουρική ⓕ ki·pu·ri·*ki*
garlic σκόρδο ⓝ *skor*·tho
gas (for cooking) πετρογκάζ ⓝ pe·tro·*gaz*
gas (petrol) βενζίνη ⓕ ven·*zi*·ni

gas bottle φιάλη υγραερίου ⓕ fi·a·li i·ghra·e·ri·u
gastroenteritis γαστρεντερίτιδα ⓕ gha·stre·de·ri·ti·ţha
gate (airport etc) πύλη ⓕ pi·li
gauze γάζα ⓜ ya·za
gay γκέι ge·i
gelatine ζελατίνη ⓕ ze·la·ti·ni
Germany Γερμανία ⓕ yer·ma·ni·a
get παίρνω per·no
get off (transport) κατεβαίνω ka·te·ve·no
gift δώρο ⓝ ţho·ro
gig παράσταση ⓕ pa·ra·sta·si
gin τζιν ⓝ dzin
girl κορίτσι ⓝ ko·rit·si
girlfriend φιλενάδα ⓕ fi·le·na·ţha
give δίνω ţhi·no
given name μικρό όνομα ⓝ mi·kro o·no·ma
glandular fever λοιμώδης μονοπυρήνωση ⓜ li·mo·ţhis mo·no·pi·ri·no·si
glass (drinking) ποτήρι ⓝ po·ti·ri
glasses (spectacles) γυαλιά ⓝ pl yia·lia
glove γάντι ⓝ ghan·ti
gloves γάντια ⓝ pl ghan·tia
glue κόλλα ⓕ ko·la
go πηγαίνω pi·ye·no
go out βγαίνω vye·no
go out with (a male) βγαίνω με κάποιον vye·no me ka·pi·on
go out with (a female) βγαίνω με κάποια vye·no me ka·pia
go shopping πάω για ψώνια pa·o yia pso·nia
goal (score/point) γκολ ⓝ gol
goalkeeper τερματοφύλακας ⓜ&ⓕ ter·ma·to·fi·la·kas
goat κατσίκα ⓕ kat·si·ka
god (general) θεός ⓜ the·os
goddess θεά ⓕ the·a
goggles προστατευτικά γυαλιά ⓝ pl pro·sta·tef·ti·ka yia·lia
goggles (swimming) γυαλάκια κολύμβησης ⓝ pl yia·la·ki·a ko·lim·vi·sis
gold χρυσάφι ⓝ khri·sa·fi
golf ball μπαλάκι του γκολφ ⓝ ba·la·ki tu golf
golf course γήπεδο του γκολφ ⓝ yi·pe·ţho tu golf
good καλός ka·los
government κυβέρνηση ⓕ ki·ver·ni·si
gram γραμμάριο ⓝ ghra·ma·ri·o
granddaughter εγγονή ⓕ e·go·ni
grandfather παππούς ⓜ pa·pus
grandmother γιαγιά ⓕ yia·yia
grandson εγγονός ⓜ e·go·nos
grapefruit γκρέιπ φρουτ ⓝ gre·ip frut
grapes σταφύλια ⓝ pl sta·fi·lia
grass γρασίδι ⓝ ghra·si·ţhi
grateful ευγνώμων ev·ghno·mon
grave τάφος ⓜ ta·fos
gray γκρίζος gri·zos
great (fantastic) απίθανος a·pi·tha·nos
Greece Ελλάδα ⓕ e·la·ţha
Greek (language) Ελληνικά ⓝ pl e·li·ni·ka
Greek (people) Έλληνες ⓜ pl e·li·nes
green πράσινος pra·si·nos
greengrocer μανάβης ⓜ/ⓕ ma·na·vis
grey γκρίζος gri·zos
grilled ψημένο στο γκριλ psi·me·no sto grill
grocery μανάβικο ⓝ ma·na·vi·kho
groundnut αράπικο φιστίκι ⓝ a·ra·pi·ko fi·sti·ki
grow μεγαλώνω me·ga·lo·no
guaranteed εγγυημένος e·ghi·i·me·nos
guess v μαντεύω ma·de·vo
guesthouse ξενώνας ⓜ kse·no·nas
guide (audio) ηχητικός οδηγός ⓜ i·hi·ti·kos o·ţhi·gos
guide (person) ξεναγός ⓜ&ⓕ kse·na·ghos
guidebook ταξιδιωτικός οδηγός ⓜ ta·xi·ţhi·o·ti·kos o·ţhi·ghos
guide dog σκυλος οδηγός ⓜ ski·los o·ţhi·ghos
guided tour ξενάγηση ⓕ kse·na·yi·si
guilty a ένοχος e·no·khos
guitar κιθάρα ⓕ ki·tha·ra
gum μαστίχα ⓕ ma·sti·kha
gun όπλο ⓝ o·plo
gym (fitness) γυμναστήριο ⓝ yim·na·sti·ri·o
gymnastics γυμναστική ⓕ yim·na·sti·ki
gynaecologist γυναικολόγος ⓜ&ⓕ yi·ne·ko·lo·ghos
gyros γύρος ⓜ yi·ros

H

hair μαλλιά ⓝ pl ma·lia
hairbrush βούρτσα μαλλιών ⓕ vur·tsa ma·lion
haircut κούρεμα ⓝ ku·re·ma
hairdresser κομμωτής/κομμώτρια ⓜ/ⓕ ko·mo·tis/ko·mo·tri·a
halal χαλάλ kha·lal
half μισό mi·so
hallucination παραίσθηση ⓕ pa·res·thi·si
ham ζαμπόν ⓝ za·bon
hammer ⓝ σφυρί sfi·ri
hammock αιώρα ⓕ e·o·ra
hand χέρι ⓝ he·ri
handbag τσάντα ⓕ tsa·da
handball χάντμπολ ⓝ khand·bol
handicrafts εργόχειρα ⓝ pl er·gho·hi·ra
handkerchief μαντήλι ⓝ ma·di·li
handlebars τιμόνι ⓕ ti·mo·ni
handmade a χειροποίητο hi·ro·pi·i·to
handsome όμορφος o·mor·fos
happy ευτυχισμένος ef·ti·hiz·me·nos
harassment παρενόχληση ⓕ pa·re·no·khli·si
harbour λιμάνι ⓝ li·ma·ni
hard (not soft) σκληρός skli·ros
hard-boiled σφιχτός sfikh·tos
hardware store κατάστημα σιδηρικών ⓝ ka·ta·sti·ma si·ţhi·ri·kon
hash χασίς ⓝ ha·sis
hat καπέλο ⓝ ka·pe·lo
have έχω e·ho
have a cold έχω κρύωμα e·ho kri·o·ma
have fun διασκεδάζω ţhia·ske·ţha·zo
hay fever αλλεργική ρινίτιδα ⓕ a·ler·ghi·ki ri·ni·ti·ţha
hazelnut φουντούκι ⓝ fu·du·ki
he αυτός ⓜ af·tos
head κεφάλι ⓝ ke·fa·li
headache πονοκέφαλος ⓜ po·no·ke·fa·los
headlights προβολείς ⓝ pl pro·vo·lis
health υγεία ⓕ i·yi·a
hear ακούω a·ku·o
hearing aid ακουστικά βαρηκοΐας ⓝ pl a·ku·sti·ka va·ri·ko·i·as
heart καρδιά ⓕ kar·ţhia
heart attack καρδιακή προσβολή ⓕ kar·ţhi·a·ki proz·vo·li
heart condition καρδιοπάθεια ⓕ kar·ţhi·o·pa·thi·a
heat ζέστη ⓕ ze·sti
heated ζεσταμένος ze·sta·me·nos
heater σόμπα ⓕ so·ba
heating θέρμανση ⓕ ther·man·si
heatstroke θερμοπληξία ⓕ ther·mo·plik·si·a
heatwave καύσωνας ⓜ kaf·so·nas
heavy βαρύς va·ris
Hellenistic Ελληνιστικός e·li·ni·sti·kos
helmet (motorbike) κράνος ⓕ kra·nos
help βοήθεια ⓕ vo·i·thi·a
help v βοηθώ vo·i·tho
hepatitis ηπατίτιδα ⓕ i·pa·ti·ti·ţha
her (ownership / direct object) της tis
herb βότανο ⓝ vo·ta·no
herbalist βοτανοθεραπευτής ⓜ&ⓕ vo·ta·no·the·ra·pef·tis
here εδώ e·ţho
heroin ηρωίνη ⓕ i·ro·i·ni
herring ρέγκα ⓕ re·ga
high ψηλός psi·los
highchair καρέκλα για μωρά ⓕ ka·re·kla yia mo·ro
high school γυμνάσιο/λύκειο ⓝ yim·na·si·o / li·ki·o
highway εθνική οδός ⓜ eth·ni·ki o·ţhos
hike v κάνω πεζοπορία ka·no pe·zo·po·Rl·a
hiking πεζοπορία ⓕ pe·zo·po·ri·a
hiking boots μπότες πεζοπορίας ⓕ pl bo·tes pe·zo·po·ri·as
hiking route μονοπάτι πεζοπορίας ⓜ mo·no·pa·ti pe·zo·po·ri·as
hill λόφος ⓜ lo·fos
Hindu Ινδουιστής/Ινδουίστρια ⓜ/ⓕ in·ţhu·i·stis / in·ţhu·i·stri·a
hire v ενοικιάζω e·ni·ki·a·zo
his (ownership / direct object) του tu
historical ιστορικός i·sto·ri·kos
history ιστορία ⓕ i·sto·ri·a
hitchhike v κάνω ωτοστόπ ka·no me o·to·stop
HIV έιτς άι βι ⓝ e·idz a·i vi
hockey χόκεϊ ⓝ kho·ki
holiday (public) αργία ⓕ ar·yi·a
holidays διακοπές ⓕ pl ţhi·a·ko·pes
home σπίτι ⓝ spi·ti
homeless άστεγος a·ste·ghos
homemaker νοικοκύρης/νοικοκυρά ⓜ/ⓕ ni·ko·ki·ris / ni·ko·ki·ra

homeopathy ομοιοπαθητική ⓕ o·mi·o·pa·thi·ti·ki
homosexual ομοφυλόφιλος ⓜ o·mo·fi·lo·fi·los
honey μέλι ⓝ me·li
honeymoon ταξίδι του μέλιτος ⓝ tak·si·ţhi tu me·li·tos
horoscope ωροσκόπιο ⓝ o·ro·sko·pi·o
horse άλογο ⓝ a·lo·gho
horse riding ιππασία ⓕ i·pa·si·a
hospital νοσοκομείο ⓝ no·so·ko·mi·o
hospitality φιλοξενία ⓕ fi·lok·se·ni·a
hot ζεστός ze·stos
hotel ξενοδοχείο ⓝ kse·no·ţho·hi·o
hot water ζεστό νερό ⓝ ze·sto ne·ro
hour ώρα ⓕ o·ra
house σπίτι ⓝ spi·ti
housework νοικοκυριό ⓜ ni·ko·ki·rio
how πώς pos
how much πόσο po·so
hug v αγκαλιάζω a·ga·lia·zo
huge πελώριος pe·lo·ri·os
humanities φιλολογικές σπουδές ⓕ pl fi·lo·lo·ghi·kes spu·ţhes
human resources ανθρώπινο δυναμικό ⓝ an·thro·pi·no ţhi·na·mi·ko
human rights ανθρώπινα δικαιώματα ⓝ pl an·thro·pi·na ţhi·ke·o·ma·ta
hundred εκατό e·ka·to
hungry (be) v πεινάω pi·na·o
hunting κυνήγι ⓝ ki·ni·yi
hurt v πληγώνω pli·gho·no
husband σύζυγος ⓜ si·zi·ghos
hydrofoil ιπτάμενο δελφίνι ⓝ ip·ta·me·no ţhel·fi·ni

I

I εγώ e·gho
ice πάγος ⓜ pa·ghos
ice cream παγωτό ⓝ pa·gho·to
ice-cream parlour παγωτατζίδικο ⓝ pagho·ta·dzi·ţhi·ko
ice hockey άις χόκεϊ ⓝ a·is kho·ke·i
icon εικόνα ⓕ i·ko·na
identification (ID) ταυτότητα ⓕ taf·to·ti·ta
idiot βλάκας ⓜ vla·kas
if αν an
ill άρρωστος a·ro·stos
immigration μετανάστευση ⓕ me·ta·na·stef·si
important σημαντικός si·man·di·kos
impossible αδύνατος a·ţhi·na·tos
in μέσα me·sa
in a hurry βιαστικός via·sti·kos
in front of μπροστά bro·sta
included συμπεριλαμβανομένου si·be·ri·lam·va·no·me·nu
income tax φόρος εισοδήματος ⓜ fo·ros i·so·ţhi·ma·tos
India Ινδία ⓕ pl in·ţhi·a
indicator (economic) δείκτης ⓜ ţhikh·tis
indigestion δυσπεψία ⓕ ţhis·pep·si·a
indoor εσωτερικός ⓜ e·so·te·ri·kos
industry βιομηχανία ⓕ vi·o·mi·kha·ni·a
infection μόλυνση ⓕ mo·lin·si
inflammation φλεγμονή ⓕ flegh·mo·ni
inflation πληθωρισμός ⓜ pli·tho·riz·mos
influenza γρίπη ⓕ ghri·pi
information πληροφορία ⓕ pli·ro·fo·ri·a
ingredient συστατικό ⓝ si·sta·ti·ko
inject v κάνω ένεση ka·no e·ne·si
injection ένεση ⓕ e·ne·si
injured πληγωμένος pli·gho·me·nos
injury πληγή ⓕ pli·yi
inner tube (bicycle) σαμπρέλα ελαστικού ⓕ sa·bre·la e·la·sti·ku
innocent a αθώος a·tho·os
insect έντομο ⓝ e·do·mo
inside μέσα me·sa
instructor δάσκαλος/δασκάλα ⓜ/ⓕ ţha·ska·los / ţha·ska·la
insurance ασφάλεια ⓕ as·fa·li·a
interest (hobby) ενδιαφέρον ⓝ en·ţhia·fe·ron
interesting ενδιαφέρων en·ţhia·fe·ron
intermission διάλειμμα ⓝ ţhia·li·ma
international διεθνής ţhi·eth·nis
internet διαδίκτυο ⓝ ţhi·a·ţhik·ti·o
interpreter διερμηνέας ⓜ&ⓕ ţhi·er·mi·ne·as
interview συνέντευξη ⓕ si·ne·def·ksi
invite προσκαλώ pros·ka·lo
Ionian Ιωνικός i·o·ni·kos
Ireland Ιρλανδία ⓕ ir·lan·ţhi·a
iron (for clothes) σίδερο ⓝ si·ţhe·ro
iris (eye) ίρις ⓕ i·ris
island νησί ⓝ ni·si

Israel Ισραήλ ⓝ iz·ra·*il*
it αυτό af·*to*
IT πληροφορική ⓕ pli·ro·fo·ri·*ki*
Italy Ιταλία ⓕ i·ta·*li*·a
itch φαγούρα ⓕ fa·*ghu*·ra
itemised αναλυτικός a·na·li·ti·*kos*
itinerary πρόγραμμα ⓝ *pro*·ghra·ma
IUD (contraceptive)
ενδομήτριο σπείραμα ⓝ en·ţho·*mi*·tri·o *spi*·ra·ma

J

jacket ζακέτα ⓕ za·*ke*·ta
jail φυλακή ⓕ fi·la·*ki*
jam μαρμελάδα ⓕ mar·me·*la*·ţha
January Ιανουάριος ⓜ i·a·nu·*a*·ri·os
Japan Ιαπωνία ⓕ i·a·po·*ni*·a
jar βάζο ⓝ *va*·zo
jaw σαγόνι ⓝ sa·*gho*·ni
jealous ζηλιάρης zi·*lia*·ris
jeans τζιν ⓝ dzin
jeep τζιπ ⓝ dzip
jellyfish μέδουσα ⓕ *me*·ţhu·sa
jet lag τζετ λαγκ ⓝ dzet lag
jewellery κοσμήματα ⓝ pl koz·*mi*·ma·ta
Jewish Ιουδαϊκός/Ιουδαϊκή ⓜ/ⓕ i·u·ţha·i·*kos* / i·u·ţha·i·*ki*
job δουλειά ⓕ du·*lia*
jogging τρέξιμο ⓝ *trek*·si·mo
joke αστείο ⓝ a·*sti*·o
journalist δημοσιογράφος ⓜ&ⓕ ţhi·mo·si·o·*ghra*·fos
journey ταξίδι ⓝ tak·*si*·ţhi
judge δικαστής ⓜ&ⓕ ţhi·ka·*stis*
jug κανάτα ⓕ ka·*na*·ta
juice χυμός ⓜ hi·*mos*
July Ιούλιος ⓜ i·*u*·li·os
junta χούντα ⓕ *khu*·da
jump v πηδώ pi·*ţho*
jumper (sweater) πουλόβερ ⓝ pu·*lo*·ver
jumper leads καλώδια μπαταρίας ⓝ pl ka·*lo*·ţhi·a ba·ta·*ri*·as
June Ιούνιος ⓜ i·*u*·ni·os

K

kebab shop σουβλατζίδικο ⓝ suv·la·*tzi*·ţhi·ko
ketchup σάλτσα ⓕ *salt*·sa
key κλειδί ⓝ kli·*ţhi*
keyboard πληκτρολόγιο ⓝ plik·tro·*lo*·yi·o
kick v κλωτσάω klot·*sa*·o
kidney νεφρό ⓝ ne·*fro*
kilo κιλό ⓝ ki·*lo*
kilogram κιλό ⓝ ki·*lo*
kilometre χιλιόμετρο ⓝ hi·*lio*·me·tro
kind (nice) καλός ka·*los*
kindergarten νηπιαγωγείο ⓝ ni·pi·a·gho·*yi*·o
king βασιλιάς ⓜ va·si·*lias*
kiosk περίπτερο ⓝ pe·*rip*·te·ro
kiss φιλί ⓜ fi·*li*
kiss v φιλώ fi·*lo*
kitchen κουζίνα ⓕ ku·*zi*·na
kiwi fruit ακτινίδιο ⓝ ak·ti·*ni*·ţhi·o
knee γόνατο ⓝ *gho*·na·to
knife μαχαίρι ⓝ ma·*he*·ri
know v ξέρω *kse*·ro
kosher a κοσέρ ko·*ser*

L

labourer εργάτης/εργάτρια ⓜ/ⓕ er·*gha*·tis / er·*gha*·tri·a
labyrinth λαβύρινθος ⓜ la·*vi*·rin·thos
lace δαντέλα ⓕ ţha·*de*·la
lake λίμνη ⓕ *li*·mni
lamb αρνί ⓝ ar·*ni*
land ξηρά ⓕ ksi·*ra*
landlady σπιτονοικοκυρά ⓕ spi·to·ni·ko·ki·*ra*
landlord ιδιοκτήτης ⓜ i·ţhi·ok·*ti*·tis
language γλώσσα ⓕ *ghlo*·sa
laptop λάπτοπ ⓝ *lap*·top
large μεγάλος me·*gha*·los
last (previous) προηγούμενος pro·i·*ghu*·me·nos
last week περασμένη εβδομάδα pe·raz·*me*·ni ev·ţho·*ma*·ţha
late καθυστερημένος ka·thi·ste·ri·*me*·nos
later αργότερα ar·*gho*·te·ra
laugh v γελάω ye·*la*·o
launderette πλυντήριο ⓝ pli·*di*·ri·o
laundry (place) πλυντήριο ⓝ pli·*di*·ri·o
law νόμος ⓜ *no*·mos
law (study, profession) νομικά ⓜ no·mi·*ka*
lawyer δικηγόρος ⓜ&ⓕ ţhi·ki·*gho*·ros
laxative καθαρτικό ⓝ ka·thar·ti·*ko*
lazy τεμπέλης te·*be*·lis

leader αρχηγός ⓜ&ⓕ ar·hi·ghos
leaf φύλλο ⓝ fi·lo
learn μαθαίνω ma·the·no
leather δέρμα ⓝ ther·ma
lecturer λέκτορας ⓜ&ⓕ lek·to·ras
ledge (window) περβάζι ξέρες ⓕ pl per·va·zi
leek πράσο ⓝ pra·so
left (direction) αριστερός ⓜ a·ri·ste·ros
left-luggage (office) (γραφείο) φύλαξη αποσκευών ⓝ (gra·fi·o) fi·lak·si a·po·ske·von
left-wing αριστερός ⓕ a·ri·ste·ros
leg πόδι ⓝ po·thi
legal νόμιμος no·mi·mos
legislation νομοθεσία ⓕ no·mo·the·si·a
legume όσπρια ⓝ pl os·pri·a
lemon λεμόνι ⓝ le·mo·ni
lemonade λεμονάδα ⓕ le·mo·na·tha
lens φακός ⓜ fa·kos
Lent Σαρακοστή ⓕ sa·ra·ko·sti
lentil φακές ⓕ pl fa·kes
lesbian λεσβία ⓕ les·vi·a
less λιγότερο li·gho·te·ro
letter (mail) γράμμα ⓝ ghra·ma
lettuce μαρούλι ⓝ ma·ru·li
liar ψεύτης/ψεύτρα ⓜ/ⓕ psef·tis / psef·tra
library βιβλιοθήκη ⓕ viv·li·o·thi·ki
licence άδεια ⓕ a·thi·a
licence plate number αριθμός κυκλοφορίας ⓜ a·rith·mos ki·klo·fo·ri·as
lie down ξαπλώνω xa·plo·no
life ζωή ⓕ zo·i
life jacket σωσίβιο ⓝ so·si·vi·o
lift (elevator) ασανσέρ ⓝ a·san·ser
light φως ⓝ fos
light (colour) a ανοιχτός a·nikh·tos
light (weight) a ελαφρύς e·la·fris
light bulb λάμπα ⓕ lam·pa
light meter φωτόμετρο ⓝ fo·to·me·tro
lighter αναπτήρας ⓜ a·nap·ti·ras
like v μου αρέσει mu a·re·si
lime (fruit) λάιμ ⓝ lime
linen (material) λινό ⓝ li·no
linen (sheets) σεντόνια ⓝ pl se·do·nia
lip balm λιποζάν ⓝ li·po·zan
lips χείλι ⓝ pl hi·li
lipstick κραγιόν ⓝ kra·yion
liquor store κάβα ⓕ ka·va
listen (to) ακούω a·ku·o
little (quantity) λίγο li·gho
little (size) μικρός mi·kros
live (somewhere) v μένω me·no
liver συκώτι ⓝ si·ko·ti
lizard σαύρα ⓕ sav·ra
local ντόπιος do·pi·os
lock κλειδαριά ⓕ kli·tha·ria
lock v κλειδώνω kli·tho·no
locked κλειδωμένος kli·tho·me·nos
lollies καραμέλες ⓕ pl ka·ra·me·les
long a μακρύς ma·kris
look v κοιτάζω ki·ta·zo
look after προσέχω pro·se·kho
look for ψάχνω psakh·no
lookout παρατηρητήριο ⓝ pa·ra·ti·ri·ti·ri·o
loose a χαλαρός kha·la·ros
loose change ψιλά ⓝ pl psi·la
lose χάνω kha·no
lost a χαμένος kha·me·nos
lost property office γραφείο απωλεσθέντων αντικειμένων ⓝ gra·fi·o a·po·les·the·don a·di·ki·me·non
(a) lot πολύ po·li
lotion λοσιόν ⓝ lo·sion
loud δυνατός thi·na·tos
love αγάπη ⓕ a·gha·pi
love v αγαπώ a·gha·po
lover εραστής/ερωμένη ⓜ/ⓕ e·ra·stis / e·ro·me·ni
low a χαμηλός kha·mi·los
lubricant λιπαντικό ⓝ li·pa·di·ko
luck τύχη ⓕ ti·hi
lucky a τυχερός ti·he·ros
luggage αποσκευές ⓕ pl a·po·ske·ves
luggage lockers φύλαξη αποσκευών ⓕ fi·lak·si a·po·ske·von
luggage tag ταμπέλα αποσκευών ⓕ ta·be·la a·po·ske·von
lump εξόγκωμα ⓝ ek·so·gho·ma
lunch μεσημεριανό ⓝ me·si·me·ria
lung πνευμόνι ⓝ pnev·mo·ni
luxury πολυτέλεια ⓕ po·li·te·li·a

M

Macedonia Μακεδονία ⓕ ma·ke·tho·ni·a
machine μηχανή ⓕ mi·kha·ni
magazine περιοδικό ⓝ pe·ri·o·thi·ko

mail (letters) αλληλογραφία ⓕ a·li·lo·ghra·*fi*·a
mail (postal system) ταχυδρομείο ⓝ ta·hi·ţhro·*mi*·o
mailbox γραμματοκιβώτιο ⓝ ghra·ma·to·ki·*vo*·ti·o
main κύριος *ki*·ri·os
main road κεντρικός δρόμος ⓜ ken·dri·*KOS* *ţhro*·mos
make v κάνω *ka*·no
make-up καλλυντικά ⓝ pl ka·li·di·*ka*
mammogram μαστογραφία ⓕ ma·sto·gra·*fi*·a
man (male) άντρας ⓜ *a*·dras
manager διευθυντής/διευθύντρια ⓜ/ⓕ ţhi·ef·thi·*dis*/ţhi·ef·*thi*·dri·a
mandarin μανταρίνι ⓝ ma·da·*ri*·ni
mango μάνγκο ⓝ *man*·go
manual work χειρωνακτική εργασία ⓕ hi·ro·nak·ti·*ki* er·gha·*si*·a
many πολλοί po·*li*
map χάρτης ⓜ *khar*·tis
March Μάρτιος ⓜ *mar*·ti·os
margarine μαργαρίνη ⓕ mar·gha·*ri*·ni
marijuana μαριχουάνα ⓕ ma·ri·khu·a·na
marine reserve θαλάσσιο πάρκο ⓝ pl tha·*la*·si·o *par*·ko
marital status οικογενειακή κατάσταση ⓕ i·ko·ghe·ni·a·*ki* ka·*ta*·sta·si
market αγορά ⓕ a·gho·*ra*
marmalade μαρμελάδα ⓕ mar·me·*la*·ţha
marriage γάμος ⓜ *gha*·mos
married a παντρεμένος/παντρεμένη ⓜ/ⓕ pa·dre·*me*·nos/pa·dre·*me*·ni
marry παντρεύομαι pa·*dre*·vo·me
martial arts πολεμικές τέχνες ⓕ po·le·mi·*kes* *tekh*·nes
mass (Catholic) λειτουργία ⓕ li·tur·*yi*·a
massage μασάζ ⓝ ma·*saz*
masseur μασέρ ⓜ ma·*ser*
masseuse μασέζ ⓕ ma·*sez*
mat χαλί ⓝ kha·*li*
match (sports) ματς ⓝ mats
matches (for lighting) σπίρτα ⓝ pl *spir*·ta
mattress στρώμα ⓝ *stro*·ma
May Μάιος ⓜ *ma*·i·os
maybe ίσως *i*·sos
mayonnaise μαγιονέζα ⓕ ma·yi·o·*ne*·za
mayor δήμαρχος ⓜ&ⓕ *ţhi*·mar·khos
me εγώ e·*gho*
meal γεύμα ⓝ *yev*·ma
measles ιλαρά ⓕ i·la·*ra*
meat κρέας ⓝ *kre*·as
mechanic μηχανικός ⓜ mi·kha·ni·*kos*
media μέσα ενημέρωσης ⓝ pl *me*·sa e·ni·*me*·ro·sis
medicine (medication) φάρμακο ⓝ *far*·ma·ko
medicine (study, profession) Ιατρική ⓕ i·a·tri·*ki*
meditation διαλογισμός ⓜ di·a·lo·ghis·*mos*
Mediterranean Μεσόγειος ⓕ me·*so*·yi·os
meet v συναντώ si·nan·*do*
melon πεπόνι ⓝ pe·*po*·ni
member μέλος ⓝ *me*·los
menstruation περίοδος ⓕ pe·*ri*·o·ţhos
menu μενού ⓝ me·*nu*
message μήνυμα ⓝ *mi*·ni·ma
metal μέταλλο ⓝ *me*·ta·lo
metre μέτρο ⓝ *me*·tro
metro (train) μετρό ⓝ me·*tro*
metro station σταθμός μετρό ⓝ stath·*mos* me·*tro*
microwave (oven) φούρνος μικροκυμάτων ⓜ *fur*·nos mi·kro·ki·*ma*·ton
midday (noon) μεσημέρι ⓝ me·si·*me*·ri
midnight μεσάνυχτα ⓝ pl me·sa·nikh·ta
migraine ημικρανία ⓕ i·mi·kra·*ni*·a
mild ήπιος *i*·pi·os
military a στρατιωτικός stra·ti·o·ti·*kos*
military base στρατιωτική βάση ⓕ stra·ti·o·ti·*ki* *va*·si
military service στρατιωτική θητεία ⓕ stra·ti·o·ti·*ki* thi·*ti*·a
milk γάλα ⓝ *gha*·la
millimetre χιλιοστό ⓝ hi·li·o·*sto*
million εκατομμύριο ⓝ e·ka·to·*mi*·ri·o
mince κιμάς ⓜ ki·*mas*
mineral water μεταλλικό νερό ⓝ me·ta·li·*ko* ne·*ro*
Minoan Μινωικός mi·no·i·*kos*
minute λεπτό ⓝ lep·*to*
mirror καθρέφτης ⓜ ka·*thref*·tis
miscarriage αποβολή ⓕ a·po·vo·*li*
miss (feel absence of) μου λείπει mu *li*·pi

mistake λάθος ⓝ la·thos
mix v ανακατεύω a·na·ka·te·vo
mixed plate ποικιλία ⓕ pi·ki·li·a
mobile phone κινητό ⓝ ki·ni·to
modem μόντεμ ⓝ mo·dem
modern μοντέρνος mo·der·nos
moisturiser ενυδατική κρέμα ⓕ e·ni·ţha·ti·ki kre·ma
monarchy μοναρχία ⓕ mo·nar·hi·a
monastery μοναστήρι ⓝ mo·na·sti·ri
Monday Δευτέρα ⓕ def·te·ra
money χρήματα ⓝ pl khri·ma·ta
monk καλόγερος ⓜ ka·lo·ye·ros
monk seal φώκια μοναχός ⓕ fo·ki·a mo·na·HOS
month μήνας ⓜ mi·nas
monument μνημείο ⓝ mni·mi·o
moon φεγγάρι ⓝ fe·ga·ri
more περισσότερος pe·ri·so·te·ros
morning πρωί ⓝ pro·i
morning sickness πρωινή ναυτία ⓕ pro·i·ni naf·ti·a
mosaic μωσαϊκό ⓝ mo·sa·i·ko
mosque τζαμί ⓝ dza·mi
mosquito κουνούπι ⓝ ku·nu·pi
mosquito coil φιδάκι για κουνούπια ⓝ fi·dha·ki yia ku·nu·pia
mosquito net κουνουπιέρα ⓕ ku·nu·pi·e·ra
motel μοτέλ ⓝ mo·tel
mother μητέρα ⓕ mi·te·ra
mother-in-law πεθερά ⓕ pe·the·ra
motorbike μηχανή ⓕ mi·kha·ni
motorboat μηχανοκίνητο σκάφος ⓝ mi·kha·no·ki·ni·to ska·fos
motorcycle μοτοσυκλέτα ⓕ mo·to·si·kle·ta
motorway (tollway) αυτοκινητόδρομος ⓜ af·to·ki·ni·to·ţhro·mos
mountain βουνό ⓝ vu·no
mountain bike ποδήλατο βουνού ⓝ po·ţhi·la·to yia vu·nu
mountain path μονοπάτι ⓝ mo·no·pa·ti
mountain range οροσειρά ⓕ o·ro·si·ra
mountaineering ορειβασία ⓕ o·ri·va·si·a
mouse ποντίκι ⓜ po·di·ki
mouth στόμα ⓝ sto·ma
movie ταινία ⓝ te·ni·a
Mr Κος ⓜ khi·ri·os
Mrs Κα ⓕ khi·ri·a
Ms Δις ţhe·spi·nis
mud λάσπη ⓕ la·spi
muesli μούσλι ⓝ mu·zli
mum μαμά ⓕ ma·ma
mumps μαγουλάδες ⓜ pl ma·ghu·la·thes
murder δολοφονία ⓕ ţho·lo·fo·ni·a
murder v δολοφονώ ţho·lo·fo·no
muscle μυς ⓜ mis
museum μουσείο ⓝ mu·si·o
mushroom μανιτάρι ⓝ ma·ni·ta·ri
music μουσική ⓕ mu·si·ki
music shop κατάστημα μουσικών ειδών ⓝ ka·ta·sti·ma mu·si·kon i·ţhon
musician μουσικός ⓜ&ⓕ mu·si·kos
Muslim Μουσουλμάνος/Μουσουλμάνα ⓜ/ⓕ mu·sul·ma·nos / mu·sul·ma·na
mussel μύδι ⓝ mi·ţhi
mustard μουστάρδα ⓕ mus·tar·ţha
mute a βουβός vu·vos
my μου mu
Mycenaean Μυκηναϊκός mi·ki·na·i·kos
mythological μυθολογικός mi·tho·lo·yi·kos

N

nail clippers νυχοκόπτης ⓜ ni·kho·kop·tis
name όνομα ⓝ o·no·ma
napkin χαρτοπετσέτα ⓕ har·to·pe·tse·ta
nappy πάνα ⓕ pa·na
nappy rash σύγκαμα ⓝ si·ga·ma
national park εθνικός δρυμός ⓜ eth·ni·kos dri·mos
nationality εθνικότητα ⓕ eth·ni·ko·ti·ta
NATO ΝΑΤΟ ⓝ na·to
nature φύση ⓕ fi·si
naturopathy φυσιοπαθητική ⓕ fi·si·o·pa·thi·ti·ki
nausea ναυτία ⓕ naf·ti·a
near(by) κοντά ko·da
nearest το πιο κοντινό to pio ko·di·no
necessary αναγκαίο a·na·ge·o
neck λαιμός ⓜ le·mos
necklace κολιέ ⓝ ko·li·e
nectarine νεκταρίνι ⓝ nek·ta·ri·ni
need v χρειάζομαι khri·a·zo·me
needle (sewing) βελόνα ⓕ ve·lo·na
needle (syringe) σύριγγα ⓕ si·ri·ga
negative a αρνητικός ar·ni·ti·kos
neither κανένα ka·ne·na
net δίχτυ ⓝ ţhik·ti
Netherlands Ολλανδία ⓕ o·lan·ţhi·a

never ποτέ po·*te*
new νέος *ne*·os
New Year's Day Πρωτοχρονιά ⓕ pro·to·khro·*nia*
New Year's Eve Παραμονή Πρωτοχρονιάς ⓕ pa·ra·mo·*ni* pro·to·khro·*nias*
New Zealand Νέα Ζηλανδία ⓕ *ne*·a zi·lan·*ţhi*·a
news νέα ⓝ pl *ne*·a
newsagency πρακτορείο εφημερίδων ⓝ prak·to·*ri*·o e·fi·me·*ri*·ţhon
newspaper εφημερίδα ⓕ e·fi·me·*ri*·ţha
newsstand περίπτερο ⓝ pe·*rip*·te·ro
next a επόμενος e·*po*·me·nos
next to δίπλα *ţhi*·pla
nice ωραίος o·*re*·os
nickname παρατσούκλι ⓝ pa·rat·*su*·kli
night νύχτα ⓕ *nikh*·ta
night out έξοδος ⓕ *e*·kso·dos
nightclub νάιτ κλαμπ ⓝ *na*·it klab
no όχι *o*·hi
noisy θορυβώδης tho·ri·*vo*·ţhis
none κανένα ka·*ne*·na
nonsmoking μη καπνιζόντων mi kap·ni·*zo*·don
noodles νουντλς ⓝ pl *nu*·dels
noon μεσημέρι ⓝ me·si·*me*·ri
north βορράς ⓜ vo·*ras*
Norway Νορβηγία ⓕ nor·vi·*yi*·a
nose μύτη ⓕ *mi*·ti
not όχι *o*·hi
notebook σημειωματάριο ⓝ si·mi·o·ma·*ta*·ri·o
nothing τίποτε *ti*·po·te
November Νοέμβριος ⓜ no·*em*·vri·os
now τώρα *to*·ra
nuclear energy πυρηνική ενέργεια ⓕ pi·ri·ni·*ki* e·*ner*·yi·a
nuclear testing πυρηνικές δοκιμές ⓕ pl pi·ri·ni·*kes* ţho·ki·*mes*
nuclear waste πυρηνικά απόβλητα ⓝ pl pi·ri·ni·*ka* a·*pov*·li·ta
number αριθμός ⓜ a·rith·*mos*
numberplate αριθμός κυκλοφορίας ⓜ a·rith·*mos* ki·klo·fo·*ri*·as
nun καλόγρια ⓕ ka·*lo*·ghri·a
nurse νοσοκόμος/νοσοκόμα ⓜ/ⓕ no·so·*ko*·mos / no·so·*ko*·ma
nut ξηρός καρπός ⓜ ksi·*ro* kar·*pos*

O

oats βρώμη ⓕ *vro*·mi
ocean ωκεανός ⓜ o·ke·a·*nos*
October Οκτώβριος ⓜ ok·*tov*·ri·os
off (food) μπαγιάτικος ba·*yia*·ti·kos
office γραφείο ⓝ ghra·*fi*·o
often συχνά sikh·*na*
oil (cooking) λάδι ⓝ *la*·ţhi
oil (car) λάδι αυτοκινήτου ⓝ *la*·ţhi af·to·ki·*ni*·tu
old παλιός pa·*lios*
olive ελιά ⓕ e·*lia*
olive oil ελαιόλαδο ⓝ e·le·o·la·ţho
Olympic Games Ολυμπιακοί Αγώνες ⓜ o·li·bi·a·*ki* a·*gho*·nes
omelette ομελέτα ⓕ o·me·*le*·ta
on πάνω *pa*·no
on time στην ώρα stin *o*·ra
once μια φορά mia fo·*ra*
one ένα *e*·na
one-way (ticket) απλό εισιτήριο ⓝ a·*plo* i·si·*ti*·ri·o
onion κρεμμύδι ⓝ kre·*mi*·ţhi
only μόνο *mo*·no
open a ανοιχτός a·nikh·*tos*
open v ανοίγω a·*ni*·gho
opening hours ώρες λειτουργίας ⓕ pl *o*·res li·tur·*yi*·as
opera (house) όπερα ⓕ *o*·pe·ra
operation (medical) εγχείρηση ⓕ eng·*hi*·ri·si
operator χειριστής/χειρίστρια ⓜ/ⓕ hi·ri·*stis*/hi·*ri*·stri·a
opinion γνώμη ⓕ *ghno*·mi
opposite απέναντι a·*pe*·na·di
optometrist οπτομέτρης ⓜ&ⓕ op·to·*me*·tris
or ή i
oracle μάντης ⓜ *man*·dis
orange (fruit) πορτοκάλι ⓝ por·to·*ka*·li
orange (colour) a πορτοκαλί por·to·ka·*li*
orange juice χυμός πορτοκάλι ⓜ hi·*mos* por·to·*ka*·li
orchestra ορχήστρα ⓕ or·*hi*·stra
orchid ορχιδέα ⓕ or·hi·*ţhe*·a
order σειρά ⓕ si·*ra*
order v διατάζω ţhia·*ta*·zo

ordinary συνηθισμένος si·ni·thiz·me·nos
orgasm οργασμός ⓜ or·ghaz·mos
original πρωτότυπος pro·to·ti·pos
Orthodox Ορθόδοξος/Ορθόδοξη ⓜ/ⓕ or·tho·ţhok·sos / or·tho·ţhok·si
other άλλος a·los
Ottoman a Οθωμανικός o·tho·ma·ni·kos
our μας mas
outside έξω ek·so
ouzo ούζο ⓝ u·zo
ouzeria ουζερί ⓕ u·ze·ri
ovarian cyst κύστη ωοθήκης ⓕ ki·sti o·o·thi·kis
ovary ωοθήκη ⓕ o·o·thi·ki
oven φούρνος ⓜ fur·nos
overcoat πανωφόρι ⓝ pa·no·fo·ri
overdose υπερβολική δόση ⓕ i·per·vo·li·ki ţho·si
overnight τη νύχτα ti nikh·ta
overseas εξωτερικό ek·so·te·ri·ko
owe οφείλω o·fi·lo
owner ιδιοκτήτης ⓜ i·ţhi·o·kti·tis
oxygen οξυγόνο ⓝ ok·si·gho·no
oyster στρείδι ⓝ stri·ţhi
ozone layer σφαίρα του όζοντος ⓕ sfe·ra tu o·zo·dos

P

pacemaker βηματοδότης ⓜ vi·ma·to·ţho·tis
pacifier (dummy) πιπίλα ⓕ pi·pi·la
package δέμα ⓝ ţhe·ma
packet πακέτο ⓝ pa·ke·to
padlock κλειδαριά ⓕ kli·ţha·ria
page σελίδα ⓕ se·li·ţha
pain πόνος ⓜ po·nos
painful οδυνηρός o·ţhi·ni·ros
painkiller παυσίπονο ⓝ paf·si·po·no
painter ζωγράφος ⓜ&ⓕ zo·ghra·fos
painting (a work) πίνακας ⓜ pi·na·kas
painting (the art) ζωγραφική ⓕ zo·ghra·fi·ki
pair (couple) ζευγάρι ⓝ zev·gha·ri
palace παλάτι ⓝ pa·la·ti
pan τηγάνι ⓝ ti·ya·ni
pants (trousers) παντελόνι ⓝ pa·de·lo·ni
panty liners σερβιετάκι ⓝ ser·vi·e·ta·ki
pantyhose καλτσόν ⓝ kal·tson
paper χαρτί ⓝ khar·ti
papers (documents) έγγραφα ⓝ pl e·gra·fa
paperwork προετοιμασία ⓕ εγγράφων pro·e·ti·ma·si·a e·gra·fon
paprika πάπρικα ⓕ pa·pri·ka
pap smear τεστ παπ ⓝ test pap
paraplegic παραπληγικός ⓜ pa·ra·pli·yi·kos
parcel δέμα ⓝ ţhe·ma
parents γονείς ⓜ pl gho·nis
park πάρκο ⓝ par·ko
park (a car) παρκάρω par·ka·ro
parliament Βουλή ⓕ vu·li
part (component) εξάρτημα ⓝ ek·sar·ti·ma
part-time μερική απασχόληση me·ri·ki a·pas·kho·li·si
party (night out) πάρτυ ⓝ par·ti
party (politics) κόμμα ⓝ ko·ma
pass v περνάω per·na·o
passenger επιβάτης/επιβάτισσα ⓜ/ⓕ e·pi·va·tis / e·pi·va·ti·sa
passion fruit πάσιον φρουτ ⓝ pa·si·on frut
passport διαβατήριο ⓝ ţhia·va·ti·ri·o
passport number αριθμός διαβατηρίου ⓜ a·rith·mos ţhia·va·ti·ri·u
past παρελθόν ⓝ pa·rel·thon
pasta ζυμαρικά ⓝ pl zi·ma·ri·ka
pastry φύλλο ⓝ fi·lo
path μονοπάτι ⓝ mo·no·pa·ti
patisserie ζαχαροπλαστείο ⓝ za·kha·ro·pla·sti·o
pay v πληρώνω pli·ro·no
payment πληρωμή ⓕ pli·ro·mi
pea αρακάς ⓜ a·ra·kas
peace ειρήνη ⓕ i·ri·ni
peach ροδάκινο ⓝ ro·ţha·ki·no
peak (mountain) κορυφή ⓕ ko·ri·fi
peanut αράπικο φιστίκι ⓝ a·ra·pi·ko fi·sti·ki
pear αχλάδι ⓝ a·khla·ţhi
pedal πεντάλ ⓝ pe·dal
pedestrian πεζός ⓜ pe·zos
pelican πελεκάνος ⓜ pe·le·ka·nos
pen (ballpoint) στυλό ⓝ sti·lo
pencil μολύβι ⓝ mo·li·vi
penis πέος ⓝ pe·os
penknife σουγιάς ⓜ su·yias
pension σύνταξη ⓕ si·dak·si

pensioner συνταξιούχος/συνταξιούχα ⓜ/ⓕ si·dak·si·*u*·khos/ si·dak·si·*u*·kha
people κόσμος ⓜ *koz*·mos
pepper πιπέρι ⓝ pi·*pe*·ri
pepper (bell) πιπεριά ⓕ pi·per·i·*a*
per ανά a·na
per cent τοις εκατό tis e·ka·*to*
perfect a τέλειος *te*·li·os
performance απόδοση ⓕ a·*po*·ţho·si
perfume άρωμα ⓝ *a*·ro·ma
period pain πόνοι περιόδου ⓜ *po*·ni pe·ri·*o*·ţhu
permission άδεια ⓕ *a*·ţhi·a
permit άδεια ⓕ *a*·ţhi·a
person πρόσωπο ⓝ *pro*·so·po
petition λίστα υπογραφών ⓕ *li*·sta i·po·ghra·*fon*
petrol βενζίνη ⓕ ven·*zi*·ni
petrol station βενζινάδικο ⓝ ven·zi·*na*·ţhi·ko
pharmacist φαρμακοποιός ⓜ&ⓕ far·ma·ko·pi·*os*
pharmacy φαρμακείο ⓝ far·ma·*ki*·o
photo φωτογραφία ⓕ fo·to·gra·*fi*·a
photographer φωτογράφος ⓜ&ⓕ fo·to·*ghra*·fos
photography φωτογραφική ⓕ fo·to·ghra·fi·*ki*
phrasebook βιβλίο φράσεων ⓕ viv·*li*·o *fra*·se·on
pickaxe τσεκούρι ⓝ tse·*ku*·ri
pickles τουρσί ⓝ tur·*si*
picnic πίκνικ ⓝ pik·*nik*
pie πίτα ⓕ *pi*·ta
piece κομμάτι ⓝ ko·*ma*·ti
pig γουρούνι ⓝ ghu·*ru*·ni
pill χάπι ⓝ *kha*·pi
the Pill το Χάπι ⓝ to *kha*·pi
pillow μαξιλάρι ⓝ mak·si·*la*·ri
pillowcase μαξιλαροθήκη ⓕ mak·si·la·ro·*thi*·ki
pine πεύκο ⓝ *pef*·ko
pineapple ανανάς ⓜ a·na·*nas*
pink ροζ roz
pistachio κελυφωτό φιστίκι ⓝ ke·li·fo·*to* fi·*sti*·ki
place θέση ⓕ *the*·si
place of birth γέννησης ⓜ *to*·pos ye·*ni*·se·os
plane αεροπλάνο ⓝ a·e·ro·*pla*·no
planet πλανήτης ⓜ pla·*ni*·tis
plant φυτό ⓝ fi·*to*
plastic a πλαστικός pla·sti·*kos*
plate πιάτο ⓝ *pia*·to
plateau οροπέδιο ⓝ o·ro·*pe*·ţhi·o
platform (train) αποβάθρα ⓕ a·po·*va*·thra
play (theatre) θεατρικό έργο ⓝ the·a·tri·*ko* *er*·gho
play cards v παίζω χαρτιά *pe*·zo khar·*tia*
play guitar v παίζω κιθάρα *pe*·zo ki·*tha*·ra
plug (bath) τάπα ⓕ *TA*·pa
plug (electricity) βύσμα ⓝ *viz*·ma
plum δαμάσκηνο ⓝ ţha·*ma*·ski·no
poached ποσέ po·*se*
pocket τσέπη ⓕ *tse*·pi
pocket knife σουγιάς ⓜ su·*yias*
poetry ποίηση ⓕ *pi*·i·si
point σημείο ⓝ si·*mi*·o
point v δείχνω *ţhi*·khno
poisonous δηλητηριώδης ţhi·li·ti·ri·*o*·ţhis
police αστυνομία ⓕ a·sti·no·*mi*·a
police officer αστυνόμος ⓜ a·sti·*fi*·la·kos
police station αστυνομικό τμήμα ⓝ a·sti·no·mi·*ko* t·*mi*·ma
policy πολιτική ⓕ po·li·ti·*ki*
politician πολιτικός ⓜ&ⓕ po·li·ti·*kos*
politics πολιτική ⓝ pl po·li·ti·*ki*
pollen γύρη ⓕ *yi*·ri
pollution ρύπανση ⓕ *ri*·pan·si
pool (game) μπιλιάρδο ⓝ bi·*liar*·ţho
pool (swimming) πισίνα ⓕ pi·*si*·na
poor a φτωχός fto·*khos*
popular δημοφιλής ţhi·mo·fi·*lis*
pork χοιρινό ⓝ hi·ri·*no*
pork sausage χοιρινό λουκάνικο ⓝ hi·ri·*no* lu·*ka*·ni·ko
port (sea) λιμάνι ⓝ li·*ma*·ni
positive a θετικός the·ti·*kos*
possible πιθανός pi·tha·*nos*
post v ταχυδρομώ ta·hi·ţhro·*mo*
postage ταχυδρομικά τέλη ⓝ pl e·kso·ţha a·po·sto·*lis*

postcard καρτ-ποστάλ ⓕ kart·po·*stal*
postcode έξοδα κώδικας ⓜ ta·hi·ţhro·mi·*kos* *ko*·ţhi·kas
post office ταχυδρομείο ⓝ ta·hi·ţhro·*mi*·o
poster αφίσα ⓕ a·*fi*·sa
pot (ceramics) κεραμικό ⓝ ke·ra·mi·*ko*
pot (dope) χόρτο ⓝ *hor*·to
potato πατάτα ⓕ pa·*ta*·ta
pottery αγγειοπλαστική ⓕ a·gi·o·pla·sti·*ki*
pound (money) λίρα ⓕ *li*·ra
pound (weight) λίβρα ⓕ *li*·vra
poverty φτώχεια ⓕ *fto*·hia
powder πούδρα ⓕ *pu*·ţhra
power δύναμη ⓕ *ţhi*·na·mi
prawn γαρίδα ⓕ gha·*ri*·ţha
prayer προσευχή ⓕ pro·sef·*hi*
prayer book προσευχητάρι ⓝ pro·sef·khi·*ta*·ri
prefer προτιμώ pro·ti·*mo*
pregnancy test kit τεστ εγκυμοσύνης ⓝ test e·gi·mo·*si*·nis
pregnant a έγκυος *e*·gi·os
prehistoric προϊστορικός pro·i·sto·ri·*kos*
premenstrual tension προεμμηνορροϊκή ένταση ⓕ pro·e·mi·no·ro·i·*khi* *e*·da·si
prepare προετοιμάζω pro·e·ti·*ma*·zo
prescription συνταγή ⓕ si·da·*yi*
present (gift) δώρο ⓝ *ţho*·ro
present (time) παρόν ⓝ pa·*ron*
president πρόεδρος ⓜ&ⓕ *pro*·e·ţhros
pressure πίεση ⓕ *pi*·e·si
pretty όμορφος *o*·mor·fos
price τιμή ⓕ ti·*mi*
priest παπάς ⓜ pa·*pas*
prime minister πρωθυπουργός ⓜ&ⓕ pro·thi·pur·*ghos*
printer (computer) εκτυπωτής ⓜ ek·ti·po·*tis*
prison φυλακή ⓕ fi·la·*ki*
prisoner φυλακισμένος ⓜ fi·la·kiz·*me*·nos
private a ιδιωτικός i·ţhi·o·ti·*kos*
problem πρόβλημα ⓝ *pro*·vli·ma
produce v παράγω pa·*ra*·gho
profit κέρδος ⓝ *ker*·ţhos
programme πρόγραμμα ⓝ *pro*·gra·ma
projector προτζέκτορας ⓜ tze·kto·*ras*
promise v υπόσχομαι i·*pos*·kho·me
prostitute πόρνη ⓕ *por*·ni
protect προστατεύω pro·sta·*te*·vo
protected (species) προστατευόμενα (είδη) ⓝ pl pro·sta·te·*vo*·me·na (*i*·ţhi)
protest διαμαρτυρία ⓕ ţhi·a·mar·ti·*ri*·a
protest v διαμαρτύρομαι ţhi·a·mar·*ti*·ro·me
provisions προμήθειες ⓕ pl pro·*mi*·thi·es
prune (dried fruit) ξηρό δαμάσκηνο ⓝ ksi·*ro* ţha·*ma*·ski·no
pub (bar) παμπ ⓕ pub
public gardens εθνικός κήπος ⓜ eth·ni·*kos* *ki*·pos
public relations δημόσιες σχέσεις ⓕ pl ţhi·*mo*·si·es *she*·sis
public toilet δημόσια τουαλέτα ⓝ pl ţhi·*mo*·si·a tu·a·*le*·ta
pulse σφυγμός ⓜ sfigh·*mos*
pull v τραβάω tra·*va*·o
pump τρόμπα ⓕ *tro*·ba
pumpkin κολοκύθα ⓝ ko·lo·*ki*·tha
puncture τρύπα ⓕ *tri*·pa
punch (ticket) v ακυρώνω a·ki·*ro*·no
pure a καθαρός ka·tha·*ros*
purple μωβ mov
purse πορτοφόλι ⓝ por·to·*fo*·li
push v σπρώχνω *sprokh*·no
put βάζω *va*·zo

Q

quadriplegic τετραπληγικός ⓜ te·tra·pli·yi·*kos*
qualifications προσόντα ⓝ pl pro·*so*·da
quality ποιότητα ⓕ pi·*o*·ti·ta
quarantine καραντίνα ⓕ ka·ra·*di*·na
quarter τέταρτο ⓝ *te*·tar·to
queen βασίλισσα ⓕ va·*si*·li·sa
question ερώτηση ⓕ e·*ro*·ti·si
queue ουρά ⓕ u·*ra*
quick a γρήγορος *ghri*·gho·ros
quiet a ήσυχος *i*·si·khos
quit v παραιτούμαι pa·re·*tu*·me

R

rabies λύσσα ⓕ *li*·sa
rabbit κουνέλι ⓝ ku·*ne*·li
race (sport) αγώνας ⓕ a·*gho*·nas

racetrack (motor racing) πίστα ⓜ *pi*·sta
racing bike αγωνιστικό ποδήλατο ⓝ a·*gho*·ni·sti·ko po·*thi*·la·to
racism ρατσισμός ⓜ rat·sis·*mos*
racquet ρακέτα ⓕ ra·*ke*·ta
radiator ψυγείο αυτοκινήτου ⓝ psi·*yi*·o af·to·ki·*ni*·tu
radio ραδιόφωνο ⓝ ra·thi·*o*·fo·no
radish ραπάνι ⓝ ra·*pa*·ni
railway station σιδηροδρομικός σταθμός ⓜ si·thi·ro·thro·mi·*kos* stath·*mos*
rain ⓝ βροχή vro·*hi*
raincoat αδιάβροχο ⓝ a·thi·*av*·ro·ho
raisin σταφίδα ⓕ sta·*fi*·tha
rally ράλι ⓝ *ra*·li
rape βιασμός ⓜ vi·az·*mos*
rape v βιάζω vi·*a*·zo
rare (uncommon) σπάνιος *spa*·ni·os
rare (food) μισοψημένο ⓝ mi·so·psi·*me*·no
rash εξάνθημα ⓝ ek·*san*·thi·ma
raspberry σμέουρο ⓝ va·*to*·mu·ro
rat ποντίκι ⓝ po·*di*·ki
raw ωμός *o*·mos
razor ξυράφι ⓝ ksi·*ra*·fi
razor blade λεπίδα ⓕ le·*pi*·tha
read διαβάζω thia·*va*·zo
reading διάβασμα ⓝ *thia*·vaz·ma
ready έτοιμος *e*·ti·mos
real estate agent κτηματομεσίτης/κτηματομεσίτρια ⓜ/ⓕ kti·ma·to·me·*si*·tis / kti·ma·to·me·*si*·tri·a
realistic ρεαλιστικός re·a·li·sti·*kos*
rear (seat etc) πίσω *pi*·so
reason αιτία ⓕ e·*ti*·a
receipt απόδειξη ⓕ a·*po*·thik·si
recently πρόσφατα *pros*·fa·ta
recommend προτείνω pro·*ti*·no
record v καταγράφω ka·ta·*ghra*·fo
recording καταγραφή ⓕ ka·ta·ghra·*fi*
recyclable ανακυκλώσιμο a·na·ki·*klo*·si·mo
recycle ανακυκλώνω a·na·ki·*klo*·no
red κόκκινο *ko*·ki·no
referee διαιτητής/διαιτήτρια ⓜ/ⓕ thi·e·ti·*tis*/thi·e·*ti*·tri·a
reference (letter) συστατική επιστολή ⓕ si·sta·ti·*ki* e·pi·sto·*li*
reflexology ρεφλεξολογία ⓕ re·fle·kso·lo·*ghi*·a
refrigerator ψυγείο ⓝ psi·*yi*·o
refugee πρόσφυγας ⓜ&ⓕ *pros*·fi·ghas
refund ⓕ επιστροφή χρημάτων e·pi·stro·*fi* khri·*ma*·ton
refuse v αρνούμαι ar·*nu*·me
regional (administration) περιφερειακός pe·ri·fe·ri·a·*kos*
(by) registered mail συστημένη επιστολή ⓕ si·sti·*me*·ni a·po·sto·*li*
rehydration salts ηλεκτρολύτες ⓜ pl i·le·ktro·*li*·tes
relationship σχέση ⓕ *she*·si
relax v χαλαρώνω kha·la·*ro*·no
relic κειμήλιο ⓝ ki·*mi*·li·o
religion θρησκεία ⓕ thri·*ski*·a
religious a θρήσκος *thri*·skos
remote a απόμακρος a·*po*·mak·ros
remote control τηλεχειριστήριο ⓝ ti·le·hi·ri·*sti*·ri·o
rent v νοικιάζω ni·ki·*a*·zo
repair v επισκευάζω e·pi·ske·*va*·zo
republic δημοκρατία ⓕ thi·mo·kra·*ti*·a
reservation (booking) κράτηση ⓕ *kra*·ti·si
residency permit άδεια παραμονής ⓕ *a*·thi·a pa·ra·mo·*nis*
rest v ξεκουράζομαι kse·ku·*ra*·zo·me
restaurant εστιατόριο ⓝ e·sti·a·*to*·ri·o
restriction περιορισμός ⓜ pe·ri·o·riz·*mos*
résumé (CV) βιογραφικό σημείωμα ⓝ vi·o·ghra·fi·*ko* si·*mi*·o·ma
retired συνταξιούχος si·dak·si·*u*·khos
retsina (drink) ρετσίνα ⓕ ret·*si*·na
return (come back) v επιστρέφω e·pi·*stre*·fo
return (ticket) εισιτήριο μετ' επιστροφής ⓝ i·si·*ti*·ri·o me·te·pis·tro·*fis*
review (critique) κριτική ⓕ kri·ti·*ki*
rhythm ρυθμός ⓜ rith·*mos*
rib πλευρό ⓝ plev·*ro*
rice ρύζι ⓝ *ri*·zi
rich (wealthy) πλούσιος *plu*·si·os
ride (horse) ιππασία ⓕ i·pa·*si*·a
ride (horse) v ιππεύω i·*pe*·vo
right (correct) a σωστός so·*stos*
right (direction) δεξιός thek·si·*os*
right-wing δεξιά ⓕ thek·si·*a*
ring (jewellery) δαχτυλίδι ⓝ thakh·ti·*li*·thi
ring (phone) v τηλεφωνώ ti·le·fo·*no*
rip-off κλεψιά ⓕ kle·psi·*a*
risk ρίσκο ⓝ *ri*·sko
river ποτάμι ⓝ po·*ta*·mi
road δρόμος ⓜ *thro*·mos

road map οδικός χάρτης (m) o·thi·*kos* *khar*·tis
roasted ψημένος psi·*me*·nos
rob ληστεύω li·*ste*·vo
rock βράχος (m) *vra*·khos
rock climbing αναρρίχηση (f) a·na·*ri*·hi·si
rock music μουσική ροκ (f) mu·si·*ki* rok
rockfalls κατολίσθηση (f) ka·to·*lis*·thi·si
rock group μπάντα ροκ (f) *ba*·da rok
rockmelon πεπόνι (n) pe·*po*·ni
roll (bread) ψωμάκι (n) pso·*ma*·ki
rollerblading τροχοπεδιλισμός (m) tro·kho·pe·thi·lis·*mos*
Roman Ρωμαϊκός ro·ma·i·*kos*
romantic ρομαντικός ro·ma·di·*kos*
room δωμάτιο (n) tho·*ma*·ti·o
room number αριθμός δωματίου (m) a·rith·*mos* tho·ma·*ti*·u
rope σκοινί (n) ski·*ni*
round a στρογγυλός stro·gi·*los*
roundabout κυκλική διασταύρωση (f) ki·kli·*ki* thi·a·*stav*·ro·si
route δρόμος (m) *thro*·mos
rowing κωπηλασία (f) ko·pi·la·*si*·a
rubbish σκουπίδια (n) pl sku·*pi*·thia
rubella ερυθρά (f) e·ri·*thra*
rug χαλί (n) kha·*li*
rugby ράγκμπυ (n) *rag*·bi
ruins ερείπια (n) pl e·*ri*·pi·a
rule (m) κανόνας ka·*no*·nas
rum ρούμι (n) *ru*·mi
run v τρέχω *tre*·kho
running τρέξιμο (n) *trek*·si·mo
runny nose καταρροή (f) kha·ta·ro·*i*

S

sad λυπημένος li·pi·*me*·nos
saddle σέλα (f) *se*·la
safe ασφάλεια (f) as·*fa*·li·a
safe a ασφαλής as·fa·*lis*
safe sex ασφαλές σεξ (n) as·fa·*les* seks
saint άγιος/αγία (m)/(f) *a*·yi·os/a·*yi*·a
sailing ιστιοπλοΐα (f) i·sti·o·plo·*i*·a
salad σαλάτα (f) sa·*la*·ta
salami σαλάμι (n) sa·*la*·mi
salary μισθός (m) mis·*thos*
sale πώληση (f) *po*·li·si
sales tax φόρος κατανάλωσης (m) *fo*·ros ka·ta·*na*·lo·sis
salmon σολομός (m) so·lo·*mos*
salt αλάτι (n) a·*la*·ti
same ίδιος *i*·thi·os
sand άμμος (m) *a*·mos
sandal σανδάλι (n) sa·*tha*·li
sanitary napkin σερβιέτα (f) ser·vi·e·ta
sardine σαρδέλα (f) sar·*the*·la
Saturday Σάββατο (n) *sa*·va·to
sauce σάλτσα (f) *sal*·tsa
saucepan κατσαρολάκι (n) ka·tsa·ro·*la*·ki
sauna σάουνα (n) *sa*·u·na
sausage λουκάνικο (n) lu·*ka*·ni·ko
savoury αλμυρός al·mi·*ros*
say v λέω *le*·o
scalp κρανίο (n) kra·*ni*·o
scarf κασκόλ (n) ka·*skol*
school σχολείο (n) skho·*li*·o
science επιστήμη (f) e·pi·*sti*·mi
scientist επιστήμονας (m)&(f) e·pi·*sti*·mo·nas
scissors ψαλίδι (n) psa·*li*·thi
score v σκοράρω sko·*ra*·ro
scoreboard πίνακας αποτελεσμάτων (m) *pi*·na·kas ap·te·les·*ma*·ton
Scotland Σκωτία (f) sko·*ti*·a
scrambled σκραμπλ (αβγά) *skram*·bel (av·*gha*)
sculpture γλυπτική (f) ghlip·ti·*ki*
sea θάλασσα (f) *tha*·la·sa
seafood θαλασσινά (n) pl tha·la·si·*na*
(be) seasick πάσχει από ναυτία *pa*·shi a·*po* naf·*ti*·a
seasickness ναυτία (f) naf·*ti*·a
seaside παραλία (f) pa·ra·*li*·a
season εποχή (f) e·po·*hi*
seat (place) θέση (f) *the*·si
seatbelt ζώνη ασφαλείας (f) *zo*·ni as·fa·*li*·as
sea turtle θαλάσσια χελώνα (f) tha·*la*·si·a he·*lo*·na
sea urchin αχινός (m) a·hi·*nos*
second δευτερόλεπτο (n) thef·te·*ro*·lep·to
second (time) a δεύτερος *thef*·te·ros
second class (economy) οικονομική θέση (f) i·ko·no·mi·*ki* *the*·si
second-hand a μεταχειρισμένος me·ta·hi·riz·*me*·nos
second-hand shop κατάστημα μεταχειρισμένων ειδών (n) ka·*ta*·sti·ma me·ta·hi·ris·*me*·non i·*thon*

secretary γραμματέας ⓜ&ⓕ *ghra·ma·te·as*
see βλέπω *vle·po*
self-employed a αυτοαπασχολούμενος *a·fto·apas·ho·lu·me·nos*
selfish εγωιστής *e·yo·i·stis*
self-service ⓝ σελφ σέρβις *self ser·vis*
sell v πουλάω *pu·la·o*
seminar σεμινάριο ⓝ *se·mi·na·ri·o*
send στέλνω *stel·no*
sensible λογικός *lo·ghi·kos*
sensual αισθησιακός *e·sthi·si·a·kos*
separate a χωριστός *kho·ri·stos*
September Σεπτέμβριος ⓜ *sep·tem·vri·os*
serious σοβαρός *so·va·ros*
service υπηρεσία ⓕ *i·pi·re·si·a*
service charge φιλοδώρημα ⓝ *fi·lo·ţho·ri·ma*
service station βενζινάδικο ⓝ *ven·zi·na·ţhi·ko*
serviette χαρτοπετσέτα ⓕ *har·to·pe·tse·ta*
several μερικοί *me·ri·ki*
sew v ράβω *ra·vo*
sex (intercourse) σεξ ⓝ *seks*
sexism σεξισμός ⓜ *sek·siz·mos*
sexy σέξυ *sek·si*
shade σκιά ⓕ *ski·a*
shadow σκιά ⓕ *ski·a*
shampoo σαμπουάν ⓝ *sam·pu·an*
shape σχήμα ⓝ *shi·ma*
share (with) μοιράζομαι *mi·ra·zo·me*
shave v ξυρίζω *ksi·ri·zo*
shaving cream κρέμα ξυρίσματος ⓕ *kre·ma ksi·riz·ma·tos*
she αυτή *af·ti*
sheep πρόβατο ⓝ *pro·va·to*
sheet (bed) σεντόνι ⓝ *se·do·ni*
shelf ράφι ⓝ *ra·fi*
shiatsu σιάτσου ⓜ *si·at·su*
shield ασπίδα ⓕ *as·pi·ţha*
shingles (illness) έρπης ζωστήρας ⓜ *er·pis zo·sti·ras*
ship πλοίο ⓝ *pli·o*
shirt πουκάμισο ⓝ *pu·ka·mi·so*
shoe παπούτσι ⓝ *pa·put·si*
shoes παπούτσια ⓝ pl *pa·put·si·a*
shoe shop κατάστημα παπουτσιών ⓝ *ka·ta·sti·ma pa·pu·tsi·on*
shoot v πυροβολώ *pi·ro·vo·lo*
shop κατάστημα ⓝ *ka·ta·sti·ma*
shop v ψωνίζω *pso·ni·zo*
shopping ψώνια ⓝ pl *pso·nia*
shopping centre εμπορικό κέντρο ⓝ *em·bo·ri·ko ke·dro*
short (height) κοντός *ko·dos*
shortage έλλειψη ⓕ *e·lip·si*
shorts σορτς ⓝ *sorts*
shoulder ώμος ⓜ *o·mos*
shout v φωνάζω *fo·na·zo*
show επίδειξη ⓕ *e·pi·ţhik·si*
show v δείχνω *ţhikh·no*
shower ντους ⓝ *duz*
shrine βωμός ⓜ *vo·mos*
shut a κλειστός *kli·stos*
shy a ντροπαλός *dro·pa·los*
sick a άρρωστος *a·ro·stos*
side πλευρά ⓕ *plev·ra*
siesta απογευματινός ύπνος ⓜ *a·po·ghev·ma·ti·nos ip·nos*
sign πινακίδα ⓕ *pi·na·ki·ţha*
signature υπογραφή ⓕ *i·po·ghra·fi*
silk μετάξι ⓝ *me·tak·si*
silver ασήμι ⓝ *a·si·mi*
similar παρόμοιος *pa·ro·mi·os*
simple απλός *a·plos*
since (May) από (το Μάη) *a·po (to ma·i)*
sing v τραγουδώ *tra·ghu·ţho*
Singapore Σινγκαπούρη ⓕ *sig·ga·pu·ri*
singer τραγουδιστής/τραγουδίστρια ⓜ/ⓕ *tra·ghu·ţhi·stis/tra·ghu·ţhi·stri·a*
single (person) a εργένης/εργένισσα ⓜ/ⓕ *er·ye·nis/er·ye·ni·sa*
single room μονό δωμάτιο ⓝ *mo·no ţho·ma·tio*
singlet φανέλα ⓕ *fa·ne·la*
sister αδερφή ⓕ *a·ţher·fi*
sit κάθομαι *ka·tho·me*
size μέγεθος ⓝ *me·ye·thos*
skate v κάνω πατίνι *ka·no pa·ti·ni*
skateboarding πατίνι ⓝ *pa·ti·ni*
ski v κάνω σκι *ka·no ski*
skiing σκι ⓝ *ski*
skimmed milk άπαχο γάλα ⓝ *a·pa·kho gha·la*
skin δέρμα ⓝ *ţher·ma*
skirt φούστα ⓕ *fu·sta*
skull κρανίο ⓝ *kra·ni·o*
sky ουρανός ⓜ *u·ra·nos*
sleep v κοιμάμαι *ki·ma·me*
sleeping bag υπνόσακος ⓜ *ip·NO·sa·kos*
sleeping berth (ship) κουκέτα ⓕ *ku·ke·ta*

sleeping car κλινάμαξα (f) kli·na·ma·ksa
sleeping pills υπνωτικά χάπια (n) pl ip·no·ti·ka kha·pia
sleepy νυσταγμένος nis·tagh·me·nos
slice φέτα (f) fe·ta
slide (film) σλάιντ (n) sla·id
slow a αργός ar·ghos
slowly αργά ar·gha
small μικρός mi·kros
smaller μικρότερος mi·kro·te·ros
smallest ο μικρότερος o mi·kro·te·ros
smell μυρωδιά (f) mi·ro·ţhia
smile v χαμογελώ kha·mo·ye·lo
smog νέφος (n) ne·fos
smoke v καπνίζω kap·ni·zo
snack σνακ (n) snak
snail σαλιγκάρι (n) sa·li·ga·ri
snake φίδι (n) fi·dhi
snorkelling κατάδυση με αναπνευστήρα (f) ka·ta·ţhi·si me a·na·pne·fsti·ra
snow χιόνι (n) hio·ni
snow pea ζαχαρομπίζελο (n) za·ha·ro·bi·ze·lo
snowboarding σνόουμπορντ (n) sno·bord
soap σαπούνι (n) sa·pu·ni
soap opera σαπουνόπερα (f) sa·pu·no·pe·ra
soccer ποδόσφαιρο (n) po·ţhos·fe·ro
social welfare κοινωνική πρόνοια (f) ki·no·ni·ki pro·ni·a
socialist σοσιαλιστής/σοσιαλίστρια (m)/(f) so·si·a·li·stis/so·si·a·li·stri·a
sock κάλτσα (f) kal·tsa
socks κάλτσες (f) pl kal·tses
soft drink αναψυκτικό (n) a·nap·sik·ti·ko
soft-boiled μελάτο (n) me·la·to
soldier στρατιώτης (m) stra·ti·o·tis
some μερικοί me·ri·ki
someone κάποιος ka·pi·os
something κάτι ka·ti
sometimes μερικές φορές me·ri·kes fo·res
son γιος (m) yios
song τραγούδι (n) tra·ghu·ţhi
soon σύντομα si·do·ma
sore a πονεμένος po·ne·me·nos
soup σούπα (f) su·pa
sour cream ξινή κρέμα (f) ksi·ni kre·ma
south νότος (m) no·tos
souvenir σουβενίρ (n) su·ve·nir
souvenir shop κατάστημα με σουβενίρ (n) ka·ta·sti·ma me su·ve·nir
souvlaki σουβλάκι (n) suv·la·ki
soy milk γάλα σόγια (n) gha·la so·yi·a
soy sauce σάλτσα (f) σόγια sal·tsa so·yi·a
space διάστημα (n) ţhi·a·sti·ma
Spain Ισπανία (f) i·spa·ni·a
sparkling wine αφρώδης οίνος (m) a·fro·ţhis o·nos
speak μιλάω mi·la·o
spear (ancient weapon) δόρυ (n) ţho·ri
special a ειδικός i·ţhi·kos
specialist ειδικός/ειδική (m)/(f) i·ţhi·kos/i·ţhi·ki
speed (velocity) ταχύτητα (f) ta·hi·ti·ta
speed limit όριο ταχύτητας (n) o·ri·o ta·hi·ti·tas
speedometer ταχύμετρο (n) ta·hi·me·tro
spider αράχνη (f) a·rakh·ni
spinach σπανάκι (n) spa·na·ki
spoiled (food) χαλασμένος kha·laz·me·nos
spoke ακτίνα (f) ak·ti·na
spoon κουτάλι (n) ku·ta·li
sport σπορ (n) spor
sportsman αθλητής (m) a·thli·tis
sportswoman αθλήτρια (f) ath·li·tri·a
sports store κατάστημα με αθλητικά είδη (n) ka·ta·sti·ma me a·thli·ti·ka i·ţhi
sprain τράβηγμα (n) tra·vigh·ma
spring (coil) ελατήριο (n) e·la·ti·ri·o
spring (season) άνοιξη (f) a·nik·si
square (town) πλατεία (f) pla·ti·a
spray σπρέι (n) spre·i
stadium στάδιο (n) sta·ţhi·o
stairway σκάλα (f) ska·la
stale μπαγιάτικος ba·yia·ti·kos
stamp γραμματόσημο (n) ghra·ma·to·si·mo
stand-by ticket εισιτήριο σταντ μπάι (n) i·si·ti·ri·o stand ba·i
star (sky) αστέρι (n) a·ste·ri
start αρχή (f) ar·hi
start v αρχίζω ar·hi·zo
station σταθμός (m) stath·mos
stationer's χαρτοπωλείο (n) khar·to·po·li·o
statue άγαλμα (n) a·ghal·ma
stay μένω me·no
steak (beef) μπριζόλα (f) bri·zo·la
steal κλέβω kle·vo
steep απότομος a·po·to·mos
step βήμα (n) vi·ma
stereo στερεοφωνικό (n) ste·re·o·fo·ni·ko
still water μεταλλικό νερό (n) me·ta·li·ko ne·ro

sting v τσιμπάω tsi·*ba*·o
stock (food) ζωμός ⓜ zo·*mos*
stockings καλτσόν ⓝ kal·*tson*
stolen κλεμμένο kle·*me*·no
stomach στομάχι ⓝ sto·*ma*·hi
stomachache στομαχόπονος ⓜ sto·ma·*kho*·po·nos
stone πέτρα ⓕ *pe*·tra
stoned (drugged) μαστουρωμένος ma·stu·ro·*me*·nos
stop (bus etc) στάση ⓕ *sta*·si
stop (cease) v σταματάω sta·ma·*ta*·o
stop (prevent) v εμποδίζω e·bo·*thi*·zo
storm καταιγίδα ⓕ ka·te·*yi*·tha
story ιστορία ⓕ i·sto·*ri*·a
stovetop μάτια ⓝ *ma*·ti·a
straight ίσιος *i*·si·os
strange παράξενος pa·*rak*·se·nos
stranger (person) ξένος/ξένη ⓜ/ⓕ *kse*·nos / *kse*·ni
strawberry φράουλα ⓕ *fra*·u·la
stream ατμός ⓜ at·*mos*
street οδός ⓕ o·*thos*
street market λαϊκή ⓕ la·i·*ki*
strike απεργία ⓕ a·per·*yi*·a
string κλωστή ⓕ klo·*sti*
stroke (health) εγκεφαλικό ⓝ e·ge·fa·li·*ko*
stroller καροτσάκι ⓝ ka·rot·*sa*·ki
strong δυνατός thi·na·*tos*
stubborn ισχυρογνώμων is·hi·rog·*no*·mon
student (university) φοιτητής / φοιτήτρια ⓜ/ⓕ fi·ti·*tis* / fi·*ti*·tri·a
studio στούντιο ⓝ *stu*·di·o
stupid χαζός kha·*zos*
style στυλ ⓝ stil
subtitles υπότιτλοι ⓜ pl i·*po*·ti·tli
suburb προάστειο ⓝ pro·*a*·sti·o
subway a υπόγειος i·*po*·yi·os
subway (train) μετρό ⓝ me·*tro*
sugar ζάχαρη ⓕ *za*·kha·ri
suitcase βαλίτσα ⓕ va·*lit*·sa
sultana σταφίδα ⓕ sta·*fi*·tha
summer καλοκαίρι ⓝ ka·lo·*ke*·ri
sun ήλιος ⓜ *i*·li·os
sunblock αντηλιακό ⓝ a·di·li·a·*ko*
sunburn κάψιμο ⓝ *ka*·psi·mo
Sunday Κυριακή ⓕ ki·ria·*ki*
sunglasses γυαλιά ηλίου ⓝ pl yia·*lia* i·*li*·u
sunny ηλιόλουστος i·li·*o*·lu·stos
sunrise ανατολή ⓕ a·na·to·*li*
sunset ηλιοβασίλεμα ⓝ i·li·o·va·*Si*·le·ma
sunstroke ηλιοπληξία ⓕ i·li·o·plik·*si*·a
supermarket σουπερμάρκετ ⓝ su·per·*mar*·ket
superstition πρόληψη ⓕ *pro*·lip·si
supporter (politics, sport) υποστηρικτής ⓜ&ⓕ i·po·sti·rik·*tis*
surf σερφ ⓝ serf
surface mail (land) ταχυδρομική αποστολή δια ξηράς ta·hi·dro·mi·*ki* a·po·sto·*li* thi·a ksi·*ras*
surface mail (sea) ταχυδρομική αποστολή δια θαλάσσης ta·hi·dro·mi·*ki* a·po·sto·*li* *thi*·a tha·*la*·sis
surfboard σανίδα του σερφ ⓕ sa·*ni*·tha tu serf
surfing σέρφινγκ ⓝ *ser*·fing
surname επώνυμο ⓝ e·*po*·ni·mo
surprise έκπληξη ⓕ *ek*·plik·si
sweater πουλόβερ ⓝ pu·*lo*·ver
Sweden Σουηδία ⓕ su·i·*thi*·a
sweet a γλυκός ghli·*kos*
sweets γλυκά ⓝ pl ghli·*ka*
swelling πρήξιμο ⓝ *prik*·si·mo
swim v κολυμπώ ko·li·*bo*
swimming (sport) κολύμπι ⓝ ko·*li*·bi
swimming pool πισίνα ⓕ pi·*si*·na
swimsuit μαγιό ⓝ ma·*yio*
Switzerland Ελβετία ⓕ el·ve·*ti*·a
sword σπαθί ⓝ spa·*thi*
synagogue συναγωγή ⓕ si·na·gho·*yi*
synthetic a συνθετικός sin·the·ti·*kos*
syringe σύριγγα ⓕ *si*·ri·ga

T

table τραπέζι ⓝ tra·*pe*·zi
tablecloth τραπεζομάντηλο ⓝ tra·pe·zo·*ma*·di·lo
table tennis πινγκ πονγκ ⓝ ping pong
tail ουρά ⓕ u·*ra*
tailor ράφτης/ράφτρα ⓜ/ⓕ *raf*·tis / *raf*·tra
take παίρνω *per*·no
take a photo βγάζω φωτογραφία *vga*·zo fo·to·gra·*fi*·a
talk v μιλάω mi·*la*·o
tall ψηλός psi·*los*
tampon ταμπόν ⓝ ta·*bon*
tanning lotion αντηλιακό ⓝ a·di·li·a·*ko*

tap βρύση ⓕ *vri*·si

tap water νερό βρύσης ⓝ ne·*ro* *vri*·sis

tasty νόστιμος *no*·sti·mos

taverna ταβέρνα ⓕ ta·*ver*·na

tax φόρος ⓜ *fo*·ros

taxi ταξί ⓝ tak·*si*

taxi stand πιάτσα ταξί ⓕ pi·*a*·tsa tak·*si*

tea τσάι ⓝ *tsa*·i

teacher δάσκαλος/δασκάλα ⓜ/ⓕ *ţha*·ska·los / ţha·*ska*·la

team ομάδα ⓕ o·*ma*·ţha

teaspoon κουταλάκι του γλυκού ⓝ ku·ta·*la*·ki tu ghli·*ku*

technique τεχνική ⓕ tekh·ni·*ki*

teeth δόντια ⓝ *ţho*·dia

telegram τηλεγράφημα ⓝ ti·le·*ghra*·fi·ma

telephone τηλέφωνο ⓝ ti·*le*·fo·no

telephone v τηλεφωνώ ti·le·fo·*no*

telephone centre τηλεφωνικό κέντρο ⓝ ti·le·fo·ni·*ko* *ke*·dro

telescope τηλεσκόπιο ⓝ ti·le·*sko*·pi·o

television τηλεόραση ⓕ ti·le·*o*·ra·si

tell λέω *le*·o

temperature (fever) πυρετός ⓜ pi·re·*tos*

temperature (weather) θερμοκρασία ⓕ ther·mo·kra·*si*·a

temple (church) ναός ⓜ na·*os*

tennis τένις ⓝ *te*·nis

tennis court γήπεδο του τένις ⓝ *yi*·pe·ţho tu *te*·nis

tent σκηνή ⓕ ski·*ni*

tent peg πάσσαλος ⓜ *pa*·sa·los

terracotta pot αγγείο τερακότα ⓝ a·*gi*·o te·ra·*ko*·ta

terrible απαίσιος a·*pe*·si·os

test τεστ ⓜ test

thank ευχαριστώ ef·kha·ri·*sto*

that (one) εκείνο e·*ki*·no

theatre θέατρο ⓝ *the*·a·tro

their τους tus

there εκεί e·*ki*

they αυτοί af·*ti*

thick πυκνός pik·*nos*

thief κλέφτης ⓜ *klef*·tis

thin λεπτός lep·*tos*

think νομίζω no·*mi*·zo

third τρίτος *tri*·tos

thirsty διψασμένος ţhip·saz·*me*·nos

this (one) αυτός ⓜ af·*tos*

thread κλωστή ⓕ klo·*sti*

throat λαιμός ⓜ le·*mos*

thrush (health) κολπίτιδα ⓕ kol·*pi*·ti·ţha

thunderstorm καταιγίδα ⓕ ka·te·*yi*·ţha

Thursday Πέμπτη ⓕ *pem*·ti

tick τσιμπούρι ⓝ tsi·*bu*·ri

ticket εισιτήριο ⓝ i·si·*ti*·ri·o

ticket collector ελεγκτής εισιτηρίων ⓜ&ⓕ e·len·*ktis* i·si·ti·*ri*·on

ticket machine μηχάνημα έκδοσης εισιτηρίων ⓝ mi·*ha*·ni·ma *ek*·ţho·sis i·si·ti·*ri*·on

ticket office γραφείο έκδοσης εισιτηρίων ⓝ ghra·*fi*·o *ek*·ţho·sis i·si·ti·*ri*·on

tide παλίρροια ⓕ pa·*li*·ri·a

tight σφιχτός sfikh·*tos*

time ώρα ⓕ *o*·ra

time difference διαφορά ώρας ⓕ ţhia·fo·*ra* *o*·ras

timetable δρομολόγια ⓝ pl ţhro·mo·*lo*·yi·a

tin (can) κουτί ⓝ ku·*ti*

tin opener ανοιχτήρι ⓝ a·nikh·*ti*·ri

tiny μικροσκοπικός mi·kro·sko·pi·*kos*

tip (gratuity) φιλοδώρημα ⓝ fi·lo·*ţho*·ri·ma

tire λάστιχο ⓝ *la*·sti·kho

tired κουρασμένος ku·raz·*me*·nos

tissues χαρτομάντηλα ⓝ pl khar·to·*ma*·di·la

to σε se

toast τοστ ⓝ tost

toaster τοστιέρα ⓕ to·sti·*e*·ra

tobacco καπνός ⓜ kap·*nos*

tobacconist καπνοπώλης ⓜ ka·pno·*po*·lis

today σήμερα *si*·me·ra

toe δάχτυλο ποδιού ⓝ *ţhakh*·ti·lo po·*ţhiu*

tofu τόφου ⓝ *to*·fu

together μαζί ma·*zi*

toilet τουαλέτα ⓕ tu·a·*le*·ta

toilet paper χαρτί υγείας n ⓝ khar·*ti* i·*yi*·as

tomato ντομάτα ⓕ do·*ma*·ta

tomato sauce σάλτσα ντομάτας ⓕ *sal*·tsa do·*ma*·tas

tomb τάφος ⓜ *ta*·fos

tomorrow αύριο *av*·ri·o

tomorrow afternoon αύριο το απόγευμα *av*·ri·o to a·*po*·yev·ma

tomorrow evening αύριο το βράδι *av*·ri·o to *vra*·ţhi

tomorrow morning αύριο το βράδυ av·ri·o to pro·i
tonight απόψε a·pop·se
too (excess) πάρα πολύ pa·ra po·li
tooth δόντι ⓝ tho·di
toothache πονόδοντος ⓜ po·no·tho·dos
toothbrush οδοντόβουρτσα ⓕ o·tho·do·vur·tsa
toothpaste οδοντόπαστα ⓕ o·tho·do·pa·sta
toothpick οδοντογλυφίδα ⓕ o·tho·do·ghli·fi·tha
torch (flashlight) φακός ⓜ fa·kos
touch v αγγίζω a·gi·zo
tour (guided) ξενάγηση ⓕ kse·na·yi·si
tourist τουρίστας/τουρίστρια ⓜ/ⓕ tu·ri·stas / tu·ri·stri·a
tourist office γραφείο πληροφοριών ⓝ ghra·fi·o pli·ro·fo·ri·on
towards προς pros
towel πετσέτα ⓕ pet·se·ta
tower πύργος ⓜ pir·ghos
toxic waste τοξικά απόβλητα ⓝ pl tok·si·ka a·pov·li·ta
toy shop κατάστημα παιχνιδιών ⓝ ka·ta·sti·ma peh·ni·thion
track (path) μονοπάτι ⓝ mo·no·pa·ti
track (sport) στίβος ⓜ sti·vos
trade εμπόριο ⓝ e·bo·ri·o
tradesperson τεχνίτης ⓜ&ⓕ te·khni·tis
traffic κυκλοφορία ⓕ ki·klo·fo·ri·a
traffic light φανάρι ⓝ fa·na·ri
trail μονοπάτι ⓝ mo·no·pa·ti
train τρένο ⓝ tre·no
train station σταθμός τρένου ⓜ stath·mos tre·nu
tram τραμ ⓝ tram
transit lounge αίθουσα αναμονής ⓕ e·thu·sa a·na·mo·nis
translate μεταφράζω me·ta·fra·zo
transport μεταφορά ⓕ me·ta·fo·ra
travel v ταξιδεύω tak·si·the·vo
travel agency ταξιδιωτικό γραφείο ⓝ tak·si·thi·o·ti·ko ghra·fi·o
travel sickness ναυτία ⓕ naf·ti·a
tree δέντρο ⓝ the·dro
trip (journey) ταξίδι ⓝ tak·si·thi
trolley καροτσάκι ⓝ ka·rot·sa·ki
trolley bus τρόλεϊ ⓝ tro·le·i
trousers παντελόνι ⓝ pa·de·lo·ni
truck φορτηγό ⓝ for·ti·gho
trust v εμπιστεύομαι e·bi·ste·vo·me
try (attempt) προσπαθώ pros·pa·tho
T-shirt μπλουζάκι ⓝ blu·za·ki
tube (tyre) σαμπρέλα ⓕ sa·bre·la
Tuesday Τρίτη ⓕ tri·ti
tumour όγκος ⓜ o·gos
tuna τόνος ⓜ to·nos
tune μελωδία ⓕ me·lo·thi·as
tunic χιτώνας ⓜ hi·to·nas
Turkey Τουρκία ⓕ tur·ki·a
turkey γάλοπούλα ⓕ gha·lo·pu·la
Turkish (language) Τουρκικά tur·ki·ka
Turkish (people) Τούρκοι ⓜ pl tur·ki
turn v γυρίζω yi·ri·zo
TV τηλεόραση ⓕ ti·le·o·ra·si
tweezers τσιμπιδάκι ⓝ tsi·bi·tha·ki
twice δυο φορές thio fo·res
twin beds δύο μονά κρεβάτια ⓝ thi·o mo·na kre·va·ti·a
twins δίδυμα ⓝ pl thi·thi·ma
two δύο thi·o
type τύπος ⓜ ti·pos
typhus τύφος ⓜ ti·fos
typical τυπικός ti·pi·kos
tyre λάστιχο ⓝ la·sti·kho

U

ultrasound υπέρηχος ⓜ i·pe·ri·hos
umbrella ομπρέλα ⓕ o·bre·la
uncomfortable άβολος a·vo·los
understand καταλαβαίνω ka·ta·la·ve·no
underwear εσώρουχα ⓝ pl e·so·ru·kha
unemployed a άνεργος/άνεργη ⓜ/ⓕ a·ner·ghos / a·ner·yi
unfair άδικος a·thi·kos
uniform στολή ⓕ sto·li
universe σύμπαν ⓝ si·ban
university πανεπιστήμιο ⓝ pa·ne·pi·sti·mi·o
unleaded (petrol) αμόλυβδος ⓕ a·mo·liv·thos
unsafe ανασφαλής a·nas·fa·lis

until μέχρι *me*·khri
unusual ασυνήθιστος a·si·*ni*·thi·stos
UN zone ζώνη των Ηνωμένων Εθνών ⓕ *zo*·ni ton i·no·*me*·non e·*thnon*
up πάνω *pa*·no
uphill ανηφορικά a·ni·fo·ri·*ka*
urgent επείγον e·*pi*·ghon
urinary tract infection ουρολοίμωξη ⓕ u·ro·*li*·mo·ksi
USA ΗΠΑ ⓕ *i*·pa
useful χρήσιμος *khri*·si·mos

V

vacancy κενό ⓝ ke·*no*
vacant ελεύθερος e·*lef*·the·ros
vacation διακοπές ⓕ pl ţhia·ko·*pes*
vaccination εμβόλιο ⓝ em·*vo*·li·o
vagina κόλπος ⓜ *kol*·pos
validate επικυρώνω e·pi·ki·*ro*·no
valley κοιλάδα ⓕ ki·*la*·ţha
valuable πολύτιμος po·*li*·ti·mos
value (price) αξία ⓕ ak·*si*·a
van φορτηγάκι ⓝ for·ti·*gha*·ki
VAT (Value Added Tax) Φ.Π.Α. ⓜ fi·pi·a
veal μοσχάρι ⓝ mos·*kha*·ri
vegan βίγκαν ⓜ&ⓕ *vi*·gan
vegetables λαχανικά ⓝ pl la·kha·ni·*ka*
vegetarian a χορτοφάγος ⓜ&ⓕ khor·to·*fa*·ghos
vein φλέβα ⓕ *fle*·va
venereal disease αφροδίσιο νόσημα ⓝ a·fro·*ţhi*·si·o *no*·si·ma
venue χώρος ⓜ *kho*·ros
very πολύ po·*li*
vessel σκάφος ⓝ *ska*·fos
view θέα ⓕ *the*·a
village χωριό ⓝ kho·*rio*
vine κλήμα ⓝ *kli*·ma
vinegar ξύδι ⓝ *ksi*·ţhi
vineyard αμπέλι ⓝ a·*be*·li
virus ιός ⓜ i·*os*
visa βίζα ⓕ *vi*·za
visit επίσκεψη ⓕ e·*pi*·skep·si
visit v επισκέπτομαι e·pi·*ske*·pto·me
vitamins βιταμίνες ⓕ pl vi·ta·*mi*·nes
vodka βότκα ⓕ *vot*·ka
voice φωνή ⓕ fo·*ni*
volleyball ⓝ βόλεϊ *vo*·le·i
vote v ψηφίζω psi·*fi*·zo

W

wage μισθός ⓜ mis·*thos*
wait (for) περιμένω pe·ri·*me*·no
waiter σερβιτόρος/σερβιτόρα ⓜ/ⓕ ser·vi·*to*·ros / ser·vi·*to*·ra
waiting room αίθουσα αναμονής ⓕ *e*·thu·sa a·na·mo·*nis*
waitress σερβιτόρα ⓕ ser·vi·*to*·ra
wake (someone) up ξυπνάω ksip·*na*·o
walk v περπατάω per·pa·*ta*·o
wall (outer) τοίχος ⓜ *ti*·khos
wallet πορτοφόλι ⓝ por·to·*fo*·li
want θέλω *the*·lo
war πόλεμος ⓜ *po*·le·mos
wardrobe ντουλάπα ⓕ du·*la*·pa
warm a ζεστός ze·*stos*
warn προειδοποιώ pro·i·ţho·pi·*o*
wash (oneself) v πλένομαι *ple*·no·me
wash (something) v πλένω *ple*·no
wash cloth (face) πετσέτα προσώπου ⓕ pe·*tse*·ta pro·*so*·pu
washing machine πλυντήριο ⓝ pli·*di*·ri·o
wasp σφήκα ⓕ *sfi*·ka
watch v κοιτάζω ki·*ta*·zo
watch ρολόι ⓝ ro·*lo*·i
water νερό ⓝ ne·*ro*
water bottle μπουκάλι νερού ⓝ bu·*ka*·li ne·*ru*
water bottle (hot) θερμοφόρα ⓕ ther·mo·*fo*·ra
waterfall καταρράκτης ⓜ ka·ta·*rakh*·tis
watermelon καρπούζι ⓝ kar·*pu*·zi
waterproof a αδιάβροχος a·ţhi·*av*·ro·khos
waterskiing θαλάσσιο σκι ⓝ tha·*la*·si·o ski
wave κύμα ⓝ *ki*·ma
way δρόμος ⓜ *ţhro*·mos
we εμείς e·*mis*
weak a αδύναμος a·*ţhi*·na·mos
wealthy πλούσιος ⓜ *plu*·si·os
wear v φοράω fo·*ra*·o
weather καιρός ⓜ ke·*ros*
weaving ύφανση ⓕ *i*·fan·si

wedding γάμος ⓜ *gha*·mos
wedding cake γαμήλια τούρτα ⓕ gha·*mi*·li·a *tur*·ta
wedding present γαμήλιο δώρο ⓝ gha·*mi*·li·o *tho*·ro
Wednesday Τετάρτη ⓕ te·*tar*·ti
week εβδομάδα ⓕ ev·tho·*ma*·tha
weekend Σαββατοκύριακο ⓝ sa·va·to·*ki*·ria·ko
weigh ζυγίζω zi·*yi*·zo
weight βάρος ⓝ *va*·ros
weights βάρη ⓝ pl *va*·ri
welcome v καλωσορίζω ka·lo·so·*ri*·zo
welfare πρόνοια ⓕ *pro*·ni·a
well (health) καλά ka·*la*
west δύση ⓕ *thi*·si
wet a βρεγμένος vregh·*me*·nos
what τι ti
wheel τροχός ⓜ tro·*khos*
wheelchair αναπηρικό καροτσάκι ⓝ a·na·pi·ri·*ki* ka·ro·*tsa*·ki
when όταν *o*·tan
where πού pu
which ποιος pios
whisky ουίσκυ ⓝ u·*i*·ski
white άσπρος *as*·pros
who ποιος pios
wholemeal bread ψωμί ολικής αλέσεως ⓝ pso·*mi* o·li·*kis* a·*le*·se·os
why γιατί yia·*ti*
wide πλατύς pla·*tis*
wife σύζυγος ⓕ *si*·zi·ghos
wildflowers αγριολούλουδα ⓝ pl a·ghri·o·*lu*·lu·tha
win v κερδίζω ker·*thi*·zo
wind άνεμος ⓜ *a*·ne·mos
window παράθυρο ⓝ pa·*ra*·thi·ro
windscreen παρμπρίζ ⓝ par·*briz*
windsurfing γουίντ σέρφινγκ ⓝ ghu·id·*ser*·fing
wine κρασί ⓝ kra·*si*
wings φτερά ⓝ pl fte·*ra*
winner νικητής ⓜ ni·ki·*tis*
winter χειμώνας ⓜ hi·*mo*·nas
wire καλώδιο ⓝ ka·*lo*·thi·o
wish v εύχομαι *ef*·kho·me
with με me
within (an hour) εντός e·*dos*
without χωρίς kho·*ris*
wok γουόκ ⓝ ghu·*ok*
woman γυναίκα ⓕ yi·*ne*·ka
wonderful θαυμάσιος thav·*ma*·si·os
wood ξύλο ⓝ *ksi*·lo
wool μαλλί ⓝ ma·*li*
word λέξη ⓕ *lek*·si
work δουλειά ⓕ thu·*lia*
work v δουλεύω thu·*le*·vo
work experience πρακτική ⓕ pra·kti·*ki*
workout γυμναστική ⓕ ghi·mna·sti·*ki*
work permit άδεια εργασίας ⓕ *a*·thi·a er·gha·*si*·as
workshop εργαστήρι ⓝ er·gha·*sti*·ri
world κόσμος ⓜ *koz*·mos
World Cup Παγκόσμιο Κύπελλο ⓝ pa·*goz*·mi·o *ki*·pe·lo
worm σκουλήκι ⓝ sku·*li*·ki
worried ανήσυχος a·*ni*·si·khos
worship v λατρεύω la·*tre*·vo
wrist καρπός ⓜ kar·*pos*
write γράφω *ghra*·fo
writer (author) συγγραφέας ⓜ&ⓕ si·gra·*fe*·as
wrong a λανθασμένος lan·thaz·*me*·nos

Y

year χρόνος ⓜ *khro*·nos
(this) year (αυτό το) χρόνο (*af*·to to) *khro*·no
yellow a κίτρινος *ki*·tri·nos
yes ναι ne
yesterday χτες khtes
(not) yet (όχι) ακόμη (*o*·hi) a·*ko*·mi
yoga γιόγκα ⓕ *yiog*·ka
yoghurt γιαούρτι ⓝ yia·*ur*·ti
you sg inf εσύ e·*si*
you sg pol & pl inf&pol εσείς e·*sis*
young νέος *ne*·os
your sg pol & pl inf&pol σας sas
your sg inf σου su
youth hostel γιουθ χόστελ ⓝ yuth *kho*·stel

Z

zip / zipper φερμουάρ ⓝ fer·mu·*ar*
zodiac ζωδιακός ⓜ zo·thi·a·*kos*
zoo ζωολογικός κήπος ⓜ zo·o·lo·yi·*kos* *ki*·pos
zucchini κολοκυθάκι ⓝ ko·lo·ki·*tha*·ki

Dictionary

GREEK – ENGLISH

Greek nouns in the **dictionary** have their gender indicated by ⓜ masculine, ⓕ feminine or ⓝ neuter. If it's a plural noun you'll also see pl. When a word that could be either a noun or a verb has no gender indicated, it's a verb. Adjectives are given in the masculine form only – see **adjectives & adverbs** (p17) in the **phrasebuilder** for more on how to form feminine and neuter adjectives. Both nouns and adjectives are provided in the nominative case only – refer to p19 in the **phrasebuilder** for more information on **case**. You'll also find the English words marked as a adjective and v verb, sg singular, pl plural, inf informal, and pol polite where necessary.

This **Greek–English dictionary** has been ordered according to the Greek alphabet:

Α α Β β Γ γ Δ δ Ε ε Ζ ζ Η η Θ θ Ι ι Κ κ Λ λ Μ μ
Ν ν Ξ ξ Ο ο Π π Ρ ρ Σ σ/ς Τ τ Υ υ Φ φ Χ χ Ψ ψ Ω ω

Α α

άβολος a·vo·los *uncomfortable*
αγάπη a·gha·pi ⓕ *love*
αγαπώ a·gha·po *love* ⓥ
Αγγλία ⓕ ang·gli·a *England*
Αγγλικά ⓝ pl ang·gli·ka *English (language)*
αγορά ⓕ a·gho·ra *market • shopping centre*
αγοράζω a·gho·ra·zo *buy* ⓥ
αγόρι ⓝ a·gho·ri *boy*
άδεια κυκλοφορίας ⓜ a·thi·a ki·klo·fo·ri·as *registration certificate*
άδειο a·thi·o *empty* a
αδερφή ⓕ a·ther·fi *sister*
αδερφός ⓜ a·ther·fos *brother*
αδιάβροχο a·thi·av·ro·ho ⓝ *raincoat*
αδύνατος a·thi·na·tos *slim* a
αεροδρόμιο a·e·ro·thro·mi·o ⓝ *airport*
αεροπλάνο a·e·ro·pla·no ⓝ *airplane*
αεροπορική εταιρεία ⓕ a·e·ro·po·ri·ki e·te·ri·a *airline*
αίθουσα αναμονής e·thu·sa a·na·mo·nis ⓕ *waiting room*
αίθουσα τράνζιτ ⓕ e·thu·sa tran·zit *transit lounge*
αίμα e·ma ⓝ *blood*
ακριβός a·kri·vos *expensive*
ακριβώς a·kri·vos *exactly*
ακυρώνω a·ki·ro·no *cancel*
αλλαγή a·la·yi ⓕ *change*
αλλεργία a·ler·yi·a ⓕ *allergy*
αλληλογραφία a·li·lo·ghra·fi·a ⓕ *mail*
άλλος a·los *other*
άμεσος a·me·sos *direct* a
αναπηρική καρέκλα a·na·pi·ri·ki ka·re·kla ⓕ *wheelchair*
ανάπηρος a·na·pi·ros *disabled* a
αναπτήρας ⓜ a·nap·ti·ras *cigarette lighter*
ανατολή ⓕ a·na·to·li *east • sunrise*
αναχώρηση ⓕ a·na·kho·ri·si *departure*
αναχωρώ a·na·kho·ro *depart* ⓥ *• leave* ⓥ
ανεβαίνω a·ne·ve·no *board (transport)* ⓥ
ανεμιστήρας ⓜ a·ne·mi·sti·ras *fan (machine)*
άνετος a·ne·tos *comfortable*
ανθοπώλης ⓜ an·tho·po·lis *florist*
ανθοπώλισσα ⓕ an·tho·po·li·sa *florist*
ανιαρός a·ni·a·ros *boring*
άνοιξη ⓕ a·nik·si *spring (season)*
ανοιχτήρι ⓝ a·nikh·ti·ri *bottle opener • can opener • corkscrew*
ανοιχτός a·nikh·tos *light (colour) • open* a
ανταλλάσσω a·da·la·so *exchange* ⓥ
αντιβιοτικά ⓝ pl a·di·vi·o·ti·ka *antibiotics*
αντίγραφο ⓝ a·di·ghra·fo *copy*
αντιηλιακό ⓝ a·di·i·li·a·ko *sunblock*
αντισηπτικό ⓝ a·di·si·lip·ti·ko *antiseptic*
άντρας ⓜ a·dras *man*
απαίσιος a·pe·si·os *awful*
απασχολημένος a·pa·skho·li·me·nos *busy*
απεργία ⓕ a·per·yi·a *strike*
απίθανος a·pi·tha·nos *fantastic • great*

απλό εισιτήριο ⓝ a·plo i·si·ti·ri·o one-way (ticket)
απόγευμα ⓝ a·po·yev·ma afternoon
απόδειξη ⓕ a·po·thik·si receipt
αποσκευές ⓕ pl a·po·ske·ves baggage
αποσμητικό ⓝ a·poz·mi·ti·ko deodorant
απόψε a·pop·se tonight
αργά ar·gha slowly
αργότερα ar·gho·te·ra later
αριθμομηχανή ⓕ a·rith·mo·mi·kha·ni calculator
αριθμός ⓜ a·rith·mos number
αριθμός διαβατηρίου ⓝ a·rith·mos thia·va·ti·ri·u passport number
αριθμός δωματίου ⓝ a·rith·mos tho·ma·ti·u room number
αριθμός κυκλοφορίας αυτοκινήτου ⓕ a·rith·mos ki·klo·fo·ri·as af·to·ki·ni·tu car registration
αριθμός οδήγησης ⓕ a·rith·mos o·thi·yi·sis driver's licence
αριστερός a·ri·ste·ros left (direction) a
αρκετά ar·ke·ta enough
αρραβωνιασμένη ⓕ a·ra·vo·niaz·me·ni engaged (to marry)
αρραβωνιασμένος ⓜ a·ra·vo·niaz·me·nos engaged (to marry)
αρραβωνιαστικιά ⓕ a·ra·vo·nia·sti·kia fiancée
αρραβωνιαστικός ⓜ a·ra·vo·nia·sti·kos fiancé
άρρωστος a·ro·stos ill • sick
αρχιτέκτονας ⓜ&ⓕ ar·hi·tek·to·nas architect
αρχιτεκτονική ⓕ ar·hi·tek·to·ni·ki architecture
άρωμα ⓝ a·ro·ma perfume
ασανσέρ ⓝ a·san·ser lift • elevator
ασήμι ⓝ a·si·mi silver
ασθενοφόρο ⓝ as·the·no·fo·ro ambulance
άσπρος as·pros white
αστείος a·sti·os funny
αστικό λεωφορείο ⓝ a·sti·ko le·o·fo·ri·o bus
αστράγαλος ⓜ a·stra·gha·los ankle
αστυνομία ⓕ a·sti·no·mi·a police
αστυνομικός σταθμός ⓜ a·sti·no·mi·kos stath·mos police station
αστυφύλακας ⓜ a·sti·fi·la·kas police officer
ασφάλεια ⓕ as·fa·li·a insurance
ασφαλές σεξ ⓝ as·fa·les seks safe sex
ατύχημα ⓝ a·ti·hi·ma accident
αυγή ⓕ av·yi dawn
αύριο av·ri·o tomorrow
αυτοκίνητο ⓝ af·to·ki·ni·to car
αυτοκινητόδρομος ⓜ af·to·ki·ni·to·thro·mos motorway • tollway
αυτόματη μηχανή χρημάτων ⓕ af·to·ma·ti mi·kha·ni khri·ma·ton ATM
αυτός ⓜ af·tos he • this (one)
αφή ⓕ a·fi feeling (physical)
αφίξεις ⓕ pl a·fik·sis arrivals
αφτί ⓝ af·ti ear

Β β

βαγόνι ⓝ va·go·ni train car
βαγόνι εστιατορίου ⓝ va·go·ni e·sti·a·to·ri·u dining car
βαλίτσα ⓕ va·lit·sa suitcase
βαμβάκι ⓝ vam·va·ki cotton
βάρκα ⓕ var·ka boat
βαρύς va·ris heavy
βγάζω φωτογραφία vga·zo fo·to·gra·fi·a take a photo
βγαίνω vye·no go out
βελόνα ⓕ ve·lo·na needle (sewing)
βενζίνη ⓕ ven·zi·ni petrol • gas
βενζινάδικο ⓝ ven·zi·na·thi·ko service • petrol station
βήχω vi·kho cough ⓥ
βιαστικός via·sti·kos in a hurry
βιβλίο viv·li·o book ⓝ
βιβλιοθήκη ⓕ viv·li·o·thi·ki library
βιβλιοπωλείο ⓝ viv·li·o·po·li·o bookshop
βιβλίο φράσεων ⓕ viv·li·o fra·se·on phrasebook
βίζα ⓕ vi·za visa
βοήθεια ⓕ vo·i·thi·a help
βοηθώ vo·i·tho help ⓥ
βορράς ⓜ vo·ras north
βούλωμα ⓝ vu·lo·ma stopper (for a bottle)
βουνό ⓝ vu·no mountain
βούρτσα ⓕ vur·tsa brush
βράδυ ⓝ vra·thi evening
βροχή ⓝ vro·hi rain
βρύση ⓕ vri·si tap • faucet
βρώμικος a vro·mi·kos dirty
βύσμα ⓝ viz·ma plug (electricity)

Γ γ

γάλα ⓝ gha·la milk
γαστροεντερίτιδα ⓕ gha·stro·e·de·ri·ti·tha gastroenteritis

γεμάτο ye·ma·to full
γενέθλια ⓝ pl ye·ne·thli·a birthday
Γερμανία ⓕ yer·ma·ni·a Germany
γεύμα ⓝ yev·ma meal
γεφύρι ⓝ ye·fi·ri bridge
Γη ⓕ yi Earth
γήπεδο ⓝ yi·pe·ţho court (tennis)
— του γκολφ ⓝ tu golf golf course
— του τένις ⓝ tu te·nis tennis court
γιαγιά ⓕ yia·yia grandmother
γυαλιά ⓝ pl yia·lia glasses • spectacles
γυαλιά ηλίου ⓝ pl yia·lia i·li·u sunglasses
γιατί yia·ti why
γιατρός ⓜ&ⓕ yia·tros doctor
γιος ⓜ yios son
γιουθ χόστελ ⓝ yuth kho·stel youth hostel
γκαρσόν ⓝ gar·son waiter
γκαρνταρόμπα ⓝ gar·da·ro·ba cloakroom
γκέι ge·i gay a
γκρίζος gri·zos grey • gray a
γλυκός ghli·kos sweet a
γλυπτική ⓕ ghlip·ti·ki sculpture
γλώσσα ⓕ ghlo·sa language • tongue
γόνατο ⓝ gho·na·to knee
γονείς ⓜ pl gho·nis parents
γράμμα ⓝ ghra·ma letter (mail)
γραμμάριο ⓝ ghra·ma·ri·o gram
γραμματοκιβώτιο ⓝ ghra·ma·to·ki·vo·ti·o mailbox
γραμματόσημο ⓝ ghra·ma·to·si·mo stamp
γραφείο απολεσθέντων αντικειμένων ⓝ gra·fi·o a·po·le·sthe·don a·di·ki·me·non lost property office
γραφείο έκδοσης εισιτηρίων ghra·fi·o ek·ţho·sis i·si·ti·ri·on ⓝ ticket office
γράφω ghra·fo write
γρήγορος a ghri·gho·ros fast
γρίπη ⓕ ghri·pi influenza • flu
γυμναστήριο ⓝ yi·mna·sti·ri·o gym (place)
γυναίκα ⓕ yi·ne·ka woman

Δ δ

δάκτυλο ⓝ ţhak·ti·lo finger
δάσος ⓝ ţha·sos forest
δαχτυλίδι ⓝ ţhakh·ti·li·ţhi ring (on finger)
δείπνο ⓝ ţhip·no dinner
δείχνω ţhi·khno point ⓥ • show ⓥ
δεκαπενθήμερο ⓝ ţha·ka·pen·thi·me·ro fortnight
δέμα ⓝ ţhe·ma parcel
δεξιός ţhek·si·os right (direction) a
δέρμα ⓝ ţher·ma leather • skin
δεύτερη τάξη ⓕ ţhef·te·ri tak·si second grade
δημόσια τουαλέτα ⓕ pl ţhi·mo·si·a tu·a·le·ta public toilet
δημόσιο τηλέφωνο ⓝ ţhi·mo·si·o ti·le·fo·no phone box • public telephone
δημοσιογράφος ⓜ&ⓕ ţhi·mo·si·o·ghra·fos journalist
διαβατήριο ⓝ ţhia·va·ti·ri·o passport
διαδίκτυο ⓝ ţhi·a·ţhik·ti·o internet
διάδρομος ⓜ ţhi·a·ţhro·mos aisle
διαζευγμένη ⓕ ţhi·a·zev·ghme·ni divorced a
διαζευγμένος ⓜ ţhi·a·zev·ghme·nos divorced a
διαθέσιμος ţhi·a·the·si·mos free (available)
διακοπές ⓕ pl ţhia·ko·pes holiday • vacation
διάλειμμα ⓝ ţhia·li·ma intermission • break
διαμέρισμα ⓝ ţhi·a·me·riz·ma apartment
διάρροια ⓕ ţhi·a·ri·a diarrhoea
διαφορά ώρας ⓕ ţhia·fo·ra o·ras time difference
διαφορετικός ţhia·fo·re·ti·kos different
διαχωριστική γραμμή ⓕ ţhi·a·kho·ri·sti·ki ghra·mi delineation line
διερμηνέας ⓜ&ⓕ ţhi·er·mi·ne·as interpreter
διεύθυνση ⓕ ţhi·ef·thin·si address
δικηγόρος ⓜ&ⓕ ţhi·ki·gho·ros lawyer
δίκλινο δωμάτιο ⓝ ţhi·kli·no ţho·ma·ti·o twin • double room
δίπλα ţhi·pla beside • next to
διπλό δωμάτιο ⓝ ţhi·plo ţho·ma·ti·o double room
διπλό κρεβάτι ⓝ ţhi·plo kre·va·ti double bed
διψασμένος ţhip·saz·me·nos thirsty
δοκιμάζω ţho·ki·ma·zo try ⓥ
δοκιμαστήριο ⓝ ţho·ki·ma·sti·ri·o changing room (in shop)
δολάριο ⓝ ţho·la·ri·o dollar
δουλειά ⓕ ţhu·lia job • work
δρόμος ⓜ ţhro·mos road • route • way
δροσερό ţhro·se·ro cool (temperature)
δυνατός ţhi·na·tos loud • strong • possible
δύο ţhi·o two
δύση ⓕ ţhi·si sunset • west
δυσπεψία ⓕ ţhis·pep·si·a indigestion

δωμάτιο ⓝ tho·ma·ti·o *room*
δωρεάν tho·re·an *complimentary • free*
δώρο ⓝ tho·ro *gift • present*

Ε ε

εβδομάδα ⓕ ev·tho·ma·tha *week*
εθνική οδός ⓜ eth·ni·ki o·thos *highway*
εγγονή ⓕ e·go·ni *granddaughter*
εγγονός ⓜ e·go·nos *grandson*
εγγυημένος e·ghi·i·me·nos *guaranteed*
έγκαυμα ⓝ e·gav·ma *burn*
έγκυος e·gi·os *pregnant*
εγώ e·gho *me*
εδώ e·tho *here*
έθιμο ⓝ e·thi·mo *custom*
εισιτήριο ⓝ i·si·ti·ri·o *fare • ticket*
— **μετ' επιστροφής** ⓝ me·te·pi·stro·fis *return ticket*
— **σταντ μπάι** ⓝ stand ba·i *stand-by ticket*
είσοδος ⓕ i·so·thos *entry*
εκατοστό ⓝ e·ka·to·sto *centimetre*
εκεί e·ki *there*
εκείνο e·ki·no *that (one)*
έκθεμα ⓝ ek·the·ma *exhibit*
έκθεση ⓕ ek·the·si *exhibition*
εκκλησία ⓕ e·kli·si·a *church*
έκπτωση ⓕ ek·pto·si *discount*
έκτακτη ανάγκη ⓕ ek·tak·ti a·na·gi *emergency*
εκτυπωτής ⓜ ek·ti·po·tis *printer (computer)*
ελαττωματικός e·la·to·ma·ti·kos *faulty*
ελαφρύ γεύμα ⓝ e·laf·ri ghev·ma *light meal*
ελαφρύς e·la·fris *light (weight)*
ελεύθερος e·lef·the·ros *vacant • free • available*
Ελλάδα ⓕ e·la·tha *Greece*
Έλληνες ⓜ pl e·li·nes *Greek (people)*
Ελληνικά ⓝ pl e·li·ni·ka *Greek (language)*
εμβόλιο ⓝ em·vo·li·o *vaccination*
ένα e·na *one*
ένας άλλος e·nas a·los *another*
ένεση ⓕ e·ne·si *injection*
ενοικιάζω e·ni·ki·a·zo *hire* ⓥ • *rent* ⓥ
ενοικίαση αυτοκινήτου ⓕ e·ni·ki·a·si af·to·ki·ni·tu *car hire*
εξαργυρώνω ⓥ ek·sar·yi·ro·no *cash a cheque*
έξοδος ⓕ ek·so·thos *exit*
εξοχή ⓕ ek·so·hi *countryside*
εξπρές eks·pres *express* a
έξω ek·so *outside*
εξωτερικό ek·so·te·ri·ko *overseas*
επάνω e·pa·no *on*
επείγον e·pi·ghon *urgent*
— **ταχυδρομείο** ⓝ ta·hi·thro·mi·o *by express mail*
επιβάτης ⓜ e·pi·va·tis *passenger*
επιβάτισσα ⓕ e·pi·va·ti·sa *passenger*
επίδειξη ⓕ e·pi·thik·si *show*
επίδεσμος ⓜ e·pi·thez·mos *bandage*
επιδόρπιο ⓝ e·pi·thor·pi·o *dessert*
επικίνδυνος e·pi·kin·thi·nos *dangerous*
επικυρώνω e·pi·ki·ro·no *confirm (booking) • validate*
έπιπλα ⓝ pl e·pi·pla *furniture*
επισκευάζω e·pi·ske·va·zo *repair* ⓥ
επιστήμη ⓕ e·pi·sti·mi *science*
επιστήμονας ⓜ&ⓕ e·pi·sti·mo·nas *scientist*
επιστρέφω e·pi·stre·fo *come back • return* ⓥ
επιστροφή χρημάτων ⓕ e·pi·stro·fi khri·ma·ton *refund*
επιτρεπόμενες αποσκευές ⓕ pl e·pi·tre·po·me·nes a·po·ske·ves *baggage allowance*
επιχείρηση ⓕ e·pi·hi·ri·si *business*
επόμενος e·po·me·nos *next* a
εποχή ⓕ e·po·hi *season*
επώνυμο ⓝ e·po·ni·mo *surname*
εργόχειρα ⓝ pl er·gho·hi·ra *handicrafts*
ερείπια ⓝ pl e·ri·pi·a *ruins*
εσείς e·sis *you* sg pol & pl
εστιατόριο ⓝ e·sti·a·to·ri·o *restaurant*
εσύ e·si *you* sg inf
εσώρουχα ⓝ pl e·so·ru·kha *underwear*
εταιρεία ⓕ e·te·ri·a *company (firm)*
ευγνώμων ev·ghno·mon *grateful*
εύθραυστος ef·thraf·stos *fragile*
ευτυχισμένος ef·ti·hiz·me·nos *happy*
εφημερίδα ⓕ e·fi·me·ri·tha *newspaper*
έχω e·kho *have*

Ζ ζ

ζακέτα ⓕ za·ke·ta *jacket • sweater*
ζαχαροπλαστείο ⓝ za·kha·ro·pla·sti·o *cake shop*
ζεστός ze·stos *hot • warm* a
ζωγραφική ⓕ zo·ghra·fi·ki *painting (the art)*
ζωγράφος ⓜ&ⓕ zo·ghra·fos *painter*

ζώνη ασφαλείας (f) zo·ni as·fa·li·as *seatbelt*
ζωολογικός κήπος (m) zo·o·lo·yi·kos ki·pos *zoo*

Η η

ηθοποιός (m)&(f) i·tho·pi·os *actor*
ηλεκτρισμός (m) i·lek·triz·mos *electricity*
ηλιακό έγκαυμα (n) i·li·a·ko e·gav·ma *sunburn*
ήλιος (m) i·li·os *sun*
ημέρα (f) i·me·ra *day*
ημερολόγιο (n) i·me·ro·lo·yi·o *diary*
ημερομηνία (f) i·me·ro·mi·ni·a *date (day)*
— **γεννήσεως** (f) ye·ni·se·os *date of birth*
ΗΠΑ (f) i·pa *USA*
ήσυχος i·si·khos *quiet* a
ήχος κλήσης (m) i·khos kli·sis *dial tone*

Θ θ

θάλασσα (f) tha·la·sa *sea*
θέα (f) the·a *view*
θεά (f) the·a *goddess*
θεατρικό έργο (n) the·a·tri·ko er·gho *play (theatre)*
θέατρο (n) the·a·tro *theatre*
θεία (f) thi·a *aunt*
θερμοκρασία (f) ther·mo·kra·si·a *temperature (weather)*
θερμοπληξία (f) ther·mo·plik·si·a *heatstroke*
θερμοφόρα (f) ther·mo·fo·ra *(hot) water bottle*
θηλυκός a thi·li·kos *female*
θορυβώδης tho·ri·vo·ţhis *noisy*
Φ.Π.Α. (m) fpa *VAT (Value Added Tax)*

Ι ι

ιατρική (f) i·a·tri·ki *medicine (job, study)*
ιδιωτικός i·ţhi·o·ti·kos *private* a
ινστιτούτο αισθητικής (n) in·sti·tu·to es·thi·ti·kis *beauty salon*
ιππασία (f) i·pa·si·a *horse riding • ride*
ιχθυοπωλείο (n) ikh·thi·o·po·li·o *fish shop*

Κ κ

Κα (f) khi·ri·a *Mrs*
καθαρίζω ka·tha·ri·zo *clean* (v)
καθάρισμα (n) ka·tha·riz·ma *cleaning*
καθαρός ka·tha·ros *clean* a
καθαρτικό (n) ka·thar·ti·ko *laxative*
κάθε ka·the *every • per*
καθένας ka·the·nas *each • everyone*
καθετί (n) ka·the·ti *everything*
καθημερινός ka·thi·me·ri·nos *daily*
καθρέφτης (m) ka·thref·tis *mirror*
καθυστερημένος ka·thi·ste·ri·me·nos *late*
καθυστέρηση ka·thi·ste·ri·si *delay* (v)
και ke *and*
και οι δύο ke i ţhi·o *both*
κακός ka·kos *bad*
καλλιτέχνης (m) ka·li·tekh·nis *artist*
καλλυντικά (n) pl ka·li·di·ka *make-up*
καλοκαίρι (n) ka·lo·ke·ri *summer*
καλός ka·los *good* a • *kind* a
κάλτσες (f) kal·tses *socks*
καλύτερος ka·li·te·ros *better*
καλώ ka·lo *call* (v)
Καναδάς (m) ka·na·ţhas *Canada*
καπέλο (n) ka·pe·lo *hat*
καπνίζω kap·ni·zo *smoke* (v)
καρδιά (f) kar·ţhia *heart*
καρδιοπάθεια (f) kar·ţhi·o·pa·thi·a *heart condition*
καρέκλα (f) ka·re·kla *chair*
καροτσάκι (n) ka·rot·sa·ki *stroller • trolley*
κάρτα (f) kar·ta *card*
— **επιβίβασης** (f) e·pi·vi·va·sis *boarding pass*
κασκόλ (n) ka·skol *scarf*
κάστρο (n) ka·stro *castle*
κατάθεση (f) ka·ta·the·si *deposit (bank)*
κατάλογος (m) ka·ta·lo·ghos *catalogue • list*
κατάλυμα (n) ka·ta·li·ma *accommodation*
κατάστημα (n) ka·ta·sti·ma *store*
για σουβενίρ (n) yia su·ve·nir *souvenir shop*
— **ηλεκτρικών ειδών** (n) i·lek·tri·kon i·ţhon *electrical store*
— **μουσικών ειδών** (n) mu·si·kon i·ţhon *music shop*
— **ρούχων** (n) ruk·hon *clothing store*
— **παπουτσιών** pa·pu·tsi·on *shoe shop*
— **σπορ** (n) ton spor *sports shop*
κατεβαίνω ka·te·ve·no *get off • get down (train, etc)*
κατεύθυνση (f) ka·tef·thin·si *direction*
καύσωνας (m) kaf·so·nas *heatwave*

καφέ ka·fe brown a
καφενείο ⓝ ka·fe·ni·o traditional cafe
καφές ⓜ ka·fes coffee
καφεστιατόριο ⓝ ka·fe·sti·a·to·ri·o cafe -restaurant
κενή θέση ⓕ ke·ni the·si vacant seat
κέντημα ⓝ ke·di·ma embroidery
κέντρο ⓝ ke·dro centre
κέντρο της πόλης ⓝ ke·dro tis po·lis city centre
κέρματα ⓝ pl ker·ma·ta coins
κεφάλι ⓝ ke·fa·li head
κήπος ⓜ ki·pos garden
κιλό ⓝ ki·lo kilogram
κινητό ⓝ ki·ni·to mobile • cell phone
κίτρινος ki·tri·nos yellow a
κλειδί ⓝ kli·ţhi key
κλειδωμένος kli·ţho·me·nos locked
κλειδώνω kli·ţho·no lock ⓥ
κλείνω kli·no close ⓥ
— θέση the·si book ⓥ
κλεισμένος kliz·me·nos closed • booked
κλειστός kli·stos shut
κλεμμένο kle·me·no stolen
κλονισμός ⓜ klo·niz·mos concussion
κόβω ko·vo cut ⓥ
κοιμάμαι ki·ma·me sleep ⓥ
κοιμητήριο ⓝ ki·mi·ti·ri·o cemetery
κόκκινο ko·ki·no red
κολιέ ⓝ ko·li·e necklace
κολυμπώ ko·li·bo swim ⓥ
κολώνα ⓕ ko·lo·na column
κολόνια ξυρίσματος ⓕ ko·lo·ni·a ksi·riz·ma·tos aftershave
κομμωτής ⓜ ko·mo·tis hairdresser
κομμώτρια ⓕ ko·mo·tri·a hairdresser
κοντά ko·da near • nearby
κοντινός ko·di·nos close a
κοντός ko·dos short (height)
κόρη ⓕ ko·ri daughter
κορίτσι ⓝ ko·rit·si girl
Κος ⓜ khi·ri·os Mr
κοσμήματα ⓝ pl koz·mi·ma·ta jewellery
κοστίζω ko·sti·zo cost ⓥ
κοτόπουλο ⓝ ko·to·pu·lo chicken
κουβέρ ⓕ ku·ver cover charge
κουβέρτα ⓕ ku·ver·ta blanket
κουζίνα ⓕ ku·zi·na kitchen
κουμπί ⓝ ku·bi button
κουρασμένος ku·raz·me·nos tired
κούρεμα ⓝ ku·re·ma haircut
κουτάλι ⓝ ku·ta·li spoon
— τσαγιού ⓝ tsa·yiu teaspoon
κουτί ⓝ ku·ti box • can • tin
κραγιόν ⓝ pl kra·yion lipstick
κρασί ⓝ kra·si wine
κράτηση ⓕ kra·ti·si booking • reservation
κρέας ⓝ kre·as meat
κρεβάτι ⓝ kre·va·ti bed
κρέμα ⓕ kre·ma cream
— ξυρίσματος ⓕ ksi·riz·ma·tos shaving cream
κρεοπωλείο ⓝ kre·o·po·li·o butcher's shop
κρυωμένος kri·o·me·nos cold a
κτηματομεσιτικό γραφείο ⓝ kti·ma·to·me·si·ti·ko ghra·fi·o real estate agency
κτήριο ⓝ kti·ri·o building
κυλιόμενες σκάλες ⓕ pl ki·li·o·me·nes ska·les escalator
κουτί πρώτων βοηθειών ⓝ ki·ti·o pro·ton vo·i·thi·on first-aid kit

Λ λ

λάδι ⓝ la·ţhi oil
— αυτοκινήτου ⓝ af·to·ki·ni·tu oil (car)
λαϊκή ⓕ la·i·ki street market
λαιμός ⓜ le·mos throat
λάστιχο ⓝ la·sti·kho tyre • tire
λαχανικά ⓝ pl la·kha·ni·ka vegetables
λαιμός ⓜ le·mos neck
λεξικό ⓝ lek·si·ko dictionary
λεπτό ⓝ lep·to minute
λεσβία ⓕ lez·vi·a lesbian
λιγότερο li·gho·te·ro less
λίμνη ⓕ lim·ni lake
λινό ⓝ li·no linen (material)
λιπαντικό ⓝ li·pa·di·ko lubricant
λίρα ⓕ li·ra pound (money)
λίτρα ⓕ lit·ra litres (weight)
λογαριασμός ⓜ lo·gha·riaz·mos account • bill • check
λοσιόν ⓝ lo·sion lotion
— για μαύρισμα ⓝ yia mav·riz·ma tanning lotion

Μ μ

μαγαζί ⓝ ma·gha·zi shop
μάγειρας ⓜ ma·yi·ras cook
μαγείρισσα ⓕ ma·yi·ri·sa cook
μαγειρεύω ma·yi·re·vo cook ⓥ
μαγιό ⓝ ma·yio swimsuit

μαζί ma·zi together
μαθαίνω ma·the·no learn
μακριά ma·kri·a far
μακρύς ma·kris long ⓐ
μαντήλι ⓝ ma·di·li handkerchief
μαξιλάρι ⓝ mak·si·la·ri pillow
μαξιλαροθήκη ⓕ mak·si·la·ro·thi·ki pillowcase
μας mas our
μάτι ⓝ ma·ti eye
μάτια ⓝ pl ma·tia eyes
ματς ⓝ mats game • match
μαυρόασπρο (φιλμ) ⓝ mav·ro·a·spro (film) B&W (film)
μαύρος mav·ros black
μαχαίρι ⓝ ma·he·ri knife
μαχαιροπήρουνα ⓝ pl ma·he·ro·pi·ru·na cutlery
με ερκοντίσιον me er kon·di·si·on air-conditioned
μεγάλος me·gha·los big • large
μεγαλύτερος me·gha·li·te·ros bigger
μέγεθος ⓝ me·ye·thos size (general)
μεθαύριο me·thav·ri·o day after tomorrow
μεθυσμένος me·thiz·me·nos drunk
μενού ⓝ me·nu menu
μέσα me·sa in • inside
μεσάνυχτα ⓝ pl me·sa·nikh·ta midnight
μεσημέρι ⓝ me·si·me·ri midday • noon
μεσημεριανό φαγητό ⓝ me·si·me·ria·no fa·yi·to lunch
μετά me·ta after
μεταλλικό νερό ⓝ me·ta·li·ko ne·ro mineral water
μετάξι ⓝ me·tak·si silk
μετασχηματιστής ⓜ me·ta·shi·ma·ti·stis adaptor
μεταφράζω me·ta·fra·zo translate
μετρητά ⓝ pl me·tri·ta cash
μέχρι me·khri until
μη καπνίζοντες mi kap·ni·zo·des nonsmoking
μήνας ⓜ mi·nas month
μήνυμα ⓝ mi·ni·ma message
μητέρα ⓕ mi·te·ra mother
μητρόπολη ⓕ mi·tro·po·li cathedral
μηχανή ⓕ mi·kha·ni engine • machine
— **εισιτηρίων** ⓕ i·si·ti·ri·on ticket machine
μηχανική ⓕ mi·kha·ni·ki engineering
μηχανικός ⓜ&ⓕ mi·kha·ni·kos engineer • mechanic

μικρό όνομα ⓝ mi·kro o·no·ma first name
μικρότερος mi·kro·te·ros smaller
μιλάω mi·la·o speak • talk ⓥ
μισό mi·so half
μόδα ⓕ mo·ţha fashion
μοιράζομαι mi·ra·zo·me share with
μολύβι ⓝ mo·li·vi pencil
μόλυνση ⓕ mo·lin·si infection
μονό δωμάτιο ⓝ mo·no ţho·ma·tio single room
μονοπάτι ⓝ mo·no·pa·ti path • track • trail
μόνος mo·nos alone
μου mu my • to me
μου αρέσει mu a·re·si like ⓥ
μπαγιάτικος ba·yia·ti·kos off (spoiled) • stale
μπαίνω be·no enter
μπάλες από βαμβάκι ⓝ pl ba·les a·po vam·va·ki cotton balls
μπάνιο ⓝ ba·nio bath • bathroom
μπάντα ⓕ ba·da band (music)
μπαρ ⓝ bar bar
μπαταρία ⓕ ba·ta·ri·a battery
μπέιμπι σίτερ ⓕ be·i·bi si·ter babysitter
μπιζνες κλασ biz·nes klas business class
μπλε ble blue ⓐ
μπλοκαρισμένος blo·ka·riz·me·nos blocked
μπλουζάκι ⓝ blu·za·ki T-shirt
μπότα ⓕ bo·ta boot (footwear)
μπουκάλι ⓝ bu·ka·li bottle
μπουφές ⓜ bu·fes buffet
μπροσούρα ⓕ bro·su·ra brochure
μπύρα ⓕ bi·ra beer
μπυραρία ⓕ bi·ra·ri·a bar • pub
μπωλ ⓝ bol bowl
μυρουδιά ⓕ mi·ru·ţhia smell
μύτη ⓕ mi·ti nose
μωβ mov purple
μωρό ⓝ mo·ro baby

Ν ν

ναι ne yes
ναρκωτικά ⓝ pl nar·ko·ti·ka drugs
ναυτία ⓕ naf·ti·a nausea • seasickness • travel sickness
νέα ⓝ pl ne·a news
Νέα Ζηλανδία ⓕ ne·a zi·lan·ţhi·a New Zealand
νέος ne·os new • young
νερό ⓝ ne·ro water
νοικοκυρά ⓕ ni·ko·ki·ra homemaker

νοικοκύρης ⓜ ni·ko·ki·ris *householder*
νησί ⓝ ni·si *island*
νομικά ⓜ no·mi·ka *law (study, profession)*
νοσοκόμος ⓜ no·so·ko·mos *nurse*
νοσοκόμα ⓕ no·so·ko·ma *nurse*
νοσοκομείο ⓝ no·so·ko·mi·o *hospital*
νόστιμος no·sti·mos *tasty*
νότος ⓜ no·tos *south*
ντελικατέσεν ⓝ de·li·ka·te·sen *delicatessen*
ντους ⓝ duz *shower*
νύχτα ⓕ nikh·ta *night*
νωρίς no·ris *early*

Ξ ξ

ξενοδοχείο ⓝ kse·no·tho·hi·o *hotel*
ξένη ⓕ kse·ni *foreign* a • *stranger* ⓝ
ξένος ⓜ kse·nos *foreign* a • *stranger* ⓝ
ξενώνας ⓜ kse·no·nas *guesthouse*
ξυπνάω ksip·na·o *wake • wake (someone) up*
ξυπνητήρι ⓝ ksip·ni·ti·ri *alarm clock*
ξυράφι ⓝ ksi·ra·fi *razor blade*
ξυρίζω ksi·ri·zo *shave* ⓥ
ξυριστική μηχανή ⓕ ksi·ri·sti·ki mi·kha·ni *razor*

Ο ο

ο καλύτερος o ka·li·te·ros *best* a
ο μεγαλύτερος o me·gha·li·te·ros *biggest*
ο μικρότερος o mi·kro·te·ros *smallest*
οδηγός ⓜ&ⓕ o·thi·ghos *driver • guide (person)*
— **διασκέδασης** ⓜ thia·ske·tha·sis *entertainment guide*
οδηγώ o·thi·gho *drive* ⓥ
οδοντιατρική κλωστή ⓕ o·tho·di·a·tri·ki klo·sti *dental floss*
οδοντίατρος ⓜ&ⓕ o·tho·di·a·tros *dentist*
οδοντόβουρτσα ⓕ o·tho·do·vur·tsa *toothbrush*
οδοντόπαστα ⓕ o·tho·do·pa·sta *toothpaste*
οδός ⓕ o·thos *street*
οδυνηρός o·thi·ni·ros *painful*
Οθωμανικός o·tho·ma·ni·kos *Ottoman* a
οικογένεια ⓕ i·ko·ye·ni·a *family*
οικονομική θέση ⓕ i·ko·no·mi·ki the·si *economy class*
Ολλανδία ⓕ o·lan·thi·a *Netherlands*
όλοι o·li *all*
ολονυχτίς o·lo·nikh·tis *all night*
ομάδα αίματος ⓕ o·ma·tha e·ma·tos *blood group*
όμορφος o·mor·fos *beautiful • handsome*
ομοφυλόφιλος ⓜ o·mo·fi·lo·fi·los *homosexual*
όνομα ⓝ o·no·ma *name*
οπίσθιος o·pi·sthi·os *rear (body)*
οπωροπωλείο ⓝ o·po·ro·po·li·o *grocery*
όριο ταχύτητας ⓝ o·ri·o ta·hi·ti·tas *speed limit*
όροφος ⓜ o·ro·fos *floor (storey)*
όταν o·tan *when*
όχι o·hi *no • not*

Π π

πάγος ⓜ pa·ghos *ice*
παγωμένος pa·gho·me·nos *frozen*
παγωτό ⓝ pa·gho·to *ice cream*
παζάρι ⓝ pa·za·ri *flea market*
παιδί ⓝ pe·thi *child*
παιδιά ⓝ pl pe·thia *children*
παιδικό κάθισμα ⓝ pe·thi·ko ka·thiz·ma *child seat*
παιδικός σταθμός ⓜ pe·thi·kos stath·mos *creche*
παλάτι ⓝ pa·la·ti *palace*
πάλι pa·li *again*
παλιός pa·lios *old* a
παλτό ⓝ pal·to *coat*
πάνα ⓕ pa·na *nappy • diaper*
πανεπιστήμιο ⓝ pa·ne·pi·sti·mi·o *university*
παντελόνι ⓝ pa·de·lo·ni *trousers • pants*
παντρεμένη ⓕ pa·dre·me·ni *married*
παντρεμένος ⓜ pa·dre·me·nos *married*
πάνω pa·no *on • up*
παππούς ⓜ pa·pus *grandfather*
παπούτσι ⓝ pa·put·si *shoe*
πάρα πολύ pa·ra po·li *too (expensive etc)*
παραδίνω pa·ra·thi·no *deliver*
παράθυρο ⓝ pa·ra·thi·ro *window*
παραλαβή αποσκευών ⓕ pa·ra·la·vi a·po·ske·von *baggage claim*
παραλία ⓕ pa·ra·li·a *beach • seaside*
Παραμονή Πρωτοχρονιάς ⓕ pa·ra·mo·ni pro·to·khro·nias *New Year's Eve*
παράπονο ⓝ pa·ra·po·no *complaint*
παράσταση ⓕ pa·ra·sta·si *gig*
παρκάρω par·ka·ro *park a car*
Πάσχα ⓝ pas·kha *Easter*
πατέρας ⓜ pa·te·ras *father*
παυσίπονο ⓝ paf·si·po·no *painkiller*
παχύς ⓐ pa·his *fat*

πάω για ψώνια pa·o yia pso·nia *go shopping*
πεζοδρόμιο ⓝ pe·zo·thro·mi·o *footpath*
πεζοπορία ⓕ pe·zo·po·ri·a *hiking*
πεθερά ⓕ pe·the·ra *mother-in-law*
πεθερός ⓜ pe·the·ros *father-in-law*
πεινάω pi·na·o *(be) hungry* ⓥ
πελάτης ⓜ pe·la·tis *client*
πελάτισσα ⓕ pe·la·ti·sa *client*
πέος ⓝ pe·os *penis*
περιήγηση ⓕ pe·ri·i·yi·si *tour*
— **με οδηγό** ⓕ me o·thi·gho *guided tour*
περιμένω pe·ri·me·no *wait* ⓥ
περίπτερο ⓝ pe·rip·te·ro *kiosk*
περισσότερος pe·ri·so·te·ros *more*
περπατάω per·pa·ta·o *walk* ⓥ
πετάω pe·ta·o *fly* ⓥ
πετρέλαιο ⓝ pe·tre·le·o *petrol*
πετρογκάζ ⓝ pe·tro·gaz *gas (for cooking)*
πετσέτα ⓕ pet·se·ta *towel*
πετσετάκι ⓝ pet·se·ta·ki *napkin*
— **υγείας** i·yi·as ⓝ *panty liners • sanitary napkins*
πηγαίνω pi·ye·no *go*
πιάτο ⓝ pia·to *dish • plate*
πικρός pi·kros *bitter* ⓐ
πίνακας ⓜ pi·na·kas *painting (a work)*
πινακοθήκη ⓕ pi·na·ko·thi·ki *art gallery*
πίνω pi·no *drink* ⓥ
πιπίλα ⓕ pi·pi·la *dummy • pacifier*
πιρούνι ⓝ pi·ru·ni *fork*
πισίνα ⓕ pi·si·na *swimming pool*
πίστωση ⓕ pi·sto·si *credit*
πιστωτική κάρτα ⓕ pi·sto·ti·ki kar·ta *credit card*
πλατεία ⓕ pla·ti·a *square (town)*
πλάτη ⓕ pla·ti *back (body)*
πλατφόρμα ⓕ plat·for·ma *platform*
πλένω ple·no *wash* ⓥ
πληγή ⓕ pli·yi *injury*
πληγωμένος pli·gho·me·nos *injured* ⓐ
πληροφορία ⓕ pli·ro·fo·ri·a *information*
πληροφορική ⓕ pli·ro·fo·ri·ki *IT*
πληρωμή ⓕ pli·ro·mi *payment*
πλυντήριο ⓝ pli·di·ri·o *launderette • laundry • washing machine*
ποδήλατο ⓝ po·thi·la·to *bicycle • bike*
πόδι ⓝ po·thi *foot • leg*
ποδόσφαιρο ⓝ po·thos·fe·ro *football*
ποιος pios *which • who*
πόλη ⓕ po·li *city*
πολυτέλεια ⓕ po·li·te·li·a *luxury*
πολύτιμος po·li·ti·mos *valuable*
πονόδοντος ⓜ po·no·tho·dos *toothache*
πονοκέφαλος ⓜ po·no·ke·fa·los *headache*
πόνος ⓜ po·nos *pain*
πόρνη ⓕ por·ni *prostitute*
πορτοκαλής por·to·ka·lis *orange (colour)*
πορτοφόλι ⓝ por·to·fo·li *purse*
ποτάμι ⓝ po·ta·mi *river*
ποτήρι ⓝ po·ti·ri *drinking glass*
ποτό ⓝ po·to *drink*
πού pu *where*
πουκάμισο ⓝ pu·ka·mi·so *shirt*
πουλόβερ ⓝ pu·lo·ver *jumper • sweater*
πούρο ⓝ pu·ro *cigar*
πρακτορείο εφημερίδων ⓝ prak·to·ri·o e·fi·me·ri·thon *newsagency*
πράσινος pra·si·nos *green*
πρατήριο βενζίνας ⓝ pra·ti·ri·o ven·zi·nas *petrol • gas station*
πρεσβεία ⓕ prez·vi·a *embassy*
πριν prin *before*
προβολείς ⓜ pl pro·vo·lis *headlights*
πρόγραμμα ⓝ pro·ghra·ma *timetable*
προετοιμασία εγγράφων ⓕ pro·e·ti·ma·si·a e·gra·fon *preparation of documents*
προηγούμενος pro·i·ghu·me·nos *last • previous*
προκαταβολή ⓕ pro·ka·ta·vo·li *deposit (on house etc)*
προμήθεια ⓕ pro·mi·thi·a *commission*
προμήθειες ⓕ pl pro·mi·thi·es *supplies (food etc)*
προξενείο ⓝ prok·se·ni·o *consulate*
προορισμός ⓜ pro·o·riz·mos *destination*
πρόστιμο ⓝ pros·ti·mo *fine (penalty)*
προσωπική επιταγή ⓕ pro·so·pi·ki e·pi·ta·yi *check (banking) • cheque*
πρόσωπο ⓝ pro·so·po *face • person*
προϋπολογισμός ⓜ pro·i·po·lo·yiz·mos *budget*
προφυλακτικό ⓝ pro·fi·lak·ti·ko *condom*
προχθές prokh·tes *day before yesterday*
πρωί ⓝ pro·i *morning*
πρωινό ⓝ pro·i·no *breakfast*
πρώτη θέση ⓕ pro·ti the·si *first class*
Πρωτοχρονιά ⓕ pro·to·khro·nia *New Year's Day*
πτήση ⓕ pti·si *flight*
πυρετός ⓜ pi·re·tos *fever*

Ρ ρ

ράδιο ⓝ ra·thi·o *radio*
ραντεβού ⓝ ra·de·vu *appointment • date*
ράφτης ⓜ raf·tis *tailor*
ράφτρα ⓕ raf·tra *tailor*
ρεσεψιόν ⓕ re·sep·sion *check-in (desk)*
ρέστα ⓝ pl re·sta *change (money)*
ρεύμα ⓝ rev·ma *current (electricity)*
ρινική αλλεργία ⓕ ri·ni·ki a·ler·yi·a *hay fever*
ροζ roz *pink*
ρούχα ⓝ pl ru·kha *clothing*

Σ σ

Σαββατοκύριακο ⓝ sa·va·to·ki·ria·ko *weekend*
σακίδιο ⓝ sa·ki·thi·o *backpack*
σάκος ⓜ sa·kos *bag*
σαμπάνια ⓕ sam·pa·nia *Champagne*
σαπούνι ⓝ sa·pu·ni *soap*
σε se *at • to*
σεισμός ⓜ siz·mos *earthquake*
σελφ σέρβις ⓝ self ser·vis *self-service*
σεμινάριο ⓝ se·mi·na·ri·o *seminar*
σεντόνι ⓝ se·do·ni *sheet (bed)*
σεντόνια ⓝ pl se·do·nia *bed linen*
σερβιτόρα ⓕ ser·vi·to·ra *waitress*
σεξ ⓝ seks *sex*
σεφ ⓜ sef *chef • cook*
σημειωματάριο ⓝ si·mi·o·ma·ta·ri·o *notebook*
σήμερα si·me·ra *today*
σίδερο ⓝ si·the·ro *iron (for clothes)*
σιδηροδρομικός σταθμός ⓜ si·thi·ro·thro·mi·kos stath·mos *railway station*
σκάλα ⓕ ska·la *stairway*
σκιά ⓕ ski·a *shade*
σκληρός skli·ros *hard (not soft)*
σκοτεινός sko·ti·nos *dark* a
σκουλαρίκια ⓝ pl sku·la·ri·kia *earrings*
σκουπιδοτενεκές ⓜ sku·pi·tho·te·ne·kes *rubbish bin*
σκούρος sku·ros *dark (colour)* a
σκυλί ⓝ ski·li *dog*
Σκωτία ⓕ sko·ti·a *Scotland*
σοκολάτα ⓕ so·ko·la·ta *chocolate*
σορτς ⓝ sorts *shorts*
σουβενίρ ⓝ su·ve·nir *souvenir*
σουγιάς ⓜ su·yias *penknife*
σουτιέν ⓝ su·ti·en *bra*
σπασμένος spaz·me·nos *broken*
σπίρτα ⓝ pl spir·ta *matches (for lighting)*
σπίτι ⓝ spi·ti *home*
σπουδαίος spu·the·os *important*
σπουδαστής ⓜ spu·tha·stis *student*
σπουδάστρια ⓕ spu·tha·stri·a *student*
σπρέι ⓝ spre·i *spray*
σταθμός ⓜ stath·mos *station*
σταθμός λεωφορείου ⓜ stath·mos le·o·fo·ri·u *bus station*
σταθμός μετρό ⓜ stath·mos me·tro *metro station*
σταθμός τρένου ⓜ stath·mos tre·nu *train station*
στάση ⓕ sta·si *stop (bus, tram, etc)*
— **λεωφορείου** ⓕ le·o·fo·ri·u *bus stop*
— **ταξί** ⓕ tak·si *taxi stand*
σταχτοθήκη ⓕ stakh·to·thi·ki *ashtray*
στεγνός stegh·nos *dry* a
στήθος ⓝ sti·thos *chest (body)*
στην ώρα stin o·ra *on time*
στόμα ⓝ sto·ma *mouth*
στομάχι ⓝ sto·ma·hi *stomach*
στομαχόπονος ⓜ sto·ma·kho·po·nos *stomachache*
στραμπούληγμα ⓝ stra·bu·ligh·ma *sprain*
στρώμα ⓝ stro·ma *mattress*
στυλό ⓝ sti·lo *pen (ballpoint)*
σύζυγος ⓜ&ⓕ si·zi·ghos *husband • wife*
συμπεριλαμβανομένου si·be·ri·lam·va·no·me·nu *included*
συνάδελφος ⓜ si·na·thel·fos *colleague*
συναδέλφισσα ⓕ si·na·thel·fi·sa *colleague*
συνάλλαγμα ⓝ si·na·lagh·ma *exchange*
σύνδεσμος ⓜ sin·thez·mos *connection*
συνέδριο ⓝ si·ne·thri·o *conference*
συνεισφέρω si·nis·fe·ro *contribute*
συνιστώ si·ni·sto *recommend*
σύνορο ⓝ si·no·ro *border*
συνταγή ⓕ si·da·yi *prescription*
σύνταξη ⓕ si·dak·si *pension*
συνταξιούχα ⓕ si·dak·si·u·kha *pensioner*
συνταξιούχος ⓜ si·dak·si·u·khos *pensioner*
σύντομα si·do·ma *soon*
συντροφιά ⓕ si·dro·fia *company (friends)*
σύντροφος ⓜ si·dro·fos *companion*
συστημένο sis·ti·me·no *by registered mail*
σωσίβιο ⓝ so·si·vi·o *life jacket*

Τ τ

ταμείο ⓝ ta·mi·o *cash register*
ταμίας ⓜ&ⓕ ta·mi·as *cashier*

ταμπόν (n) ta·bon tampon
ταξίδι (n) tak·si·thi journey • trip
— επαγγελματικό (n) e·pal·ghe·ma·ti·ko business trip
— του μέλιτος (n) tu me·li·tos honeymoon
ταξιδιωτικό γραφείο (n) tak·si·thi·o·ti·ko ghra·fi·o travel agency
ταξιδιωτικός οδηγός (m) ta·xi·thi·o·ti·kos o·thi·ghos guidebook
ταυτότητα (f) taf·to·ti·ta identification • identification card
ταχυδρομείο (n) ta·hi·thro·mi·o mail • post office
ταχυδρομική αποστολή δια ξηράς ta·hi·thro·mi·ki a·po·sto·li thi·a ksi·ras surface mail
ταχυδρομικός κώδικας (m) ta·hi·thro·mi·kos ko·thi·kas postcode
ταχυδρομώ ta·hi·thro·mo post (v)
τελεφερίκ (n) te·le·fe·rik chairlift (skiing etc)
τέλος (n) te·los end
τέλος αεροδρομίου (n) te·los a·e·ro·thro·mi·u airport tax
τελωνείο (n) te·lo·ni·o customs
τένις (n) te·nis tennis
τέχνη (f) tekh·ni craft • art
τηγάνι (n) ti·gha·ni frying pan
τηγανίζω ti·gha·ni·zo fry (v)
τηλεγράφημα (n) ti·le·ghra·fi·ma telegram
τηλεχειριστήριο (f) ti·le·hi·ri·sti·ri·o remote control
τηλεόραση (f) ti·le·o·ra·si television • TV
τηλέφωνο (n) ti·le·fo·no telephone
τηλεφωνώ ti·le·fo·no telephone (v)
της tis her (ownership/direct object)
τιμή (f) ti·mi price
— εισόδου (m) i·so·thu admission (price)
— εξυπηρέτησης (f) ek·si·pi·re·ti·sis service charge
— συναλλάγματος (f) si·na·lagh·ma·tos currency exchange • exchange rate
τίποτα ti·po·ta nothing
το πιο κοντινό to pio ko·di·no nearest
τοπικός to·pi·kos local (a)
τοστ (n) tost toast
τοστιέρα (f) to·stie·ra toaster
του tu his (ownership/direct object)
τουαλέτα (f) tu·a·le·ta toilet
τουριστικό γραφείο (n) tu·ri·sti·ko ghra·fi·o tourist office
τράπεζα (f) tra·pe·za bank
τραπεζικός λογαριασμός (m) tra·pe·zi·kos lo·gha·riaz·mos bank account
τρένο (n) tre·no train
τρόλεϊ (n) tro·le·i trolley bus
τρώω tro·o eat (v)
τσάντα (f) tsa·da handbag
τσιγάρο (n) tsi·gha·ro cigarette
τσιμπιδάκι (n) tsi·bi·tha·ki tweezers
τσίρκο (n) tsir·ko circus
τσιρότο (n) tsi·ro·to plaster • Band-Aid
τυρί (n) ti·ri cheese
τώρα to·ra now

Υ υ

υπεραστικό λεωφορείο (n) i·pe·ra·sti·ko le·o·fo·ri·o intercity bus
υπέρβαρες αποσκευές (f) i·per·va·res a·po·ske·ves excess baggage
υπηρεσία (f) i·pi·re·si·a service
υπνοδωμάτιο (n) ip·no·tho·ma·ti·o bedroom
υπόγειος i·po·yi·os subway (a)
— σιδηρόδρομος (m) si·thi·ro·thro·mos subway train
υποδηματοποιείο (n) i·po·thi·ma·to·pi·i·o shoe shop
υπότιτλοι (m) pl i·po·ti·tli subtitles
υποχρέωση (f) i·po·khre·o·si engagement • obligation

Φ φ

φαγητό (n) fa·yi·to food
— για μωρά (n) yia mo·ra baby food
φαγούρα (f) fa·ghu·ra itch
φάκελος (m) fa·ke·los envelope
φακοί επαφής (m) pl fa·ki e·pa·fis contact lenses
φακός (m) fa·kos lens • torch • flashlight
φαρμακείο (n) far·ma·ki·o pharmacy
φάρμακο (n) far·ma·ko medicine
— για το βήχα (n) yia to vi·kha cough medicine
φαρμακοποιός (m)&(f) far·ma·ko·pi·os pharmacist
φερμουάρ (n) fer·mu·ar zip • zipper
φέρυ (n) fe·ri ferry
φέτα (f) fe·ta slice
φθινόπωρο (n) fthi·no·po·ro autumn • fall
φιλενάδα (f) fi·le·na·tha girlfriend
φίλη (f) fi·li friend

φιλμ ⓝ film *film • movie*
φιλοδώρημα ⓝ fi·lo·ţho·ri·ma *gratuity • tip*
φίλος ⓜ fi·los *boyfriend • friend*
φλας ⓝ flas *flashlight*
φλυτζάνι ⓝ fli·dza·ni *cup*
φόρεμα ⓝ fo·re·ma *dress*
φούρνος ⓜ fur·nos *bakery • oven*
— **μικροκυμάτων** ⓜ mi·kro·ki·ma·ton *microwave oven*
φουσκάλα ⓕ fu·ska·la *blister*
φούστα ⓕ fu·sta *skirt*
φρένα ⓝ pl fre·na *brakes*
φρέσκος fre·skos *fresh*
φρούτα ⓝ pl fru·ta *fruit*
φτηνός fti·nos *cheap* a
φύλαξη αποσκευών ⓕ fi·lak·si a·po·ske·von *luggage lockers*
φύλαξη παιδιών ⓕ fi·la·xi pe·ţhion *childminding*
φως ⓝ fos *light*
φωτογραφία ⓕ fo·to·gra·fi·a *photo*
φωτογραφική ⓕ fo·to·ghra·fi·ki *photography*
φωτογραφική μηχανή ⓕ fo·to·ghra·fi·ki mi·kha·ni *camera*
φωτογράφος ⓜ&ⓕ fo·to·ghra·fos *photographer*

Χ χ

χαλασμένος kha·laz·me·nos *broken down • out of order • spoiled (food)*
χαλκός ⓜ khal·kos *copper*
χαμένος kha·me·nos *lost* a
χάπι ⓝ kha·pi *pill*
χάρτης ⓜ khar·tis *map (of country/town)*
χαρτί ⓝ khar·ti *paper*
— **υγείας** ⓝ i·yi·as *toilet paper*
χαρτομάντηλα ⓝ pl khar·to·ma·di·la *tissues*
χαρτονόμισμα ⓝ khar·to·no·miz·ma *banknote*
χαρτοπωλείο ⓝ khar·to·po·li·o *stationer's shop*
χαρτοφύλακας ⓜ khar·to·fi·la·kas *briefcase*
χειμώνας ⓜ hi·mo·nas *winter*
χειροποίητο hi·ro·pi·i·to *handmade* a
χέρι ⓝ he·ri *arm • hand*
χιλιόμετρο ⓝ hi·lio·me·tro *kilometre*
χιόνι ⓝ hio·ni *snow*
χορεύω kho·re·vo *dance* ⓥ
χορός ⓜ kho·ros *dancing*
χορτοφάγος ⓜ&ⓕ khor·to·fa·ghos *vegetarian* a
χρήματα ⓝ pl khri·ma·ta *money*
Χριστούγεννα ⓝ pl khri·stu·ye·na *Christmas*
χρόνος ⓜ khro·nos *year*
χρυσάφι ⓝ khri·sa·fi *gold*
χρώμα ⓝ khro·ma *colour*
χτένα ⓕ khte·na *comb*
χτες khtes *yesterday*
χωρίς kho·ris *without*
χώρος ⓜ kho·ros *venue • place*
— **για κάμπινγκ** ⓜ yia kam·ping *camping ground • campsite*
χωροφύλακας ⓜ kho·ro·fi·la·kas *police officer*

Ψ ψ

ψαλίδι ⓝ psa·li·ţhi *scissors*
ψάρεμα ⓝ psa·re·ma *fishing*
ψηφιακός psi·fi·a·kos *digital* a
ψηλός psi·los *high • tall*
ψιλά ⓝ pl psi·la *change (money)*
ψιχάλα ⓕ psi·kha·la *drizzle*
ψυγείο ⓝ psi·yi·o *fridge • refrigerator*
ψωμί ⓝ pso·mi *bread*
ψωνίζω pso·ni·zo *shop* ⓥ

Ω ω

ώμος ⓜ o·mos *shoulder*
ώρα ⓕ o·ra *hour • time*
ώρες λειτουργίας ⓕ pl o·res li·tur·yi·as *opening hours*
ωτοστόπ o·to·stop *hitchhike* ⓥ

INDEX

D

E

F

N

O

P

Q

R

S

T

V

W

Y

Key Phrases

When's (the next bus)?	Πότε είναι (το επόμενο λεωφορείο);	po·te *i*·ne (to e·*po*·me·no le·o·fo·*ri*·o)
Where's (the station)?	Πού είναι (ο σταθμός);	pu *i*·ne (o stath·*mos*)
How much is it (per night)?	Πόσο έχει (τη βραδιά);	*po*·so e·hi (ti vra·*dia*)
I'm looking for (Ampfilohos).	Ψάχνω για (τον Αμφίλοχο).	*psakh*·no yia (ton am·*fi*·lo·kho)
Do you have (a local map)?	Έχετε (οδικό χάρτη);	e·he·te (o·ţhi·*ko khar*·ti)
Is there a (lift)?	Υπάρχει (ασανσέρ);	i·*par*·hi (a·san·*ser*)
Can I (try it on)?	Μπορώ να (το δοκιμάσω);	bo·*ro* na (to ţho·ki·*ma*·so)
Do I need (to book)?	Χρειάζεται (να κλείσω θέση);	khri·a·ze·te (na *kli*·so *the*·si)
I have (a reservation).	Έχω (κράτηση).	e·kho (*kra*·ti·si)
I need (assistance).	Χρειάζομαι (βοήθεια).	khri·a·zo·me (vo·*i*·thi·a)
I'd like (to hire a car).	Θα ήθελα να (νοικιάσω αυτοκίνητο);	tha i·the·la na (ni·ki·a·so af·to·*ki*·ni·to)
Could you (please help)?	Μπορείς να (βοηθήσεις, παρακαλώ);	bo·*ris* na (vo·i·*thi*·sis pa·ra·ka·*lo*)